Environmental Ethics and
Medical Reproduction

Environmental Ethics and Medical Reproduction

CRISTINA RICHIE

OXFORD
UNIVERSITY PRESS

Oxford University Press is a department of the University of Oxford. It furthers
the University's objective of excellence in research, scholarship, and education
by publishing worldwide. Oxford is a registered trade mark of Oxford University
Press in the UK and certain other countries.

Published in the United States of America by Oxford University Press
198 Madison Avenue, New York, NY 10016, United States of America.

© Oxford University Press 2024

All rights reserved. No part of this publication may be reproduced, stored in
a retrieval system, or transmitted, in any form or by any means, without the
prior permission in writing of Oxford University Press, or as expressly permitted
by law, by license, or under terms agreed with the appropriate reproduction
rights organization. Inquiries concerning reproduction outside the scope of the
above should be sent to the Rights Department, Oxford University Press, at the
address above.

You must not circulate this work in any other form
and you must impose this same condition on any acquirer.

CIP data is on file at the Library of Congress

ISBN 978-0-19-774518-2

DOI: 10.1093/oso/9780197745182.001.0001

Printed by Integrated Books International, United States of America

Praise page

"At a time when many ethicists are waxing eloquent about the need to maximize the happiness of the millions of possible future human beings, Dr Richie shows us, in sobering detail, the serious environmental and health costs of population growth, and particularly of using medical techniques to help people create children. The book brings an impressive amount of data to bear on a range of topics from the already-controversial (abortion, surrogacy) to the seemingly bland (medical treatment for infertility)."
—**Dr Stephen Latham**, Senior Research Scientist and Director, Yale Interdisciplinary Center for Bioethics

"This is a much needed in-depth critical analysis of the ethics of reproductive medicine in the light of environmental and climate-related considerations. It adds substantial and novel considerations to a literature on environmental reproductive population ethics that hitherto has tended to ignore the perspective of high-income countries. As such, it also adds crucial material to debates on both climate, healthcare and reproductive policy."
—**Professor Christian Munthe**, University of Gothenburg

"Cristina Richie's *Environmental Ethics and Medical Reproduction* urges us to reevaluate reproductive practices and ethics within the increasingly acute constraints of climate change. This fascinating book details the staggering environmental costs of Medical Reproduction—from infertility drugs, to gamete and embryo procurement and storage, to IVF, to genetic testing—and asks difficult and essential questions about how, why, and even whether we should bring children into the world at this particular historical juncture. The questions Richie asks are uncomfortable and she answers them with a refreshingly unapologetic straightforwardness. This book will stimulate important discussion across disciplines and, I hope, among a general audience of people interested in humanity's future."
—**Dr Jessica Pierce**, Faculty Affiliate with the Center for Bioethics and Humanities, University of Colorado Anschutz Medical Campus

"*Environmental Ethics and Medical Reproduction* by Cristina Richie provides a refreshing and much-needed outlook on healthcare through the lens of carbon emissions. Richie highlights the many under-explored demands of social justice including climate change justice, sustainable and fair resource allocation, and parenting ethics. The book is a welcome return to V.R. Potter's three pillars of global bioethics: population, peace, and pollution for an ecologically grounded approach to secure a future to our planet and species."

—**Silvia Camporesi**, Senior Research Fellow Centre for
the Study of Contemporary Solidarity,
University of Vienna & Visiting Professor of Bioethics,
Department of Global Health & Social Medicine, King's College London

"In her latest book, *Environmental Ethics and Medical Reproduction*, Cristina Richie, long one of the keenest critics of healthcare's unsustainability, provocatively and expertly argues that medical interventions into reproduction often fail to pass ethical muster once their contribution to the climate crisis are accounted for. While Richie focuses on medicalized reproduction, her argument compels readers to reassess which forms of healthcare should be immune from ecological scrutiny. And, by comprehensively tracing the ecological costs of medical reproduction—from gamete retrieval to birth—Richie offers an example of the moral imagination we will need to recognize them and reckon with healthcare's role in the climate crisis."

—**Dr Paul J. Cummins**, Bioethics Department, Earl R. and
Barbara D. Lewis School of Health Sciences, Clarkson University

"Rigorously researched and comprehensively written, this compelling book invites the reader to consider medical reproductive technologies through the fascinating lens of their environmental impacts. Its detailed ethical analysis journeys through questions of whether, when and how such impacts could or should be considered. A must read for anyone interested in medical reproductive technologies, ethics, and/or environmental sustainability."

—**Dr Gabrielle Samuel**, King's College London

"Cristina Richie's book, *Environmental Ethics and Medical Reproduction*, mounts an important challenge to prevailing moral and cultural views of human procreation. Supported by extensive scientific, sociological, and bioethical research, Prof. Richie compellingly argues that we need to take into account the ecological impact of human medical reproduction in both economically developed and developing countries. Prof. Richie counsels ecologically prudential reproductive decision-making in opposition to current mainstream medical practices. Prof. Richie's analysis not only is informed by rigorous scholarship, but also incorporates a broad range of ethical perspectives—including feminist, theological, and justice-based arguments—and proffers provocative policy recommendations to reduce medical carbon emissions. This work offers a uniquely valuable contribution to discourse regarding reproductive and ecological ethics and provides a model for interdisciplinary and ecologically-aware bioethical scholarship going forward."

—**Dr Jason T. Eberl**, Saint Louis University

"Richie offers a sustained critique of medical reproduction as an ethical and existential threat to our planet and peoples. Medical reproduction—from facilitation to formation to families—has potential impacts on people, productivity, and processes across cultures and climates. Richie's book extends a decades-old conversation about the ethics of reproduction in novel directions, compelling deeper thinking about medicalized reproduction as an environmental problem in a rapidly changing world."

—**Dr Jonathan Beever**, Director and Co-Founder,
UCF Center for Ethics, University of Central Florida

Contents

Acknowledgments	xi
Introduction: Climate Change and the Challenge of Sustainability	1

PART I: MEDICAL REPRODUCTION

1. Medical Reproduction and Gamete Retrieval	19
2. Medical Reproduction Preparing for Insemination	45
3. Medical Reproduction and Pregnant Women	72

PART II: SUSTAINABLE POLICY FOR MEDICAL REPRODUCTION

4. Healthcare and Carbon Reduction	91
5. Carbon Emissions Policies for Unsubsidized Medical Reproduction	95
6. Purpose of Healthcare	117
7. Policies for Subsidized Medical Reproduction	129
8. Rights and the Ethics of Sex and Procreation	166
9. Supporting Childwishes	181
Conclusion: Environmental Sustainability beyond Medical Reproduction	199

Notes	205
Index	287

Acknowledgments

This was "a pandemic book"—a book, like many other projects, to be fulfilled while many of the world suffered and many more sought distraction from the annihilation of social and communal life. I had come to Edinburgh from Alaska where I had spent the pandemic summer of 2020 exploring a great land where First Nation people had a significant presence and the liberty of nature offered a refuge from the restrictions of urban life. At that time, this book manuscript was only an idea, the essence of which had been previously published in the *Journal of Medical Ethics* in 2015 as "What Would an Environmentally Sustainable Reproductive Technology Industry Look Like?"

More than acknowledgments, I want to deeply thank a great number of people and institutions which have supported the writing of this book and have been companions along the way.

First, I owe gratitude and recognition to the academic institutions that recognized the value of this idea and offered me financial support to undertake the research and writing process. I started writing as a School of Social and Political Science (SSPS) Fellow at the Institute for Advanced Studies in the Humanities (IASH), University of Edinburgh in the fall of 2020. This gave me the time and (literal) space in the historic IASH building to write, revise, and think with views of the Pentland Hills before me. My thanks to the University of Edinburgh, the Institute for Advanced Studies in the Humanities, the director at the time—Steve Yearly, who encouraged me to apply for the fellowship in 2019 when I met him as a Visiting Scholar at the Just World Institute, University of Edinburgh—and Ben Fletcher-Watson, who was a constant, encouraging, and comforting face in the office. Elizabeth Cripps, my academic sponsor, was a key component of my successful application to IASH and an inspiration for my ideas on climate, ethics, and procreation.

Within two months of my fellowship at IASH, I began (remotely) as a lecturer in the Philosophy and Ethics of Technology section at Delft University of Technology. A deep thanks to the University and my section head at the time, Sabine Roeser, and the PI on the *Convergence* ethics research project,

xii ACKNOWLEDGMENTS

Samantha Copeland, for allowing me to use the IASH fellowship as research time. After the fellowship ended, they supported the book as part of the *Convergence* project, which I was part of. Thanks also to the current section head, Udo Pesch, for finding funding for the Integral Material of this book. I was humbled to be counted among the brilliant faculty in this department where innovation and ethics are synergetic and where prolific academic output is not outpaced by collegiality and good *borrels*.

While writing the book I was endorsed by the British Academy for a UK Global Talent Visa and I want to thank them for recognizing my contributions to academia and the UK. I hope this book confirms their assessment! A huge thanks to my academic sponsors—Drs. Calum MacKellar and Cathy Mungall-Baldwin—who wrote letters in support of my application.

A handful of academics based in Edinburgh have also supported the writing of this book through conversations, good-natured competition, and camaraderie, often over a pint, a dram, or a *sobremesa*. Some have gone and some have stayed. They ought to be recognized too.

In exceeding abundance above all that I could ask for or think of, I have been blessed to find a clan and a home in Edinburgh. My kin-group here has been irreplaceable. They are true Aristotelian friends—good, useful, and pleasant!

Cathy, thank you for your encouragement and free spirit.
Neri, our castle walks deepened my understandings of life and self.
Alejandra, your independence and courage is admirable.
Ana, thank you for making time to be a friend.
Calum, your wisdom exceeds your knowledge—no small feat!

Nicole, your career and humor are a fantastic combination!
Alex, thank you for being a dedicated listener and Sage.
Kat, you are the brightest person I know.
Zsuzsi, I am amazed by your tenacity and intelligence.
Carrie, the weekly walks got me through the pandemic. Thank you.
Jarita, it is a pleasure to discuss the intricacies of academic life with you.

Many others have been added to this group as the book went into production:

Jolene, thank you for being a model of hard work and success.
Emma, your balance and confidence is your strength.

ACKNOWLEDGMENTS xiii

Andrea, thank you for being an environmental ally!
Mathew, you have always challenged me intellectually and personally.
Lavinia, thank you for being positive and sincere.
Jane, my fellow Bounder, you have brought light into the world.
Paola, I admire your straightforward character.
Kritika, thanks for sharing a love of jazz with me.

To my former mentors who have shaped my thoughts in the best of ways, I am grateful; any shortcomings are my own.

Jim, I still hear your voice urging "a little less me, a little more God."
Lisa, you are still my role model of ethical praxis in life and career.
Andrea, you taught me that compassion and justice are mutually reinforcing, not exclusive.
James, thank you for forming my thought process through rigorous Rounds.

Of course, my nuclear family:

Nico, thank you for understanding me.
Pat, thank you for loving me.
Angelica, thank you for supporting me.
Matteo, thank you for trusting me.

Whether by choice or by chance, this book is dedicated to the modern environmental heroes—the childfree.

Introduction

Climate Change and the Challenge of Sustainability

Today, and for many decades, climate change has commonly been used to mean, and understood to mean, the drastic acceleration of extreme weather and weather events.[1] Among other contributing factors, climate change comes from activities that emit greenhouse gases (GHG) like carbon dioxide (CO_2). There is "clear evidence that the composition of the atmosphere is being altered as a result of human activities and that the climate is changing,"[2] according to the Environmental Protection Agency and numerous other scientific sources. Global CO_2 emissions—an indicator of human resource consumption—increased an astonishing 4.4% between 2008 and 2010 alone and is projected to continue to increase.[3] Moreover, safe amounts of global carbon emissions, measured in parts per million (PPM)—the ratio of carbon dioxide molecules to all of the other molecules in the atmosphere—have been exceeded.[4] Climate change causes a number of significant environmental problems, including extinction of non-human animals and plants.[5] Climate change also impacts humans with climate change health hazards,[6] which perpetuate environmental racism.[7]

Effects of Climate Change

The effects of climate change on the non-human world include extinction and endangerment of species, overfishing, and destruction of animal and plant habitats.[8] These affect humans, of course, as all creatures inhabit one world. The impact of anthropogenic climate change on the non-human community may be an ethical concern either because of the intrinsic value of "nature" or the instrumental value of "nature," whereas "nature" is (erroneously) conceptualized as the world outside of human life.[9] The former holds that nature is valuable in itself and should be preserved irrespective of its potential or actual use for humans; thus climate change is problematic because it

---

Environmental Ethics and Medical Reproduction. Cristina Richie, Oxford University Press.
© Oxford University Press 2024. DOI: 10.1093/oso/9780197745182.003.0001

infringes on the existence of non-human animals and plants. This is a non-anthropocentric view of nature. The latter views nature as a tool for human use; thus climate change is problematic because it compromises the resources humans can access. This is an anthropocentric view of nature.

Since the intrinsic value of nature does not hold much value outside of environmental circles, this book will not pursue this line of argumentation. However, there are many compelling arguments for the intrinsic value of nature from both religious[10] and secular[11] viewpoints. Instead, the book appeals to the instrumental value of nature and the claim that human requirements of food, land, and medicine ought to outweigh those of non-humans. This proposition is often made on the basis of theological "human dignity"[12] or secular "human exceptionalism."[13] Taking an instrumental approach to nature in this book is simply a rhetorical strategy which facilitates the largest possible dialogue, as those who recognize the intrinsic value of nature will not need to be convinced of carbon reduction. However, even when instrumentalizing nature, there are certain parameters by which rational humans must abide to maximize the cultivation, development, and excavation of resources. The instrumentalization of nature is not a blanket endorsement of overuse. The shrewd human will not foul their own nest.[14] Thus, the common environmental concerns of climate change, resource use, and population growth are placed within an anthropocentric environmental ethics. Under the instrumental view of nature, ecology is primarily a problem for other humans that impact their quality of life.

Significantly, for a book situated within biomedical ethics, *inter alia*, are the health impacts of climate change. Many health problems stem from pollution and the effects of climate change.[15] For instance, there are billions of people who cannot access the very basic resources necessary for life, which has health impacts as well as ethical implications. Malnourishment, death from exposure, and illness from contaminated drinking water are among the problems facing the developing world.[16] Moreover, climate change constitutes major challenges to public health by creating hazards associated with extreme heat, outdoor air quality, flooding, vector-borne infection, respiratory disease, and water- and food-related infection.[17] The World Health Organization reports that climate change causes over 150,000 deaths annually[18] and between the years 2030 and 2050 climate change–related health hazards will cause approximately 250,000 additional deaths per year due to extreme weather, diarrhea, malaria, other diseases, and under-nutrition as a result of famine.[19] Other aspects of global health are related to political structures and corrupt governments,[20] including effects of environmental racism, which intensify with the changing climate.

Environmental racism has been a public ethical concern since at least 1987, when *Toxic Wastes and Race in the United States: A National Report on the Racial and Socio-Economic Characteristics of Communities with Hazardous Waste Sites* was published.[21] The document found that environmental threats such as toxic waste sites, municipal dumping grounds, and hazardous waste facilities were clustered in low-income areas where racial and ethnic minorities dwelled. Impoverished locations were deliberately chosen for environmental hazards since the poor generally lack the political resources to mobilize a constituency to lobby against policies that negatively affect their health. These problematic practices still occur on a domestic as well as international level.

The climate change health hazards enumerated above disproportionately affect those in the developing world. Nancy Kass observes, "[D]omestically, there has been a longstanding concern that toxic waste sites and other environmental risks are not distributed equitably across class or racial lines. Internationally, there is growing awareness that disparities in access to clean and safe resources are growing only wider."[22] The burden of remedying poor living conditions and the effects of climate change ought to be in line with the "polluter pays principle."[23] Structural racism, including environmental racism, needs to be addressed on many levels. Governments are tasked with caring for their inhabitants and must consciously remedy unjust living conditions.[24] In the case of apathetic or corrupt governments, international bodies may need to intervene, particularly due to the rapidly escalating levels of pollution and global carbon emissions.

Causes of Climate Change

Anthropogenic, or human-caused, climate change is driven by resource use and population growth. Resource-intensive human activities are, in part, the result of the industrial revolution. Machinery has assisted humans in making labor easier, but development, deployment, and use of machinery has a significant carbon impact when it relies on fossil fuels. Similarly, the ability of humans to travel using trains, cars, and planes has accelerated not only carbon emissions, but also the myriad carbon-intensive activities that are accomplished with rapid transportation options. In highly consumptive countries,

4 ENVIRONMENTAL ETHICS AND MEDICAL REPRODUCTION

each person who immigrates to, or is born in, that country translates to greater carbon emissions that lead to climate change. The Woodrow Wilson Center for International Scholars states that "the world's richest half billion people, seven percent of the global population, are responsible for fifty percent of the world's carbon dioxide emissions. Meanwhile, the poorest fifty percent are responsible for just seven percent of emissions."[25] Humans are currently using the equivalent of 1.7 earths per year, placing the ecological debt for the future.[26] It is predicted that by 2030 humankind will be using the equivalent of two earths to sustain basic life and excessive lifestyles.[27] The planet has limited natural resources, therefore fewer people can use more resources, or more people can use fewer resources, with the same net environmental effect. However, current levels of use are unsustainable and must be reduced even if population levels are also reduced.

Human population affects the way resources are used and distributed. Population encompasses birth rate and death rate. Birth rate tracks how many children are born and is environmentally significant because each birth requires resources for each year of life. If the child comes to sexual maturity and chooses to reproduce, their birth will generate new births.[28] On the other side is the death rate, or how old people are when they die. Death rates are slowed by modern medicine, which creates longer lifespans. Everyone will die, but each additional year on the earth requires resources for life maintenance. Based on projections, the number of people on earth will grow, not stay the same or slow down.[29] The United Nations Population Division predicts that with medium fertility rates—2.53 children per woman—the world's population will reach 8.1 billion in 2025, increase to 9.6 billion in 2050, and peak at 10.9 billion by 2100. The *Proceedings of the National Academy of Sciences of the United States of America* reports, "[E]ven if the human collective were to pull as hard as possible on the total fertility policy lever . . . the result would be ineffective in mitigating the immediately looming global sustainability crises (including anthropogenic climate disruption), for which we need to have major solutions well under way by 2050 and essentially solved by 2100."[30] Of course, population policy is highly contested. Similarly, healthcare policies which would limit life-extending medicine—either by medical condition[31] or by age[32]—are generally unwelcomed.

Even so, ecologists have argued for ethically limiting procreation—with or without the incentives of policy—with some arguing on the side of zero population growth and others on the side of negative population growth, or population degrowth.[33] Zero population growth would maintain the current level of human inhabitants. Negative population growth aims to reduce the overall number of people on earth. Both zero population and negative population support some amount of new procreation, but arguments have generally focused on the numerical aspects of the population problem and therefore target the developing world. This approach is neither fair nor sensible, as it overlooks the massive resource use incurred by each birth in the developed world.

It is morally problematic to assign the burden of environmental responsibility primarily to those in developing countries, where a variety of social and political factors necessarily lead to larger families. Such factors include patriarchalism, limited contraceptive choices, a lack of educational and job opportunities for women, high infant and child mortality and morbidity, and an unstable political life that leads to general uncertainty.[34] Moreover, it is ethically inadequate and unfair to blame planetary destruction on the poorest of the world, who live on a fraction of the earth's resources. Attention must be paid to the developed world as well.

Population growth alone is not problematic for sustainability. Imagine, for instance, that the world contained only 1 billion people—instead of the current 7.5 billion—and that population was growing. Assuming that resource use was maintained at a sustainable level, that carbon dioxide was being emitted safely, and that everyone in the world had enough to live a rather good life, including just access to food, water, shelter, and other capabilities,[35] then population growth would not be ethically problematic from either a non-anthropocentric or an anthropocentric environmental standpoint. It is not the case, however, that population growth, particularly in high-carbon countries, is sustainable. Reproduction-related CO_2 is primarily due to choices of those who have children in the developed world where national carbon emissions are highest.[36]

The global problem of climate change comes from population pressure combined with resource use resulting in excess carbon emissions. As such, Maura Ryan rightly notes that "many have questioned the importance of meeting personal needs or desires or rights to bear genetically related children in a world that does not need any more children."[37] While Ryan offers an important critique of numerical reproduction, current levels of climate change must expand the concept of reproductive and sexual ethics as it relates to population growth from numbers of children born to the resource impact of each child. Resource impact includes not only the effects of children once

6 ENVIRONMENTAL ETHICS AND MEDICAL REPRODUCTION

born, but also the resources invested in creating these children, that is, with the assistance of the medical industry.

Addressing Climate Change

If resources were sustainably used and distributed equitably, an increase in population would not necessarily be a matter of concern for environmental ethics. "Sustainable" is the key word here.[38] Current rates of population are not sustainable and the recent population explosion has jeopardized the health and well-being of many people in the past century.[39] As such, evaluating the consumptive and reproductive practices of humans is appropriate, since there is widespread consensus that climate change is caused by humans, that climate change is undesirable, and that humans ought to intervene in climate change. Strategies for addressing climate change may include population degrowth,[40] carbon reduction,[41] or some combination of both.[42]

Population Degrowth in the Developing World

In the developing world, where birth rates are well beyond the replacement rate of 2.1 children per woman,[43] population degrowth would be an appropriate strategy. The most compelling—although not original—strategy for ethical population degrowth put forth by the *Lancet* in 2020[44] and numerous world organizations is addressing the unmet need for contraception.[45] In 2014, the Joint United Nations Programme on HIV/AIDS reported that "if all women wanting to avoid pregnancy used modern family planning methods, unintended pregnancies would decline by 71%."[46] As more widespread dissemination of birth control would also reduce maternal mortality and morbidity, it is a significant health priority. Healthcare providers could further address anthropogenic climate change by ensuring that all forms of birth control are available to those who request it. There are still many physicians who deny women the contraception of their choosing.[47]

More widespread implementation of the United Nations Sustainable Development Goal (SDG) of educating women would also reduce birth rates.[48] Population degrowth in the developing world would reduce both short-term and long-term resource use. Short-term, reducing population immediately decreases the everyday resources that are needed to sustain humans. Long-term, population degrowth has the benefit of relieving the pressure on earth's carrying capacity. Reduced population has an additional long-term benefit of attenuating the reproductive rates, which grow in geometric, not arithmetic, proportions.[49] But, population growth in the developing world is only one part of the population problem.

Population Degrowth in the Developed World

Population degrowth in the developed world must focus on the carbon and resource impact of new births rather than the raw number of births. Within this scope, attention must be paid to total country carbon emissions, per capita emissions, total population, birth rate, and migration. In 2018, China, the United States, and India had the highest per country carbon emissions at 10.06, 5.41, and 2.65 gigatons (GT), respectively.[50] However, population does not necessarily correlate to emissions. In 2017, the national population of China was 1,412.48 million, the US was 324.84 million, and India was 1,380.56 million.[51] As such, the per capita emissions of China, the US, and India varied and were 7.05, 16.56, and 1.96 tons, respectively.[52] Individuals in India and China emit drastically fewer carbon emissions than people in the US.

The rate at which these per-capita emissions multiply—and therefore negatively impact climate change—hinges on birth rate and immigration. In 2020, the birth rate of China was estimated at 12.3 births per 1,000 people, the US was 12.5 per 1,000 people, and India was 19 per 1,000 people.[53] The net migration rate of China was -0.2 per 1,000 population from 2015 to 2020, in the US it was 2.9 per 1,000 population from 2015 to 2020, and in India it was -0.4 per 1,000 population from 2015 to 2020.[54] These numbers only represent legally documented immigration. Thus, while population is dropping in some industrialized countries like the United States,[55] emissions are not. Environmental ethics insists that reducing the birth rate in carbon-intensive countries, as well as populous ones, is an important strategy[56] since there is consensus around two points: first, "there is such a thing as global climate change, it is at least substantially anthropogenic, and there are moral reasons to try to minimise it,"[57] and second, "one of the most significant ways that individuals in Western countries can reduce global carbon emissions is by having fewer children."[58] While ethicists and policymakers have been unforthcoming in suggesting reasons for limiting the number of children born

8 ENVIRONMENTAL ETHICS AND MEDICAL REPRODUCTION

in low-population nations—indeed, by actively working against population degrowth in some cases[59]—population degrowth in the developed world will be a key component of reducing resource use and therefore carbon emissions going forward.

In the developed world, an individual or couple without children will typically use fewer resources than an individual or couple with children of similar geographical and economic background. Likewise, an individual or couple with one child will generally produce less carbon emissions than an individual or couple with two children, and so on. Instead of feeding and transporting a family of two (the couple), doing the same for a family of four will eventually double resource use as the children become adults, even though small children do not require an adult's share of food, transport, and housing. Ostensibly, instead of living comfortably in a two-bedroom home, a family with children requires a larger home.[60] Generally, the family with children requires a less fuel-efficient, larger vehicle to transport the children to lessons, school, and church.[61]

In general, the individual or couple who decides to procreate must provide at an exponential rate for the lives that they have created, whereas the child-free couple in the corresponding demographic does not. There is some evidence that once a couple or family reaches a certain level of financial security their carbon impact tapers as they start buying low-impact, high-expense items such as tuition for higher education, investments in stocks and bonds, retirement plans and health insurance.[62] Yet this carbon "reduction" comes only after one is past the sustainable threshold. When emissions do not peak and drop off, the "Diderot effect,"[63] which drives consumerism, is at play.

Of course, it is always possible that a childfree individual or couple could be environmentally reckless and live in a profligate manner, thus expending more resources than a family of two parents and two children during their lifetime. Yet, when the childfree individual or couple dies, their carbon contribution dies too. Not so with those who leave a carbon legacy by having children that reproduce themselves.[64]

Carbon Reduction

Population degrowth is one necessary, but insufficient, way to resolve the environmental crisis. A complementary path focuses on carbon reduction. Carbon reduction is essential in all aspects of private and personal life in every country. Since carbon emissions are tied to structures of production, lifecycle assessments—which examine resource use from "cradle to grave" of a particular item—are important.[65]

Suggestions made by ecologists for carbon reduction are well known and include minimizing the use of fossil fuels, reducing the amount of meat consumed,[66] limiting disposable goods, and re-engineering packaging. These are valuable contributions in indicating highly visible, high-carbon human activities. But these suggestions, even if voluntarily adopted by individuals and implemented in various sectors, are ineffective in reducing global carbon emissions for several reasons.

First, international leadership on climate change is not uniform. For instance, the United States, one of the largest carbon emitters in the world, withdrew from the Paris Climate Agreement in 2019 and has not made any significant environmental commitments that support sustainability.[67] Carbon reduction has to be ubiquitous. Second, sustainable technologies and strategies that could contribute to the infrastructure of more sustainable commerce are not widely used.[68] Carbon reduction has to be accessible. Third, consumer habits, including shopping, eating, and transportation, are hard to break.[69] Carbon reduction has to be easy. Fourth, many aspects of life are viewed as exempt from carbon scrutiny. This includes reproductive choices, of course. It also includes the way people view and use healthcare services.

Climate Change and Medicalized Reproduction

Medicalized reproduction (MR) is a phrase this book will use to summarize the intervention of technology into human reproduction, from pre-conception gamete retrieval, to in-vitro fertilization (IVF), to birthing suites. It is broader than assisted reproductive technologies (ARTs) and includes any form of human reproduction that relies on medical resources. MR is, very often, a lifestyle procedure that is given to meet a reproductive project. Its purpose is not necessarily to address, cure, or treat infertility, but to provide options in reproduction. MR is thus poised for environmental evaluation not only as a procedure which increases population and uses resources, but also as a healthcare offering which is a clinically unnecessary carbon expenditure.

The ethical evaluation of MR is not new. Indeed, since the first successful birth resulting from IVF in 1978,[70] ethicists have debated a wide spectrum of moral questions raised by reproductive technologies and technological reproduction including "economic exploitation, profiteering, health effects in women's bodies, interference with traditional family norms, and children's welfare."[71] Yet, the environmental impact of MR is rarely discussed,[72] despite its exceptional impact on the environment and its profound uniqueness as an environmentally intensive and unnecessary "healthcare" offering.

Unlike other areas of high-carbon healthcare, such as organ transplantation or chemotherapy, MR does not save life. Nor does MR cure, treat, or prevent disease. The most well-known forms of MR—like IVF—temporarily circumvent infertility to permit pregnancy, when used by the infertile. However, offerings on the MR spectrum are used by both fertile and infertile people. Fertile people using MR include gestational surrogates,[73] some couples using pre-implantation genetic diagnosis and sex selection, and some single people and same-sex couples.[74] Uniquely, medicalized reproduction contributes to carrying capacity, population growth, and resource use.

To rule out all environmental evaluation of MR as "unfair" to those with infertility is founded on a faulty premise. MR caters to the fertile and infertile, with growing numbers of people availing themselves of services. Environmental ethics must hold all people who attempt biological parenthood accountable for their carbon emissions, regardless of the way the children were created, that is, naturally or with medicalized reproduction. Instead of conflating fertility with natural reproduction and infertility with medical reproduction, this book acknowledges that some people diagnosed with infertility will reproduce naturally through spontaneous pregnancy[75] and some people who are fertile use MR. The environmental impact of MR, and of MR infants in particular, does not necessarily mean that medical reproduction should be totally abolished now and in the future, although there are many strong ethical and environmental arguments to this end.[76] Rather, MR, at this time of environmental urgency calls for careful ethical investigation followed by an obligation to act if it is found to be ecologically unsustainable.

MR and Population Growth

While MR is broader than assisted fertilization, as of 2018, approximately 8 million babies were born through in-vitro fertilization alone,[77] with over a quarter of a million coming from the UK.[78] Rates of MR births continue to expand exponentially. In 2011, 4.6 million infants were born from MR.[79] MR is becoming an increasingly common way to reproduce. While in the United States, IVF contributed to 1.7% of all births in 2017,[80] Daphna Birenbaum-Carmeli reports that "IVF births already exceed 5% of the total in Japan, Spain, Denmark, Greece, Austria, Czech Republic and Slovenia."[81] In Spain, 7.6% of all births come from IVF.[82] Numbers from 2018 indicate that if MR numbers "stagnate at current levels of about 400,000 babies per year, an estimated 157 million people alive at the end of the century will owe their lives to assisted reproductive technologies (1.4% of global population)."[83] This will impact earth's carrying capacity through an additional 394 million people alive, or 3.5% of the global population.[84] More important than numbers, however, is carbon impact. For instance, one child born in the developed world increases carbon emissions up to the equivalent of 20 children born in a developing nation.[85] Thus an MR birth is not simply an addition to the population and carrying capacity, but also to global resource use and carbon emissions.

MR and Resource Use

The carbon footprint of infants born from MR in the United States is 1,644 tons of CO_2 per child.[86] Instead of having a one-time medical carbon footprint, like a surgery, MR leaves a carbon legacy from MR children who reproduce ad infinitum. The carbon legacy (the child) born from MR is 9,441 tons of carbon dioxide for the parent who uses MR.[87] Despite the work of ecologists on earth's carrying capacity,[88] carbon emissions, and population growth, the medical industry continues to develop new areas of medicalized reproduction, such as uterus transplantation[89] and three-person IVF,[90] which go beyond treating clinical infertility.[91] Karen Peterson-Iyer observes that "the huge medical infrastructure necessary to develop and implement technologies inevitably drain[s] personnel and resources away from other, perhaps more pressing, medical and public health needs."[92] These technologies are just one small part of resource use on the MR spectrum.

While the "output" of MR—the infants—is perhaps the most visible carbon impact, enormous amounts of resources are used along the spectrum of MR. Resource use prior to MR includes hormonal fertility treatments,[93] production of fertilization devices,[94] gamete retrieval,[95] and gamete storage.[96] Resource use during MR includes in-vitro fertilization,[97] artificial insemination,[98] and unproven "add-ons" like embryo glue.[99] Resource use from MR pregnancy includes selective reduction of embryos,[100] medical care for anticipated miscarriage,[101] scheduled cesarean sections,[102] and premature delivery.[103] Resource use after MR includes caring for premature infants in neonatal intensive care units[104] and cosmetic procedures for vaginal tightening[105] as part of the upselling of medicalized reproduction. Resource use with MR infants includes treating statistically significant increased duration, frequency, and severity of medical complications.[106] Activities from MR tourism include plane travel,[107] use of surrogates,[108] country infrastructure,[109] and vacation-associated activities.[110] All of these depend on a larger carbon-intensive infrastructure (see Figure I.1), which includes medical device engineers, distributors, fertility clinics, doctors, medical educational and training programs, healthcare insurance, and the pornography industry.

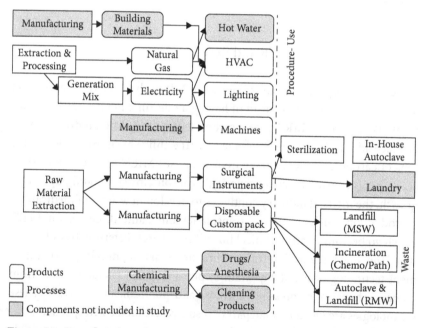

Figure I.1 Data flowchart for cesarean section and vaginal births as an example of resource-intensive medical infrastructures

From: Nicole Campion, Cassandra L. Thiel, Justin DeBlois, Noe C. Woods, Amy E. Landis, and Melissa M. Bilec, "Life Cycle Assessment Perspectives on Delivering an Infant in the US," *Science of the Total Environment* 425 (2012): 192.

Environmental Impact of Medicalized Reproduction	Resource Use	Carrying Capacity	Population Growth	Carbon Footprint	Carbon Legacy
Prior to MR	X			To be calculated	
During MR	X			To be calculated	
MR pregnancy	X			To be calculated	
After MR	X			To be calculated	
MR infants	X	X	X	+1,644 tons	+9,441 tons
MR tourism	X			To be calculated	

Some aspects of MR overlap with basic reproductive healthcare, including birthing care packs,[111] delivery assistance,[112] and emergency abortion.[113] Environmental concerns of children born from medicalized reproduction also overlap with unassisted reproduction—such as population growth and resource use. That is, naturally conceived infants will have the same carbon footprint as MR infants. However, the technological way in which MR children are conceived, gestated, and birthed contributes to carbon emissions in a way that natural procreation does not, since it utilizes the medical industry.

Environmental Problem	Population Growth	Resource Use
Natural Reproduction (intercourse)	X	
Medicalized Reproductive Healthcare		X
Medicalized Reproduction	X	X

The areas of medical reproduction and non-medical reproduction which do not overlap are the most ethically problematic from an ecological perspective, particularly since the majority of MR births occur in high-carbon countries. Given the frequency of MR due to factors such as delayed motherhood,[114] use by fertile people,[115] and increased medical consumerism,[116] the connection between climate ethics and MR deserves special attention.

MR: An Ethical Assessment

Thus, the triplicate nexus of this book is (1) the way in which the medical industry exacerbates carbon dioxide emission through facilitating reproduction—mostly in high-carbon, low-population-growth nations, (2) the way in which global carbon emissions are increased through

14 ENVIRONMENTAL ETHICS AND MEDICAL REPRODUCTION

medically assisted procreation as a medical procedure linked to other medical procedures, and (3) the way MR children contribute to the birth rate and global carbon emissions.[117] These can each be addressed as separate ethical concerns, in that even if one aspect is defeated or dismissed, the other two would stand. Instead of looking at these as separate ethical issues, a threefold ethical methodology, encompassing biomedical ethics, environmental ethics, and reproductive ethics, addresses each of these intersections and orients this book toward the aim of ethical evaluation.

Biomedical ethics maintains that the healthcare industry has a corporate social responsibility to reduce carbon emissions while also providing lifesaving medicine to all; thus, the provision of MR as a non-clinically necessary procedure, given in a time of environmental precarity, is evaluated. Environmental ethics argues that global carbon emissions must be reduced in all private and public sectors; therefore, MR as an elective service that produces carbon emissions is evaluated. Sexual, procreative, and parental ethics must include environmental impact of reproductive decisions; therefore, MR in a time of population growth and climate change is considered and, with it, decades of work on reproductive ethics. These ethical commitments are also connected to broader ethical issues of justice, sexism, economics, and well-being, thus making each argument against MR in a time of climate change more compelling.

Part I offers a systematic review of MR in all its forms, which concretizes the enormity of the environmental problem, while also acting as a case study for the carbon impact of healthcare procedures in general. Each of the three chapters explores a different phase of MR, with Chapter 1 analyzing MR prior to insemination, which is underpinned by fertility pharmaceuticals and supported by resource-intensive gamete storage units. Chapter 2 surveys MR and impregnation, from gamete assessment to fertilization techniques. Chapter 3 examines MR and pregnancy, which includes selective reduction of embryos, scheduled childbirth, and follow-up cosmetic procedures. Emphasis on use by fertile people reinforces the argument that MR should be evaluated by reproductive ethics, as well as biomedical and environmental ethics. Part II turns to policy, which highlights the threefold ethical methodology, as ethical theory grounds each chapter. Chapter 4 provides the purposes of healthcare and healthcare insurance, which are foundational commitments of biomedical ethics. From there, Chapter 5 offers policies for subsidized medical reproduction. Chapter 6 discusses the metric of carbon and carbon capping as tools of environmental ethics, with application for unsubsidized medical reproduction. Chapter 7 addresses human and reproductive rights, as well as parenting ethics, which comprise aspects of modern reproductive ethics. Chapter 8 is therefore situated to examine practices that support childwishes—the desires that some people have for children. The conclusion, much like this introduction, returns to environmental ethics more broadly and reaffirms that population degrowth, resource reduction, and carbon mitigation are ethical imperatives of all aspects of life. Sustainability must be broader and more far-reaching than medical reproduction. It must go beyond healthcare as well.

To be sure, the healthcare industry, and those who use it, are often viewed in isolation from global environmental ethics; medical developments are given to individual patients by individual doctors for their individual needs and desires. Yet, this is a naïve and simplistic view of healthcare. We live in an interconnected society. Thus, allocation of high-carbon medical procedures is a corporate social concern;[118] they are a matter for society to debate.[119] Climate change and ever more medicalized ways of reproducing are not two separate issues. At the core they reveal a death drive not to extinction through a slow dying out, but to obliteration through a war on ourselves and our planet. Bill McKibben notes that humans "have to conquer our desire to grow in numbers."[120] These are not only numbers in our nuclear family, this is also the emotional aggrandizement which is purchased with the carbon of the MR industry. It is the inflated, but false, hope of being cared for by, and only caring about, a certain type of child. It is the megalomaniacal illusion of control over all aspects of human existence, illusory because it so frequently fails.

MR is part of a medical lifestyle that an increasing number of couples and singles pursue. Indeed, the general consensus that MR is really "just another way to make a baby" is evident not only by its frequency, but also through international recognition, such as the granting of the 2010 Nobel Prize in Medicine to Dr. Robert G. Edwards, one of the innovators of reproductive technologies.[121] MR is dependent on an economized, regulated medical industry, and as such, they are open for ethical scrutiny in addition to the one that would be applied to natural procreation. Technology has fundamentally changed the discussion on biomedical ethics, environmental ethics, and reproductive ethics. This book considers how.

PART I
MEDICAL REPRODUCTION

1

Medical Reproduction and Gamete Retrieval

In order to reproduce by medical means, gametes—the sperm and eggs—must be taken from the human body. Oftentimes this requires the use of pharmaceuticals to enhance or stimulate fertility. Once gametes are taken, they require storage. After the appropriate diagnostic tests are run, gametes are used for inseminating procedures such as in-vitro fertilization (IVF) or artificial insemination (AI). Gamete retrieval and storage are part of the early phases of medical reproduction (MR). Each of these steps has many substeps along the way. This chapter will detail some of the processes of MR prior to insemination that use resources and release carbon dioxide.

It should be noted that not every phase of the MR spectrum is used by all clients. Some people may avail themselves of gamete retrieval but do not proceed to storage; others may eventually use the stored gametes for fertilization but not have a live birth. Some will have an MR birth without needing to use a neo-natal intensive care unit (NICU), while other medical consumers will use every aspect of the MR spectrum. Regardless of which MR procedures are used, carbon is emitted from a variety of sources in each step. It should also be remembered that people using the MR industry are not necessarily suspected to be, or diagnosed with, infertility. Since the MR industry caters to lifestyle choices surrounding reproduction, it eagerly serves preferences of fertile people who want a particular reproductive experience, as well as the preferences of the infertile. Both can, and do, use MR prior to insemination.

Pharmaceuticals and Carbon Emissions

Fertility pharmaceuticals are part of healthcare carbon emissions. Globally, the pharmaceutical industry's carbon emissions are more than 50% higher than the automotive sector's.[1] Over the past two decades, the environmental impact of prescription drugs has been flagged as a significant

Environmental Ethics and Medical Reproduction. Cristina Richie, Oxford University Press.
© Oxford University Press 2024. DOI: 10.1093/oso/9780197745182.003.0002

20   ENVIRONMENTAL ETHICS AND MEDICAL REPRODUCTION

public health and ecological concern. In 2001, Jessica Pierce and Andrew Jameton recognized that carbon emissions from "pharmaceutical products with complex manufacturing processes, [have] environmentally significant precursors . . . as well as complex and hazardous solid, air and water emissions, including toxic, infectious and radioactive wastes."[2] The term "biohazard" initially defined environmental harm done by healthcare and pharmaceuticals. These public health considerations are still relevant ethical factors in drug development, manufacturing, prescription, and disposal. More recently, the language of "carbon emissions" has become an additional way of quantifying pharmaceutical harm to human health and the ecosystem.

In 2007, the United Kingdom's National Health Service (NHS) reported that pharmaceuticals accounted for nearly a quarter of the 18 million tons of carbon dioxide emitted each year by the NHS, or 4 million tons of carbon per year.[3] Significantly, the pharmaceutical emissions from the NHS in England was "comparable to emissions from either building energy use or travel sectors."[4] Ten years later, in 2017, the amount of carbon from pharmaceuticals dropped to 3.29 million tons, but pharmaceuticals were still the second most carbon-contributing component of the NHS, public health, and social care sectors.[5] A disproportionally carbon-intensive pharmaceutical sector is reflected in other healthcare systems as well.

In 2009, the *Journal of the American Medical Association* (*JAMA*) reported that the US healthcare sector, "including upstream supply-chain activities, contributed an estimated total of 546 million metric tons of carbon dioxide equivalent (MMTCO2Eq), of which 254 MMTCO2Eq (46%) was attributable to direct activities. The largest contributors were the hospital and prescription drug sectors (39% and 14%, respectively)."[6] In 2016, the distribution of healthcare carbon emissions was reconfirmed. Matthew Eckelman and Jodi Sherman reported that hospital care and physician/clinical service sectors contributed the most CO_2 to healthcare, with structures/equipment and pharmaceuticals at third and fourth, respectively.[7] Data from 2021 shows that the carbon emissions from pharmaceutical preparation manufacturing in the US alone accounted for 30.2 tons of CO_2.[8]

Since the biohazards and carbon emissions of pharmaceuticals have been a vexing environmental issue for decades, once the metric of carbon emissions was attached to pharmaceuticals, attempts at carbon emission reduction became strategic priorities. Calls from individuals to reduce the carbon of pharmaceuticals began to appear in the early 2010s.[9] Institutionally, the NHS *Carbon Reduction Strategy* identified reduction of unused pharmaceuticals to combat climate change,[10] thus clearly indicating their concern for the high emissions of the drugs, as well as potential for hazardous waste and disposal. Later, the NHS report from 2018, *Reducing the Use of Natural Resources in Health and Social Care*, indicated that the carbon impact of pharmaceuticals will need to be addressed as carbon reduction in healthcare moves forward.[11] While these initiatives are laudable, focusing on reduction of drugs generally instead of elimination of particular lifestyle pharmaceuticals capitulates to the mentality that every pharmaceutical is an indispensable part of healthcare, which need not be the case.[12] Moreover, it reveals the fusion of profitability and pharmaceutical interests, which so patently manifest in fertility drugs.

Fertility Pharmaceuticals

While information on the specific carbon impact of individual drugs is rare,[13] fertility pharmaceuticals obviously contribute to the overall emissions of pharmaceuticals and the healthcare industry. Even if a person is known or suspected to be fertile, fertility drugs may be given to women or men prior to attempted gamete retrieval. In women, drugs are used for hyperovulation— whereby a woman will ovulate more than one egg during a menstrual cycle.[14] In men, fertility drugs are used to increase sperm mobility or motility.[15]

Fertility drugs are part of the vast pharmaceutical industry, which is a major contributor to environmental destruction and healthcare carbon emissions. Pharmaceuticals are resource-intensive during both upstream and downstream processes. "With its high energy costs of manufacturing and researching drugs, combined with high transportation costs for drug distribution"[16] upstream pharmaceutical carbon emissions are significant. Moreover, Willis Jenkins points out that oftentimes medical "research is overwhelmingly focused on treatment rather than causation, for much of it is funded by pharmaceutical companies with incentive to produce more chemicals, not question their long-term ecological function."[17] These pharmaceuticals, once produced, contribute to a cycle of carbon expenditure. Downstream carbon emissions come from prescribing practices such as overprescription,[18] pharmaceutical waste,[19] antibiotic resistance,[20] routine prescriptions,[21] non-adherence,[22] non-compliance,[23] drug dependency,[24] drugs given due to a lack of preventive healthcare,[25] and lifestyle prescriptions.[26]

22 ENVIRONMENTAL ETHICS AND MEDICAL REPRODUCTION

Fertility drugs are also connected to multiple categories contributing to downstream carbon emissions. If infertility is age-related, for instance, over-prescription is relevant, as age is the cause of infertility, which is a naturally occurring condition, not something that signals a deficit.[27] Thus, the prescription for fertility-boosting pharmaceuticals would be unnecessary as it would not address a biologically abnormal or harmful condition. In pharmaceutical waste, fertility drugs that are unused or stopped prematurely, for a variety of reasons, are disposed of without consumption.[28] Sometimes, fertility drugs are given as part of a routine prescription prior to running diagnostic tests, thus producing unnecessary carbon if there is not a clinical indication of infertility. In some cases, non-adherence or non-compliance characterizes those who use fertility drugs; the side effects of the fertility drugs may cause one to stop use or reduce the amount or frequency of drugs taken. Fertility drugs can also be related to a lack of preventive healthcare, as some forms of infertility are caused by untreated sexually transmitted diseases.[29] And, in all cases, fertility drugs are a lifestyle prescription, as the inability to make pregnant or become pregnant is a personal preference that does not support health or maintain one's own life. Moreover, there are a number of medical concerns of fertility drugs, including the toxicity,[30] risk of death from severe ovarian hyperstimulation syndrome,[31] and emotional fluctuations.[32]

Given the carbon impact of pharmaceuticals and the fact that fertility drugs are at the beginning of MR use—thus creating the potential for more people to access them as the entry point into other stages of MR—their environmental impact is significant. It should be noted that sometimes fertility drugs to bolster hormones are the only part of MR used, because pregnancy occurs. This makes their use as part of the total MR carbon footprint overlooked, as it is not part of what people typically envision as medical reproduction—which is usually IVF. Yet, carbon emissions are expended by a person using MR who only uses fertility drugs. It should also be noted that sometimes fertility drugs do not result in viable or usable gametes[33] and thus carbon is expended without the desired effect—fertilization and pregnancy. And, although "successful" fertility drugs that eventually contribute to creating a pregnancy will produce more carbon overall because of the new birth, on the other hand there is still the unnecessary carbon from a "treatment" that does not meet its objectives, that is carbon is wasted when pregnancy does not occur.

From both biomedical and environmental perspectives, reducing carbon emissions from fertility drugs is an ethical requirement. Yet, this will be challenged on numerous fronts. The pharmaceutical industry is tied to global economic activity[34] and may not be willing to change lucrative production models unless they can be persuaded that sustainability itself is profitable.[35] Moreover, drug companies have a stronghold on the medical industry because they are viewed—oftentimes accurately—as supporting standards of care.[36] Healthcare insurance policies, or the governments that provide healthcare, face pressure to fund high-carbon drugs when effective lower-carbon alternatives exist.[37] Some pharmaceutical companies have quotas that give bonuses to doctors who meet the targeted prescription of certain drugs,[38] which leads to overprescription as well. Even so, policies and practices for the carbon reduction of pharmaceuticals must include assessment of drugs used as part of medical reproduction. Not only because of the environmental effects of the drugs themselves, but also because of the environmentally detrimental effects of the intention of the drugs—human reproduction.

Gamete Retrieval—Process

If fertility drugs are not used in the MR process because the couple or individual is known to be fertile, then gamete retrieval might be the first step of MR.

Sperm Retrieval

The procedure for obtaining sperm is straightforward: samples may be obtained either through masturbation—oftentimes with the use of pornography or with the aid of one's sexual partner, that is through manual stimulation or sexual intercourse with a perforated condom. The production and distribution of pornography, either in print or in visual form, is a multi-billion-dollar industry[39] which also has a carbon footprint. From travel time to erotic sets to media dissemination of pornography, this carbon-associated activity of MR should not be overlooked from an environmental perspective.[40] If pornography is not used, but a perforated condom instead, this too takes resources. Condoms are generally produced to protect against pregnancy and sexually transmitted disease, and thus are a good environmental investment since they can prevent population growth and medical care from maternal mortality and morbidity. However, they still take resources in the excavation of rubber, latex, or natural fibers and in the production,

24 ENVIRONMENTAL ETHICS AND MEDICAL REPRODUCTION

manufacturing, and distribution process.[41] Condoms are not recyclable and although perforated condoms are less rare in sperm retrieval, they too contribute to carbon.

There are other resource-intensive medical means to obtain sperm, such as cutaneous vibratory stimulation and rectal probe electroejaculation.[42] This technique is used in anejaculate men, those who are paralyzed, those with spinal injury, and boys who are pre-pubescent and too young to achieve an erection with ejaculation. Cutaneous vibratory stimulation requires the use of a vibratory device, which also has to be produced and manufactured, leading to environmental toxins.[43] Likewise, rectal probes require engineering materials, use of minerals and metals, packaging, fuels for transportation, and distribution. Associated materials might be numbing creams or relaxing drugs.

Postmortem sperm retrieval is another way to retrieve male gametes. In human males, sperm is viable up to 24 to 36 hours after cardiac death, depending on the method of extraction.[44] For men who are dead by neurological criteria, postmortem sperm retrieval is done with en-bloc orchiectomy with epididymectomy and vasal sperm aspiration; orchiectomy plus epididymectomy; epididymectomy alone; or electroejaculation, or sperm retrieval from the penile tract.[45] En-bloc orchiectomy is surgical castration, which requires scalpels and other medical tools to remove the testicles, but, significantly does not require high-carbon anesthetic gasses, since the man is dead. Epididymectomy removes the epididymis, which is inside the testicles. This too requires a set of medical tools which also have a carbon footprint. Vasal sperm aspiration punctures the testicles to retrieve sperm. Electroejaculation has been explained above on cutaneous vibratory stimulation and rectal probe. Recent studies have examined the efficaciousness of sperm retrieval from the penile tract from corpses[46] which also requires a set of medical tools. In each case the sperm retrieval from a dead man takes a similar set of resources.

For Catholics, who may follow the interpretation of ecclesiastical teachings that have prohibited intentional sexual activity without the possibility of procreation (such as masturbation),[47] aspiration of the testes with a needle or biopsy gun can be used. Like other medical tools, these require production, manufacturing, and sterilization if used multiple times. They also require engineering and distribution. There may be some recovery time from sutures. In any of these cases, medical accidents and errors are always possible, which would require follow-up care.[48] Sperm retrieval may need to be done multiple times in order to get a quality sample. In this case each of the resources used will be repeated.

There are a handful of adjunctive ethical issues associated with sperm retrieval. Besides the religious objection related to sexual ethics and the feminist objections to the use of pornography, the way men are treated during the sperm retrieval process—and their direct experience—must also be considered. Some men have argued that "the process of providing sperm degrades and objectifies men."[49] According to personal interviews regarding the sperm donation experience, one man reported, "I felt like a piece of meat almost. I felt like a cow. I'm being milked for something that I can provide."[50] If the man is alive, this feeling may be compounded with negative emotions related to being infertile, or going through the process of fertility treatments.[51] Humiliation, shame, and stress which are tied to providing a sperm sample are problematically overlaid with the otherwise enjoyable activity of sexual intercourse and orgasms during this medicalized process.[52] Men undergoing postmortem sperm retrieval avoid these negative feelings since they are deceased. However, if gamete retrieval is performed on a man who is dead, the thought of castration might be repugnant or horrifying. Some men, of course, will not be troubled by this form of sperm retrieval. In either case informed consent while alive is an important process in understanding the man's wishes after death.[53]

In addition to the other ethical issues, sperm retrieval is part of the carbon footprint of MR and the medical industry. Each method of obtaining sperm has a unique resource impact, but in itself has no clinical benefit. That is, obtaining sperm does not cure, treat, or prevent disease. It has no therapeutic benefit for either the patient—the man giving sperm—or the recipient of the sperm and requires carbon-intensive supply chains both prior to and after sperm is obtained.

Egg Retrieval

Whereas the procedure for obtaining sperm ranges from simple to more complex, due to the many methods of sperm retrieval and external anatomy of male genitalia, the process for obtaining eggs is standard. Eggs are retrieved by passing a thin tube through the vagina and past the cervix into the fallopian tubes to the ovaries.[54] The surgical tube is made of plastic and requires manufacturing, production, distribution, and disposable packaging. Both the

26 ENVIRONMENTAL ETHICS AND MEDICAL REPRODUCTION

device and the packages may contain toxins and chemicals.[55] Using suction, the tube retrieves the eggs. Laparoscopy guides the tubes. The laparoscopic machine requires the use of energy and, as a technological development, depends on metals and other materials for resources.[56] Local anesthetic is used for the woman's comfort. This too has a carbon footprint. Anesthetic carbon emissions vary, depending on the mode of delivery, for instance, topical or by injection, and the pharmaceutical being given.[57] The egg retrieval procedure is then performed on the other ovary. Because cramping is likely, women may be given a muscle relaxant after or during the procedure.[58]

As with sperm donation, ethical issues of egg retrieval are medical, environmental, and feminist-social. Medical concerns include unnecessary pain[59] and medical complications[60] for an elective treatment that does not cure or treat infertility. The drugs that are required to induce the hyperovulation necessary for egg retrieval have been discussed in biomedical and feminist ethics, while the environmental effects have been overshadowed. Occasionally, parallels between environmental health and women's well-being have been drawn. For instance, Janice Raymond highlights how many of these medical invasions in the female body are a "glaring pollution of women."[61] But the resource use of the treatments themselves remains overlooked. That is, environmental assessments of egg retrieval tend to be unidirectional—from environmental toxins to women—when in fact it is this and also the carbon output of the treatments from the women using MR services which go into the environment—that also require ethical evaluation.

Gamete Storage for Short-Term Access

Gametes may be retrieved and stored for a variety of reasons and for a variety of timeframes. These sections will distinguish between "short-term access," that is, gamete retrieval with the intention of use as soon as possible, but no longer than three years, and "long-term access," that is, gamete retrieval with the intention of waiting longer than three years before first use. This chronological distinction is flexible and has been selected because often, people who want to use gametes in the short term for a first pregnancy may return to the gametes for a second pregnancy in a period of time parallel to natural child spacing.[62] Moreover, one study has demonstrated that there is an effect on the total fertility rate of couples who use IVF before and after three years.[63] Research shows that better maternal and child outcomes occur when births are spaced at least 18 to 24 months apart[64] and better growth rates occur when children are spaced three years apart.[65] As a part of premeditated parenthood, gamete use in this time period will likely become standardized as health data and medicalization of reproduction become more scientific and prescribed.

Gametes Storage for Couples and Singles Currently Undergoing Fertility Treatments

Couples and singles who are undergoing treatments for infertility may have their gametes retrieved with the intention of short-term use. Since gametes cannot be used at the exact time of retrieval—due to the testing done on samples[66]—there is an interval between retrieval and use while the gametes are temporarily stored in cryogenic units. Cryogenic units are very cold storage facilities which rely on constant subzero temperatures. Once screening of the gametes is complete, the "fittest" or most desirable are selected for further storage and the remainder are discarded.[67] Gametes can be stored indefinitely in cryopreservation units, thus the initial carbon investment of fertility drugs and gamete retrieval is extended both by amount of resources used and by number of years in storage.

Simultaneously, the couple or single person may want to obtain donor sperm or eggs. These donated gametes may come from the same storage facility, or from another facility. If the woman is receiving artificial insemination, the stored semen is used; if the woman or couple is using in-vitro fertilization, both the stored egg and the stored sperm are united, and then the fertilized egg is implanted in the woman. The fertilization process may include non-fertility-related adjunctive procedures like pre-implantation genetic diagnosis.[68] Since success rates of both AI and IVF vary, usually multiple attempts are necessary.[69] Thus, there is a "bank" of stored gametes which can be used during the months or years of fertility treatments.

Another variation on short-term access of gametes storage for couples and singles currently undergoing fertility treatments is embryo storage.[70] It may be the case that, in consultation with the doctor, a couple or single person using in-vitro fertilization chooses to let the fertilized eggs develop into embryos and then store the embryos. Embryo storage has the advantage of efficiency, since numerous eggs can be fertilized with sperm simultaneously. However, there are lower rates of MR pregnancy with the more complicated thawing process of the embryos compared with the use of thawed gametes.[71]

If fertilization is successful, then the unused embryos are either stored in case of future use or discarded. Some ethicists have objected to the disposal of unused embryos on stronger terms than the disposal of unused sperm or eggs on the basis that embryos are human beings and their disposal is akin to "murder."[72] This has led to the rarely used option of "embryo adoption" whereby couples or singles seeking fertility treatments use unwanted, surplus embryos in storage rather than their own gametes or donor gametes. For instance, the US Southern Baptist Convention has encouraged members to adopt embryos otherwise destined for destruction.[73] Although embryo adoption bypasses personal carbon emissions related to gamete retrieval and storage, the couple or single person still uses resources during fertilization, as IVF is required for embryo adoption, thus making the balance of environmental cost a significant ethical consideration even in embryo adoption, particularly because pregnancy is not a medical need and fertility treatments are unnecessary to sustain life.

Gamete storage for singles and couples currently undergoing fertility treatments is a very clear—and widespread—example of resource use in the early spectrum of the MR process. Like many other aspects of MR, gamete storage is also used by fertile people.

Gamete Storage for Donation for Use by Infertile People

Gamete "donation" is one example of fertile people participating in the MR industry at the point of gamete storage. Because gamete donation—giving egg or sperm—depends on viable gametes, the people donating do not need fertility treatments to become pregnant or impregnate and may bypass the use of fertility pharmaceuticals. Yet, they are still fertile people using MR. Both egg and sperm donation require that the gametes are stored until they are selected for use. The gametes may be stored for a prolonged period of time without use while waiting for selection, thereby wasting resources. If they are eventually used, these donated gametes will require larger MR infrastructures, depending on the configuration of the people or person seeking fertilization from donor gametes.

In the case of heterosexual infertile couples, if either the male or female partner is clinically infertile and wants to reproduce biologically, the couple will choose donated sperm or egg, resulting in a child who is genetically related to half of the couple. In the case of male infertility using donated sperm, the woman may use artificial insemination or in-vitro fertilization. If the woman is infertile and a donor egg is used, artificial insemination is not possible, so IVF or a related form of insemination, such as intracytoplasmic sperm injection (ICSI), is required. IVF and ICSI are more resource-intensive than artificial insemination as there are more steps involved. This will be elaborated on in the next chapter.

In the case of infertile same-sex male couples, if one man is infertile and the other is fertile, and the fertile man has acceptable sperm, then the same-sex male couple will need a donor egg and a womb to reproduce biologically. The donor egg and womb may be provided by a gestational surrogate, using artificial insemination or IVF with the donor sperm, or with one woman for an egg and another woman as the gestational surrogate, with the donor sperm, using in-vitro fertilization or intracytoplasmic sperm injection. The child will be genetically half of one partner and unrelated to the other partner. If both men in the couple are infertile, donor sperm will be required as well as a donor egg and a womb. The same inseminating configurations as above will be required and the child would be genetically unrelated to both men.

In the case of infertile same-sex female couples, if one woman is infertile and the other is fertile, and the fertile woman has acceptable eggs, then the same-sex female couple will need donor sperm to reproduce biologically. In this case, artificial insemination, IVF, or ICSI would be used. If both women in the couple are infertile, but one of them is able to carry a pregnancy to term, donor sperm and a donor egg would be needed, but one of the women could gestate the fetus with her own womb. IVF or ICSI would be used and the child would be genetically unrelated to both women. If neither woman has viable eggs nor can carry a pregnancy to term, they will require donor sperm, egg, and womb. AI could be used if the surrogate also provided the eggs; IVF or ICSI would be used with a separate egg donor and surrogate, again making the child genetically unrelated to both women.

Infertile single men (of any sexual orientation) seeking to reproduce biologically will need donor sperm, donor egg, and a gestational surrogate. The child would be genetically unrelated to the man, but the appeal of using MR for a child created in this way would be the selection of the possible genetic makeup of the child and the involvement in the process of child creation from fertilization to pregnancy to birth. Therefore, the man might feel more connected to the child than when adopting an infant or older child.

30 ENVIRONMENTAL ETHICS AND MEDICAL REPRODUCTION

An infertile single woman (of any sexual orientation) seeking biological children will need donor sperm and egg, and possibly a surrogate if she cannot carry the pregnancy to term. If the woman can gestate the fetus, she will still require donor egg and sperm. In either scenario, the child is genetically unrelated to the woman, but in the former situation, the woman would carry the fetus in her body. Similar to the infertile man, the only advantage might be the selection of a particular genetic profile of the sperm donor and egg donor and watching the gestational process.

The question may arise about the frequency of gay and single infertile people wanting to use MR to reproduce and therefore its significance for environmental ethics. This question is complicated by a few factors. First, while the numbers of gay and single infertile people who use subsidized MR are likely low, especially when compared to heterosexual infertile couples (mostly due to factors such as healthcare access,[74] lack of recognition of same-sex partnerships,[75] and other logistical barriers), actual use does not necessarily correlate to desire to use MR. Thus, there is a latent environmental threat. Indeed, second, with the increase in lobbying for subsidized MR beyond infertile straight couples[76]—inclusive of access to gestational surrogates[77]—rates of use by gay and single infertile people will likely increase. Third, many countries, such as the US, do not track use of MR by sexual orientation or by partner status, so numbers may be underreported. Fourth, given the variety of configurations of donor sperm, donor egg, and gestational surrogates, some forms of MR for infertile same-sex couples and singles may be less visible—such as sperm donation for a single woman or a woman in a same-sex partnership. In all of these cases, it should be remembered that gamete donation depends on the participation of the fertile people in the MR retrieval and storage process. MR, in these cases, requires fertile people, thus destabilizing understandings of MR as "only" a procedure for infertile people, and opening the realm of ethical inquiry into environmental and reproductive ethics as well as medical ethics.

Gamete Storage for Donation for Use by Fertile People

Fertile people use MR both to donate gametes and to use gametes. In contrast to those who cannot reproduce using their own eggs or sperm, heterosexual fertile couples—who are able to produce and sustain a pregnancy—may wish to create a particular type of child, for instance with a desirable ethnicity or height disposition that they are unlikely to produce naturally. The couple would then avail themselves of donated egg, sperm, or both. Similarly, a fertile heterosexual couple may want to avoid the "burdens" of pregnancy—either because it is medically dangerous for the woman in the couple to carry the pregnancy or because it is merely inconvenient—and hire a surrogate.[78]

Depending on the couple's own genetic makeup and desires, if only one of the gametes is donated either AI will be used for donor sperm and IVF or intrauterine insemination (IUI) for donor eggs. The child will be genetically related to one of the partners and unrelated to the other partner. This assumes that if the woman in the fertile heterosexual couple can carry the pregnancy, she will. If both gametes are donated, the child is genetically unrelated to either socializing parent. There is the possibility that the woman in the fertile heterosexual couple could gestate the fetus, regardless of genetic tie. In this case, she would essentially be the surrogate for her genetically unrelated child. However, the woman may not want to gestate the fetus and the couple could have one or both gametes donated, with use of a surrogate.

Both fertile heterosexual couples and fertile same-sex couples may use donated gametes to create a custom child. In the case of fertile same-sex male couples seeking a particular genetic profile, they may want both donor egg and sperm and will need a gestational surrogate. There would be no genetic tie to either of the men. Another possibility is that one of the fertile men's sperm will be used and they select a donor egg, with a gestational surrogate. If the surrogate also provides the eggs, AI, IVF, or IUI would be necessary to reproduce. In this scenario, the genetic tie would be to only one of the men in the couple.

In case of fertile same-sex female couples seeking a particular genetic profile, they may select donor egg, donor sperm, and use the womb of one of the women in the couple. This would require IVF or IUI. The child would be genetically unrelated to either woman. In another scenario, donor sperm may be chosen and one woman would supply both the eggs and the womb. AI could be possible and the child would be related to only half of the couple. In a third scenario, the fertile women may use donor sperm and one woman would supply her eggs to be gestated in the other woman's womb. This would require IVF or IUI and the child would be related to half of the couple, although both women in the couple would participate in the reproductive process. While the feeling of proximity to the child might be closer through gestation, it would not necessarily be the case that the child is related to either mother.

32 ENVIRONMENTAL ETHICS AND MEDICAL REPRODUCTION

Fertile single men seeking a particular genetic profile will need a donor egg and a gestational surrogate to reproduce biologically, but they may also opt for donor sperm. As in other cases, the donor egg may come from the surrogate, or it may be obtained from a different woman. Fertile single women seeking a specific genetic profile may also want to select a particular type of sperm to be inseminated with and use their own eggs and womb. Or a fertile single woman could use her eggs with donor sperm in a surrogate womb. Alternatively, a fertile single woman could use donor egg and sperm and she could gestate the child in her womb. She would be genetically unrelated to the child, but still have the experience of pregnancy.

Ethical discussions of the use of donated gametes have tended to focus on the emotional difficulties of raising a child that one is not genetically related to. These difficulties have been dismissed and rightfully so; adoption is one parenting option—and a low-carbon one at that—where children who are not biologically related to the parents can thrive.[79] Thus, the arguments for access to donor egg or sperm for infertile couples on the basis of poor child outcomes is unfounded. Children from gamete donation are not "biologically" from the two parents; neither is an adopted child. On balance, there is not persuasive reasons for gamete donation over adoption because of genetic tie.

The preference for use of MR under the lines of wanting "a child of one's own" can also be dismissed when donor gametes are used. Use of MR and donor gametes therefore requires additional ethical justification beyond biological connection, particularly with the amount of natural resources used in the process. When couples use gamete donation under the guise of "wanting a biological child" they are misleading the conversation. A child that comes from donated gametes is not biologically from both people in the couple—gay or straight. The single person only avoids this commentary on lack of biological connection by virtue of being unpartnered; the child is only half genetically theirs, but there is not a partner who is absent from the reproductive process.

Gamete Retrieval and Storage for Long-Term Access

In some cases, gamete retrieval and storage are not intended for short-term access. These gametes can be stored indefinitely and while they are in storage, they absorb resources from the cooling facilities. Some governmental health insurance covers storage for a certain period of time. For instance, in 2018 the UK's NHS England policy was to pay for storage of gametes for up to five years, even after the person no longer meets the criteria for "infertility"—which includes having a biological child—or for as long as the patient continues to meet the guidelines for "infertility."[80] If the single person or couple exceeds this timeframe, or if subsidized healthcare does not cover storage, they may pay for storage independently.

Stored gametes have other resource-intensive infrastructures such as the monitoring of the facilities during storage and, of course, the steps preceding the retrieval, from fertility drugs and retrieval devices to transportation of gametes and assessment of viability. There are several categories of gamete storage for long-term access, which are used by both infertile and fertile people.

Gametes for Couples and Singles Who May Undergo Fertility Treatments in the Future

Gametes may be retrieved and stored by singles or couples who are fertile and not considering fertility treatments at the present time, but who nonetheless want to store their fertile gametes for use in the future, in anticipation of potential infertility. The growing popularity of MR use by fertile people indicates that this is becoming more common.

In some cases, gamete freezing has become institutionalized. Servicepeople in the armed forces may be encouraged to store eggs or sperm for long-term access based on anticipated vocational hazards. In many countries, military service is still mandatory.[81] This does not necessarily mean that these individuals will be placed in a combatant situation. However, if they are entering a place where injury or death is possible, then both female and male servicepeople may be offered fertility preservation.[82] The motivation is severalfold. First, severe pelvic wounds in either sex could compromise the ability to procreate.[83] Violence or injury which may cause castration or paralysis in males would have infertility as a secondary effect.[84] Before this happens, a fertile serviceperson may store gametes.

Second, if the person dies in the course of service, their partner, if they have one, may want to use the stored gametes for postmortem procreation. Beyond this, parents may want to use their children's gametes for grandchildren. In Israel, parents of dead soldiers have been able to access the

34   ENVIRONMENTAL ETHICS AND MEDICAL REPRODUCTION

gametes of their children for postmortem grandparenthood and a number of parents have successfully petitioned courts for postmortem sperm retrieval (PMSR) as well as postmortem egg retrieval from their single, adult children.[85] Between 2003 and 2010, 10 of the 21 petitions for PMSR and freezing were made by a parent for posthumous grandparenthood.[86] Most people would not consider death as a criterion of infertility, yet the utilization of MR by surviving family members after a person's death points to expansive use of MR not only by fertile and infertile, but also by the living and the dead.

Third, servicewomen who become pregnant while enlisted reduce the numbers of possible combatants; pregnancy is a liability for the strength of the armed forces. In 2009, the US military proposed a policy that female personnel in Iraq could face a court-martial for getting pregnant. The rationale was that "the redeployment of the pregnant soldier creates a void in the unit and has a negative impact on the unit's ability to accomplish its mission. Another soldier must assume the pregnant soldier's responsibilities."[87] Among the many criticisms of this policy what the fact that the male serviceman who impregnated the soldier, thus rendering her unfit to serve, was treated much less harshly. The double standard, albeit rooted in biological differences in reproduction, was not implemented. Yet, the concerns around female soldier pregnancy remain. Thus, this military has offered a "security net" program that gives women the option of gamete storage in hopes of deterring pregnancy.[88] Of course, storage does not safeguard the servicemen's and -women's health or life. Nor does it guarantee the ability to reproduce after their service is done. Moreover, these gametes may be stored and never used, either because postmortem reproduction is unappealing to surviving partners and parents or because ex-servicepeople reproduce naturally, or because they do not want additional MR fertilization services as a matter of preference or ethical principle. Besides the resources required for these fertility preservation programs, the unnecessary medical procedure of gamete retrieval and infrastructure required for gamete storage and possible later use must be considered from an environmental perspective. The carbon of the military is significant,[89] as is the carbon of military hospitals.[90] Added to this is the routinization of fertility preservation programs.

Outside of the military, many gamete cryopreservation advertisements are marketed to young professional women in the developed world.[91] Civilian women may be advised—or may feel the compulsion to—store eggs while they are in their peak fertility years and choosing to postpone pregnancy.[92] A woman's motivation for delaying pregnancy varies, from wanting to complete education, to not being economically ready for a pregnancy, to not having a willing or desirable partner.[93] Egg cryopreservation for fertile women may be financially supported by employers. The tech companies Facebook, Apple, and Google offer cryopreservation of women's eggs as part of their healthcare plan.[94] These policies have been met with criticism. The motivation for employer-sponsored egg storage seems less about reproductive choice than worker productivity; women stay active in the company's workforce instead of taking a maternity break under the guise of future MR use and success. However, MR has lower success rates than natural conception, and fertility declines with age, so it is not the case that employer gamete storage schemes seamlessly allow management of pregnancy. Rather, they avoid pregnancy during peak working years and make actual pregnancy more difficult later.

Significantly, men are not advised to store gametes for later use under the pretense of wanting to achieve certain work goals or complete education. This binary approach to fertility preservation is indicative of sexism that expects women to be the primary caregiver,[95] thus incentivizing a later pregnancy and minimizing the "motherhood penalty" during a career.[96] Moreover, it is not the possible inconvenience of being pregnant during a program of academic study which would lead a woman to want to store eggs, since there are institutional supports for these women,[97] but rather the interlocking factors of institutionalized maternity leave being more accepted than paternity leave,[98] the expectations that women will be the first to sacrifice a career, the pressure women face to take on caregiving roles associated with children,[99] and the stigma against proper parenting responsibility from men.[100] Men do not face these challenges of balancing fatherhood during education or career, thus cryopreservation is not an appealing way to manage sexism.

To be sure, women's fertility declines more precipitously than men's with age.[101] However, factors contributing to birth complications and birth defects include older age of both men and women, which is an underdiscussed factor in gamete storage for long-term access. Autism in children, among other forms of life-altering neurodiversity, is associated with higher paternal age.[102] Down syndrome, among other genetic disorders, is associated with higher maternal age.[103] Pregnancy is also medically riskier later in life.[104] Moreover, storing eggs for future use does not solve the underlying problems of sexism. Nor does it guarantee a pregnancy on demand. Hence, women have also been warned not to rely on fertility preservation,[105] thus leading to contradictory messages.

36 ENVIRONMENTAL ETHICS AND MEDICAL REPRODUCTION

Finally, some clinicians have suggested that men or women who voluntarily seek contraceptive sterilization or sex-reassignment surgery—even after informed consent has been performed and the clients are aware that their fertility will be terminated—should be offered gamete storage for long-term access.[106] The resources to retrieve and store the gametes would be unnecessary if contraceptive sterilization or sex-reassignment surgery were performed after procreative choices were complete. In fact, this sequence of medical interventions underpins the logic behind non-coverage of IVF for women who have chosen sterilization.[107] While contraceptive sterilization and sex-reassignment surgery are directly related to possible loss of fertility, if performed during fertile years, other medical treatments are indirectly associated with loss of fertility and may lead to gamete retrieval and storage for long-term access.

Oncofertility

Oncofertility, or "fertility preservation," is the process of gamete retrieval and storage for potential future use with medical reproduction following cancer treatments.[108] Cancer treatments—even those unrelated to cancers of the reproductive organs—may cause loss of fertility due to the toxicity of the drugs.[109] However, not all people will become infertile from cancer treatments. Also, some people who are undergoing cancer treatments are already biological parents and not advised to avail themselves of oncofertility options. Other cancer patients, such as children, are only potentially fertile and do not lose any reproductive functioning from cancer treatments, they simply do not develop that capacity.

Oncofertility is primarily available in the developed world, where people have a very good chance of surviving some cancers. Options have been developed for both men and women. Oncofertility options for men parallel those enumerated above. Sperm retrieval, either through masturbation, sexual intercourse, electrovibration, or aspiration of the testis, would be done prior to cancer treatments and the gametes subsequently stored.[110] Males make sperm before they are physically able to ejaculate, so a male child could have sperm retrieval imposed on him by electrovibration or aspiration of the testis.

Oncofertility possibilities for women include oocyte cryopreservation and ovarian tissue cryopreservation. Oocyte cryopreservation has been discussed above and can be used for women who are sexually mature and undergoing chemotherapy.[111] Ovarian tissue cryopreservation involves a surgery to obtain ovarian tissue.[112] Ovarian tissue cryopreservation is available for females who are too young to be fertile, as well as women who are reproductively mature. In 2012, the youngest girl to forcibly undergo ovarian tissue removal was two years old.[113]

Finally, oncofertility options for either men or women undergoing cancer treatments include embryo cryopreservation.[114] In this case, the cancer patient and their partner (or possibly a gamete donor) will each have their gametes retrieved, then the egg will be fertilized with the sperm. Once it develops into an embryo, the embryos will be stored. As of 2007, there were "over 400,000 frozen embryos in cryopreservation storage facilities in the United States."[115] From the period of 2004 through 2013, 1,954,548 embryos were cryopreserved in the United States alone.[116] Embryos can be stored indefinitely and require environmental resources for each year stored. The emotional attachment to embryos may delay disposal[117] and this ought to be considered in cryopreservation decisions.

There are a number of ethical concerns with oncofertility itself. First, oncofertility is often suggested as a part of cancer treatments,[118] but itself does not cure, treat, or prevent cancer. Rather, it is an elective service that is within the jurisdiction of medical reproduction, although the precipitating factor for use is medical: the cancer treatments. Oncofertility sets into motion a series of medical procedures centered on reproductive technologies that cannot increase the chance of surviving cancer. While some argue that oncofertility is an adjunct to oncology, it is truly situated in MR. The intention of all forms of oncofertility is reproduction, not cancer care. Moreover, in some cases, oncofertility is not for the benefit of the cancer patient, who might die in the course of treatments, but for the surviving partner or parents, who will use the gametes or embryos to reproduce posthumously.[119] This violates biomedical principles of treating the patient, not the family.[120] It also, significantly, does not medically benefit the recipient of the gametes who will use them for pregnancy, unlike organ donation after death, which prolongs life. Oncofertility treatments are not related to medical care of cancer, take resources, and expend carbon unrelated to the goals of medicine.

Second, if the person survives cancer and their fertility is compromised, they must use medical reproductive techniques such as in-vitro fertilization or artificial insemination with their stored eggs or sperm. If ovarian tissue

38 ENVIRONMENTAL ETHICS AND MEDICAL REPRODUCTION

has been frozen, it can be retransplanted into the woman's own body after cancer treatments.[121]

These initial procedures to provide the possibility of impregnation have low success rates. The American Pregnancy Association records that, in the United States, the live birth rate for one round of in-vitro fertilization per age group is as follows: 41–43% for women under age 35; 33–36% for women ages 35 to 37; 23–27% for women ages 38 to 40; and 13–18% for women over 40.[122] These success rates of IVF are comparable to pregnancy rates by ovarian tissue transplantation, which offers an average 30% chance of pregnancy and birth.[123] Oncofertility and assisted reproductive technologies always use resources, but the desired outcome is not guaranteed. It could be pointed out that the low success rates of oncofertility are better for the environment, as a child will not be created, so it might still be ethically pursued. In this case, the purpose of oncofertility would not be the output of a child, but rather the intangible hope for pregnancy, or the "peace of mind" associated with fertility preservation.[124] However, these are emotional and psychological benefits and very far away from either cancer care or the intentions of medical reproduction. Non-physical "benefits" of oncofertility are best addressed by lower-carbon branches of healthcare such as psychotherapy[125] or another discipline discrete from oncology.[126]

Third, pediatric oncofertility raises significant ethical concerns about informed consent and risk. Minors cannot consent to medical treatments, but they may assent to treatments.[127] Parents or legal guardians act as surrogate decision-makers and are tasked with making medical choices in the best interest of their child. While this holds true for both the cancer treatments and fertility preservation, it is ethically dubious to compel children to have invasive non-lifesaving treatments.[128] Moreover, children cannot be made fertile with oncofertility treatments and fertility cannot be *preserved* in children since preservation implies that something already exists. Children with cancer can have procedures that can aid them in medical reproduction later in life, if the cancer treatments compromise fertility, but a child undergoing cancer treatment, who survives to puberty, does not lose anything that they ever had. The risks associated with fertility retrieval and storage for children is incommensurate. Oncofertility for children also raises unique ethical concerns due to the longer time interval between gamete retrieval, storage, and access. The extended time that must be invested in the maintenance and payment for gamete storage in facilities[129] and limitations on gamete storage[130] put additional pressures on the parents who want oncofertility for their children. These practicalities may be resolved with enough money, but if money is not available, it can cause stress as fertility options in the future are foreclosed. As gametes are stored, technical errors, such as possible malfunctions in cryopreservation units which destroy viable samples,[131] are another concern. The longer gametes are stored, the more time there is for potential issues with storage facilities.[132] If the child does live to be an adult and the gametes are stored for a decade or more, there may be stress around the perceived obligation to use the gametes to procreate, even in the absence of partnership or heterosexuality. Pressure to reproduce—especially in a pronatalist society—is already strong.[133] The added financial investment of fertility preservation, possible trauma or side effects from the (unconsented to) procedures of gamete retrieval,[134] and the disparity between a parental choice for a child with cancer and the adult cancer patient's desire for fertility preservation also present a power dynamic[135] that may lead to additional ethical concerns associated with oncofertility for children.

Fourth, and related to the point above, is the pressure that adults feel for fertility preservation, especially in time-sensitive situations. A late-stage cancer diagnosis puts the clock into motion in a race for effective treatments.[136] While sperm can be obtained quite quickly, egg retrieval may take weeks or months,[137] which is significant in the face of spreading cancer. A woman may have to debate between starting lifesaving cancer treatment or pursuing the rather frivolous-by-comparison, non-lifesaving process of fertility preservation. Similarly, some women when faced with a cancer diagnosis while pregnant will have a dilemma to continue carrying the pregnancy to term and postpone cancer treatments,[138] or terminate the pregnancy and immediately begin cancer treatment, if they are fortunate enough to live in a place with accessible, safe, and legal abortion.

Fifth, medical professionalism entails being non-directive, which means that clinicians are not to persuade medical decisions or suggest one course of treatment over another.[139] Yet, many factors, like the stress of diagnosis, uncertainty over future fertility desires, and of course, availability of MR services, lead doctors to *encourage* fertility preservation.[140] While it may be argued that the opposite decision—not to preserve gametes or continue a pregnancy—is also influenced by stress, the same rationale is not applied to the cancer treatments themselves.[141] Doctors accept that aggressive cancer treatments will proceed, even in times of stress, but struggle to understand refusal of fertility preservation.[142] Hasty fertility preservation in the case of adults is below the threshold of truly informed consent as any adult must

40   ENVIRONMENTAL ETHICS AND MEDICAL REPRODUCTION

have the ability to consider the benefits and drawbacks of a particular procedure without direction from a physician and without it being framed as "just an option for the future."[143] Oncofertility, in these cases, raises the ethical red flags of paternalistic boundary crossing.

Sixth, fertility drugs are known carcinogens and have been linked to increases in cancer in women following MR use.[144] Thus, a woman facing a cancer diagnosis should be informed that starting the egg retrieval process might place her at additional risk for other cancers, thus making the decision for cancer treatment and gamete retrieval counterintuitive. The harm from oncofertility itself, whether actual or potential, needs to be considered, as well as the medical resources that will then be required to treat an additional, and potentially self-selected, form of cancer. Simultaneously, cancer treatments themselves are becoming more resource-intensive. The West Midlands Cancer Intelligence Unit (UK) found that "data comparisons from 1999 and 2004 showed that there has been a 214% increase in total car miles travelled which equates to over 400 tonnes of carbon associated with radiotherapy treatment in the West Midlands."[145] Their study, which only looked at the cancer registry for treating breast cancer, is a reminder that all medical carbon cumulates in the atmosphere, causing extensive environmental problems.

The treatments before, during, and after fertility preservation use substantial medical, intellectual, and natural resources. Oncofertility—even when separated from cancer care—has a twofold consumptive effect: that of the initial gamete retrieval, preservation, and storage, and that of the MR industry following cancer treatments. From an environmental perspective, oncofertility and cryopreservation are an unmitigated resource drain without concomitant medical benefit, since the inability to make or become pregnant does not threaten life or physical well-being. Certainly, medicine should attempt to prevent, treat, and cure cancer in all parts of the world, but oncofertility is part of the MR industry, not cancer care.

Ultimately, it must be remembered that not all men or women who are rendered infertile by cancer treatments will see this as a loss. Yet, the discussions in oncofertility—as with the entire medical reproduction industry—reify the notion that biological parenthood is a life goal of adults that should not be disrupted by cancer. For women, in particular, this narrative is particularly strong. Academic literature, unhelpfully, adds valence to what should be value-neutral descriptions of the effects of cancer treatments. For instance, saying that women "*suffered* from ovarian failure"[146] instead of "had ovarian failure" emotionalize what is a normal and predictable result of chemotherapy. Moreover, the narrative of women "needing" to become pregnant or needing to "preserve" fertility reinforces the idea that biological reproduction is the height of feminine achievement, thus perpetuating a discriminatory atmosphere for women who are childless and childfree both inside and outside of the medical industry. The pronatalist narrative that often drives MR in the face of life-threatening cancer is so tenacious that it persists even after death.

Postmortem Sperm Retrieval

Postmortem sperm retrieval is a form of gamete retrieval that takes sperm from a man who has been dead for a short period of time, or a man who has been declared dead by neurological criteria and is being kept alive artificially. It is part of the spectrum of MR related to posthumous reproduction. While postmortem egg[147] and uterus[148] retrieval exist, but are rare, postmortem sperm retrieval is common enough that multiple countries have produced policies and laws governing its acceptability.

The first case of PMSR occurred in 1995, when British woman Diana Blood requested sperm harvesting of her comatose husband. Using electroejaculation, the doctors procured his sperm and cryopreserved it. After a legal battle in the UK,[149] "Mrs. Blood [sic] traveled to Belgium for insemination,[150] in the first case of postmortem reproductive tourism. Through the harvested sperm, two children were born using MR—one in 1999[151] and another in 2002."[152] Thus, the sperm was stored for a total of seven years. PMSR is currently legal in the UK under the Human Fertilisation and Embryology (Deceased Fathers) Act of 2003[153] and in other countries.

As of 2016, PMSR is conditionally legal in the UK, Canada, Netherlands, and Greece with prior written consent of the man, but prohibited by law in Germany, Sweden, and France.[154] In Eastern Europe, the Czech Republic practices PMSR with written consent; Estonia allows PMSR if assisted reproduction treatments are already in progress and attempted pregnancy occurs within one month of the death; Cyprus, Latvia, Lithuania, Malta, Poland, and Slovakia do not mention PMSR in legislation or guidelines; and Hungary and Slovenia prohibit PMSR by law.[155] Japan allows postmortem sperm retrieval "if blood relationship and husband's agreement are confirmed."[156] Sri Lanka has no guidelines or rules for PMSR, Pakistan forbids it, and Nepal, Bhutan,

42   ENVIRONMENTAL ETHICS AND MEDICAL REPRODUCTION

Bangladesh, and India have no guidelines in place.[157] In Australia and New Zealand, there are inconsistent, ambiguous, or absent laws regarding the retrieval and use of sperm after death. In some cases, there are guidelines without laws.[158]

In the United States, the earliest institutional guidelines on postmortem sperm retrieval were published in 2003.[159] Ten years later, the Ethics Committee of the American Society for Reproductive Medicine (ASRM) issued *Posthumous Collection and Use of Reproductive Tissue: A Committee Opinion*. The 2013 opinion stated, in short, "Posthumous gamete [sperm or oocyte] procurement and reproduction are ethically justifiable if written documentation from the deceased authorizing the procedure is available."[160] They further clarified that "in the absence of written documentation from the decedent, programs open to considering requests for posthumous gamete procurement or reproduction should only do so when such requests are initiated by the surviving spouse or life partner."[161] By 2016, a survey of 50 major academic medical centers in the United States found that five had policies on postmortem sperm retrieval (Columbia University, Cornell University, Tufts University, University of Iowa at Carver, and University of Virginia).[162]

In a typical case of postmortem sperm retrieval, the person requesting the sperm is the wife or partner of the dead man and the potential child will be the offspring of the man and woman who were in a relationship. The Ethics Committee of the American Society for Reproductive Medicine affirms, "The desire of a surviving partner to have a child with the gametes of the deceased, in light of their intention to have a family together, may be viewed with sympathy."[163] However, there are also cases where family members outside of a romantic relationship request PMSR.

The same ASRM report opines, "A more troubling situation is when the request for gametes for posthumous reproduction does not come from a spouse or life partner, but from the parents of the deceased, who see this intervention as promulgating the legacy of their child or as the only way to become grandparents. Ethically, these situations are not comparable. In the case of a surviving parent, no joint reproductive project can ever be said to have existed. Nor do the desires of the parents give them any ethical claim to their child's gametes."[164] The Ethics Committee therefore recommends rejection of requests for posthumous grandparenthood in the absence of written instructions from the adult child. However, it is worth noting that Israel has permitted requests for posthumous grandparenthood, thus confronting some of the aforementioned concerns about proximity to sperm donor.

In Israel, petitions for PMSR are processed according to the non-legally-binding *Israel Attorney General Guidelines*.[165] The guidelines support PMSR requests from a widow or partner on the basis of presumed consent of the dead man.[166] However, cases outside of these guidelines can be superseded by court order.[167] Israel appears to be moving toward accepting requests for PMSR from parents without these safeguards, thus expanding the reach of MR and concomitant potential for resource use. Yael Hashiloni-Dolev and Silke Schicktanz report that in 2014, the courts granted a request for PMSR from parents of a dead man without reference to their son's wishes and in 2016 "an Israeli judge decided in favour of parents who are planning to raise their grandchild on their own, using a surrogate and an egg donor who will not actively parent the child."[168] Recent qualitative data indicates that post-humous grandparenthood is against the wishes of a majority of men.[169]

Beyond the typical ethical concerns of PMSR that have been raised and addressed through law and policy, such as consent and privacy,[170] one underconsidered factor is the environmental impact of PMSR, as a form of medical reproduction. An ecological assessment of PMSR indicates that resource use, from retrieval with the intention of cryopreservation and later insemination, to reproduction, are contributing factors to the carbon of MR. PMSR must also be accountable in biomedical ethics as a procedure that does not cure, treat, or prevent disease, or directly or indirectly benefit the patient—the dead man. As such, it is a clinically unnecessary part of the carbon emissions of the medical industry. And, with all reproductive ethics, the intention to create a child that one will never know because of death must be seriously assessed.

Summary

When viewed from an ethical lens of environmental resource use and carbon emissions, the early stages of MR, such as fertility drugs which support gamete retrieval, are significant. Given the purpose of gamete retrieval is further resource use through storage for short-term or long-term access, medical reproduction prior to insemination indicates numerous ecological concerns. The various reasons that one might use stored gametes highlight not only the numerous ways MR leaves a carbon footprint—which is an

44 ENVIRONMENTAL ETHICS AND MEDICAL REPRODUCTION

environmental problem—but also their use by the fertile and infertile, living and dead.

When viewed from the lens of biomedical ethics, the lack of clinical indication for MR use by fertile people highlight a disjuncture between the goals of medicine and actual MR use. The elective nature of MR as a "medical procedure" which does not treat or cure a disease demands a critical reassessment from the medical industry.

MR as an elective mode of reproduction, which may be used by fertile people, renders it subjected to criticism from sexual and parental ethics on a number of fronts, ranging from fairness to children who need to be adopted, impact on lives of women who bear the brunt of medical interventions related to MR, and the additional human carbon footprint, which contributes to both population growth and resource consumption.

The intersection of technology and medicine renews the questions and "assumptions made about reproduction—is it a privilege, or is it an unquestionable and unalienable right? Is it a mere want, a deeply held desire, or a need so profound and fundamental as to trump the rights of others?"[171] These assumptions obfuscate the ethical concerns about MR. Every step along the MR spectrum comes at an environmental cost that all people bear. This includes, of course, people using MR and their potential children. Fundamentally, MR is not only about resolving infertility, as can be seen from the many ways fertile people use even this first step of MR. Rather, MR is a means of facilitating reproductive projects. Any of the stages of MR are environmentally significant enough to warrant reevaluation, but the entire process of medical reproduction is long and laborious. When taken in aggregate, the MR spectrum must be viewed as a total environmental menace which demands serious reconsideration.

2

Medical Reproduction Preparing for Insemination

After gametes have been retrieved they are brought to a storage unit for further processing. Transportation-associated activities are among the largest contributors to the medical industry carbon footprint.[1] This primarily includes the transportation of clients and healthcare workers to and from clinics, but also the transportation of gametes from fertility clinics to cryopreservation units.

Cryopreservation units use resources related to maintaining a constant, very cold temperature.[2] The containers that store the gametes, the electronic medical records that track the arrival of gametes, and various scanners, barcode printouts, disposable personal protective equipment, and other associated tools, which are minimal requirements of a safe lab, also take resources.[3]

These "behind the scenes" aspects of MR are often overlooked as part of the carbon impact of medicalized reproduction because people using the MR industry do not see them personally; because cryopreservation units are not part of the experience of the person using MR, they are almost invisible. However, it is significant that these centers are constant-use locations. Fertility storage units demand resources no matter how many gametes are being stored. They are a building, like other healthcare clinics, that require a constant source of energy. Moreover, since the storage units seem to exist a priori, they are not questioned as excessively contributing to carbon emissions, even though the growing MR industry depends on building and constructing new and additional storage units to accommodate the number of people using MR. Usually, these are new storage units in different parts of the country,[4] due to the sensitive material that is being transported. Rather than expanding current storage units, which would "only" add to the carbon of already existing facilities, new infrastructures and locations appear.

After the carbon-intensive gamete retrieval and storage, gamete assessment and fertilization are the next stages of medical reproduction. Once obtained, the gametes are assessed for fitness, that is, desirability, which has

Environmental Ethics and Medical Reproduction. Cristina Richie, Oxford University Press.
© Oxford University Press 2024. DOI: 10.1093/oso/9780197745182.003.0003

three basic components: viability, or potential for successful fertilization, genetic health, and genetic features unrelated to health, like sex or physical characteristics. Only after this stage of MR does the most identifiable feature—assisted reproductive technologies—occur. Assisted reproductive technologies (ARTs) are the techniques of MR that attempt to impregnate women. As with other MR procedures, both fertile and infertile people avail themselves of gamete assessment and fertilization, thus causing carbon emissions and resource use, even when there is no medical reason for seeking treatments.

Gamete Assessment—Viability

Viability includes both the ability of a sperm to fertilize an egg and the ability of an egg to be fertilized by sperm. All gametes are screened for viability even though some people who are assumed to be fertile have their gametes retrieved and stored. This includes egg and sperm donors, those preserving gametes before military deployment or cancer treatments, people who will use MR as a lifestyle option—for instance by planning a timed pregnancy, as a substitution for an opposite-sex partner, and for genetic selection of embryos. Other people who are assumed to be infertile may have a clinical diagnosis confirmed after their gametes are assessed for viability.

Definitions of infertility and diagnostics of infertility are different aspects that determine which fertility treatments may be offered or clinically indicated. For instance, a definition of infertility for women has certain criteria like age range,[5] but a woman may be fertile beyond the "average" age of fertility, or have more limited ovarian reserves before the upper age limit of the definition is met. Moreover, "infertility" as a proxy for the inability to make pregnant or become pregnant might be affected by a variety of factors such as stress, which would not necessarily impact the quality of the gamete samples given, although it could affect the process of sexual intercourse and effective ejaculation and fertilization.[6] Furthermore, infertility might be caused by biological factors such as blocked reproductive tubes, which would not affect the viability of the gametes, only their ability to be accessed.[7] Regardless, a diagnostic test of the gametes is performed to ensure that a baseline level of fertility is being met, and also as a way to more closely identify the possible cause of infertility (if any) so further treatments can be recommended.

Assessment of Sperm

Sperm will be tested for quantity as well as motility. Quantity is one factor that may cause infertility. The semen volume, total number of sperm, and sperm concentration are related to quantity.[8] This is an important indicator of fertility, as the sheer number of sperm available to inseminate an egg is important. Lower numbers indicate fewer chances of fertilization and therefore pregnancy. However, the number of sperm will not matter if the sperm are not motile. Motility is the ability of the sperm to "swim" properly, that is, with enough speed and force to penetrate the egg. Without this ability, the sperm are called asthenospermia or asthenozoospermia.[9]

Some of the forms of MR have been developed to address these specific issues. Fertility drugs can bolster low sperm counts. Men with low motility can have their sperm directly inserted into an egg if they are asthenospermiac. The testing of gametes should be seen, not as a final step before insemination, but as a diagnostic tool that may refer back to the previous steps of MR described in Chapter 1—fertility drugs and gamete retrieval—or toward the next steps of gamete assessment related to health, or genetic features unrelated to health, before insemination. It is a (?) fork to determine which additional resources will be used, rather than a completion of some form of resource use in the assessment process.

Assessment of Eggs

The number of eggs a woman has may affect her fertility.[10] Tests for these are done prior to gamete retrieval, because the egg is a single gamete and so the number taken will be mathematically obvious, unlike the sperm which are numerous and can be quantified only after retrieval. Thus, the quality of eggs is the primary factor that can be assessed. A low-quality egg might have reduced oocyte mitochondrial efficiency or oxidative stress.[11] This form of infertility may be age-related.

As with male-related infertility, some forms of MR can be used as a workaround for infertility in women. Fertility drugs can increase the number of eggs that can be withdrawn at one time, but there is little that can be done to increase the quality of eggs in human women prior to insemination. In studies involving mice, the deletion of kinase 2 (*Chk2* or *Chek2*) can "restore fertility to females that would otherwise be sterile because of a meiotic

48 ENVIRONMENTAL ETHICS AND MEDICAL REPRODUCTION

recombination mutation or radiation exposure,"[12] but this technique does not exist for humans. Thus, if the egg is of low quality, obtaining an egg donor may be advised, which would close off the possibility of the woman having a biologically related child.

Gamete Assessment—Genetic Health

Viable gametes are a prerequisite for attempted fertilization but the genetic health of gametes is essential too. MR clinics will usually advise against fertilizing genetically unhealthy gametes, although there are some exceptions where people select for a disabled child, discussed below. If the single person or couple using MR wants to decrease the chances of a disabled child, then the genes that are targeted for assessment range from serious genetic disorders, to objective features like sex, to trivial characteristics like eye color.[13] Of the hundreds of genetic conditions that can be tested for, some of the most common inherited diseases include various cancers, cardiac disease, muscular dystrophy, Alzheimer's, and congenital malformations.[14] The test for genetic health is called pre-implantation genetic diagnosis (PGD). In the future, genetic editing may be done with CRISPR-Cas9, which could replace or supplement PGD.

Pre-implantation Genetic Diagnosis (PGD)

Pre-implantation genetic diagnosis, or PGD, is a technique that falls under the umbrella of MR. It requires first gamete retrieval and storage, with the intention of use with in-vitro fertilization. PGD is used on embryos to determine their genetic makeup. PGD, although it is often offered as part of MR, is not a cure or treatment for infertility. As an elective part of MR, PGD embryos with the desired traits or health conditions are identified, and they are implanted into the woman's womb in hopes of fertilization.

Indeed, with the isolation of the first gene, "researchers shift[ed] emphasis from concern about childlessness to control of genetic anomalies."[15] Both fertile and infertile people can use PGD, including couples who already have children, couples with a disposition for genetic diseases—which is an increasing number of people worldwide[16]—and those who want to select the features of their potential children, like sex and physical characteristics.

MEDICAL REPRODUCTION FOR INSEMINATION   49

Pre-implantation genetic diagnosis can also be done with the intention of creating a "savior sibling," that is a child who will be selected as a perfect genetic match for an older sibling with a rare disease that requires marrow, or blood platelets, from a donor. The new child will have their genetic material taken from them without permission and given to the older child one or more times throughout their life.[17]

Aside from the environmental impact, major ethical concerns about PGD have centered on its possible eugenic implication and social consequences for those with disabilities. Genetic counseling, which was a forerunner to pre-implantation genetic diagnosis, was first offered to couples with known genetic diseases who wished to have a biological child. Genetic counseling traces back to the 1940s, when the "genetic hygiene centers" emerged. In the United States, for instance, the University of Minnesota's center, co-funded by the American Eugenics Society and the Rockefeller Foundation, offered genetic counseling. At the time, the director was "concerned the term 'hygiene' connoted personal care products; he changed the term to 'counseling'—and the new field of 'genetic counseling' was born."[18] Given the historical situation of the emergence of these centers—the eugenics of Hitler's Reich and various programs of forced sterilization in the United States, Sweden,[19] and Guatemala,[20] compounded by legal support for these sterilizations,[21] the concerns about genetic counseling leading to PGD are apparent.

To be sure, genetic diagnosis need not imply eugenics, particularly when it is separate from MR and selective abortion as a result of disability. For instance, Catholic theologian Janet Smith argues that prenatal diagnosis "is permissible . . . to provide an ailing or effective fetus with treatment in the womb, or in order to prepare to treat the child more effectively after birth."[22] This approach avoids the concerns that PGD might only be used to "vaccinate the social body against the birth of [a disabled] child,"[23] as it embraces the child instead of eliminating them. Indeed, as PGD has become more widely available and MR a more common way of reproducing, the ethical concerns—and thus arguments in favor for, or against, pre-implantation genetic diagnosis for genetic health—have moved from the obligations of parents to society (similar to eugenics) to the duties to vulnerable groups that may be impacted by mass genetic testing.

The disability rights movement has pointed out that conversation about "genetic hygiene" has shifted from research institutes to medical facilities as "many eugenic ideas have jumped the gap from yesterday to today, bridging the chasm between overtly coercive eugenics and purportedly voluntary

50   ENVIRONMENTAL ETHICS AND MEDICAL REPRODUCTION

parental and social responsibility."[24] Now, with the availability of genetic testing, potential parents are able to screen out disability, which, purportedly, not only make their children healthier, but make their own lives easier. But beyond this self-interest is the idea that parents have an obligation to make life easier—whereas "easy" is a code word for health—for society. Particularly when taxes are tied to social support for the disabled, there is an economic argument for making "healthy" children.[25] In this sort of world, only the fittest survive, not only because they have been engineered that way, but because the social and financial supports that would have previously gone to parents who had disabled children "by accident," that is, naturally, would disappear as fewer and fewer of these children were born.

The arguments from the disability rights movement then indicate that as disability becomes a "choice," the obligation of care and financial support for disabled children ought to be on the ones who chose—the parents—virtually removing the free choice to use PGD,[26] when available or abort an "abnormal" fetus if PGD fails or is unavailable. Moreover, if social and financial supports remained for the few who refused PGD, then there is a fear that resentment would build toward those with disabled children, since the financial "burden" was avoidable. Eventually, with a shrinking pool of children born with disabilities, social and financial supports would be thought to be mismanaged, with lobbyists asking for money to be put into more "important," that is, ableist, programs.

One key medical-ethical problem of pre-implantation genetic diagnosis from this perspective centers on the loss of autonomy to freely choose PGD or have children naturally.[27] Moreover, parental ethics intersect with the disability rights movement as the function of having a biological child is interrogated. PGD may indicate prejudicial thinking that at once limits potential children to their genetic makeup and also devastates parents when children do not "perform" as expected. This instrumentalization of children is a concern on several different levels, from objectifying a human being, to the issue of how children may be commodified[28] and economized.

Feminists have pointed out that the same sort of biological determinism that places female-sex children at a disadvantage socially, and in the eyes of parents, is at work with concepts of disability.[29] Female children are assumed to have limited potential because of their sex; they are seen as weaker, less intelligent, or less capable in a sexist society. So too are disabled children seen as weaker, less intelligent, or less capable in an ableist society. Social constructs of what it means to be "female" or "disabled" often drive

PGD, since the actual female or disabled child will be an individual, not a stereotype.

The reliance on PGD for an ideal child is dangerous, since a parent's investment in creating a particular type of child will be thwarted if the boy child wants to wear a dress, play with dolls, and become a ballet dancer. Likewise, the parents selecting against disability may be devastated if their child is in an accident and becomes physically or intellectually dependent for life.

Larger anthropological concerns have also been raised about PGD. Pioneers of the disability rights movement in the United States, Erik Parens and Adrienne Asch, write, "[D]o these technologies lead us, one might ask, towards the commodification of children, towards thinking about them and treating them as products rather than as 'gifts' or 'ends in themselves'? Is it making us as a society ... less willing to acknowledge the essential fragility of our species?"[30]

Ultimately, in all cases of PGD, unsatisfactory embryos are destroyed. Many conservative bioethicists discuss the ethical implications of creating a human life only to "kill it."[31] From an environmental perspective, the ethical issue is a waste of resources, that of oversupply. While the environmental impact of discarding embryos is certainly very small, it must be remembered that the embryos that are not implanted have used all of the MR resources along the way. Like research that never gets published,[32] there is a carbon impact without meeting the aims of the procedure: ostensibly fertilization and live birth, in this case. On the other hand, it could be argued that creating and destroying embryos is better environmentally than creating and implanting embryos, and this is true. In any case, PGD is not a medical treatment for infertility. It is part of MR services that both fertile and infertile couples and singles may use, which contributes to the global carbon emissions.

Clustered Regularly Interspaced Short Palindromic Repeats (CRISPR)

In recent years an alternative to PGD has emerged: clustered regularly interspaced short palindromic repeats (CRISPR) technology. In humans and animals, CRISPR technology uses the protein Cas9 to cut targeted strands of DNA, which then are replaced or repaired within the body. Through this genome-editing process, the DNA of human cells, or embryos, is altered.[33] In 2013, CRISPR-Cas9 was used to edit human cells in an experimental setting.[34] Worldwide, it was not approved for use in human cells that would become embryos and then humans.[35] However, in 2015 scientists in China edited a human embryo and by 2018 had used CRISPR-Cas9 and in-vitro fertilization to bring a gene-edited embryo to full-term pregnancy, with a live birth.[36] Public and scientific outcries were global, and genome editing[37]—particularly at the germline level which would pass on alterations in the genetic relatives of gene-edited humans—remained unapproved as of 2023.

As CRISPR becomes more effective and ethical concerns, particularly around unknown future outcomes, are assuaged, it will certainly become a more frequently offered part of MR, surpassing even PGD.[38] The benefit of CRISPR, so it is said, is that genetic disease can be prevented in embryos and generations to come.[39] This mentality assumes both a therapeutic and a reproductive purpose of CRISPR and indeed may be seen as a "waste" of a technology if the gene-edited person did not reproduce. The obligation or pressure to reproduce in the face of extraordinary medical treatment has been addressed in the section on oncofertility and "fertility preservation."[40]

The ethical issues that have been raised by genome editing technology thus far have engaged neither environmental ethics nor environmental bioethics,[41] aside from the hyperbolic article on genetic engineering for environmental benefit by Matthew Liao, Anders Sandberg, and Rebecca Roache in 2012.[42] Yet, the environmental impact of CRISPR reproduction, as it relates to the MR process, should be assessed.

Similar to PGD, CRISPR will be used to create new humans. Although it may, in the future, be used on adults, the intention is to alter the human genome at the embryonic level. Obviously, CRISPR requires gamete retrieval (or in the future synthetic gametes)[43] and storage. If done on embryos it requires IVF. And if the embryos are brought to term it depends on the fertilization, implantation, MR pregnancy, and the same risks of infant prematurity as standard MR. CRISPR is fundamentally a pronatalist technology that is not medically necessary as it does not address the goals of medicine for a person who is already alive. Rather, like PGD, it uses resources to create potential humans, who otherwise may not have come into being, simply for the purpose of giving a couple a child of choice. But, unlike PGD, the CRISPR child would bear additional reproductive expectations, in excess of average social norms around procreation, since they would have a "genetic incentive" to pass on healthy genes.[44] If the CRISPR child was socially or clinically infertile, the pressure to reproduce would again result in offering MR, thus causing a cycle of medical resource use and carbon expenditure with minimal clinical benefit.

Scientific advancement should certainly be lauded and pursued, but in a time of environmental precarity the wisdom of technologies that support reproduction and use resources must be seriously questioned and analyzed through the appropriate lens of medical, reproductive, and environmental ethics,[45] not only research[46] and engineering ethics.[47]

A further environmental ethical concern is that of proportion of resources used. Both PGD and CRISPR are avoidable; unlike healthcare resources that go toward unforeseen catastrophe and acute illnesses, genetic testing or alteration is chosen and pursued, along with the attendant resource use. Adults do not have to reproduce; genetics do not need to be selected if biological children are desired. Prevention of pregnancy also avoids genetic disease. Beyond this, both PGD and CRISPR have the potential to be used for more than just disease prevention. They are also a way of producing a child for the fertile and infertile, based on desirable, non-health-related characteristics.

Gamete Assessment—Genetic Features Unrelated to Health

Gamete assessment can also be done with the intention of selecting embryos with conditions unrelated to genetic health. For instance, fertile and infertile couples and singles can choose an embryo with a particular sex (male or female), or with a certain eye color or disposition to height. However, sex selection, when related to a sex-linked disorder, may serve two purposes: one is a desire for a particular sex of the embryo and the other is in pursuit of health. Genes may also be selected in relation to the health of another person, including human leukocyte antigen (HLA) compatibility for "savior siblings." Genetic selection may also create a child with a particular "disability" such as achondroplasia or deafness. As an option related to MR, PGD is not a medical treatment, since it invokes beings into existence and then addresses the genetics or medical conditions of the embryo. This is categorically unlike treating people who are currently alive with medicine. Thus, it is even more ethically concerning, from a biomedical perspective, to use PGD for selections of genetic traits totally unrelated to genetic health or with the intention of creating a disability since it first increases the population and then adds to resource use.

54 ENVIRONMENTAL ETHICS AND MEDICAL REPRODUCTION

Options in gamete assessment for genetic features unrelated to health are offered to couples using MR to bypass infertility or for those that are fertile and seeking a first or additional child with a particular makeup, ostensibly on the disappointed hopes that their first child did not fulfill. In each case, it should be remembered that procreating is not obligatory, however, and potential parents must defend their use of PGD for non-health reasons beyond simply the desire to procreate, given the environmental impact.

Human Leukocyte Antigen (HLA) Compatibility

Singles and couples who have reproduced naturally may have a child with a serious medical condition. Some conditions, such as organ failure,[48] leukemia or lymphoma,[49] or Fanconi anemia[50] may be cured or treated through human leukocyte antigen (HLA) compatibility treatments.[51] The human leukocyte antigen system in humans is responsible for regulating the immune system and thus connected to immune response, genetic autoimmune diseases, and the ability of a body to accept tissue grafts, organs, and other biological materials like blood or marrow.[52] Since there is a genetic basis of HLA systems, genetically related family members may be matches for HLA-compatible treatments, thus family members of an affected child who needs medical care on the basis of HLA misfunctioning are usually tested first for compatibility. If there are no familial matches, and no other donors are histocompatible, then pre-implantation genetic diagnosis with HLA matching may be sought after gamete retrieval, storage, and assessment.[53] Here, the primary objective is to produce a child that will be an HLA match for their sick sibling, that is, a "savior sibling."[54] The secondary objective is another child free from that illness, if genetic selection is successful.[55] Tertiary objectives may be sex selection for birth order or family balancing.[56]

"Savior siblings" are legal in some situations and have been used in the United Kingdom, funded through subsidized healthcare, since at least 2004.[57] There have been numerous ethical concerns with PGD for HLA compatibility, primarily related to the third party—the embryos being selected whose role is to provide biological materials which will alleviate or treat the older sibling's condition.[58] A first ethical concern is the instrumentalization of the new child, since they are being created specifically to "serve" the purposes of another human being in a direct and corporeal way. This violates Kant's categorical imperative that states that people ought to be treated as a means

MEDICAL REPRODUCTION FOR INSEMINATION   55

in themselves and not only as an end.[59] To be sure, these new infants may be loved and cherished, but the lingering thoughts of the intention of their creation—to exist for another—may shadow personal social development.[60]

A second ethical concern is that the provision of HLA-compatible material may range from invasive and painful, such as bone marrow,[61] to painless, like umbilical cord blood.[62] Since these procedures do not cure or treat the person undergoing them, the risk and pain of the procedure must be evaluated against the benefit for another person. In some cases, healthy people do undergo procedures for the medical benefit of others, such as organ donation, marrow donation, and even medical reproduction or gestational surrogacy. However, those are generally consenting adults who understand the risks and benefits.[63] HLA-based procedures do not guarantee that a sibling will be cured, that the treatment will produce the desired effects, or that additional treatments will not be necessary. In the UK, although PGD with HLA compatibility was approved in 2004, it was not until 2010 that the first successful savior sibling treatment occurred.[64] The interval between legality and success indicates numerous attempts at unsuccessful procedures where the new infant may have to undergo frequent and more burdensome procedures.[65]

Thus, a third ethical concern is that the new infant cannot consent to these treatments. Consent is an important part of healthcare ethics, based on the principle of respect for autonomy.[66] Essentially, no one should be compelled to have medical treatments against their will or without their express consent. Certainly, children and infants cannot provide consent to whether or not they will be created through MR; children do not consent to being born or called into existence even with natural procreation.[67] Thus, parents are the legitimate and legal decision-makers who are tasked with making medical (and social, educational, and moral) choices on the basis of the best interest of each individual child.[68] With savior siblings, the parents are faced with a conflict of interest between the two children.[69] Medical decisions for the new "savior" child have, in a way, been predetermined, as the infant being created is compelled to be used for biological harvesting. Thus, the parents are forcing medical procedures on one child for the benefit of another. To be sure, parents have trade-offs to make in child rearing, and sometimes favor one child's needs over another for family cohesion.[70] But, making ethical choices within the context of the family unit does not usually extend to violating physical safety or bodily integrity of any other family member.[71] Compounded with these ethical concerns are the environmental effects not

56 ENVIRONMENTAL ETHICS AND MEDICAL REPRODUCTION

only of MR, and the new birth, but the medical procedures that are implied in the birth of a savior sibling child.

Selecting for Disability

Some forms of PGD offer the opportunity to intentionally select for conditions that have been considered a "disability."[72] There is ongoing ethical debate about using PGD to provide parents with a "disability" a similarly "disabled" child. Among the "desirable disabilities" that have relied on PGD, achondroplasia (dwarfism) and deafness have received the most attention. Indeed, a 2008 survey of 186 US IVF-PGD clinics found that 3% "report having provided PGD to couples who seek to use PGD to select an embryo for the presence of a disability."[73] The primary ethical concern is the instrumentalization of the child, which is particularly noticeable in the creation of any MR child of choice.[74] Additionally, another significant bioethical concern is that of ensuring a child's "right to an open future."[75] Concretely, this right to an open future would not foreclose possibilities to a child, such as the ability to hear or being of a "normal" stature. The child might choose to be deaf,[76] or participate in a community of people with achondroplasia,[77] but it is argued that they should make that significant choice once they are mature; parents ought not impose it on then.

On the other side of the debate are people from "disabled" communities who insist that either they are not disabled,[78] or that PGD will ensure that their child will be a better fit in their communities.[79] These groups might even point to the ableism that shuns disability or sees it as deficient. Yet, there is a fine line between supporting the needs of those who may require alternative accommodations because of a disability and eliminating opportunities for future children by choosing for a condition that may come with social and physical disadvantages.[80] In reaction to the latter, it is not on eugenic grounds, since all people with disabilities and these conditions would still be valued and valuable. Rather, the rejection is an ethical concern for the best interests of the child. In this case, the doctor or insurance company may decide to refuse PGD with selection for disability. For instance, the American Society for Reproductive Medicine Ethics Committee advises that physicians may withhold services "when significant harm to future children is likely."[81]

Moreover, the couple with the "disability"—if it is genetic—may still have a child with that disability naturally, thus MR is a redundant or duplicate procedure. Pursuing unnecessary medical treatments is considered health-care overuse and is one of the causes of excess carbon in the medical industry.[82] When the couple or single person is fertile and using MR for selection of disabled children, there is twofold medical waste: that of not needing medical assistance to reproduce and that of not needing medical intervention for a disabled child.

Sex Selection

A further aspect of PGD unrelated to genetic health is sex selection. Sex selection is when an embryo's sex chromosomes are identified and the desired sex—either male or female—is implanted. Embryos of the undesirable sex are disposed of. Intersex embryos are typically discarded as they are considered genetically abnormal.[83] In the United States, a 2017 study showed that 72.7% of fertility clinics reported offering sex selection.[84] Both fertile and infertile people use PGD for sex selection. This lucrative form of MR[85] may be used for several reasons.

One "clinical" reason may be family history of X-linked disorders, such as Duchenne muscular dystrophy and hemophilia.[86] Here, "sex selection against healthy female carrier embryos would have the same 2-fold purpose of (i) avoiding difficult reproductive decisions for the future child and (ii) avoiding transmission of the mutation to a possible third generation."[87] One social reason for PGD and sex selection might be preference for a female or male child, based on the gender stereotypes associated with that sex in that culture.[88] That is, a single person or couple may want a female child because they assume she will be feminine (e.g., be docile, dress up, play with dolls, be a wife and mother), or a male child because they assume he will be masculine (e.g., be assertive, play sports, take over the family business). Preference for a sex-specific child may also be placed in the context of birth order (e.g., first, middle, last children)[89] or for "family balancing" where a single person or couple has one or more (sometimes several) children of a particular sex and desire another child of a different sex.[90] In the same study from 2017, 93.6% of the fertility clinics offering sex selection for those with infertility did so for "family balancing, and 81.2% reported performing for elective purposes (patient preference, regardless of rationale for the request). For couples without infertility, 83.5% of clinics offered sex selection for family balancing and 74.6% for non-specific elective reasons."[91] Like other aspects

58 ENVIRONMENTAL ETHICS AND MEDICAL REPRODUCTION

of MR, sex selection is a separate treatment from fertilization to bypass clinical infertility. Like other forms of PGD, sex selection does not address medical conditions of an existing person.

Even when there are medically based reasons for sex selection—such as risk of disease—the PGD process does not meet a goal of medicine or cure, treat, or prevent infertility. Instead, PGD relies on the MR industry to create a new being, who may have a higher risk for genetic disease, and then proceeds with fertilization on the basis of sex, whereby sex is an indicator of potential for disease. Ethicists are right to point out the implications of PGD on the disabled community[92] and the potential to slip into eugenics.[93] Moreover, by using PGD and sex selection, medical resources and carbon emissions are produced in the pursuit of mere parental desires and aspirations, not medical needs that benefit existing human beings.

To be sure, parents may have a vested interest in healthy children, as people may have an interest in avoiding disease. But, parenthood is possible without reproduction and PGD does not guarantee health after birth. Thus, the bioethical problem is not simply that a person may be born with a disease or condition unless the parents use PGD. It ought to be reiterated that, even in cases where PGD is used for sex selection related to clinical conditions and the child is born healthy, PGD does not guarantee a healthy life, free from diseases or accidents.

In the case that PGD and sex selection are done for sex preference, there is not a concomitant clinical concern for the child. Certainly, women and men are susceptible to different diseases, but parents are not concerned with, for instance, having a male child who might be at higher risk for violent suicide.[94]

There are many additional ethical problems with sex selection which have been highlighted by feminists[95] and economists.[96] However, the primary ethical problem from an environmental perspective are the resources used for a purely elective procedure that does not cure, treat, or prevent a disease (unless being male or female is considered a medical condition).

Whereas PGD and sex selection for clinical reasons and PGD and sex selection for sex preference may be offered to both the fertile and the infertile, "family balancing"—by definition—is only offered to the fertile, that is a couple or single person who already has one or more biological children. Not only is this intensively wasteful, it is based on the fallacy that sex and gender align. Although PGD can produce a child of a particular sex, it cannot guarantee performativity[97] of the gender stereotypes associated with that sex. With an ever-increasing number of people identifying as transgender,[98] sex selection does not ensure that parents will get the gendered child of their desire.[99] This raises many other questions in reproductive ethics about the medicalization of gender, gender conformity, and parental expectations of children.[100]

Designer Babies

Both fertile and infertile couples, those with suspected genetic disease and those without, may use PGD for selection of characteristics that are more "cosmetic" or superficial, such as eye color, disposition to intelligence, and height.[101] Already, "designer babies" are available to couples who pay out of pocket,[102] indicating that it is socially acceptable—typically on the basis of reproductive liberty and scientific advancement. But, as Maura Ryan notes, "advocating a model where children are brought into this world chiefly for that purpose (the liberty of adults who want to procreate) gives too much weight to parental desires and too little protection of the offspring's essential autonomy."[103]

If liberty is not a sufficient reason to accept PGD for selection of superficial traits, then claims for "progress" on the side of science and medicine push PGD into the forefront of ethically endorsable elective MR procedures. One doctor clarifies this position by stating, "[O]nce I've got this science, am I not to provide this to my patients? I'm a physician. I want to provide everything science gives me to my patients."[104] From an ecological standpoint, the interests of the potential child not to be brought into a world with a deteriorating ecosystem, face risks of climate change health hazards, and other environmental threats that may undermine autonomy may also be considered.

Yet, there are numerous stakeholders who develop and promote PGD. Scientists continue to develop new applications of genetic knowledge in reproductive engineering. Practitioners "control access to assisted conception, determine the boundaries of acceptable risk, and make judgments that often extend well beyond their technical expertise, such as embryo selection to circumvent the transmission of genetic anomalies."[105] Adults who want to reproduce using MR may avail themselves of these genetic options with very few moral qualms. The biomedical, feminist, and disability-based ethical issues highlighted above are serious. While various realms of academic inquiry have addressed PGD as an ethical concern, when placed within

60 ENVIRONMENTAL ETHICS AND MEDICAL REPRODUCTION

environmental ethics, and the tandem issues of population growth and resource use—particularly when there is no medical benefit—make the continual provision and developments of these services morally suspect. In a zero-sum environment, medical carbon is not wisely spent on desires, but needs; not on creating new people, but taking care of existing ones.[106]

Assisted Reproductive Technologies— Fertilization Techniques

Artificial insemination in non-human animals has been a long-standing technique used to breed desired characteristics in offspring.[107] Although it has been used, likely since the beginning of husbandry and farming—in tandem with botany techniques like grafting—with the advent of Mendelian genetics, better understanding of reproduction and expressed genetic traits increased.[108] Techniques in managed breeding in non-human animals have ranged from rudimentary to sophisticated. Developments in tools that facilitate breeding have made selection of "good" animal stock—from food sources to racing horse speed to quality wool—a highly skilled area of work.[109] Thus, as humans have gained mastery over animal and plant reproduction, the same framework has been applied to our own species.

Medical reproduction includes the procedures that facilitate human reproduction before and after conception. Conception has been the central focus of many biomedical issues because it indicates the presence of a new human life (whether or not that has an absolute normative value) and because it is the place where natural and artificial reproduction intersect. Once a woman is fertilized by MR techniques, the pregnancy may be seen as natural, even though the embryo contained within is still a creation of MR. Nonetheless, for people outside of the medical industry, and for couples and singles who have only a cursory understanding of medicalized reproduction, the idea of conception from assisted (or artificial) reproductive technologies (ART) is the most well understood, likely due to education on the topic from news sources,[110] popular media,[111] and conversations among peers. ARTs are one small part of MR that require resources, expend carbon, and must be assessed for environmental sustainability.

Assisted reproductive technologies for humans were first created to circumvent—not cure—infertility. Infertility is sometimes traced to biological factors such as blocked tubes and low sperm count; in other cases, it is correlated to advanced age. Every person who lives to middle age and beyond will become infertile, as fecundity declines with age. In this manner it is a normal physical process of aging. Other factors that influence fertility and infertility are related to lifestyle, like obesity,[112] or untreated sexually transmitted diseases.[113] ARTs are "a breeding technique, not a medical therapy. A woman isn't 'cured' of anything, she is 'made pregnant' by a team of IVF technicians."[114] Infertility itself can only be cured if it is caused by physical factors that can be reversed, like blocked tubes which can be repaired or obesity-related infertility which can be ameliorated by weight loss.

ART Adjuncts and Add-ons

After the gametes have been obtained, stored, and checked for viability, health, and sometimes other desirable traits, the fertilization process can begin. There are a variety of techniques used for fertilization, each of which may have a different clinical indication, such as injection of slow sperm into an egg (IVF), to providing the experience of pregnancy through a donated, single-use womb. There are also different MR adjuncts which are purported to increase the chances of fertilization. Both adjunctive procedures and ARTs may allow a pregnancy to be produced, but since they do not treat the underlying condition, some ethicists, policymakers, and doctors do not consider ARTs a medical treatment. Nonetheless, they add to the carbon of the medical industry and global carbon emissions.

In recent years, a number of fertilization "adjuncts" and "add-ons" have been offered in fertility clinics as an intermediate step between gamete retrieval and fertilization. These include "embryo glue and adherence compounds, sperm DNA fragmentation, time-lapse imaging, preimplantation genetic screening, mitochondria DNA load measurement and assisted hatching."[115] Fertility clinic customers have been warned about the limited efficacy of these services and, in 2017, the UK's Human Fertilisation and Embryology Authority (HFEA) released a statement regarding their proper use and potential for misuse.[116] From a biomedical lens, these add-ons may indicate overuse of medicine, which is an additional environmental burden. As a consumer choice that is often clinically unnecessary, add-ons at the

62 ENVIRONMENTAL ETHICS AND MEDICAL REPRODUCTION

point of pre-fertilization should be monitored for potential to become more widely used in the course of MR treatments. While underdeveloped right now, the future of MR moves toward more services, as is evidenced in the course of, not only MR options, but also services and techniques.

If fertilization adjuncts are not available, or not desired, then assisted reproductive technologies are the next step in MR. Artificial insemination (AI), in-vitro fertilization (IVF), and intracytoplasmic sperm injection (ICSI) are the most common.

Artificial Insemination

Artificial insemination (AI) was the earliest type of assisted reproductive technology used in humans. One of the first documented artificial inseminations was in London in the 1770s. A physician, John Hunter, advised a man to "collect the semen (which escaped during coitus) in a warmed syringe and inject the sample into the vagina."[117] The basic idea behind this technique has remained the same. Throughout the history of AI, sperm that has been ejaculated is collected and, in some manner, placed in the vagina. AI is generally a choice for couples with male-factor infertility, fertile single women, fertile women in same-sex couples, and fertile women in opposite-sex couples who want to have control over the timing of conception.

Techniques in AI have developed in both sophistication and precision, from the "turkey baster baby"[118] (a reference to the cooking tool used to moisten a turkey being roasted in the oven) to the cervical spoon,[119] some of which are still used by those who cannot access more technological medical reproduction. In the developed world, a woman will go to a clinic to have the sperm—either donated or from a known partner—inserted into her cervix, fallopian tubes, or uterus, depending on her clinical indications for infertility, if any, and the predicted potential for success. The latter may also be called intrauterine insemination (IUI).[120] Techniques and tools for AI vary by practitioner and available resources.

Resources used in the AI process include fertility drugs, gamete retrieval, pornography use, storage, sperm assessment, sperm preparation, use of different disposable instruments, and other associated medical facility requirements, like energy and heating of buildings, transportation, disposable gowns, and sterilization devices.[121] If AI is not successful the first time, which is often the case, the procedure and resources will have to be expended

MEDICAL REPRODUCTION FOR INSEMINATION   63

again. AI (IUI) has a success rate of about 11%,[122] so many cycles may be used before there is a pregnancy.

In-Vitro Fertilization (IVF)

IVF is used by fertile and infertile single and coupled men and women in both same-sex and opposite-sex unions (where relevant). Each IVF client has a different reason for using IVF, ranging from timing of fertilization, to number of children desired, to selection of certain genetic profiles. In-vitro fertilization requires more resources than AI because it depends on gametes from a man and a woman. After both eggs and sperm are retrieved, stored, and assessed, the gametes are placed together in a petri dish. Fertilization, if it occurs, is outside of the body, hence the term "in vitro." Unlike AI, in which only one egg can be fertilized at a time, the IVF procedure allows multiple fertilized eggs (zygotes) to be implanted. The zygotes may be left to develop into embryos for genetic testing and selected implantation. If this is not desired, then the zygotes are inserted into the uterus by passing a long thin tube through the vagina. The first successful birth resulting from IVF occurred in England in 1978.[123] At the time, a single fertilized egg was the standard and that standard continued for some time. However, the 1980s and 1990s saw a preference for multiple fertilized eggs for financial and social reasons. IVF is expensive and has limited success—around 26% by some studies.[124] Thus, a number of expensive cycles will be pursued, each with compounded costs. Moreover, many couples feel the need to accelerate plans around reproduction and view twin or higher order preference as a way to make up for lost time. That is, they have desires for multiple children born during a certain time frame and infertility or delayed pregnancy derails these reproductive plans. Although the children will not be spaced apart in a desired interval, the total number of children born could still meet the adult expectations about reproduction and family size.

There are some medical reasons for implanting multiple zygotes as well. Some implanted zygotes might not attach to the uterine wall. Thus, if more are implanted, the likelihood of successful pregnancy is higher. Even if all the zygotes attach, there is the option to "selectively reduce" when they develop to the point of an embryo. Selective reduction is performed if some embryos are not as "fit" as others, or to obtain the desired number that will develop

64   ENVIRONMENTAL ETHICS AND MEDICAL REPRODUCTION

into fetuses.[125] Despite the financial and social reasons for implanting multiple zygotes, singleton pregnancies are widely preferred for health reasons[126] and patients ought to expect selective reduction after multiple implantations. Thus, it is medically redundant to implant so many zygotes that they would be beyond the safe, healthy, or desirable number of embryos.

There are numerous ethical issues with in-vitro fertilization and IVF has been criticized by ethicists since it was first used. Feminists have voiced some of the strongest concerns, noting that "women undergoing IVF treatment talk of feeling objectified, denigrated, and humiliated as they become embodiments of a medical tutorial for resident physicians learning the techniques."[127] Many of these concerns have been elaborated upon by feminists, queer[128] and gender[129] theorists, theologians,[130] and those concerned with just distribution of medical resources.[131] To be sure, the environmental aspects of IVF have also been raised.[132] Particularly with the preference for twins, population growth and in particular, carbon emissions related to births in the developed world are germane when examining the rationale for requesting and receiving IVF with multiple fetuses coming to term. Moreover, since IVF is also given to fertile singles and couples, either in tandem with PGD and other adjuncts or not, there is no clinical indication, thus the medicalized reproductive process produces carbon and the outcome of those processes: the MR children.

Intracytoplasmic Sperm Injection (ICSI)

If traditional IVF methods do not work because of male-factor infertility, intracytoplasmic sperm injection (ICSI) may be attempted. ICSI is a sub-type of IVF in which a single sperm is taken and injected directly into the egg to increase the chance of fertilizing the egg. The fertilized egg is then implanted into the uterus. ICSI does not increase the chances of implantation, only the chances of fertilizing the egg. ICSI is also used in non-human animals and studies on the efficacy of this technique translate to human use.[133] Like the other forms of assisted reproduction, ICSI may require many cycles, during which numerous resources are used. Unique to this form of ART is the additional tools used to inject the sperm into the egg and the tools which are used to select the individual sperm from the semen sample. As with IVF, ICSI can be used by fertile and infertile single and coupled men and women in both same-sex and opposite-sex unions (where relevant).

Assisted Reproductive Technologies— Gestational Options

The increase in MR use has contributed to a new lexicon in social and medical conversations about parenthood. Adults are now distinguished between "reproductive parents"—those who supply genetic material—and "socializing parents"—those who raise the child. To be sure, prior to MR, there were these constitutive differences, such as in adoptions, fostering children, or being cared for by relatives. But MR, and particularly surrogacy, has complicated the concept of "parenthood," raising new ethical issues in gestational options.

Gestational Surrogates

Gestational surrogacy—often simply written as "surrogacy," within the context of ARTs—is where a woman who is not intended to be the socializing mother of the child is fertilized in an attempt to carry a pregnancy to term and give birth to one or more live infants. The term "intended" is important; sometimes the single person or couple who has hired the surrogate no longer wants the child, usually due to "genetic defects" and ask to terminate the pregnancy.[134] The surrogate may then keep the child, or not. In other, more rare cases, the surrogate has refused to give up the child.[135] Surrogacy is often tied to remuneration, and this complicates both the autonomy of the surrogate to do as she wishes with her body and the control that the person or people who have hired her have over another human being. One publication from 2018 reported that surrogacy accounted for about 2.4% of pregnancies in the United States between the years 2010 and 2014,[136] up from less than 1% based on data from 2009.[137]

AI, IVF, or ICSI can be used on a surrogate, depending on the specific childwish. Fertile and infertile single and coupled men and women in both same-sex and opposite-sex unions (where relevant) may opt for surrogacy. Thus, the children born from a gestational surrogate may have many different configurations of reproductive and socializing parents. A surrogate may be inseminated with the male socializing parent's sperm and use her own eggs and uterus (AI). Or, a surrogate could have an embryo implanted in her using the male and female socializing parents' gametes, thus only providing her womb (IVF). In another scenario, the socializing parents may choose donor sperm and a donor egg for implantation of embryos into the surrogate (IVF).

The fetus would not be genetically related to either of the socializing parents or the surrogate, but the couple (or single person) would have the experience of watching a child of choice grow in a woman of choice, and having a new infant to raise. This scenario may occur if a single man or woman is infertile and therefore need to obtain a gamete to replace theirs and an opposite-sex gamete as well. Particularly for single and same-sex coupled men who do not have a uterus of their own, surrogacy is appealing.[138] However, surrogacy may also be appealing for women who are fertile and do not want the stress, inconvenience, or danger of pregnancy themselves.[139]

Surrogacy, whether domestic or international, has been heavily criticized for its objectification of women as "fetal containers."[140] The exploitation of developing world women in the international reproductive tourism market[141] and the negative impact on the already scarce resources of the destination country[142] are also ethical concerns. Moreover, the deregulation of surrogacy leaves these women unprotected since surrogacy agreements are made between independent parties[143] instead of overseen by fertility clinics and healthcare insurance. For instance, while a woman seeking fertility treatments may be evaluated for mental health by a fertility doctor, the person or couple who has hired a surrogate may not be subject to psychological assessments. The surrogate has an evaluation done on her, while the qualifications of the socializing parent or parents are left unassessed.

In addition to these ethical concerns, the environmental burden of using a fertility technique on a person who is fertile (the surrogate) makes the medical treatment redundant, as ARTs are not required to make the woman receiving the treatments pregnant. MR for fertile people—like surrogates—is not clinically indicated. It does not address a health need. Moreover, pregnancy is a health risk in itself. While risk of medical injury may be acceptable in, for instance, organ donation, due to the balance of saving the life of the person receiving the organ, in pregnancy there is not a concomitant balance of saving a life for the person receiving the infant. It may be stated that sometimes a pregnancy is risky for the socializing mother and thus a surrogate could be lifesaving. But this merely places the medical risk on another instead of avoiding it altogether.

Having a biological child is not necessary for life, whereas functioning organs are. The extra resources used to fertilize fertile woman are not environmentally justified. It might be argued that there is little ecological difference between hiring a surrogate and using IVF or having a couple who uses IVF, but in fact many of the aspects of MR—from fertility testing, to gamete retrieval and storage, to transportation time to and from clinics—are duplicated as the genetic parents and the gestational carrier undertake all these steps. Carbon externalities from reproductive tourism, flights, surrogate interviews, and associated vacation activities might also be considered, even in the cases of domestic reproductive tourism.[144]

Uterus Transplants

In 2013, the first live birth from a human uterus transplant was reported in Sweden.[145] Since then, the technique has developed and other countries have followed, with India reporting a live birth from a uterus transplant in 2017.[146] The purpose of the donated uterus is purely for the sake of the experience of pregnancy,[147] not having a biological child, which may be accomplished through surrogacy, or having a child, which can be obtained through any number of non-procreative means. Moreover, there is no clinical indication that would support uterus transplant. That is, the uterus's primary function is to provide the option to gestate a child, but abstaining from gestation does not compromise health.

In the future, men may be offered this form of MR.[148] This could be especially appealing to male-to-female transgender individuals, men in opposite-sex relationships who want to make the burden of bearing children more equal, and single men and men in same-sex couples who do not have a uterus and do not want to use a surrogate. In many of the above cases, the fertility of the men's sperm can be assumed, based on the average distribution of fertility in a population. They could thus fertilize an egg and carry the pregnancy while needing only a donor egg.

There are two additional places of MR resource use in uterus transplants. First, from the woman giving the womb and, second, for the woman (or man) receiving the womb. Medical criteria for the donor uterus include being able to carry a pregnancy, thus a fertile donor with a known history of procreation will have her uterus removed and implanted in another woman. This invasive, elective, and medically laborious procedure is another part of unnecessary MR carbon emissions. For the woman (or man) receiving the womb, recovery time, complications, and medical sequelae, such as pain and painkiller addiction,[149] incontinence,[150] and psychological, physical, and sexual consequences of hysterectomy[151]—without a proportionate reason, like uterine cancer—are both biomedical and environmental concerns.

68 ENVIRONMENTAL ETHICS AND MEDICAL REPRODUCTION

Uterus transplants—much like organ transplantation—can come from a living or a dead donor. Unlike organ donation, pregnancy does not support or maintain life. However, much like organ donation, surgery and immunosuppressant drugs are required,[152] thus adding to the resources used for this type of MR. Recovery time from receiving the uterus takes about a year. Complications and side effects are possible in the process of uterus transplantation. Even before fertilization, the body may reject the uterus, which will require medical care, including removal of the uterus, recovery time, medical risk for errors, and infection.[153]

If the transplant is successful, then in-vitro fertilization is used, which can be done with the uterus recipient's eggs or with donated eggs. Again, the success of IVF is not ensured. If the zygote attaches to the uterus and comes to term, the fetus is born and the uterus may be removed at that time, or after the desired number of children have been born.[154] Like other forms of IVF, success rates are low and numerous cycles—all demanding medical resources—are required.

Ethical questions about medical risk of an elective, experimental procedure have been in the forefront of uterus transplant cases.[155] Feminists have been cautious about endorsing uterus donation, as it may be seen to be part of the expected sacrificial nature of women.[156] Feminists have also highlighted how uterus transplantations reify pressure to reproduce when it was seemingly impossible just a few years prior, indicating that the hetero-medical model[157] which regards reproduction as the norm of a healthy woman—despite the fact that pregnancies and childbirth do not make women healthier and carry a significant disease burden worldwide[158]—is harmful to women. Similarly, the disability critique of health is germane, as the medical industry and MR seek to "fix" those without a uterus, or with a "faulty" uterus, whether that is a natal sex woman or part of sex reassignment surgery,[159] whereby cis and transwomen are viewed as physically insufficient if they are not born with a uterus. These ethical issues have been under-addressed when compared with biomedical concerns over resource allocation and risk. Completely overlooked is the extreme carbon requirements, particularly because of the numerous ways to become a parent apart from pregnancy.

Uterus transplantation demands medical resources from beginning to end unparalleled in other forms of MR. While the ingenuity of the technique may be admired from scientific and medical perspectives, the balance of clinical indication, resource use, and impact on the environment are disproportionate. Uterus transplantation is still relatively rare, but like

MEDICAL REPRODUCTION FOR INSEMINATION   69

other forms of MR, will continue to develop in efficacy and prevalence, thus creating another drain on natural resources and carbon emissions that affect all people—those who use this service and their children included.

ARTs and Fertile People

Although ARTs have been most closely associated with married, infertile couples, they are not limited to infertile couples, and are becoming a more frequently used option for fertile couples who view ARTs as a lifestyle choice, as well as single people. For people who do not want to "deal with the stress of trying to get pregnant"[160] or are no longer in a relationship but wish to provide a biological sibling for a child from the now-dissolved marriage,[161] ARTs facilitate the desires of individualistic ideals about life and reproduction. As such, they are incredibly lucrative. The assisted reproductive technologies business grossed $16.1 billion in 2013 and is growing at a tremendous rate.[162] There were 443 reporting fertility clinics in the United States alone in 2010.[163]

In the United States, where the MR industry is decentralized, data is not collected on how many fertile people are utilizing ARTs compared to how many infertile people. By deduction, however, there are some ways to understand the far reach of ARTs for fertile people. Those couples who use heterologous gametes (donor egg or sperm) may only have one person in the couple who is infertile, while the other is fertile. In 2005, 12% of IVF cycles used donor eggs. Donor sperm are not reported in data on ARTs in the US, but the numbers are probably similar, making a quarter of all IVF children unrelated to both their socializing parents.[164]

Gestational surrogates are chosen for their ability to become pregnant, remain pregnant, and give birth, thus it is recommended that surrogates already have "at least one child" of their own.[165] The number of people who use surrogates is increasing both nationally[166] and internationally,[167] as the global reproduction business flourishes. These fertilization cycles are reported without distinguishing the fertility status of the surrogate, only that a surrogate is used, and only in some cases where the data is managed in this way.[168]

Since the majority of people who reach sexual maturity are fertile—by some counts about 85–90%, since 10–15% are suspected to be infertile[169]— most single women and women in same-sex couples who seek ARTs are fertile. Notably, fertile single women and fertile women in same-sex couples

70 ENVIRONMENTAL ETHICS AND MEDICAL REPRODUCTION

may be eligible for funded ARTs. In America, 15 of the 50 states mandate that health insurance policies have some provision for coverage of infertility, but 14 do not specify that a woman be married or in a couple.[170] Many other countries, from Australia,[171] to Canada,[172] to Great Britain,[173] have moved from not funding to funding ARTs for women in this category.

In addition to fertile singles and couples who have no previous children, another group of fertile people who use MR are those who have one or more children via natural reproduction and seek additional children with MR. The ethical problems with this approach to ARTs was highlighted by the "octomom" incident in 2009, when Nadya Suleman, a US single mother of several children, sought assisted fertility treatments and gave birth to eight more children.[174]

Additionally, using ARTs for "gender balancing," that is, sex selection, with the desire to create at least one male child and at least one female child means that the single person or couple already has at least one child, otherwise there would be nothing to balance. A 2006 survey by Johns Hopkins University found that 42% of fertility clinics offered sex selection for the purpose of "family balancing."[175] Likewise, all people using PGD for "savior sibling" treatments already have at least one child. PGD is also a way for fertile couples to select for a specific genetic characteristic or disability, as discussed above. Women with children who have secondary infertility—whereby they were able to conceive and deliver a fetus at one point, but are no longer able to do so—may also use ARTs for additional children.[176]

Recently, financially stable and emotionally mature fertile women in the industrialized world who become pregnant opt for abortions when the timing of the pregnancy is not ideal and then use ARTs in later years.[177] This is a risky strategy, as a pregnancy, even if it is unwanted, is closer to the ultimate goal of a biological child than waiting to use ARTs, which may not succeed. Of course, women and their life choices are more complicated than risk assessment. While being fertile and making use of it at the appropriate time may not be ideal, these choices impact the environment and reiterate the redundancy of ARTs for fertile people.

Highlighting the various uses of ARTs by fertile people both reorients the ethical discussion from a medical treatment to an elective, lifestyle choice. At the same time, it highlights the fact that ARTs are becoming "just another way to have a child" and must be subjected to the same ethical standards that parents who have naturally conceived children must be held to. These standards include those of population growth, resource use, instrumentalization, the possibility for a good life, lack of harm, and other social values. They also include environmental stewardship.

Summary

The technical aspects of the impregnation process of MR may be the most widely understood by people, as it is front and center in social life. Yet the phases of the MR impregnation process, from gamete assessment to assisted reproduction, are resource-intensive. Many of them are unrelated to infertility, with many more being unrelated to the health of the future child. As such, they are largely a lifestyle procedure, which is only justified by appealing to personal liberty or economic stimulus. Although ARTs are not as efficient as natural procreation,[178] they are, in terms of environmental impact, another mode of procreation, which carry the additional environmental burden of healthcare use, from beginning to end. ARTs may be more appealing to the infertile who do not have the physical option to have a biological child naturally, but as use and acceptability increase, alongside financial support from healthcare insurance programs, the ecological implications of assisted reproductive technologies must be considered. The ethics of MR based on environmental impact, resource use, population growth, and carrying capacity must be evaluated. Each aspect of MR, as well as MR in aggregate, can be assessed for resource use. The global obligation for sustainability is relevant in every part of MR and the entire process; the ethics cannot only be parsed by the MR phase or overall impact.

3
Medical Reproduction and Pregnant Women

MR is a spectrum of medical procedures—all of which have a carbon footprint and use resources. Pregnancy is situated in the middle of this spectrum, with gamete retrieval and storage, fertilization and embryonic assessment leading up to "successful pregnancy," and the aftereffects of pregnancy—from cosmetic vaginal procedures to the impact on the newly created children—filling out the final stages of MR. Although fertilization leading to pregnancy may be the most obvious development of MR, it is not in isolation from other procedures, as the pregnancy depends on the MR industry. Thus, the environmental impact must be evaluated at the point of use and in tandem with the other supportive procedures.

This chapter concretizes the use of MR as a carbon-intensive procedure offered by healthcare—but not necessarily meeting a goal of medicine—by highlighting the unnecessary environmental demands of medicalized pregnancy. Indeed, it has been argued that "the most characteristic aspect of modern antenatal care is the clinical instance in the probability of pathology in all childbearing,"[1] which then "requires" continual dependence and use of the medical industry for what can be considered a non-medical experience. Here, the environmental resources of natural conception and MR conception dovetail.

Medical procedures related to fetuses, such as selective reduction, miscarriage prematurity; medicalization of childbirth, whether vaginally or with an elective cesarean section; and the cosmetic procedures that may be offered to women post-partum are part of medicalized reproduction for pregnant women, which absorbs natural resources and emits carbon. While academic work on the medicalization of pregnancy has been present for nearly four decades, its environmental impact has been overlooked. Calling for environmental accountability—given the preventability and lack of clinical indication, the impact on the population and ecosystem, and the risks for infants and women—is the only logical reaction.

Environmental Ethics and Medical Reproduction. Cristina Richie, Oxford University Press.
© Oxford University Press 2024. DOI: 10.1093/oso/9780197745182.003.0004

Selective Reduction

After fertility drugs have been used, gametes retrieved, assessed, and stored, fertilization adjunctives and genetics diagnosis has occurred, and the mode of fertilization has been chosen and implemented, pregnancy may occur. A woman may be fertilized with one or more zygotes which develop into embryos. The number of zygotes might exceed the number of desirable embryos or fetuses; thus selective reduction manages the number of potential MR children which will gestate in the woman. Both surrogates and women carrying their own children utilize this option.

Selective reduction, whereby one or more embryos will be removed from the uterus, may take place within days of implantation.[2] If, however, the embryos are left to develop to a further stage, selective reduction can occur at a later time in pregnancy, which is a clinical abortion. This is often done to maximize the growth and potential of one "stronger" fetus over another. "Stronger" may be defined by genetics or growth relative to statistical norms.[3] In order to determine this, medical monitoring must occur. This is also done for the woman's health. Women with higher-order pregnancies are more likely to have hemorrhaging or die in childbirth than women who are pregnant with only one child at a time.[4] This is true whether the fetuses are from MR or naturally occurring twins or higher-order pregnancies.

The monitoring of pregnant women in this case requires sophisticated diagnostic tools, numerous doctors' appointments, clinical determinations and assessment, and medical treatments, where indicated. Diagnostic tools may include ultrasounds, which view the uterus; measuring devices which chart growth; tissue sampling; and processing of this data. These use resources and emit carbon. Under the medical model of pregnancy, detailed tracking of fetuses must be done in a clinic and cannot be done at home—due to the internal nature of pregnancy; transportation to and from the clinic at regular intervals is required. The carbon emission of transport in healthcare is one of the key places that have been identified as needing to be reduced.[5] For it is not just the pregnant woman who must commute to appointments, but the doctors and administrative and support staff as well.

While there is no medical need to track a "normal" pregnancy and women have been enduring pregnancies for millennia without medical monitoring, the MR industry views pregnancy and the fetus as a condition to be managed rather than simply experienced. The medicalization of both MR and natural

74 ENVIRONMENTAL ETHICS AND MEDICAL REPRODUCTION

pregnancy therefore rarely has a clinical indication and serves only the curiosity of a data-driven world, obsessed with quantifying and controlling.

While statistical norms may be helpful to alert a physician to a potentially dangerous pregnancy, the practice of implanting multiple zygotes actually places the woman at risk for a dangerous pregnancy—that of higher-order multiples—thus monitoring the fetuses for selective reduction is a correction in pregnancy control rather than a solution to a spontaneous problem. Essentially, this practice sets up the need for more resource use instead of taking the simple, more parsimonious path or implanting only the number of zygotes that will be brought to term.

A clinical determination of attenuated fetal growth or weaker fetus may result in a recommendation for selective reduction to redirect the previous action of multiple implantations. This should be discussed as part of informed consent prior to implantation not only as a standard of care, but also to conserve resources. The woman or couple may not wish to pursue selective reduction for one or more reasons. A first reason would be the objection to the technique of selective reduction itself, as a form of abortion.[6] A second reason would be the hope that the weaker fetus may regain some fitness and catch up developmentally.[7] In these cases, the clinical recommendation would be more monitoring.

If, on the other hand, the woman accepts that one or more of the fetuses has to be eliminated, she will undergo a clinical abortion. The clinical abortion is a short surgery that requires local anesthesia, guided ultrasonic tools to perform the abortion, and disposal of the biohazard waste.[8] Both paths result in resource use and carbon emissions. If the woman pursues a non-reductive path, she will continue to be monitored. If the fetus does not perform well, or is impacting the growth of the other, stronger fetus due to intrauterine growth restriction, selective reduction will again be offered. If the woman pursues this clinical recommendation, the above steps will proceed. If she does not, she will attempt to give birth to more than one fetus.

Sharp critiques of medicalized reproduction have come from feminists who are concerned with the socio-medical control of women and dependence on medical services. Ann Oakley, in her seminal work on medicalization and pregnancy, observes that "the A-Z [x ray] test launched the modern era in which obstetricians would eventually be able to claim a knowledge superior to that possessed by the owners of the wombs themselves, as to the presence of a guest, invited or uninvited, within."[9] Women concede power to doctors when they use healthcare for pregnancy; this is true, but what is often

MEDICAL REPRODUCTION AND PREGNANT WOMEN 75

overlooked is the environmental impact of these procedures. Submitting to medical treatments demands carbon expenditure, compounding the ethical objections to antenatal "care."

Furthermore, the economic commentary on the medicalization of pregnancy has also been a cause of concern. For instance, it has been pointed out that the function of the ultrasound and other pregnancy-related evaluations is not necessarily the pursuit of health, but profitability. In many countries, "the healthcare system is insurance-based, and in private practice, the existence of the technique has substantially boosted the profits to be made from pregnancy surveillance as an area of medical work."[10] Profitability is not inherently unethical, but it is often antithetic to sustainability,[11] since all activities that drive the economy produce carbon emissions. Economic growth is therefore dependent on making non-essential services appealing to consumers. This in turn puts pressure on the environment as desires, and not needs, are pursued. It is not simply that monitoring a pregnancy or selecting the fittest embryos or fetuses to be allowed to develop to term is a desire predicated on a reproductive plan, but rather the entire system of MR is built upon a highly choreographed system of self-perpetuating steps that each, in turn, emit carbon. The desire is not problematic; rather the consequence is.

Miscarriage

After the desired number of embryos are in the womb, pregnancy will continue to be monitored. At any time, miscarriage, or spontaneous abortion, could occur. Miscarriage is the natural death of a fetus in the womb. Although there are myths about miscarriages being caused by a woman's actions, either intentionally or unintentionally, most cannot be controlled. Common reasons for miscarriage are the inadequacy of the embryo or fetus, meaning that it is not strong enough to survive or has chromosomal abnormalities and therefore dies.[12] Miscarriage is a common result of both MR and non-MR pregnancies. It is estimated that 10–20% of pregnancies result in a miscarriage,[13] with some number occurring before the woman realizes she is pregnant. However, rates of miscarriage are higher for MR pregnancies.

Eli Y. Adashi and Rajiv C. McCoy report that "the incidence of fetal loss among women aged 36 or younger is < 15% but rapidly increases to 29 and > 50% in women aged 40 and 44 and older, respectively."[14] MR pregnancies have several features that predispose toward miscarriage.

76   ENVIRONMENTAL ETHICS AND MEDICAL REPRODUCTION

Endometriosis is a significant factor in MR miscarriage.[15] Researchers from the Reproductive Medical Center in Zhengzhou University (China) identified the presence of polycystic ovary syndrome, uterus malformation, and frozen embryo transfer[16] as three features impacting miscarriage after in-vitro fertilization. Note that the first three—endomitoses, polycystic ovary syndrome, uterus malformation—may be indicative of infertility or subfertility. Women with these conditions therefore rely on in-vitro fertilization over artificial insemination to counteract their body's configuration. If they are using their own eggs, the presence of infertility as a condition with possible genetic ties may explain higher miscarriage rates related to embryonic aneuploidy. However, the fourth—frozen embryo transfer—would be a technique both fertile and infertile people would use.

Embryos can be transferred to a woman either "fresh" or "frozen."[17] Fresh embryo transfer will use in-vitro fertilization and transfer to the womb without freezing; frozen embryo transfer takes the fertilized egg and stores it cryogenically, defrosts the embryos, and then transfers to the womb. Frozen embryo transfer is consistently tied to lower rates of pregnancy, poorer maternal outcomes, and high rates of miscarriage.[18] Although rates have improved, between 12% and 30% of pregnancies from cryogenically frozen embryos result in spontaneous termination.[19] By way of comparison, one study from 2016 put miscarriage rates at 22% for fresh embryo transfer and 32.7% for frozen.[20] Another study from 2008 places miscarriage rates at 13.8% for fresh cycles and 23.0% for frozen-thawed embryo.[21] Even when fresh embryos are used, the average percentage of women who will miscarry is still higher than the average miscarriage rate for non-MR pregnancies.[22] Miscarriage is therefore a predictable outcome of MR with significant ethical implications.

First, MR pregnancies obviously use resources, including the process of gamete retrieval, storage, fertilization, and embryo transfers. When miscarriage occurs, as it predictably will, then medical care for those women is required. From a bioethics perspective, embryo transfer that results in miscarriage causes unnecessary pain and follow-up treatments; they are unnecessary since pregnancy is not a lifesaving need and embryo transfer is not a medical procedure; it is a fertilization technique. Moreover, if the embryos spontaneously abort, it is likely that the woman or couple will attempt repeated fertilization.[23] This will absorb more resources as subsequent MR cycles are pursued. The emotional and financial toll[24] must also be factored in to the ethics of MR, as well as the environmental cost of a high-risk procedure for a non-medical necessity that likely has to be repeated. Finally, since rates of miscarriage are higher with embryo transfer versus natural pregnancy, fertile people should avoid using MR and embryo transfer as it is not the most efficient way to ensure a pregnancy. If they do use it, the balance of extra resources, not only for MR itself but for the increased chances of miscarriage, must be confronted. The use of MR by fertile people is "redundant" in that it uses medical resources but these resources are not required for the goal of pregnancy. Simultaneously, the predictability of miscarriage indicates misdirection of resources and the consequence that singles and couples using MR will return to the previous steps of MR.

Premature Delivery

Premature delivery is often connected to children conceived by MR, and particularly MR twins and higher-order pregnancies. Singles and couples seeking medical fertilization often choose to become pregnant with twins.[25] This reflects the choice to transfer multiple embryos with the intention of multiple implantations. Many MR clients prefer to go this route to "make up for lost time," thus having two or more children in one pregnancy. There is a direct correlation between using MR for conception and early birth, which burdens the medical industry needlessly. The *European Journal of Obstetrics & Gynecology and Reproductive Biology* indicates that "the incidence of twins after ART born at < 32 weeks increased 27-fold from 1987 to 2010 and has not reduced from its peak incidence over the last decade."[26]

Twins or higher-order pregnancies often result in premature and low-birth-weight infants for a variety of reasons. The first is simply a division of nutrition and internal support while in the womb. More fetuses have to compete for the same resources, even if the pregnant woman is being diligent with safeguarding her health, thus "intrauterine growth retardation (IUGR) is a frequent occurrence in twin pregnancy."[27] This has been described as the "lifeboat" phenomenon:[28] too many beings vying for the safety of one, limited space. While individual fetal growth is attenuated in twin pregnancy, having two or more fetuses extends the overall capacity of the womb more quickly than a singleton. As such, the fetuses are more likely to be born prematurely and with low birth weight. A 2013 report indicated that 8% of babies born in the US were low birth weight and 11.4% were premature.[29] Associated conditions of prematurity and low birth weight include subdued cardiac and respiratory development.[30] Moreover, the European Society of

78   ENVIRONMENTAL ETHICS AND MEDICAL REPRODUCTION

Human Reproduction and Embryology Capri Workshop Group indicated that "multiple gestation children may suffer long-term consequences of perinatal complications, including cerebral palsy and learning disabilities."[31] Some of these medical problems will require extra healthcare support after birth and sometimes throughout life.[32]

Moreover, women put themselves at risk when carrying twins or higher-order pregnancies. A 2019 article in *Obstetrics & Gynecology* found that, "compared with women with singleton pregnancies, women with twin pregnancies have a fourfold increased risk for severe maternal complications both before and after delivery."[33] Women carrying twins are more likely to suffer from preeclampsia and other health risks such as gestational hypertension.[34] Higher-order pregnancies may be categorized as high risk[35] because of the extra strain on the woman's reproductive and circulatory system, which will require extra monitoring and visits prior to birth and sometimes medical interventions to sustain the pregnancy until delivery is viable, followed by follow-up care from any complications.

Due to the factors of prematurity, poorer health outcomes from prematurity, and increased risks for the mother, twins and higher-order multiple births are extremely costly to healthcare.[36] In 2014, *JAMA Pediatrics* determined that "the mean hospital costs of a singleton, twin, and HOM [higher-order multiple] child to age 5 years were \$2,730, \$8,993, and \$24,411 (in 2009–2010 US dollars), respectively."[37] Beyond the hospital care, there are additional costs to taxpayers. In 2013, *The Lancet* estimated that the total economic cost of each preterm birth in the United States in 2005 was \$51,600.[38] When the various financial aspects of prematurity are combined, "preterm births place a multibillion-dollar burden on business, with employers billed more than \$12 billion annually in excess health care costs."[39] In Canada, there are "total national costs of \$123.3 million for early preterm infants" over the first 10 years of life.[40] Economic cost is tied to the cost of healthcare procedures, which require resources and emit carbon.[41] Prematernity, economic drain, and unnecessary resource use are predictable outcomes of MR; they can be avoided by not using the technology.

Childbirth

If the fetus or fetuses do not need to be delivered prematurely and come to full term, birth will occur either "naturally" (vaginally) or through a

MEDICAL REPRODUCTION AND PREGNANT WOMEN 79

cesarean section. For decades, critical commentary on the medicalization of childbirth has appeared, pointing out the discrepancy between what has, for thousands of years, been a non-medical event and the current technological approach toward childbirth.[42] To be sure, childbirth has often been attended by a midwife.[43] A lack of access to medical care of pregnant women contributes to preventable maternal mortality and morbidity.[44] Thus, the objection to healthcare rituals associated with pregnancy is not about their use, but the overuse and overreliance on the healthcare system, which takes resources and removes autonomy from women.

Ann Oakley observes that the co-opting of pregnancy from something natural into a medical event coincided with the disappearance of midwives. In the Western world, more pregnancies became categorized as "abnormal." However, Oakley clarifies, "the normal/abnormal distinction was not to be consistently held over the many years, the boundaries around the two notions were shifting constantly. . . . [W]hile 70% of childbirths were thought normal enough to be delivered at home in the 1930s, 70% were identified as abnormal enough to be delivered in the hospital in the 1950s."[45] The move toward hospital birth is striking.

Medicalization of pregnancy is partially explainable by economics. In the US, the rise of third-party insurers led to higher costs of pregnancy. David Crippen indicates "the bill for a typical 6-day hospital stay for childbirth in 1951 was $85—well within the range of most families. A 6-day hospitalization for cardiac workup at a large urban hospital in 2010 has recently been calculated to be $19,254; the facility lost $2,695 of that amount after reimbursement."[46] The economic stronghold on pregnancy in tandem with medicalization has led to removal of birthing options from women. In fact, in some places women have to fight for home delivery, which is viewed as nearly criminal.[47] Sociologist Victoria Pitts notes, "[B]ecause certain groups are more closely scrutinized under the medical gaze, and pathologized more readily than others (women, people of color, sexual minorities), pathologization is never politically neutral."[48] Indeed, "it is no longer the woman who wants to have her baby in a hospital who has to fight, but the woman who wants a home birth."[49]

The change in approach toward pregnancy—as something that can be reasonably managed by oneself, or with the aid of a doula or other birthing professional—and the current view that childbirth is a medical event reaffirm that "today the object of antenatal care is to screen a population suffering from the pathology of pregnancy from the few women who are normal

80   ENVIRONMENTAL ETHICS AND MEDICAL REPRODUCTION

enough to give birth with the minimum of midwife attention."[50] This has removed the power and experience of safe childbirth from women and placed it in the hands of the medical industry. "Hospitals, by aligning normal parturition with the confinement of the sick, created a medical label for pregnancy," which allowed for it to be "a legitimate subject of medical discourse and treatment."[51] This has the double effect of causing distress for women who want options in birthing[52] and environmental impacts of hospital surveillance which are, oftentimes, unnecessary. Interestingly, the environmental impact of childbirth is one of the few forms of medical reproduction that has been given attention. While neither comprehensive nor exhaustive, some aspects of childbirth have been evaluated for carbon emissions and therefore are a case study in one very small part of MR.

Vaginal Childbirth

Vaginal childbirth, often referred to as "natural childbirth" to distinguish it from a cesarean section, does not imply sustainability, as many vaginal births utilize medical resources, including transport to and from the hospital and care in the hospital.[53] All medicalized vaginal childbirths will make use of a disposable custom birth pack, which Campion et al. define as "a set of sterile, disposable products prepackaged for a specific procedure with the aim of reducing time, errors, and contamination risk."[54] These packs are premade and ready to use in hospitals. Research quantified the environmental impact of the disposable custom birth packs and found that there is 8.7 kg of CO_2[55] (range 2.4–19.8 kg of CO_2) for each vaginal birth custom pack in the United States.[56] In 2019, the Centers for Disease Control recorded 2,558,882 vaginal deliveries in the United States alone,[57] making the carbon from only the birth packs of only vaginal deliveries only in the US in only one year 22,262,273.4 kg of CO_2. This is equivalent to 11,131 round-trip flights from Boston to London,[58] or the amount of carbon generated by worldwide emails in one year, assuming the lowest email carbon estimate.[59] Custom birth packs are only one source of carbon and resources used in medicalized pregnancy, only one aspect of MR, and only one small part of healthcare carbon.

Since childbirth is a medicalized event, the carbon from inpatient admissions must also be considered. In England, the CO_2 of one hospital admission is 92 kg and the impact of each inpatient day has been calculated

MEDICAL REPRODUCTION AND PREGNANT WOMEN   81

to be 80 kg.[60] In the UK, there are approximately 800,000 births annually, costing the NHS over £2.5 billion per year.[61] Bowers and Cheyne report that "in the late 1970s and 80s it was expected that women would remain in hospital for around 6 days." This number has decreased: "[B]y 1990 56% of women in England remained in hospital for three or more days following birth. . . . In Scotland the mean postnatal hospital stay fell from 2.8 days in 2001 to 1.9 days in 2013."[62] Using the mean number for Scotland in 2013, the admission and inpatient carbon is 244 kg of CO_2 per birth and 195,200,000 kg of CO_2 per year for admission and hospital stay for birth only in Scotland only in one year. Clearly, these calculations could be done for each step of medicalized reproduction related to childbirth, in each country and year, making the aggregate of carbon significant. Vaginal births can often be done safely at home[63] with less environmental impact. However, not all childbirth is low-risk and may truly require medical intervention.

Cesarean Section

A cesarean section (C-section), whereby the fetus is taken from the uterus by cutting through the abdominal wall, may be necessary or clinically indicated in some cases. For instance, when the fetus is in a breached position, with its feet heading toward the birth canal, vaginal childbirth is difficult and risky and a cesarean section can prevent harm to both fetus and mothers.[64] Sometimes if the fetus or mother is in distress, a cesarean section can be a quicker way of delivering the infant to provide medical treatment or relieve the mother from clinical distress. Healthcare disparities, some of which are rooted in systemic racism that lead to high-risk pregnancies,[65] may also be a clinical indication for cesarean section. Moreover, cesarean sections have a prophylactic purpose by reducing the risk of transmitting human immunodeficiency virus (HIV) during birth.[66] All of the above scenarios are medical ways of addressing a medical need. However, cesarean sections are not without risks, and the forcible imposition of C-sections on women constitutes a serious ethical and legal problem.[67]

Delivery by cesarean can also be a threat to women's health, as it is correlated with higher post-partum antibiotic treatment, severe maternal morbidity and mortality, and worse outcomes for the infants.[68] In 2012, research presented at the Society for Maternal-Fetal Medicine annual meeting

82 ENVIRONMENTAL ETHICS AND MEDICAL REPRODUCTION

in Dallas found that "small, premature infants born by cesarean section are at 30 percent higher risk for serious breathing problems than those delivered vaginally."[69] These breathing problems are a result of fluid in the fetus's lungs, which is normally cleared in the course of vaginal birth.[70] Since cesarean sections come with a variety of health risks, they ought only be used when necessary. Yet, C-sections are an elective part of MR for some women.

Women using MR for pregnancy or MR for childbirth may elect for a cesarean for several reasons. First is if the woman is pregnant with twins or higher-order multiples. In this case, the C-section may be a necessity either because of the prematurity associated with twins[71] or to hasten the rather long process of birthing multiple fetuses.[72] Women may also choose C-sections as part of MR independent of the number of fetuses she will deliver.

Cesarean sections are a cosmetic choice for many, but not all, women.[73] Since cesarean sections avoid vaginal childbirth, the vagina is not permanently stretched, which purportedly makes sexual intercourse more pleasurable for hetero-sexed couples.[74] Thus, some women view it as merely another option that the medical industry can provide. An unpublished interview with Gena Corea and Dr. Herbert discussing C-sections in 1979 reads, in part: "[D]eep down the American (male) physician thinks he's doing women a favor in preserving her vagina for sexual activities. . . . [T]hey're doing this in good part for the husband, but behind it if the wife can function better for the husband, she's happier too." (parenthetical mine) Note, both rationales are phallocentric: the pleasure of the husband and the pleasure the wife gets as a sexual object for her husband. No mention is made of the wife's pleasure or desire and heterosexuality is implied. Thus, if cesarean sections are done with the primary intention of retaining the elasticity of the vagina, then it is clearly a symptom of medical consumerism marketed to women. In the US, "American (male) surgeons, have been known to offer women . . . reassurance that a caesarean section will keep them 'honeymoon fresh.' "[75] (parenthetical mine) These elective options use resources, emit carbon, and endanger the health of women and infants, primarily for the purpose of male satisfaction.

In addition to the "benefit" of avoiding the natural consequences of natural childbirth, some women prefer to pick a significant date, a convenient day, or a lucky time to give birth and will schedule an appointment to deliver the child or children via cesarean section.[76] This is another aspect of medicalized reproduction which is fueled by growing consumer markets for MR and increasing prevalence in some places.[77]

The United States has one of the highest number of elective cesarean sections in the developed world—at nearly a third of all deliveries.[78] These numbers are related to cosmetic use for birth of singletons and necessity due to multiple fetuses from using MR. In other parts of the world, more frequent use of cesarean sections or birthing "interventions" have been attributed to medicalization. For instance, the increase of C-sections in London in the early 20th century "clearly had something to do with the increased medical surveillance of pregnancy, and with the battle that was being fought between the different professional groups interested in acquiring control over obstetric care."[79] Yet, the ethical implications of elective cesarean sections extend beyond control over pregnant women, which is a matter of reproductive ethics, and into wider aspects of biomedical ethics and justice.

The World Health Organization cites overuse of unnecessary cesarean as a "barrier to universal (medical) coverage."[80] The medical resources dedicated to this elective surgery, like all other elective medical procedures, take away from other healthcare services in the world. The doctors, facilities, and training programs which are funneled toward the medical demands of the developed world cluster resources in wealthy areas, leading to unjust distribution of medical resources, typically in high-impact areas.

The environmental impact of cesarean sections is higher than that of natural childbirth. In addition to the carbon emissions of medicalized childbirth from any form of delivery—transportation, hospital admission, hospital stays, and drugs—"the production of the disposable (birth) custom packs makes up a significant percentage of the ozone depletion and smog categories, due largely to the production of cotton and manufacturing of polyvinylchloride components in the packs."[81] When the entire life cycle of childbirth is assessed, a C-section is nearly five times higher than vaginal birth, not only in terms of CO_2 but also other environmental impacts, like acidification, smog, respiratory effects, ozone depletion, eutrophication, carcinogenics, non-carcinogenics, and ecotoxicity.[82]

Childbirth has been a very common experience for most women throughout time. The medicalization of it in the modern day has been hastened by a variety of social, economic, medical, and personal factors. These have had consequences for the environment. It is very clear that MR pregnancies are not just for those who use assisted reproductive technologies, but are indeed a core of medicalized reproduction, which is both significant enough and widespread enough to warrant significant ethical attention.

84   ENVIRONMENTAL ETHICS AND MEDICAL REPRODUCTION

Cosmetic Procedures

After medicalized childbirth, postpartum medical care may be clinically required. For instance, the danger of a prolapsing uterus may indicate a clinical need for a hysterectomy.[83] The physical pressure of a fetus on the uterus and organs may cause internal stress and incontinence.[84] The vaginal mesh was one very harmful procedure that was designed to meet the clinical needs of some women after childbirth.[85] Fistulas because of labor are still a major concern in the developing world, which needs more attention in biomedical and feminist ethics. Women who suffer from fistulas and cannot access medical care are often stigmatized and socially ostracized, thus leading to poverty and dangerous living situations.[86] While addressing incontinence and fistulas from childbirth does require use of medical resources, they are not part of MR, as they meet a basic need for healthcare related to hygiene. Furthermore, when pregnancy is not chosen—as in the case of rape or lack of access to contraception—antenatal care is simply an unforeseen medical requirement which resources should be saved for. When pregnancy can be avoided and some women, mostly in the developed world, pursue cosmetic procedures associated with the natural effects of pregnancy and childbirth, then limited natural resources are not used wisely.

Cosmetic procedures afterbirth vary and are defined as part of MR, as they place a distinctly non-medical need into the realm of healthcare, emitting carbon at the same time. Cosmetic procedures after birth may focus on the effects of pregnancy, the effects of childbirth, or the effects of breastfeeding. First are the effects of pregnancy. To "correct" the stretched torso that comes with pregnancy, a "tummy tuck"[87] may be sought. Here, the stretched skin of the stomach is sewn together. Second are the effects of childbirth. Since childbirth itself stretches the vagina, and original elasticity will never be regained, vaginal tightening, whereby a woman's vagina is partially sewn shut to mimic a nulliparous woman's, is becoming more common.[88] The connection with female genital mutilation—which essentially does the same thing, but without the consent of the young girl or woman—is striking.[89] The procedure, technique, and even rationale (i.e., male pleasure) are the same for both female genital mutilation and voluntary vaginal tightening. Third are the effects of breastfeeding. Mastopexy of post-nursing breasts, similar to the tummy tuck, cuts and sews the sagging skin of breasts.[90] All cosmetic procedures rely on clinics, infrastructure, medical equipment,[91] drugs, aftercare, and follow-up care, which demand resources and emit carbon.[92]

MEDICAL REPRODUCTION AND PREGNANT WOMEN 85

The social movement of medicalized reproduction causes unnecessary resource use. Whereas a century ago, doctors had the "concern of getting women to use and accept medical technological approaches to maternity care"[93] for women's safety, now the ubiquitous presence of the medical industry in pregnancy and after birth dominate. In this way, cosmetic procedures are not seen as something discrete from MR pregnancy, but indeed as a concluding step, or merely an extension of it. Likewise, the carbon of these procedures cumulates as women move from one phase of MR to the next.

Though not cosmetic, breast pumps are one additional example of the medicalization after birth. In 2008, the healthcare insurance company Blue Cross began to offer free breast pumps to members who live in Massachusetts.[94] Alison Stuebe, an ob-gyn and assistant professor of maternal and child health at the University of North Carolina, believes, "[W]hat this (provision) says is that breastfeeding is a real part of the health care continuum. . . . [I]t is not gratuitous."[95] Breast pumps can certainly be helpful, and there are few ethical debates there. The aspect which requires evaluation is the reason for making breast pumps available, which appears to be a commercial partnership between the companies manufacturing the devices and the healthcare insurance companies and the broadening understanding of pregnancy care. In the former, all commercial endeavors have hazardous waste effects and environmental manufacturing costs. In the latter, the areas for resource use are expanded. Both must be regarded with suspicion from biomedical, reproductive, and environmental ethics.

Summary

Medical reproduction and its association with pregnancy is relevant to women who have used MR prior to pregnancy and women who have conceived naturally. It is an unfounded assumption that MR is only for those who are utilizing the entire spectrum of MR. The medicalization of pregnancy and everything connected with it—from selective reduction, to miscarriage and abortion, to the manner of delivery, to the final stages of afterbirth, which include cosmetic procedures—require resources and emit carbon. In many cases, these medical options are not clinically necessary and not even desired by women. Particularly given the modern movement to de-medicalize pregnancy,[96] it is striking that so many resources would be

86 ENVIRONMENTAL ETHICS AND MEDICAL REPRODUCTION

given to something that has solid ground to be removed from the spectrum of medical reproduction. Medical reproduction is not simply an endeavor for the infertile. At the intersection of pregnancy and childbirth, it seriously and almost ubiquitously affects all women in the developed world.

Simultaneously, the risks and hazards of pregnancy are overlooked in the glamorization of gestation and parturition. Reproductive ethics evaluates these harms. In 1970, Shulamith Firestone called pregnancy "barbaric."[97] This line of thought has been extended throughout the decades. Rory E. Kraft asserts, "[F]rom medical, philosophical, and social perspectives, it seems clear that pregnancy should be perceived as a harm to the woman. Pregnancy involves not only the carrying of the fetus, but also enduring of physical, emotional, and intellectual changes that are by no means short-lived."[98] His conclusion draws on medical facts, feminist literature, and legal precedent in the United States. Several court cases ruling on non-voluntary pregnancy as a result of rape speak to the burdens of pregnancy. These include *United States v. Yankton*,[99] *Fenelon v. State*,[100] and *People v. Sargent*.[101] While rape has an additional aspect of harm in the sexual transgression, pregnancy has the same range of physiological effects regardless of whether it is consensual, planned, medicalized, or natural. *United States of America v. Defabian C. Shannon* argues:

> Apart from the nontrivial discomfort of being pregnant (morning sickness, fatigue, edema, back pain, weight gain, etc.), giving birth is intensely painful; and when the pregnancy is involuntary and undesired, the discomfort and pain have no redemptive features and so stand forth as a form of genuine and serious physical injury, just as in the case of an undesired surgical procedure (a pertinent example being involuntary sterilization). Most surgical procedures cause discomfort and pain; we bear these by-products to cure or avert a greater injury or illness; when there is no greater injury or illness to avert, the by-products become pure injury.[102]

Concretely, pregnancy, even when desired and valuable to the woman, is a harm to the body. And the ethics of this mostly avoidable experience, in tandem with the expenditure of resources so that this harm can occur, should at least cause a second glance at the entire endeavor of reproduction and its facilitation through healthcare, which has its first obligation to "do no harm." In fact, Kraft argues, "once we acknowledge pregnancy as harm, society has an obligation to assist in the amelioration of the impact of the harm. . . . [W]e all have been part of the harming of our own mothers, and many of us have already or will in the future be participants in the harming of women through their impregnation. (We might also consider whether fertility specialists carry additional obligations toward pregnant women, because they have participated in the harming of so many)."[103] His points are well taken, yet do not touch upon the larger environmental harm for women, infants, and others who suffer from the climatic effects of resource consumption. The very fact that "every human being born constitutes a draft on all aspects of the environment—food, air, water, unspoiled scenery, occasional and optional solitude, beaches, contact with wild animals, fishing and hunting"[104]—is a serious ethical consideration. The facilitation of pregnancy, not only in its medicalized form but particularly since it is not clinically necessary, speaks to the severity of ethical issues associated with MR.

PART II

SUSTAINABLE POLICY FOR MEDICAL REPRODUCTION

4

Healthcare and Carbon Reduction

Healthcare directly impacts the environment through use of resources to cure, treat, and prevent diseases. Healthcare indirectly impacts the environment by extending lifespans, decreasing child mortality, and creating not only the possibility of new births (for instance, by preventing infertility and helping people to reach sexual maturity), but also actually creating new humans through reproductive technologies. The indirect environmental impact of healthcare resource use contributes to climate change and climate change health hazards. The direct environmental impact of healthcare puts pressure on earth's carrying capacity and contributes to overpopulation. Medicine also has the capacity to reduce population growth and resource use and relieve pressure on earth's carrying capacity through contraception and more sustainable healthcare. The carbon emissions of medical care have been underconsidered in part because of the belief that all medical care is clinically necessary and therefore carbon emissions are morally irrelevant. However, safe amounts of carbon in the atmosphere have been exceeded—in part because of medical lifestyles, which include both essential and elective treatments.[1]

National carbon emissions include the carbon of the healthcare industry. Put another way, part of the per capita emissions of individuals is their use of healthcare. The carbon emissions of global healthcare activities make up 4–5% of total world emissions,[2] placing the healthcare industry on par with the food sector.[3] Healthcare carbon emissions come from external and internal sources. External healthcare carbon is produced by hospitals and clinics and includes water sourcing, energy use, and food services. External healthcare carbon also comes from patient transportation to and from hospitals and doctors commuting to work, as well as shipping products to healthcare facilities.[4] Internal healthcare carbon, also referred to as healthcare delivery, comes from medical tests, bedside care, single-use instruments, and pharmaceuticals,[5] among others.

Environmental Ethics and Medical Reproduction. Cristina Richie, Oxford University Press.
© Oxford University Press 2024. DOI: 10.1093/oso/9780197745182.003.0005

Healthcare carbon, per capita emissions, and the percentage of carbon the healthcare industry contributes to national carbon emissions vary by country. Data from 2019 shows that China's healthcare carbon is 600 million metric tons (MMT), .44 tons per capita, comprising 6.6% of the national carbon footprint. Germany's healthcare carbon is 55.1 MMT, .68 tons of carbon per capita, comprising 6.7% of the total national carbon footprint. Japan's healthcare carbon is 114 MMT, .9 tons per capita, and comprises 7.6% of the total national carbon footprint.[6] The US healthcare carbon is 479 MMT, 1.51 tons per capita, and comprises 7.9% of the total national carbon footprint. China's total healthcare carbon is the highest in the world, with the US being second. However, the per capita emissions in the US are 3.4 times higher than China's. These details are important for biomedical ethics, particularly in relation to justice and allocation of resources.

Data on the carbon emissions of national healthcare industries—even when estimated per capita—does not correlate to healthcare access and cannot capture the success or clinical necessity of medical treatments. Disparities between substantial healthcare emissions and deficient medical quality of life[7] are indicative of healthcare waste,[8] misdistribution of medical resources,[9] and non-medically indicated lifestyle procedures. Moreover, it is not the case that greater healthcare carbon translates to better healthcare outcomes. The World Health Organization ranked Germany's healthcare system's "overall efficiency" at 25 worldwide, Japan's at 10, the US's at 37, and China's at 144.[10] Large and unjust healthcare disparities are concealed in the carbon impact of many healthcare systems. As an industry, healthcare must be accountable for not only its raw carbon emissions, but also for where those emissions are expended.[11]

Carbon Dioxide (CO_2) Emissions as a Metric of Sustainability

Using the metric of carbon dioxide (CO_2) emissions is believed to be one of the most efficient and effective ways of quantifiably limiting carbon dioxide emissions.[12] Carbon reduction is not the only approach to sustainability in healthcare, but it does have several pragmatic advantages. First, it is widely recognized as an indicator of resource use. CO_2 has become a familiar term in the lexicon of environmentally aware citizens, thus making it easier for the average healthcare consumer to understand the impact their healthcare use has on the environment.[13] Second, much has already been written on national carbon emissions, with some significant initiatives in carbon reduction already in place. Globally, countries may join an international initiative like the Paris Accord[14] or Kyoto Protocol[15] to limit emissions. Other countries may place additional taxes on highly polluting industries, such as energy.[16] Thus, there is global backing for methodical carbon dioxide reduction. Third, there is an increasing amount of literature on the carbon emissions of healthcare services worldwide and nationally, which can lead to effective policies in carbon reduction.[17] In the United Kingdom, healthcare carbon reduction is part of a national plan to reduce overall emissions.[18] In other countries, the carbon of individual medical developments, techniques, and procedures and healthcare divisions is being calculated.[19] Once known, carbon can be reduced through quantifiable measures. Fourth, arguments for carbon reduction in one's personal life have been put forth in environmental studies,[20] thus making an additional entry point for understanding the carbon impact of healthcare.

Carbon Reduction in Healthcare Delivery

All medical treatments have a direct carbon impact, calculated on a medical life cycle from initial doctor's appointment, to the delivery of the procedure, to follow-up care, and an indirect environmental impact. For instance, a cataract operation emits 181.8 kg of CO_2[21] and requires resource use. A heart bypass operation emits 1.1 tons of CO_2,[22] requires resource use, and also puts pressure on earth's carrying capacity by extending lifespans. Similarly, conventional hemodialysis for kidney disease emits 10.2 tons of CO_2 per patient annually and also extends life for an average of five years.[23] Medicalized reproduction in its many phases has yet to be totally quantified. However, the outcome of MR—a child—has been calculated. The carbon footprint of one child in the US is over 1,644 tons of CO_2, and the carbon legacy of the person using MR is over 9,441 tons of CO_2. MR adds to resource use, carrying capacity, and population growth.

94 ENVIRONMENTAL ETHICS AND MEDICAL REPRODUCTION

Environmental Impact of Healthcare	Resource Use	Carrying Capacity	Population Growth	Carbon Footprint	Carbon Legacy
Cataract Surgery	X			181 kg	
Heart Bypass Operation	X	X		1.1 tons	
Hemodialysis for Diabetes	X	X		10.2 tons per year	
Medicalized Reproduction	X	X	X	+1,644 tons	+9,441 tons

Numerous other studies have been published on the carbon emissions of individual medical procedures, including cesarian sections and vaginal childbirth,[24] reproduction,[25] hysterectomies,[26] Critical Care Unit stays,[27] randomized controlled trials,[28] and a variety of dental[29] and mental health[30] services. Carbon reduction of internal healthcare, or healthcare delivery, may come from "greening" the medical life cycle of individual procedures[31] or by targeting high-impact treatments.[32] Some medical procedures can be made more sustainable by examining care pathways, engineering processes, user techniques, and disposal, thus evaluating each step from "cradle to grave." Healthcare delivery can also be made more sustainable by eliminating the need for procedures, through, for instance, preventive medicine, alternatives to high-impact care, or limitations on the number of procedures done overall.

As with historical debates in biomedical ethics about resource allocation, carbon emission reduction of healthcare delivery is an important but debatable topic.[33] From an environmental ethic, prioritizing certain forms of healthcare delivery may be justified on grounds of clinical benefit and carbon output. Medical procedures that sustain life by meeting the goals of medicine of curing, treating, and preventing life-threatening diseases should be prioritized since basic healthcare[34] is a human right and must be provided regardless of carbon impact. However, not all medical treatments prevent, cure, or treat disease. MR and indeed other elective medical procedures that do not meet the goals of medicine and have a significant carbon impact must be assessed for sustainability, with the intention of carbon reduction.

5

Carbon Emissions Policies for Unsubsidized Medical Reproduction

Many healthcare organizations, including Health Care Without Harm,[1] Practice Greenhealth,[2] the Healthier Hospitals Initiatives,[3] and the Catholic Health Association,[4] have recognized the connection between the carbon emissions of external healthcare and climate change and implemented initiatives such as recycling and clean energy purchasing. However, current voluntary resource reduction programs have been imported from general business frameworks, which focus only on the external aspects of sustainability,[5] making them inadequate to address carbon unique to the medical industry. In addition to managing the carbon of external healthcare facilities, internal healthcare must be evaluated, since it is a significant contributor to healthcare carbon.

Of particular interest for environmentally sustainable healthcare is the environmental impact of healthcare developments, techniques, and procedures. The healthcare developments, techniques, and procedures that are commercially available and accessible for public use are the first place policymakers could examine in making healthcare more environmentally sustainable since they overlap with ecological economics. In places where they are provided under subsidized healthcare, they should be the first to be reduced when resources are limited[6] or premiums are inflated and the last to be expanded.

Medical reproduction has hitherto been unregulated by any environmental standards and has avoided the scrutiny of environmental policymakers, likely because healthcare delivery has been seen as outside the self-defined scope of environmental ethics until recently.[7] But, as the world grapples with climate change, population growth, resource use, carbon emissions, and earth's carrying capacity, any healthcare development that promotes fertility must be evaluated.

Environmental Ethics and Medical Reproduction. Cristina Richie, Oxford University Press.
© Oxford University Press 2024. DOI: 10.1093/oso/9780197745182.003.0006

96 ENVIRONMENTAL ETHICS AND MEDICAL REPRODUCTION

To be sure, all medical treatments have the possibility of perpetuating carbon emissions. It is legitimate to ask, therefore, how MR is different from other medical interventions that use resources, produce carbon emissions, and contribute to earth's carrying capacity and therefore why it should be a target for carbon policies in a way that other healthcare delivery is not. Essentially, all healthcare must be made more sustainable; MR is not the only medical procedure that should be examined. However, MR is exceptional in six significant ways which highlight the necessity of urgent sustainability policy.

First, other forms of healthcare that impact earth's carrying capacity (usually by extending lifespans), such as hemodialysis, typically fit within the goals of medicine, defined as "the prevention of diseases and injury and the promotion and maintenance of health; the relief of pain and suffering caused by maladies; the care and cure of those with a malady, and the care of those who cannot be cured; the avoidance of premature death and the pursuit of a peaceful death."[8] MR does not treat, cure, or prevent infertility or any other disease. Reproduction is not a medical necessity. MR is elective, and all elective treatments should be examined when conservation is a concern. It would be unethical to curtail life-extending medicine, even though it does impact carrying capacity. However, elective procedures—regardless of how socially valuable—may be restricted in times of extraordinary medical or social concerns.[9]

Second, there is widespread consensus that healthcare insurance should continue to provide uncontroversial life-extending medicine and therapies to patients even though they absorb resources. Bioethicists do not spill ink attempting to convince the healthcare industry that standard forms of medicine are unethical because they have passed necessary ethical constraints. In contrast, MR continues to be subject to feminist, policy, environmental, social, sociological, religious, and financial debates.[10] They are ethically contested as a form of "healthcare."

Third, MR leaves a carbon legacy, and not just a carbon footprint. Whereas all healthcare uses resources and life-extending medicine may result in additional years of individual CO_2 emissions, only the carbon footprint of the individual is expanded. In contrast, carbon emissions from lineage-extending fertility treatments continue after the parent dies and are often perpetuated in additional descendants of the MR child who reproduces. There is an exponential carbon legacy impact in MR. Even if the child does not reproduce, the bulk of the carbon legacy is already emitted through the first descendent, who is most proximate to the legacy.[11]

Fourth, while a pre-reproductive person who has received life-extending medical treatments may or may not go on to have children, this is merely an environmental side effect of the medicine; it is not the direct intention. People who use MR are deliberately seeking a carbon legacy. Numerous ethical theories highlight the moral difference between direct and indirect,[12] intended and unintended, and foreseen and unforeseen consequences. While healthcare may be able to claim ignorance on the reproductive decisions of those using life-extending medicine, the direct outcome of MR is the creation of carbon-emitting humans.

Fifth, in terms of sexual ethics, even when comparing the carbon legacy of parents who use MR with parents who conceive naturally, MR has far greater environmental effects. Medical reproduction uses scarce communal resources such as intellectual research, government funding for development of new MR techniques, and medical buildings. Natural procreation *qua* procreation does not. That is, a woman wishing to become pregnant through MR has to go to a clinic, visit a doctor, and use the carbon-intensive resources of the medical industry. In contrast, a natural pregnancy takes no extra physical resources to achieve conception. And considering that many fertile people who could reproduce without any extra resources use MR, this is an environmental waste that contributes to the excessive carbon footprint of the medical industry. When the infertile use MR and it is successful, there is a creation of a new being who might not have existed without medical intervention. Even when MR is used without success, resources are expended in the process.

Sixth, the unnecessary use of MR to create a child who could have been born without medical assistance is a matter of medical ethics. Healthcare ought not to give treatments that are not medically unnecessary, yet fertile people who use MR do not need medical assistance for reproduction and thus drain healthcare resources and emit carbon without clinical benefit.

Category of Additional Resource Use	Resources of MR	Birth of New Person
MR infertile—successful	X	X
MR infertile/fertile—unsuccessful	X	
MR fertile—successful	X	

98 ENVIRONMENTAL ETHICS AND MEDICAL REPRODUCTION

Carbon Emissions Policies for MR

All areas of life must be analyzed for ecological impact and made more sustainable through supportive structures like laws and policies. Legal systems vary by country, yet some international standards of law exist.[13] These laws are effective, even in areas like climate change.[14] Although MR is distinct from sexual ethics, distinct from medical ethics, and distinct from ecological ethics, since it is an interdisciplinary ethical concerns, it has not been targeted as a place for policy in any three of these areas. Sexual ethics may contribute a rationale for social and familial policies on reproduction, but policies or laws that limit children are controversial. In the developed world, individuals and couples, by and large, have full discretion to make reproductive choices without interference. Medical ethics may address the policies associated with subsidized healthcare but is less effective in commenting on healthcare delivery, which overlaps with consumer preferences. There are few legal structures outside of subsidized healthcare except for professional liability. While there is probably a stronger case for regulating MR in subsidized healthcare fertility—since the cost is shared among many people who have an interest in minimizing healthcare costs—placing environmental policies on elective treatments, whatever they may be,[15] also has strong justification.

Unsubsidized medical reproduction is an elective treatment, although given by the same industry that provides clinically necessary medical services. This area of overlap requires constant ecological discretion. Like a dentist who provides preventive oral healthcare but also elective teeth whitening procedures,[16] carbon emissions must be directed at greatest medical benefit. The rationale for policies to minimize the carbon impact of MR has been made clear: through the use of MR millions of children are born, adding to global carbon emissions, which burdens the already over-taxed ecosystem. Hence, environmental policies are appropriate for unsubsidized MR as a reproductive choice which perpetuates population growth without reliance on financial subsidization. The environmental policies suggested here are the first place for healthcare institutions, governments, fertility clinics, and those considering MR. Some of these policies for unsubsidized medical reproduction may eventually be a cornerstone of law.

Subsidiarity and Policy

Policies allow for broader interpretation and implementation in a variety of contexts and are often more expedient in effecting institutional change as well, since they can be decided on a lower level than law. That is, policy can be made with the principle of subsidiarity, which states that "a community of a higher order should not interfere in the internal life of a community of a lower order, depriving the latter of its functions, but rather should support it in case of need and help to coordinate its activity with the activities of the rest of society, always with a view to the common good."[17] Subsidiarity requires a process of dialogue with people from all areas of life and places limits on governmental, or top-down, decision-making by "insisting that no higher level of organization should perform any function that can be handled efficiently and effectively at a lower level of organization by persons who, individually or in groups, are closer to the problems and closer to the ground."[18] Concomitantly, as global carbon emissions impact everyone in the world, no single institution or individual is exempt from limiting their resource use.

Environmental policies on the global level would simply regard MR as one among many aspects of life that would need to be made more sustainable.[19] This approach benefits from ethical theories of justice, as MR would not be singled out for sustainability, but would be made more sustainable along with other forms of healthcare, as well as agriculture, travel, and energy. This does not imply that MR would be eliminated. For instance, the opportunity for carbon trade-offs could be proposed globally—MR and healthcare may continue, but private vehicles (or a carbon equivalent) would be banned.[20] A similar approach could be made in individual countries; however, due to the immense carbon of the total lifecycle of MR—the child—in some countries there are not enough trade-offs to balance the carbon of that one person.[21] Thus, another, conjunctive approach would have to be made to reduce global carbon emissions, such as carbon trading,[22] immigration policies,[23] or reducing population growth ethically.[24] Policies on sustainable MR which have an international scope can also be flexible and may be taken as seriously as the international policy of, for instance, the UN.[25]

In the next level of subsidiarity, policy for unsubsidized MR can be proposed based on previous work on carbon reduction in the healthcare industry. MR is not only a medical treatment for the infertile. When MR

100 ENVIRONMENTAL ETHICS AND MEDICAL REPRODUCTION

treatment goes beyond the realm of providing infertility service and seeps into specialized reproduction for fertile couples and singles, there is an even stronger precedent for limiting the offerings until human lifestyles come closer to sustainability. In this case, MR would be rightfully viewed as any other consumeristic purchase that releases a high amount of carbon, subject to policy.[26]

Domestic and Sectoral Policies

Some of the most recognizable forms of carbon limitations are carbon capping, carbon cap and trade programs, and carbon taxes. Each of these three may be voluntary or legally compulsory. Moreover, each could be applied at the global, national, local, or sectoral level. These models can also complement family and individual carbon structures. While a consumer considering MR may opt for natural reproduction, the very large environmental burden of procreation still needs to be considered, so carbon policies could be "applied equally to those who conceive naturally and those who require [sic] artificial reproductive treatment."[27] The briefest of overview of carbon reduction through these systems will be given here to demonstrate that there are several environmentally sustainable models in place that could be explored.

Carbon Capping

Carbon capping limits the amount of CO_2 released over a set period of time. It is reliant on available carbon calculations. The Kyoto Protocol[28] was an example of an international carbon capping scheme which "operationalized the United Nations Framework Convention on Climate Change by committing industrialized countries and economies in transition to limit and reduce greenhouse gases (GHG) emissions in accordance with agreed individual targets."[29] The Kyoto Protocol was an important first step in international carbon capping, but there were many logistical and political problems in implementation, including an eight-year gap between adoption and ratification and the reluctance of major polluters, like the United States, to implement meaningful carbon reduction measures.[30] Yet, the Protocol remains an example for international and national accountability for carbon emissions,

POLICIES FOR UNSUBSIDIZED MEDICAL REPRODUCTION   101

which compels each sector to examine their consumptive practices, while simultaneously giving latitude to each sector for how much they will commit to carbon reduction.

While carbon capping is one of the most widely accepted and, in some aspects, simplest metric to limiting the environmental impact of particular nations or sectors, there are several downsides to this approach. First, carbon caps are difficult to implement in some countries—like the United States—and there has been reluctance to initiate any sort of carbon caps, trading, or binding measures to reduce the amount of carbon emitted internationally.[31] Without the endorsement of the most-emitting countries, carbon capping will be insufficient. Second, the vast majority of lifestyle choices have yet to be assigned carbon footprints. Calculating carbon numbers on all aspects of life, in every country, will take an enormous amount of time and human resources. Ironically, the carbon calculations themselves emit carbon.[32] It could certainly be argued that these calculations are an important carbon expenditure, but in the interim, another strategy has to be in place. The global industrial economy and everything therein is simply too enormous to accurately and rapidly compute. Moreover, carbon calculations can be elusive: just as reliable data appears, the inputs change. For instance, a carbon calculation of a cataract surgery will vary based on available resources, human efficiency, patient medical condition, and sourcing of energy, which are all moving targets.[33]

Third, the fundamental idea underscoring carbon calculations is carbon reduction, either through carbon capping or carbon allocation. However, this assumes that there is a sustainable amount of carbon that can be emitted on a yearly basis. This is untrue. The amount of "safe" carbon in the atmosphere—calculated to be 350 parts per million—has already been exceeded.[34] Allocating carbon to each country does not address the urgency of a zero-emission solution. More significantly, however, is that no amount of voluntary carbon capping will affect sustainability unless the major polluters in the world—the US, India, and China[35]—are convinced to reduce their emissions.

Fourth, carbon calculations are morally reductionistic and fail to inculcate virtue into a person. Reducing environmental ethics to the carbon number associated with a given item ultimately absolves individuals from thoughtful consideration and inner motivation for conservation. Michael S. Northcott argues, "[M]arkets in carbon are idols that legitimate the continuation of a consumptive industrial economy and the continuing sacrifice

102   ENVIRONMENTAL ETHICS AND MEDICAL REPRODUCTION

of the common goods of a stable climate and a livable earth for future generations."[36] While the outcome of carbon capping might be a more sustainable planet, society should not renounce holistic moral development in the pursuit of ecology. Rather, environmental sustainability must respect the ethical frameworks with which it engages—be it economics, national defense,[37] or healthcare—and also move individuals toward inner motivation for conservation that will outlast the immediate environmental problem. Merely identifying a carbon number and then declaring a product "sustainable" or "not" is simplistic. Carbon calculations are disposable in an ethical system that does not find intrinsic value in a clean, healthy planet.

Fifth, simply identifying a carbon number and then declaring a product "sustainable" or "not" is meaningless since humankind is beyond the point of finding a carbon equilibrium and must live in a carbon recession.[38] A carbon number, much like caloric information on a soft drink, is merely descriptive unless it is set within a normative context. Unlike calories, however, there is no recommended daily carbon emissions which can be sustainably produced.

Nonetheless, carbon assessment does provide a quantifiable measure of environmental impact and will be discussed here in part, with the caveat that while society waits for the inevitable carbon calculation of each aspect of life, principles of carbon reduction can be applied: because the carbon impact of medical care and MR is correlated to national emissions, it is appropriate to target MR in high-emitting countries first, through multiple strategies, including carbon capping.

Carbon Capping and Healthcare

Carbon capping for healthcare at the national level will be particularly effective in countries that have government-sponsored medical care. In 2007, the Welsh Labour and Plaid Cymru Groups in the National Assembly made an agreement entitled "One Wales: A Progressive Agenda for Wales,"[39] which highlighted the importance of sustainability in the country. This contributed to the 2008 UK Climate Change Act,[40] which set a target to cut the greenhouse gas emissions of the entire UK by at least 80% of their 1990 levels by 2050 through legally binding carbon budgets. As the UK has socialized healthcare, in 2009 the National Health Service's *Saving Carbon, Improving Health: NHS Carbon Reduction Strategy for England*[41] outlined strategies for

POLICIES FOR UNSUBSIDIZED MEDICAL REPRODUCTION   103

carbon reduction, including carbon-neutral transportation—like walking and biking—eliminating animal-based foods from menus, and reducing water waste in healthcare facilities.[42] A complementary document from the National Institutes for Health Research, "Carbon Reduction Guidelines," "highlights areas where sensible research design can reduce waste without adversely impacting the validity and reliability of research."[43] In 2010, the *Climate Change Strategy for Wales* was released.[44] Later, NHS Scotland put a *Climate Change Plan*[45] into place with support from the Scottish Public Health Network and Scottish Managed Sustainable Health Network, the latter of which also addresses climate change health hazards.[46] North Ireland has a broader healthcare system, with their Health and Social Care providing medical services,[47] and little data is available on their carbon reduction measures.

The NHS continues to systematically address methods for minimizing the carbon impact of healthcare through carbon capping. Current initiatives include a commitment to reduce single-use plastics[48] and decrease the use of certain anesthetic gasses.[49] Moreover, a thorough evaluation of pharmaceutical prescribing practices has the potential to dramatically decrease carbon in healthcare, since prescription drugs are the second largest contributor to healthcare carbon emissions in the NHS, after medical instruments and equipment.

Current calculations of the United Kingdom's National Health Services medical carbon are at 27 million metric tons.[50] Although the raw number is higher than the 2007 levels, it is because the "care" sector has been expanded to include "health." Overall, carbon emissions are declining. Significantly, the UK is the only region of the world that integrates sustainable healthcare policy into their national health system.

Carbon Capping and MR

If unsubsidized MR treatments were subjected to carbon caps and placed under healthcare emissions, the MR business would be included among other technological offerings of the medical industry. To be sure, MR treatments are not medically necessary, but as they do use the resources of medical infrastructure they might be placed under the medical sector's emissions. In this case, the MR industry would not have to reinvent the wheel as carbon capping has been widely considered a means toward sustainability. "In

104 ENVIRONMENTAL ETHICS AND MEDICAL REPRODUCTION

step with the dramatic rise in CO_2 emissions and other pollutants in recent years, a variety of new financial markets have emerged, offering businesses key incentives—aside from taxes and other punitive measures—to slow down overall emissions growth and, ideally, global warming itself."[51] These incentives include meeting carbon emission limitations through capping the amount of carbon released.

However, even if individual fertility clinics lowered carbon emissions by using recycled energy and renewable materials they still could not offset the carbon output of their products under current production models, since the carbon emissions of a human's life are so large. Currently, when health-care systems examine the carbon of medical offerings there is no accountability for the yearly environmental impact, carrying capacity, or population growth. The total product lifecycle must be calculated in order to make carbon caps effective.

As with other sector-specific caps, only the process of manufacturing is calculated and the environmental effects of those products are not taken into account. Without the entire scope of the carbon process, carbon reduction is fragmented. Total carbon emissions must be accounted for. Thus, instead of a partial assessment of the carbon output of each sector, calculating the net environmental effects will provide accurate numbers with which to reduce carbon. With MR, this means the impact of that new person, as well as the resources used in the process.

Carbon Emission Cap and Trading

In addition to carbon capping, a country or sector could cap their emissions and then trade others for more or fewer emissions, depending on how well they met their target. A cap and trade (C&T) system allows nations or sectors to voluntarily join a legally binding international or national carbon cap and trading scheme. Before or after they form the alliance, each participating nation or industry calculates their annual carbon emissions and sets targets for meeting an overall lower standard of emissions. The target emissions goals are disseminated to the group, and at regular intervals carbon is recalculated. The C&T scheme then facilitates "trading"; those who have "excess" or unused carbon quotas may sell or trade to those who are over their carbon allotment.[52] Put another way, nations or sectors that produce too much carbon can buy or trade "unused" carbon from nations or sectors that are more sustainable.

Cap and trade policies have had some limited success. For instance, the Chicago Climate Exchange (CCX) was "the world's first and North America's only voluntary, legally binding greenhouse gas reduction and trading program for emission sources and offset projects in North America and Brazil."[53] The CCX began trading in 2003 and ended in 2010 and had over 400 "members" enrolled, spanning chemical, automotive, transportation, environmental, medical, and education industries. Prominent companies included British Petroleum (BP), Bank of America, and Fortune 500 powerhouses like DuPont, Ford, and IBM.[54] Although the CCX is now defunct, the European Union Emission Trading Scheme, which started in 2005 and is still operational, is "a major tool of the European Union in its efforts to meet emissions reduction targets now and into the future"[55] and will continue to be a leader in cap and trade.

There are some climate benefits of the cap and trade system. First, instead of upstream accountability for carbon, "C&T requires emitters rather than suppliers to obtain permits"[56] for carbon emissions. Thus, there is accountability at the point of emissions. Second, cap and trade recognizes the variation in year-to-year production of carbon, which allows for more flexibility when carbon meets economic realities. Third, since nations or sectors are incentivized to reduce carbon as much as possible to profit from the sales of their excess carbon quotas, those that are already more sustainable have the opportunity for economic mobility. A developing country could be allotted a large share of carbon, but sell most of it. Similarly, fourth, cap and trade policies ensure that countries and sectors are held proportionately accountable for their emissions. Voluntary carbon cap and trade—as opposed to simple carbon capping—is more likely to be appealing to countries or sectors that would balk at blanket carbon emission reduction, like the US.

Carbon Emission Cap and Trading and Healthcare

Healthcare relies on many different sectors, from engineering for the production of medical devices and equipment, to agricultural systems to supply food, energy for buildings, as well as adjunctive healthcare structures like pharmaceutical companies and human resources. Thus, healthcare emissions come from a variety of sources which require a broad infrastructure. Upstream carbon comes from raw material extraction, manufacturing, and transportation, which in turn emits carbon dioxide and other environmental

106 ENVIRONMENTAL ETHICS AND MEDICAL REPRODUCTION

pollutants.[57] These resources are then turned into healthcare delivery—the medical goods and services, including consultations, procedures, pharmacy services, hospitalization, and medical research.[58] Other associated carbon from healthcare delivery includes supporting activities such as administrative services, procurement, food services, operation management,[59] and transportation of patients to and from hospitals.[60] Downstream carbon impacts include waste services, recycling or sterilization of tools, and of course the resource requirements of longer lifespans.

In countries with socialized medicine—like the UK—a cap and trade scheme would make each sector internally responsible for lowering carbon emissions to meet cross-sectorial goals. Then the nation would be free to buy or sell other carbon credits. Since the government oversees healthcare and all of the supportive sectors, it would be a rather straightforward process to allocate carbon. However, in countries without socialized medicine—like the US—healthcare carbon is at once decentralized and highly variable by region. Private healthcare insurance companies, like Blue Cross Blue Shield,[61] choose to participate in certain private hospital systems, like Kaiser Permanente.[62] These hospitals may offer exclusive access to doctors through in-network primary care providers and specialists. Thus, instead of a carbon capping within a national healthcare system, an individual healthcare network (either an insurance company or a hospital system) would join a cap and trade scheme with other, multisectoral industries across the country, which may or may not include other healthcare providers. While this might not guarantee that the healthcare providers are sustainably sourcing their materials, every supportive sector in the healthcare chain is an opportunity for voluntary carbon capping with the possibility of trading.

Carbon Emission Cap and Trading and MR

In industrialized countries, healthcare contributes a significant percentage to national carbon footprints,[63] although the actual amount of healthcare carbon, in terms of metric tons, varies dramatically. For instance, in 2007 the US healthcare sector expended an estimated 546 million metric tons of carbon dioxide, over 30 times higher than in the UK.[64] Carbon cap and trading may be effective in lowering the carbon of the healthcare sectors

POLICIES FOR UNSUBSIDIZED MEDICAL REPRODUCTION 107

overall, but would be unlikely to effect a drastic reduction in the carbon emissions from unsubsidized MR treatments for several reasons.

First, fertility businesses that accept private-party payments are decentralized,[65] although they may be owned by larger healthcare companies.[66] Since they operate outside of wider healthcare infrastructures, a cryogenic storage facility or a sperm banking center that joined on to C&T would make a rather insignificant impact in sectoral or national carbon reduction, as they are on such a small scale. Second, and similarly, individual doctors and fertility technicians do not have a way to join a cap and trade scheme. Since these are the professionals that facilitate MR, they might have the most opportunity to reduce MR emissions through ecological commitments to provide MR within sustainable limits. While it might be incongruent for an individual to have high environmental values and work in an area dedicated to reproduction,[67] the possibility for ethical growth is always present and each medical sector—especially those that support reproduction—must be agile in meeting environmental responsibilities. As with carbon capping, a third problem with C&T for the MR business is the lack of calculations of the carbon life cycle of the MR service. As MR produces people, that would have to be assessed, perhaps with each step of MR taking a certain percentage of carbon responsibility, as well as the actors—the healthcare providers and people using MR.

Since unsubsidized medical reproduction is not under one umbrella of commerce—at least not in the US, and certainly not in other countries that require out of pocket payments for MR[68]—an alternative within the carbon emission cap and trading scheme, which might be more suitable for the MR industry, is a cap-and-dividend system which "sets an economy-wide cap on the total level of CO_2 emissions, and requires fossil fuel suppliers to obtain a permit for each unit of CO_2 contained in recovered resources."[69] By reversing the burden of responsibility from the emitter to the supplier, carbon emissions would be more effectively reduced. Instead of a handful of individual MR clinics joining a cap and trade scheme, the medical manufacturers that supply MR tools to all clinics would be beholden to carbon standards. From the energy company that generates the power, to the distribution centers that send fertility devices, to the builders responsible for the construction of clinics and hospitals, a commitment to capping and dividends would mean more selective, or at least greener, power, distribution, and construction of MR processes, thus acting as a trickle-down form of sustainability.[70]

Carbon Taxes

Carbon taxes penalize those who exceed their voluntary or legally imposed carbon limitations.[71] These are most effective between countries that share a common financial sector.[72] A carbon tax "can be imposed at multiple stages of economic activity, from the early extraction or processing point (upstream) right up to the point immediately preceding combustion before the carbon dioxide is released (downstream)."[73] Carbon taxes work as a disincentive to emit carbon emissions through "punitive" means of financial imposition, rather than an incentive not to emit carbon through cap and trade.[74] The tax then goes toward sustainability initiatives which directly offset the carbon of the business.[75]

Carbon taxes are effective in as much as they compel companies or sectors to reduce their emissions in certain targeted areas, lest they pay a penalty. Carbon taxes may be calculated annually by sector or added at the time of "purchase," depending on the overall carbon reduction strategy. For instance, an annual carbon tax is simpler with long-term infrastructures like manufacturing plants, whereas disposable goods,[76] like clothes, are more suited for a tax at the time of purchase.[77] When carbon taxes are passed along to the consumer they result in more expensive products. These products may be viewed as "value added," as is the case with organic or local food in some places,[78] or may be viewed as consumers paying their fair share for participating in highly emitting activities, such as air travel.[79] A carbon tax increases the price of carbon-intensive products with the expectation that "consumers would likely respond by consuming fewer such goods and services."[80] Of course, some activities are seen as so indispensable to well-being (like procreation)[81] or have a lack of satisfactory alternatives (such as travel by train when flying is less expensive)[82] that some sectors would have little success in passing on the carbon tax to the consumer.

One downside of carbon taxing—other than the risk of unmitigated emissions due to the willingness to pay higher prices—is that carbon taxes are localized to the company or industry and do not account for the environmental impact of their product once it has entered the marketplace.[83] For instance, carbon taxes on automobile companies are localized to each specific business (e.g., the Tesla plant, the Ford warehouse); the manufacturer is not responsible for the way in which the natural resources are excavated, the carbon costs of transporting the materials for manufacturing, or, most importantly, the emissions of their cars once driven off the lot.[84] Individual cars must follow carbon emissions standards set by outside governing bodies, such as the Environmental Protection Agency (EPA) in the United States.[85] But the number of miles put on a vehicle, the type of fuel it uses, and other emission factors—like how fast a driver goes and whether they are on city or county roads—are not considered.[86] Instead of assessing only a fraction of the carbon output of each company—that which is localized to the manufacturing plant—the net carbon effects of the business must be taken into account as well.

There are several other downsides to carbon taxes. If passed along to the consumer, they disproportionately affect the poor. This has been the center of arguments on "sugar" taxes, or extra cost for unhealthy food and drinks.[87] Simultaneously, the rich may regard the carbon tax as a fee and not a fine.[88] Like a speeding ticket, it may be viewed as an acceptable monetary necessity in order to live the high-carbon life that they want. And in the case of either an upstream or a downstream tax, for the organization or the consumer, it should be remembered that the atmosphere already has more than the safe amount of carbon[89] and that all emissions need to be reduced.

Carbon Taxes and Healthcare

If a carbon tax were to be considered for the healthcare industry, it could be placed in one or more areas. First, it could be levied on the healthcare sector generally. In this scenario all medical procedures, or elective procedures which utilize medical resources, such as cosmetic dentistry, medicalized reproduction, and aesthetic medicine, would have a carbon tax added. The cost could be absorbed by the consumers at the point of use[90] or distributed across all medical procedures.[91] Second, a carbon tax could be placed on individual hospitals or the hospital network they are part of. Hospitals and clinics facing a carbon tax may choose to eliminate certain high-carbon procedures, such as long-term intensive care stays,[92] or minimize the number of carbon-intensive procedures given.[93] Like other forms of carbon markets, a simple carbon tax may prove to be ineffective if only the carbon of the procedures is subjected to taxes, rather than the entire life cycle of procedures.

Carbon Taxes and MR

A carbon tax on unsubsidized MR would be sensible in a number of areas. A carbon tax could be placed on any specific stage of MR, or on all the steps within the spectrum of MR. This path would directly link the environmental cost with the specific procedure to a financial disincentive, offering a proportionately high reason for incurring the lifestyle-related tax.[94] In this way, MR would be regarded as any other environmentally harmful positional good[95] which is taxed at a higher rate. Status symbols of wealth, which are unnecessary for basic human living, are more easily justified for high taxes—such as alcohol and private transportation.

Second, a carbon tax on MR would be more effective if it took account of the environmental externalities of the treatments. In the most basic sense, an externality is a cost that is not incorporated into the price of an action. William C. French writes that an externality occurs when "the price of a commodity or service fails to incorporate the full costs of the production and delivery of that good or service and the full costs imposed on others or future generations by the consumption of that good or service."[96] Calculating the carbon emission of each live MR birth by taking the lifetime consumption of the average resident and dividing it across the various stages of MR would give a more accurate view of the carbon emissions of the procedures.

For instance, the average lifetime carbon expenditure of the average American is 1,656 metric tons, or 3,651,480 metric pounds.[97] The carbon emissions of individuals are, of course, different in each country. Average lifetime consumption does not account for a number of factors, like sex (as women tend to live longer than men), place of residence (as cities dwellers may be more sustainable than those in the suburbs), or amount of medical needs, diet, and transportation preferences.[98] However, taking the high end of consumption, which would more closely align with the wealth and lifestyle of those who choose to avail themselves of unsubsidized MR,[99] would provide a solid baseline for a carbon tax on unsubsidized MR and align it with other higher-carbon purchases. Just as the automotive industry could be held responsible for the emissions of each car,[100] so too could the fertility business be responsible for the carbon of each child.

While it is right and sensible to ask the MR industry for accountability in matters of the carbon of their products—the babies that are made—MR is not always successful. Certainly, it would not be right to include carbon of unborn children in the carbon taxes of MR phases. Therefore, MR taxes might best be placed in each step of MR, whether that is retrieval, insemination, pregnancy, live birth, or post-partum treatments. Carbon taxes that include total life cycle emissions of MR would be a more comprehensive approach to carbon reduction than taxes only at point of use.[101] While

POLICIES FOR UNSUBSIDIZED MEDICAL REPRODUCTION   111

not impossible, this goal may be unpopular. Thus, cooperation from many sectors will be required.

The MR industry is just one small piece of the jigsaw puzzle of rampant consumption that leads to climate change. Yet, the extreme impact of MR use requires strategic measures to reduce carbon. Like other forms of consumerism, the MR industry can become more sustainable through environmental regulations. While a moratorium on all fertility clinics would be the most ecologically sound decision in this purview, it is unlikely that established fertility procedures or treatments would be effectively "banned" until global CO_2 emissions stabilize. Both carbon "carrots" and "sticks" are needed to make the MR industry more sustainable. In addition to environmental policies on unsubsidized MR itself, the people who use unsubsidized MR may also be subjects for carbon policies.

Individual and Family Carbon Policies

While the public sector does emit a significant amount of global carbon, about "40% of all energy use occurs at the individual and household levels";[102] thus, some ecologists have been critical of targeting the carbon emissions of businesses without attending to the consumers who use their services. Proposals from both the private and public sector for comprehensive environmental solutions include carbon reduction policies for individuals and families. These suggestions, which would constrain individuals to carbon emissions guidelines, include carbon budgets[103] and carbon taxes on new children.

Individual and Family Carbon Budgets

Families and individuals must be cognizant of their effects on the environment and could be subject to carbon budgets.[104] As with the commercial sector, a set number of carbon could be allocated to each person, either at birth—with parents overseeing responsibility for use until maturity—or at the age of maturity itself (16 or 18 years old). Similarly, once a person joins a family unit by birth, adoption, or marriage, their carbon budget could be added to the unit[105] or kept separate. Personal carbon budgets would require careful consideration in how they are designed. If a family allowance

112 ENVIRONMENTAL ETHICS AND MEDICAL REPRODUCTION

increased with family size, the purpose would be defeated. However, setting a standard, such as two new budgets for children per couple, and then incrementally reducing the amount of carbon for additional children over that number (e.g., 80% budget for a third child; 60% budget for a fourth), would limit the amount of resources a family is using. Having a set couple budget would also be an alternative. This may be created upon cohabitation or marriage. If couples had to choose between living modestly with one child or living a very simple life with three children, there would be some balance in carbon output. Of course, the childfree, or those who choose to adopt, may be able to live the highest standard of living.

Calculating the appropriate carbon number could be based on objective factors like carbon targets and conceptual aspirations like values. One way to distinguish between necessary and unnecessary resource use are the terms "subsistence" versus "luxury" carbon emissions.[106] Subsistence emissions are an unavoidable part of human activity and include the emissions related to basic food, shelter, and other fundamental human needs, including medical care. Luxury emissions, in contradistinction, do not impact the basic requirements of human life. As such, they can be targeted for carbon reduction. Analysis of "luxury" lifestyle choices, from eating meat[107] to using private transportation,[108] have been proposed, but rarely translate to policy. Therefore, efforts for personal and family carbon reduction are mostly dependent on the initiative of the individual.[109] The person has to opt in to a low-carbon lifestyle, which is occasionally supported by, for instance, financial credits that incentivize clean energy—such as the addition of solar panels in homes.[110]

A personal carbon budget could also utilize a carbon trading plan.[111] Here, each individual would be given "an equal number of tradable energy units per year. ... [I]ndividuals who are left with carbon credits (i.e., those who are frugal with non-renewable energy use) are then able to sell these back into the marketplace, thereby gaining financial benefit. Those who overuse their quota pay a premium price for extra energy use."[112] Personal carbon budgets respect the differences in people's views about having a good life while also recognizing that not all subjectively good lives are good for the environment everyone inhabits.

Because of these differences in lifestyle values, an individual or family carbon budget could be active in one or more sectors—such as transportation, housing, and entertainment—or it may be a net carbon budget.[113] A net carbon budget would allow a person to choose which high-carbon activities they prefer—travel by plane,[114] or meat consumption, or procreation, for example. Indeed, reproduction as a high-carbon activity could also have a sectoral allowance. Individual or family carbon budgets could be placed on MR either as part of a medical carbon budget or as part of a reproductive carbon budget.

Medical carbon budgets could be an effective path for individual healthcare consumers to mitigate their emissions.[115] There are a number of ethical concerns about medical carbon budgets, but many are similar to healthcare allocation in general, including the cost of care,[116] access to healthcare,[117] differences in baseline personal health,[118] social determinants of health,[119] longevity,[120] and ability to be proactive in one's health.[121] All of these aspects of health factor into general use of healthcare, and therefore the carbon emissions of medical use. Thus, if medical carbon budgets were to be implemented, an equity-based approach,[122] situated within a capabilities model,[123] rather than a homogenizing arithmetic equality[124] in the distribution of healthcare or health carbon can assuage some of the ethical concerns. Unsubsidized MR could potentially be subsumed under a medical carbon budget, since it uses the resources of the medical industry. In this way an individual or couple may choose to "spend" their medical carbon on MR or save it for other procedures, perhaps those that are medically necessary. However, since unsubsidized MR is not medically necessary it may be outside of a medical carbon budget and regarded as other lifestyle preferences, which are discretionary.

MR may also be placed under a reproductive carbon budget. Adults who wish to avail themselves of MR would be required to balance the carbon of reproduction with the rest of their lifestyle. The benefit of this approach is the flexibility and potential for assertion of preferences in a carbon market, since it is clearly a value for people to create a child in this way. The downside of this strategy is that it merely shuffles the burden of resource use from healthcare to a private life, which may not be as effective in reducing global carbon emissions. Moreover, the carbon budget assumes there are safe amounts of carbon being emitted and that each person is entitled to a new share of resources. While this was certainly true when carbon emissions and population were at a sustainable level, it is no longer the case. The "carbon pie" has already been cut and all pieces taken.[125]

Finally, in the absence of regulated carbon budgets, individuals may choose to self-limit emissions. As people educate themselves about sustainable practices, they may use carbon calculations to determine the carbon

114   ENVIRONMENTAL ETHICS AND MEDICAL REPRODUCTION

impact and alternatives of their lifestyle and may balance their consumption habits in one area, like housing, with being intentionally more sustainable in other areas of life, like family planning.

Individual and Family Carbon Taxes

In America and many other countries, like the UK,[126] parents get paid to have children. In the US the Child Tax Credit offers up to $1,800 for each qualifying child age 5 and younger and up to $1,500 for each kid between the ages of 6 and 17.[127] While child credits are not much to displace the more than $12,980 annually ($233,610 over the life course of 18 years) it takes to raise a child in the US (per child per year),[128] it is certainly not a deterrent to having children either. Furthermore, those birthing multiple children with MR get a larger handout per pregnancy and subsequently every year on their annual tax return. Similarly, the Australian government and other localities where birth rates are declining pay people who reproduce. "Far from penalizing large families, in 2007 the government awarded a $4,000 (£1,724) 'baby bonus' to the parents of each child born in Australia, part of a plan to reverse falling birthrates."[129] This incentive to procreate at a time of environmental decline is perplexing.

The discrepancies in policies that pay people to reproduce and the urgent need to tackle climate change are disharmonious. Because of this, some have suggested a baby *tax* instead of a baby *credit*. In a letter to the editor of the *Medical Journal of Australia*, Professor Barry Walters contended that every couple with more than two children should be taxed $5,000 upon the birth of the child in addition to an annual carbon tax of $400–$800 per child thereafter.[130] His plan combines both the dissuasion of having multiple children and accounts for the carbon legacy of the child once born, not only to deter people from having excessive numbers of children, but also to align policy with human interests in alleviating the rapid decline of the environment.

An individual or family carbon tax could be applied to natural births, but a tax on MR children could be applied either on each phase of MR or at the birth of the MR child, and then annually. Since MR is not always successful— or used—in producing a live birth, but requires resources, a tax on each phase which compounds at birth might be useful. Alternatively, a tax on MR children could be deferred to the children themselves. Much like an inheritance, which requires payment upon use,[131] an MR child may have to pay for their excessive carbon existence after a certain age, such as 18, or for a certain duration of time, perhaps during their reproductive years. However, imposing an existence tax on an MR child would be unfair, as children do not ask to be brought into existence, and it is the moral agents themselves—the users and providers of MR—who ought to be responsible for their carbon use.

Instituting a carbon tax on MR children accounts for the environmental externalities of elective medical reproduction. By "putting a price on carbon,"[132] individuals and families can "internalize" the true "social cost"[133] of MR, thus ensuring that couples and singles are aware of their carbon impact. Carbon taxes on new individuals will allow people considering unsubsidized medical reproduction to evaluate the appeal of using the medical industry to reproduce versus the carbon impact and financial cost, remembering that unsubsidized MR is not used to treat infertility and these people do not need MR to reproduce biologically.

Summary

Unsubsidized MR is a profitable endeavor. By growing the economy through creating more people, and thus more purchasers, MR is antithetical to the conservationist motto of "reduce, reuse, recycle" and instead thrives on a notion of "increase, consume, dispose." MR cycles through resources in pursuit of offering the best consumer experience of creating a child despite carbon impact. And while beneficial for the economy, it is a disaster for the environment since it employs "capitalistic methods that . . . [direct] the productive process of society primarily towards the creation of private profit rather than the service of human needs."[134] While reproduction may be a very strong desire, it is neither a medical nor a biological need. Moreover, accessing unsubsidized MR as part of a reproductive project is clearly in the area of fee-for-service; thus as a business opposed to ecological conservation, MR is fundamentally open to policy constraints. As such, carbon limitation and taxes are appropriate, as they would be with any other industry.

Simultaneously, reproduction-related CO_2 is primarily due to choices of those who have children naturally. In the US each single child will use the equivalent in resources of seven children in China,[135] and there is nothing that a potential parent can do—short of moving to another country—to offset the carbon of a biological child.[136] This is environmentally significant and makes "green parenting" in some countries oxymoronic. Thus,

116   ENVIRONMENTAL ETHICS AND MEDICAL REPRODUCTION

individual and family carbon budgets or taxes on children encourage "rational self-interested economic actors"[137] to find more sustainable ways of parenting, with the understanding that fertile people who use MR can indeed be more sustainable by reproducing naturally. These options make environmental policies more persuasive.

Beyond MR there is a better life for all people. The Aristotelian "account of the basic human functioning shows . . . (that) you cannot pay for the absence of one function by using the coin of another."[138] A clean, healthy planet for all cannot be substituted by reproduction for some. Thus, in addition to environmental policies, larger social supports must be recognized as ways around medicalized procreation. Building a family—whether biological or chosen—should not be in competition with healthcare, accessing food and shelter, a safe home, or clean air. Policymakers can and should ask carbon-emitting countries, sectors, and individuals to change their habits to align with conservation. When policy reflects values of environmental concern, society can stand united against climate change instead of indifferent in the face of perhaps the most pressing problem of the 21st century.

6

Purpose of Healthcare

Prior to institutionalized healthcare, all medical treatments were bartered, or paid, for between the individuals giving and receiving services.[1] By 1978, when the first live human birth from artificial reproduction occurred, many industrialized countries had moved to a third-party payer system. In the United States, private[2] or employer-sponsored[3] healthcare insurance paid doctors on behalf of the individuals using medical treatments. Other developed countries, such as the UK, had national healthcare schemes, such as the National Health Service (NHS), in place, whereby individuals with an income are taxed for healthcare services and those without an income are given free healthcare.[4] Communist countries had been providing socialized healthcare for citizens for nearly a century.[5] These have all been attempts at meeting the basic human need for healthcare while balancing rapidly growing costs of medical treatments.

Healthcare insurance premiums, or healthcare taxes, serve a dual function of minimizing the out-of-pocket expense to the average individual by subsidizing some treatments and benefiting other individuals who have more medical needs through cost sharing.[6] In the former, healthcare insurance is seen as a way to balance the financial risk of medical costs to the individual by regular payments to health insurance companies—or through tax deductions in countries with socialized medicine. The latter illustrates the ethical goals of distributive and social justice, since people's health needs and income vary and because certain diseases are unpredictable.

Third-party payer systems are not perfect, and there are many practical and ethical issues with the actualization and implementation of these healthcare programs. Private health insurance is cost prohibitive and excludes certain groups of people.[7] Employee-sponsored healthcare may not be offered to those with part-time jobs and can be very expensive even for those with full-time jobs.[8] National healthcare schemes do not guarantee healthcare access, only the right to use the healthcare system.[9] Some communist and post-communist countries' healthcare systems tend to be bureaucratic with inadequate medical coverage. These issues do not imply that third-party

Environmental Ethics and Medical Reproduction. Cristina Richie, Oxford University Press.
© Oxford University Press 2024. DOI: 10.1093/oso/9780197745182.003.0007

118   ENVIRONMENTAL ETHICS AND MEDICAL REPRODUCTION

payer systems should be abolished, although healthcare reform remains a perennial political topic.[10]

As both the scope and cost of healthcare have expanded, so has healthcare insurance. With it, ever more complex infrastructures for payment and patient processing are established. Both private and national healthcare services rely on massive systems of documentation which justify and classify the subsidized treatments that are offered.[11] In the United States, for instance, "billing codes" refers to the appropriate designation for provision of medical treatments when healthcare insurance is used. Within these codes, there are typically sub-codes. For instance, when an individual has cancer, their treatments are covered under health insurance since it is widely recognized as a clinical disease, with an underlying cause and a specific treatment course. All treatments must be documented and coded to indicate what should be paid to the clinician, hospital, and healthcare company. By contrast, if an individual wants elective calf implants unrelated to muscle degeneration, these are not covered under healthcare insurance since it is widely recognized that the aesthetic contours of one's legs are a personal preference and not a medical condition.[12] Calf implants could be purchased out of pocket, as aesthetic and supplemental "medical" services can be bought in the free market. Other countries have similar protocols for documentation and billing of healthcare services.[13]

Underlying billing codes are the regulations which support the choices that have been made to include or exclude certain treatments in subsidized care. Policymakers, clinicians, economists, and other relevant stakeholders—for instance, the public[14]—determine the best or most appropriate use of subsidized healthcare funds.[15] Since medical and human resources are limited, healthcare "rationing" or "prioritization" is a task of every healthcare system, whether private or governmental. In recent years, attempts to engage policyholders through democratic deliberation[16] and shared decision-making[17] have had some success. The most notable example of democratic deliberation about coverage of healthcare services is the state of Oregon's "Prioritized List of Health Services." Once a list of reimbursable treatments has been determined, the list may change. For instance, the addition or discontinuation of certain treatments, lowering or raising costs to the insurance policyholder in the form of "co-pays," and placing limits on the number of treatments offered or dollar amount[18] are ways that healthcare systems balance medical resources with financial gain, usually to the benefit of the shareholders, not the patients.

As healthcare insurance evolved alongside free market economies and the commodification of healthcare services, satisfying the fundamental requirement for just access to healthcare has been overshadowed by satisfying the consumerist demands, most clearly seen in direct-to-consumer advertising.[19] In the Unites States, annual healthcare marketing was $17.7 billion in 1997 and jumped to $29.9 billion in 2016.[20] As medical desires—fueled by marketing—increase, so do options for medical consumerism. In addition to out-of-pocket payments for elective treatments, many healthcare plans offer the option to purchase additional "healthcare" coverage through "levels" or tiers of healthcare insurance. For instance, the Affordable Care Act in the United States offers Bronze, Silver, Gold, and Platinum tiers of healthcare.[21] The monthly cost and services covered differ in each tier. While only the basic tier is required to avoid the fee for being uninsured, the other tiers are available on demand.

In biomedical ethics, it is widely agreed that individuals have a right to healthcare, which includes access to clinicians, medicine, and medical services.[22] However, this argument does not necessarily imply that individuals have a right to healthcare *insurance*.[23] As Ross Hofmeyr observes, "[W]hile an essential component of any Constitution [is] the enshrined right to care [it] has been warped into an expectation that *all*, rather than *basic* care, is a human right."[24] Yet, owing to the great expense of healthcare, and the financial penalties that one may face if one does not acquire healthcare insurance,[25] it may be argued that third-party payer systems support the goals and aims of healthcare. In this way, it can be a social good. But, as a social good it must work within certain parameters to meet the goals and aims of healthcare. Thus, Tom Beauchamp and James Childress, among others, have endorsed a multi-level approach to healthcare insurance, whereby basic healthcare plans ought to include "public health measures and preventive care, primary care, (and) acute care,"[26] with more rarified, expensive, or elective treatments covered at higher levels.

Subsidized healthcare, whether through governmental or private insurance schemes, was initially established to provide limited treatment of illnesses and make efforts to contain diseases.[27] Today's healthcare insurance often goes beyond basic medical needs and preventive and catastrophic care. Thus, one of the perennial topics in biomedical ethics is defining the parameters of healthcare that is covered under insurance, while also seeking to provide care for the widest number of citizens possible and recognizing that healthcare resources, personnel, and institutional budgets are limited.[28]

120   ENVIRONMENTAL ETHICS AND MEDICAL REPRODUCTION

This is done through revisiting and evaluating healthcare insurance policies. Assessments of healthcare policy may be undertaken based on a number of financial, social, and practical considerations.

Ronald Bayer and Amy L. Fairchild affirm that "limitations on the rights of individuals in the face of public health threats are firmly supported by legal tradition and ethics. All legal systems, as well as international human rights, permit governments to infringe on personal liberty to prevent a significant risk to the public."[29] An additional, compelling reason to evaluate policy is the carbon emissions of healthcare and the moral requirement to minimize climate change,[30] particularly because climate change is a "significant risk" to the public. However, in biomedical ethics, the purpose of healthcare—that is, proximity to the goals of medicine—often leads to the prioritization of certain treatments over others.

Reasons for Evaluating Healthcare Policies

Understandably, most people would prefer not to pay out of pocket for medical procedures—either necessary or elective. However, many fine arguments—as well as general public consensus—note that it is manifestly unjust to have all holders of healthcare insurance finance non-medically necessary, lifestyle procedures. Most healthcare premiums, or healthcare taxes, absorb a significant percentage of many people's salary.[31] Cost is related to services—treatment courses, success of treatment, specialization, and availability, and associated in-patient or out-patient services.[32] People who purchase healthcare insurance have a vested interest in both having essential services covered and minimizing costs. Thus, policyholders might rightly object to services which are considered unnecessary, such as Botox,[33] while also petitioning for access to free or reduced costs for lifesaving needs, like contraception[34] and HIV medication.[35]

Cost containment is a matter of justice not only for the person who pays for healthcare but for global health. Lifestyle and non-medically indicated procedures threaten national and global distributive justice by clustering doctors and medical resources in affluent areas where basic healthcare needs are often met and exceeded. Thus, regulations on subsidized healthcare may come from a variety of directions.

First, economic constraints may force certain treatments to be cut from healthcare funding or place limitations on provision of certain medical services. In 2009, the president of the German Association of Anesthetists maintained, "[N]o health care system works without rationing. Effective intensive care medicine will not be possible in the future without limiting therapeutic interventions."[36] The COVID-19 pandemic highlighted that governments can legitimately prioritize essential medical treatments and postpone elective and non-urgent treatments based on limited budgets, inclusive of medical costs of patients and healthcare workers' salary.

A second parameter in healthcare policies is utilitarian benefit. International models of prioritization of healthcare delivery "take into account firstly protection from loss of life and protection from severe pain, secondly protection from severe damage of body parts or body function, and, on third and fourth rank, to protect from less severe or temporary disorders."[37] Those treatments within the goals of medicine, or with highest clinical benefit, are easy to justify, while those that are further from the goals of medicine may be attenuated.

Third, and related, federal laws may require access to basic healthcare services. For instance, "since 2006 the health care system has changed significantly in the Netherlands. It is based on the conviction that solidarity is a very important driving force in our society. . . . The government decides every year which treatments are covered by the insurance."[38] Basic healthcare is then broadly distributed, while extra services are omitted from subsidized healthcare but remain discretionary options.

Fourth, environmental regulations restrict provision of some medical treatments. Some countries are moving toward carbon capping in healthcare. The United Kingdom has already implemented legally binding carbon reduction measures in both the National Health Service[39] and the National Institute for Health Research.[40] The *NHS Carbon Reduction Strategy* targets specific medical developments, techniques, and procedures for carbon reduction, based on quantitative data on environmental impact. A number of studies on the carbon emissions of anesthetic gases,[41] laparoscopic surgery,[42] and pharmaceutical distribution[43] indicate that there are more sustainable ways to perform surgery or achieve a desired health outcome.[44] Even before this, medical-environmental concerns included hazard waste standards which dictate how biological materials are disposed of.[45] Incineration or burial of toxic healthcare material must also conform to environmental standards.[46]

Many of these financial, utilitarian, legal, and environmental concerns are tied to justice. Ostensibly, the purpose of healthcare insurance is to meet the

122 ENVIRONMENTAL ETHICS AND MEDICAL REPRODUCTION

health needs of as many individuals as possible in a way that is financially manageable, as the Central German Ethics Committee statement on the prioritization of medical services of statutory health insurance affirmed by opining that all citizens should continue to have access to a basic healthcare system instead of allowing access to high-end medicine for only a fraction of the population.[47]

Criteria for Evaluating Healthcare Policies

Despite arguments for lowering healthcare costs,[48] increasing medical efficiency,[49] and providing sustainable healthcare,[50] in many countries healthcare insurance covers a range of services that go beyond the goals of medicine. Medicine, or the goals of medicine, are classically understood to be "the prevention of disease and injury, and the promotion and maintenance of health; the relief of pain and suffering caused by maladies; the cure of those with a malady, and the care of those who cannot be cured; and the avoidance of premature death and the pursuit of a peaceful death."[51] Therefore, healthcare and healthcare insurance are ethically bound to meet these goals, especially when resources—whether financial, human, or environmental—are scarce.

Once the goals of medicine are apparent, then healthcare is developed and disseminated in service to the goals of medicine. "Healthcare," that is healthcare delivery or healthcare services, refers to the scientific breakthroughs and sophisticated technologies which have yielded effective medical developments, techniques, and procedures.[52] Healthcare first uses diagnostic tests to determine a diagnosis. Tests are usually given based on reported or observed symptoms. Since clinical indication depends on a diagnosis, if there are no symptoms, diagnostic tests may not be clinically indicated. Where there are no suspected or actual reasons for a disease or condition, then diagnostic tests are indictive of overuse of healthcare.[53]

After the tests have been run and there is a diagnosis, medical treatments may be offered. Medical treatments ought to be given based on a clinical indication.[54] Clinical indication is the medical reason for providing the treatment(s). In the modern era, biomedical ethics has moved from physician-driven healthcare to patient participation through shared decision-making,[55] whereby a clinician determines possible treatment plans that are scientifically validated, close in terms of efficacy, and within their clinical competence,[56] and offers these treatment options to the patient. Then the patient decides among clinically indicated treatments to address their medical need. Healthcare delivery ought to support at least one of the goals of medicine based on clinical indication, which is derived from a diagnosis based on tests. For instance, hemodialysis is a treatment for renal failure. Thus, the clinical indication is renal failure, the medical service is hemodialysis, and it meets the goal of medicine of maintaining life. Medical developments, techniques, and procedures which are not clinically indicated are not provided in alignment with the disease, such as neurosurgery for renal failure. If there is no disease, then no treatment is indicated. After the clinical indication is recognized, a particular treatment might be medically appropriate or medically necessary.

Medical developments, techniques, and procedures which are medically appropriate are connected to the diagnostic tools of the physician[57] and clinical indication. Medically appropriate treatments include a range of options that support a goal of medicine. For instance, if a person has cancer, chemotherapy, surgery, or drugs may be medically appropriate. Each of these options would address the disease and support the goal of medicine to treat and cure disease. Medical developments, techniques, and procedures which are not medically appropriate do not address a disease or condition, or do not meet a goal of medicine related to the condition. Inducing a coma in a cancer patient would not be medically appropriate since it would not cure, treat, or prevent cancer and would not support a goal of medicine in that clinical situation.

Medical developments, techniques, and procedures which are medically necessary imply that they are necessary for continuing or maintaining life.[58] Of course, no medical treatments are medically necessary unless a person wants to live. But, as most people do want to live for an extended period of time, a medically necessary treatment might be, for instance, antiretroviral treatments for HIV. Antiretroviral treatments are clinically indicated and a medical development necessary to reduce viral loads. It supports the goal of medicine of treating disease. Medical developments, techniques, and procedures which are not medically necessary either have no clinical indication or are outside of the goals of medicine related to the clinical condition. A heart bypass operation is not clinically indicated to treat HIV and is not medically necessary to survive HIV (unless there was an unforeseen cardiac event in the course of treatments). The bypass operation would not support a goal of medicine related to the clinical indication of HIV.

124 ENVIRONMENTAL ETHICS AND MEDICAL REPRODUCTION

To be sure, some medical developments, techniques, and procedures were originally developed for a particular clinical indication and then moved "off label."[59] In some case, these do treat a medical condition with a new and different clinical indication. It was discovered, for instance, that off-label use of bedaquiline and delamanid is effective in treating multidrug-resistant tuberculosis.[60] Both the original purpose of the drugs and the new purpose met a clinical indication and were medically appropriate. In contrast, some medical developments, techniques, and procedures move off label into a consumerist market and fail to have any clinical indication. For example, the techniques originally used in reconstructive plastic surgery to correct eating difficulties resulting from a severe cleft palate can also be used in cosmetic surgery to give a person a different and more "aesthetically desirable" face.[61]

Healthcare has a fundamental obligation to meet the goals of medicine, but subsidized healthcare has the obligation to do so in a way that is financially accountable to those paying for the services, even when the "payments" are made via taxes and not directly into a private insurance company. Since subsidized healthcare requires the financial contribution of many stakeholders, there are real reasons to limit healthcare coverage to only those services that are medically necessary and a strong motivation for prioritization of healthcare services.

International Perspectives on ARTs Regulation in Healthcare

At the center of medicalized reproduction, and at many healthcare debates, is the artificial fertilization process. It is significant that time and attention are dedicated to the prioritization of IVF or ARTs in healthcare because this indicates that these fertility treatments are not widely accepted as medically necessary and thus lends additional support for evaluating their provision from an environmental lens.

Following shortly after the first human birth from in-vitro fertilization in 1978, ARTs became a feature of the medical industry. ARTs are regulated in every country, for instance, by age limitations, rationale for seeking or providing ARTs—such as the health of the mother—or available technologies. In the United States, the American Society for Reproductive Medicine Ethics Committee advises that physicians may withhold fertilization services if they believe patients will be unable to provide adequate child rearing. But it is also clear that physicians are not morally obligated to do so except "when significant harm to future children is likely."[62] Each doctor judges on a case-by-case basis the suitability of potential parents and holds an ethical standard for how many children should be produced using ARTs.

While initially paid for out of pocket, eventually ARTs became partially subsidized by healthcare insurance, or government healthcare provisions, in some countries.[63] In countries that provide subsidized ARTs, they are assimilated and regulated within the larger management of healthcare systems, including "which percentage of the gross domestic product a nation should earmark for public health expenses and its apportionment between the needs of research, prevention and care . . . while dealing with a demand side which often exceeds supply."[64] National debates about the categorization of infertility as a "disease" or a "condition," the use of scarce medical resources for an elective procedure,[65] and the financial impact of covering artificial reproductive technologies on healthcare insurance policyholders' premiums, or the general public's taxes,[66] have been additional ethical considerations that drive regulation since "infertility, much like plastic surgery is an *elective* treatment, undergone at the patient's request to alter their lives but not improve their health."[67] Healthcare insurance often recognizes the low prioritization of ARTs by placing stricter limits on artificial fertilization than actual treatment or cure of infertility.[68] Each country's approach to subsidized ARTs highlights that regulation is necessary and that it is accepted, as well as acceptable.

National Regulations on Subsidized ARTs

Israel has had one of the most liberal subsidized fertility policies. Modern social and political concerns, including ability to defend the country, territory wars, and shrinking numbers of Israelis, have led to permissive policies and laws encouraging medicalized reproduction.[69] Prior to 2011, IVF was freely available to all Israeli citizens. There were no limits on the number of IVF cycles or lifetime IVF cost. The only limitations were an upper age of 45 and a maximum of two live births per woman.[70] By 2013, Israel had the highest percentage of babies born from in vitro fertilization in the world, at 4%.[71] Israel continues with liberal MR policies, maintaining the 4–5% rate of ART births,[72] but has since been exceeded as the country with the highest percentage of ART children by Spain, which has 7.6% of children currently born from ARTs.[73]

126 ENVIRONMENTAL ETHICS AND MEDICAL REPRODUCTION

Belgium has also had lavish ART subsidies, with limits focused on upper age of the women and number of cycles. In 2001, "the Belgian government changed its reimbursement policy for IVF-related procedures to allow for the reimbursement of up to six cycles in a lifetime provided reimbursement of IVF centre costs were linked to a 50% reduction in twin pregnancies and higher order multiple pregnancies were minimized to almost zero."[74] The rationale behind these limitations are both medical and financial. Twin and multiple pregnancies are associated with a variety of healthcare issues for the neonates, which are costly. However, many couples prefer to have multiple pregnancies due to the inconvenience of pregnancy and age-related declines in fertility. Striking a balance between parent desires and clinical outcomes has ultimately driven Belgian policy. By 2003, Belgian policy was refined to cover "6 cycles of ART for women ages 42 and under. Women 43 years and over are ineligible for coverage. This coverage comes with strict limits on the number of embryos transferred per cycle, to a maximum of 2 for women under the age of 36 and a maximum of three for women under the age of 40."[75]

Similarly, in the UK there are strict age limits for governmental provision of ARTs, with both a lower age limit and an upper age limit of 23–39 years, up to 3 cycles, and, up until recently, mandatory opposite-sex partnering,[76] even if a single or coupled gay person was clinically infertile. The UK tends to be more restrictive than other European countries with their ART policy. ARTs that produce twins and higher-order pregnancies have been "draining" the National Health Services,[77] not only because there are two births instead of one, but also because of the rates of prematurity which require medical attention. Thus, in 2007, the United Kingdom Human Fertilization and Embryology Authority Code of Practice required "a 'multiple births minimization strategy' with the aim of reducing the rate of multiple pregnancies from 24% to 10%."[78] Their three-year goal took 10 years to meet.[79]

In countries without socialized healthcare, such as the United States, regulation on ARTs is checkered. Healthcare insurance in the United States is often provided by one's employer and can extend to spouses, and children under the age of 25. This is "private" healthcare insurance. It is very expensive, even with employer subsidization. Private healthcare insurance is also offered for those who wish to purchase additional or supplementary coverage. Prior to the 2010 Affordable Care Act,[80] "public" or government-sponsored healthcare was offered for those below a certain threshold of income (Medicaid) and those over a certain age (Medicare). Military healthcare was a sub-set of government healthcare that was unavailable for civilians.

Government programs that did not cover ARTs include the Federal Employee Health Benefits Programs, the Medicaid program, and Tricare—the military's healthcare program. The US government does not subsidize ARTs for either couples or individuals as it is not a basic healthcare service.[81] Further, the US government is not involved in regulating insurance coverage for fertility treatments outside of their own programs as "there is no federal law that mandates insurers to provide or offer infertility coverage for women."[82] Hence, even those with private healthcare insurance may not have subsidized access to ARTs since coverage varies by state law and healthcare insurance policies.[83] In some cases, fertility services are not covered by insurance because of a number of factors, like expense, lack of medical necessity, low success rate, or experimental nature of procedures. In cases where ARTs are covered, subsidized healthcare is not uniform in its criteria for qualification for treatments. Some healthcare plans set higher or lower limits on qualifying criteria, such as age, partnership, or a documented history of infertility. As of 2014, 15 of the 50 states in America provided infertility care or ARTs.[84] Note that infertility care might be a low-level intervention—like repairing blocked tubes or treating an underlying disease—and may be offered to the exclusion of ARTs. In cases where ARTs are covered, health insurance companies themselves determine what, if any, infertility services they will provide for policyholders, thus leaving some couples and individuals in certain states totally without coverage, and others with virtually unlimited coverage.

Singles and couples wishing to use ARTs outside of subsidized insurance must, then, pay out of pocket. In response to the lack of coverage, certain interest groups provide "scholarships" to offset the cost of unsubsidized fertility treatments. RESOLVE: The National Infertility Association lists several organizations that offer "grants"[85] for ARTs. The "applicants" are women who have insurance, and so are able to access the healthcare system, but whose insurance does not subsidize ARTs. The funds are for the explicit purpose of obtaining reproductive technologies.[86]

Summary

Healthcare insurance's primary purpose is to subsidize the cost of medically necessary and medically appropriate care. Subsidized healthcare has an epistemological obligation to provide medically appropriate treatments based on clinical indication. In the absence of clinical indication, these aims are not met. As such, there is justification for evaluating healthcare policy. Policies regulating healthcare will almost always be controversial. Ethicists in Italy write, "[T]he most difficult problem in the distribution of resources remains the finding of a convincing criterion to provide guidance, when often painful and dramatic choices have to be made, as health care providers have to do in the face of all too real inadequacies in the availability of resources. 'Who should have priority? What fairness criteria should be applied in this case? What type of legality are we appealing to?'"[87] When limited human and medical resources are combined with the environmental rationale for regulation of healthcare, there is a very solid case for far less provision of subsidized MR.

Countries that subsidize ARTs provide a handout of a non-lifesaving treatment. Hence, there is ethical support for putting limitations on access to the treatments, just as policymakers may put limits on other elective healthcare offerings, like cosmetic surgery, contact lenses, and acupuncture.[88] The entire spectrum of MR demands attention, as MR is decidedly different from natural reproduction since fertility centers provide a service for a fee, and therefore are subject to economic, social, and bioethical scrutiny. Indeed, artificial reproduction was initially subjected to broad concerns in social ethics, such as the anthropological implications of natural versus artificial ways of procreating, the status of the embryo,[89] exploitation of women, gendered norms related to reproduction,[90] and justice for the poor who cannot afford MR,[91] but the medical industry and health insurance companies rarely take these ethical considerations into account when drafting policy. Even less considered is environmental impact. Given the global magnitude and urgency of climate change, healthcare policies can no longer ignore the environmental effects of elective, high-carbon medical procedures like ARTs.

7

Policies for Subsidized Medical Reproduction

Artificial reproduction was initially developed as a workaround for clinical infertility in opposite-sex couples attempting to reproduce. As such, it is still often viewed as a clinical solution to the clinical condition of infertility. The common perception of why people use artificial reproduction—and concomitant pressure to include it as a medical service within subsidized healthcare—still hinges on a narrative of infertility. However, infertility is not a universal concept, and definitions of infertility—even by leading healthcare organizations—change over time. These alterations represent better scientific understandings of infertility. Changing definitions of infertility are also influenced by social concerns like gender equity, stigmatizing language, and the new concept of "social infertility" whereby a person does not have an inseminating or gestational partner but is biologically fertile.[1] Definitions of infertility are also situated within relevant factors in patient history such as age, underlying health conditions, sexual activity, and previous pregnancies.[2] For instance, a 60-year-old woman may not be able to conceive, but her "infertility" would be understood to be related to natural menopause.[3]

"Infertility" needs to be contextualized before it can be defined. Importantly, not all people value fertility or procreation, as is evidenced by the large number of childfree people and childfree lifestyles[4] and the near ubiquitous use of contraception at some point in adult life.[5] After infertility is situated within the subjective scope of socially desirable or undesirable, then it can be defined based on diagnostic tests and assessment, which then justify its inclusion or exclusion in subsidized healthcare insurance, with normative implications for healthcare insurance policy.

Environmental Ethics and Medical Reproduction. Cristina Richie, Oxford University Press.
© Oxford University Press 2024. DOI: 10.1093/oso/9780197745182.003.0008

Defining Infertility

The World Health Organization (WHO) is one major institution which has changed its definitions of infertility. In 2006, the WHO defined epidemiological infertility as "women of reproductive age (15–49 years) at risk of becoming pregnant (not pregnant, sexually active, not using contraception and not lactating) who report trying unsuccessfully for a pregnancy for two years or more."[6] By 2018, the definition had changed to "a disease of the male or female reproductive system defined by the failure to achieve a pregnancy after 12 months, or more, of regular unprotected sexual intercourse."[7] In an update a few years later, the World Health Organization redefined infertility as "the inability of a sexually active, non-contracepting couple to achieve pregnancy in one year" and included a recommendation that "the male partner can be evaluated for infertility or subfertility using a variety of clinical interventions, and also from a laboratory evaluation of semen."[8] Changes to definitions of infertility have been seen in national organizations as well.

In 2008, the American Society of Reproductive Medicine (ASRM) defined infertility as "the failure to achieve a successful pregnancy after 12 months or more of appropriate, timed unprotected intercourse," and also adds that earlier evaluation and treatment may be justified "after 6 months for women over 35 years."[9] Later, in 2020, the ASRM stated that "infertility is the result of a disease (an interruption, cessation, or disorder of body functions, systems, or organs) of the male or female reproductive tract which prevents the conception of a child or the ability to carry a pregnancy to delivery. The duration of unprotected intercourse with failure to conceive should be about 12 months before an infertility evaluation is undertaken, unless medical history, age, or physical findings dictate earlier evaluation and treatment."[10] Notice that the definition reorients infertility from the subject (the infertile woman) to the object—the disease—and also offers broad guidance for infertility testing.

In both newer definitions of infertility, the WHO and the ASRM recognized male infertility and, importantly for the economic inflation of subsidized healthcare, the shortened timespan before infertility may be suspected. The latter is, in part, a result of healthcare insurance companies needing external authorities to validate or produce definitions of infertility to justify the period of time before reimbursement of infertility treatments. While some aspects of the definition of infertility have changed, both the earlier and the later WHO and ASRM definitions rightfully describe a biological, scientific, clinical factor which leads to infertility. That is, a person must be sexually active with a heterosexual partner to be considered infertile. Of course, diagnostic tests for infertility may not meet all of these criteria. For instance, some single and partnered gay and straight men and single and partnered gay and straight women are epidemiologically infertile. Thus, it may be clinically recommended to provide a diagnostic test for infertility in the absence of heterosexual sex, if there is a reason to suspect infertility (like male impotence or known endometriosis). However, neither sexual activity nor sexual orientation indicates or produces infertility. This concept will be returned to in the section on "social infertility."[11]

Despite the complexities involved in defining infertility, a working definition that encompasses WHO and ASRM definitions, while also clarifying the difference between social and biological infertility, might be "a person who desires, but does not have, a biological child and who has not become pregnant or impregnated their partner after 12–24 months of regular non-contraceptive intercourse with a person of the opposite sex during one's fertile years." While this is an inelegant definition, it underscores the intentions of the WHO and ASRM, particularly with the distinction between primary infertility—when one has never had a child—and secondary infertility, which may occur after one has a biological child. This also recognizes that biological infertility does not necessarily correlate to a desire to have a biological child and therefore infertility can go undiagnosed and unreported in childfree people. An accurate and specific definition is important for understanding clinical infertility and thus the justification for providing fertility treatments in subsidized healthcare plans in so far as they might meet a goal of medicine.

Goals of Medicine and MR

Many procedures on the spectrum of MR are already covered, without objection, under subsidized healthcare. These include fetal monitoring and cesarean sections, since there is typically a clinical indication, such as fetal distress or breach birth. Many other aspects of MR are not covered, such as PGD in selection for (not against) disability or cosmetic postpartum procedures because there is no clinical indication. Thus, debates in biomedical ethics focus not on subsidized access to medicalized reproduction

132 ENVIRONMENTAL ETHICS AND MEDICAL REPRODUCTION

more broadly, but to the more specific ARTs, which were—and still are—considered to be an elective medical treatment and a bypass for infertility.

Artificial reproductive technologies do not cure, treat, or prevent infertility and do not meet a goal of medicine. ARTs temporarily circumvent infertility to permit pregnancy. While one of the goals of medicine is the "care" of those who cannot be cured, this refers to end-of-life care for terminal diseases—particularly palliative care[12]—not care for diseases or conditions that do not cause physical pain. Infertility does not cause pain. Some conditions that may cause infertility, such as endometriosis, may cause pain,[13] and treatment of that underlying condition would meet a goal of medicine. However, infertility itself does not harm the body. Infertility cannot cause death and does not impact other vital functions the way lung disease might make it difficult to breathe. Indeed, choosing to use one's fertility may cause death by maternal mortality.[14] As the impact of infertility—as a biological condition—on other physical systems is minimal, and can be advantageous to health, its priority in healthcare insurance may be contested as it is unclear how it may meet a goal of medicine.

Indeed, since many MR treatments do not meet the goals of medicine, the understanding of healthcare insurance has been, in some countries, expanded beyond clinical indication to personal lifestyle preferences. Jurgen De Wispelaere and Daniel Weinstock highlight the oft-provided argument that medicalized reproduction ought to be situated within a right to reproduce rather than a right to basic healthcare, based on the goals of medicine. They write:

> [T]o think that reproductive freedom demands a particular set of state services seems to require an additional argument. One such argument would be to think of ART as an aspect of *reproductive* (italics theirs) health.[15] On this view, the state has an obligation to provide for assisted reproduction as part of a more general obligation to remedy a poor state of health. Conceiving of assisted reproduction within the reproductive health context implies that we regard a failure to reproduce naturally as a dysfunction of an important bodily function, and ARTs as a kind of medical intervention that is supported by the state in the context of its commitment to securing the basic health needs of its population.[16]

While their argument hinges on a diagnosis of clinical infertility, there is another view latent in the way their argument is phrased: that poor health might also include an existential sadness of not being able to reproduce. Once the step is made from clinically poor health to the impact of poor health on one's social standing, artificial fertilization pivots from the core of healthcare to a broader understanding of the purpose of healthcare and as such legitimizes the provision of non-fertility-related forms of MR in support of reproductive projects, as well as MR to "correct" a clinical condition. The goals of medicine as the foundational rationale for subsidized healthcare are left behind and superseded by an individualistic, commercial understanding of healthcare insurance as servant to medical desires.

Prioritization of ARTs

With the growth of ARTs in the private sector, and diminishing concerns about the ethics of medicalizing reproduction, subsidized healthcare plans faced pressure to include numerous reproductive treatments and expand coverage of infertility-related services.[17] Although the World Health Organization and American Society of Reproductive Medicine use a biological basis for defining infertility, subsidized healthcare may not consider these definitions when offering ARTs. This leads to a relative understanding of infertility that is not necessarily based on physical factors, but rather lifestyle choice. Accessing artificial reproduction then becomes conflated with subsidized healthcare, a broad acceptance of disease unrelated to objective clinical factors, and increased provision of ARTs, much to the detriment of the environment. Instead of yielding to these trends, healthcare must have sustainability at the forefront of policymaking without losing its foundational commitment to biomedical ethics and the goals of medicine. Thus, as healthcare insurance is to be directed at the goals of medicine and offered to subsidize the cost of medically necessary or medically appropriate treatments, based on clinical indication derived from diagnostic tests, ARTs must be prioritized under these criteria.

The first level of prioritization is basic healthcare that is clinically indicated and medically necessary and which meets a goal of medicine. This includes acute, catastrophic, palliative, and preventative care. For instance, a breast cancer patient may be treated with chemotherapy or mastectomy as part of acute care.[18] In another example, contraception is clinically indicated to prevent maternal mortality and morbidity. While basic healthcare may include a preferential component—such as barrier or hormonal contraception—the outcome and intention of these services meet the goals of medicine.

134 ENVIRONMENTAL ETHICS AND MEDICAL REPRODUCTION

The second level of prioritization includes preferential medical choices that have an underlying chronic clinical indication whose treatments meet a goal of medicine. For instance, myopia is addressed by corrective lenses (glasses), but contact lenses and Lasik eye surgery are also medically appropriate. These treat the underlying medical condition.[19] In some cases, there is a clinical indication for fertility services, and a single person or couple may be offered medically appropriate treatments ranging from fertility drugs to repair of blocked tubes. Although it is still debated in healthcare if infertility is a "disease" or a "condition" and thus, if treating it fits within the goals of medicine, many clinicians do see it as a disease.

The third level of prioritization encompasses preventative, non-medical services that have no clinical indication. One example is a discount for a gym membership.[20] While these "perks" do not cure or treat disease, they do have a public health benefit and also reduce healthcare costs for payers overall.[21] Although "perks" may be appealing for the healthcare policyholders, this would not be an ethical requirement of either a national healthcare system or private health insurance companies. Moreover, these benefits ought to be minimized in places where private healthcare insurance is expensive, for example, the United States. On the other hand, preventative healthcare is more financially sensible within socialized medicine, as monthly deductions for healthcare are stable and more people benefit from social services. ARTs would not fit in the third level of prioritization since they are not a form of preventative healthcare. Moreover, ARTs increase, rather than decrease, healthcare costs to payers overall since they often result in using multiple, additional healthcare resources.[22]

The fourth level of prioritization is for elective choices, expressing a preference that does not cure, treat, or prevent disease and has no clinical indication. Breast pumps[23] and Botox[24] are examples. Inclusion of these services under healthcare insurance has significant grounds for contestation. Primary objections center on access, cost-sharing, and fairness of resource allocation. Secondary objections, which include medicalization, demand significant moral attention as well.[25] In some cases, ARTs are given without a clinical indication. That is, they are used without evidence of infertility, or used in the presence of fertility, for instance with fertile single women and men.[26] Providing medical treatments when there is no clinical indication falls short of medical standards and breaches professionalism.[27] Also known as over-treatment, this form of healthcare delivery is "ethically reprehensible and unanimously condemned, since it indicates an inappropriate use of health care."[28]

To be sure, some physicians choose to provide elective, lifestyle, or cosmetic "medicine" which does not require a clinical indication. However, these services are usually outside of healthcare insurance. When ARTs are used as an elective lifestyle choice expressing a preference that does not have a clinical indication they cannot rightly be subsumed under subsidized healthcare since they do not address a goal of medicine.

One may want to use medical resources to facilitate a specific reproductive project and it may be appealing to medical consumers to have treatments that do not meet a goal of medicine covered, but in policymaking both success rate and frivolity of treatments ought to be evaluated in addition to cost and environmental impact. In 2007, the central German ethics committee[29] outlined the main criteria for healthcare distribution. They placed, "in order of relevance . . . medical need, individual benefit of treatment and cost-effectiveness."[30] While both ARTs and Botox are frivolous, ARTs have a low success rate[31] and Botox is nearly 100% effective.[32] Thus, as a financial investment on the part of insurance policyholders, aesthetic treatments are easier to justify than ARTs. And yet, cosmetic procedures are not often offered since there is no clinical indication,[33] thus calling into question the basis for ARTs as well.

Exclusionary Criteria—Clinically Fertile People

ARTs must first be prioritized within healthcare before further policies can be proposed. ARTs can be justified only in the second level of prioritization of healthcare, when there is a clinical indication, and only when infertility is viewed as a disease. From there, exclusionary and inclusionary criteria for subsidized healthcare may be developed, clarified, and refined along the lines of clinical infertility. The purpose of healthcare policy reform is reducing the environmental impact of MR and realigning the carbon-intensive medical industry with the goals of medicine, which will also be more sustainable.[34]

Objections to exclusionary criteria for subsidized MR often center on the issue of "fairness." It seems unfair to exclude certain people from accessing subsidized MR. Or, it may seem unfair to limit certain types of MR or the number of ART cycles, or put financial limits on the money spent on MR per person. The latter two limitations—on MR and not on people—seem less unfair, perhaps because they are applied equally in every situation. However, both sets of criteria are required. In the first set of criteria, the person or

136 ENVIRONMENTAL ETHICS AND MEDICAL REPRODUCTION

people seeking MR will be addressed. Ethically, the claim that a fertile person ought to have the right to create a child in the manner that they see fit and have government assistance in their reproductive project, which is unrelated to a goal of medicine, is very hard to defend, since "experience teaches that, like interests and goods, rights cannot be absolutely unqualified."[35] Thus, the first exclusionary criteria for use of subsidized MR is fertile individuals and couples.

In the second set of criteria, the type of MR being used will be addressed. Again, the main exclusionary criteria will be forms of MR which do not cure, treat, or prevent infertility and therefore do not meet a goal of medicine. By framing the second set of exclusionary criteria for subsidized MR in alignment with the concept of infertility as a disease—as contested as that is—places it within the purpose of subsidized healthcare and the goals of medicine. Thus, the second exclusionary criteria for subsidized MR are treatments that are unrelated to clinical infertility. These two sets of exclusionary criteria for subsidized MR provide clear guidance, which is then useful for the inclusionary criteria later in the chapter. This chapter will not address limitations on MR cycles or amount of money spent, primarily because healthcare policies already do this, and secondarily because it assumes access to MR without other preceding qualifications, like clinical infertility.

Placing policy limitations on subsidized MR for fertile singles and couples is less controversial than limitations on unsubsidized MR, since all people have an interest in financially affordable healthcare insurance. The primary weakness of only examining subsidized MR is that it may risk too wide provision of MR, as the so-called "reproductive project" or reproductive preferences of individuals and couples may not be prohibited; unsubsidized treatments would be available. This is addressed in another chapter. However, the main strength of the approach is that the negative right to procreation would be untouched and the goals of medicine could be met as well as the purpose of healthcare insurance. Policy reform for subsidized MR is a necessary and essential first step in sustainability and a requirement of both biomedical and environmental ethics.

Secondary Infertility

Medical reproduction has become a multi-billion-dollar industry, primarily in industrialized countries where singles and couples have many options available to them in terms of how they would like their children to be conceived. Although those who do not have children may seek MR, fertile singles and couples with children also use MR to produce additional children. These people may have secondary infertility, whereby they had a first child naturally but cannot conceive or carry to term a second child.[36] The WHO and ASRM definitions of infertility seem to define a person as infertile if they do not have any biological children. Although it is not specified, the spirit of the definition and indeed, the common understanding of infertile, is a person without a biological child who wants one. While one child may not be the desired or ideal number of children one may want to generate, it is ethically very difficult to justify provision of subsidized MR for those with secondary infertility, both medically and environmentally.

It may seem unfair to use secondary infertility as an exclusionary criterion for subsidized MR, as most people agree that adults have a right to have as many children as they want.[37] But, in reality, the notion of "unlimited procreation" is uncomfortable for many people.[38] The idea that an adult should be able to have as many children as they want is a proxy for, first and foremost, the negative right of procreation which only says that there should not be interference with people reproducing.[39] There is a second, unspoken assumption about parental ethics and responsibility, which limits procreation by socially desirable criteria like competency, age (in both the lower and upper limits), being in good or fair health, having a stable income, and displaying certain dispositions and characteristics, such as patience, self-control, kindness, and perseverance.[40] Even when these criteria are met by adults, creating a family size of one's choice is still very much tied to modern Western norms of average rates of procreation.[41] That is, the proposal that subsidized MR should be offered for secondary infertility on the basis of procreative rights quickly becomes modified to subsidized MR for a second or third child, but no more than that. Endorsing MR for people with secondary infertility is more connected to the notion that being an only child is undesirable,[42] rather than the claim to reproductive rights, which would, ostensibly, point toward an unlimited number of MR children funded through subsidized healthcare. The question for healthcare policy then becomes whether the purpose of subsidized MR is to provide a childless person with a biological child or to provide unlimited biological children to adults.

Interestingly, the answer to this question is also related to the metaphysical pursuit of MR as one (among many) means to parenthood. Only one child is required to be a parent; if a woman has twins from MR, the second

138 ENVIRONMENTAL ETHICS AND MEDICAL REPRODUCTION

is redundant in the ontological change of parenthood. Indeed, one infamous example of MR use in an individual who already had children was the case of American Nadya Suleman. Also known as "Octomom," Ms. Suleman was a single woman raising several biological children.[43] She utilized (unsubsidized) MR for further insemination and bore eight more infants.[44] The case was widely publicized, drawing public outrage and resulting in the dismissal of the doctor who provided the fertility treatments.[45] To be sure, the situation was criticized for a number of reasons, including risk of higher-order multiples, dependence on governmental support for raising the children after birth, the stigma of being a single parent, and also the number of children she had in total. Conceptually, the purpose of MR as a means to the social experience of rearing the desirable number of biological children is highlighted as subsidized MR for people with secondary infertility is linked to reproductive projects and desirable family size, not cure or treatment of infertility, in as much as these people cannot be considered infertile by standard definitions. Framed through the lenses of clinical superfluity and minimum criteria for parenthood, secondary infertility as an exclusionary criterion of subsidized MR is sensible.

Currently, no reproductive policy to my knowledge specifies that a woman or couple seeking subsidized fertility treatments has to be childless. The Primary Care Trust in the UK does recommend that women with (biological) children from a previous relationship should not be eligible for treatment, but it does not enforce this.[46] Furthermore, the Primary Care Trust does not account for blended, step-, foster, or adopted children. This gap in policy may lead to excessive carbon emissions from MR use. Placing secondary infertility as an exclusionary criterion of subsidized MR would still permit a person or couple with secondary infertility to use unsubsidized MR or pursue another form of parenting, like adoption or fostering. However, the use of MR by parents of biological children must be regulated for the sake of environmental and medical ethics.

Abortion

The early termination of a pregnancy through medical means, also known as abortion, invokes very strong emotions in many people. Indeed, abortion as a clinical procedure is overlaid with many social issues, like a woman's right to access an elective abortion, fetal rights, women's autonomy, patriarchal use

POLICIES FOR SUBSIDIZED MEDICAL REPRODUCTION   139

of women's reproductive services, the financial hardship of raising children, and the impact that motherhood has on women's ability to fully participate in public, economic, political, and intellectual life.[47] Therefore, abortion—although a medical procedure—is also in the scope of broader ethical concerns.

Abortion is often a polarizing issue, and international and national laws that permit or prohibit abortion are not uniform.[48] Even in countries with access to safe and legal abortion, such as the United States, new laws are continually being introduced to restrict access,[49] and "many on both sides of the abortion debate continue to romanticize pregnancy and motherhood. This romantic myth blinds many to the real problems and devastating conflicts pregnant women frequently face. It blinds others to the work, delayed gratification, suffering, and sacrifice constitutive of even planned, ordinary pregnancies. Romanticism about motherhood reflects a failure of persons on both sides of the abortion debate to take the experience of women seriously."[50] Yet, there needs to be serious self-reflection on the part of each voting citizen about the lines between their personal choice to obtain an abortion, their understanding of living in a pluralistic, non-authoritarian society, and the place of healthcare in providing a service which can prevent maternal mortality and morbidity. Simultaneously, governments, healthcare policies, and other relevant stakeholders should attempt to seek consensus on the social issues that surround abortion in an attempt to meet the common goal of reducing the need for abortion as a medical procedure that has risks. Some places of consensus include social policies that prevent unwanted pregnancies—like wider availability of contraception—and the need for men to take responsibility for procreation.[51]

Even in countries with excellent social supports, women may choose to abort for a variety of reasons, and at many different stages in life. It is not the case that only teenagers, or single women, or even women without children have abortions. Certainly, a woman ought to be able to organize her procreative schedule in the manner that suits her life. But when the medical industry subsidizes MR in cases where the single person or couple has already capitalized on their fertility, it is a redundant and therefore unsustainable use of resources.

Whereas previously the modern medical industry was used only for management (suppression) of fertility,[52] now it is more common for women and men to rely on the medical industry to both produce and eliminate fertility. Indeed, reports from the UK document that some financially stable,

140   ENVIRONMENTAL ETHICS AND MEDICAL REPRODUCTION

emotionally mature women who become accidentally pregnant in their 30s terminate and then seek MR in the next few years.[53] This new technological lifestyle is becoming so prevalent that "both popular media and medicine have encouraged women not to intentionally delay procreation with the goal of seeking IVF in the years of declining fertility."[54] Thus, exclusionary criteria for subsidized access to MR for fertile people can first include couples and singles who have been pregnant, carried that pregnancy to term, and have secondary infertility, then, second, to singles and couples who have been pregnant and chosen not to carry the pregnancy to term.

There are several ethical considerations in using past pregnancy as an exclusionary criterion for subsidized MR. First, one might argue that if the medical industry subsidizes contraception as part of women's rights, then it ought to subsidize MR. However, this argument is based on a faulty premise, namely that healthcare insurance is to support women's rights. Healthcare insurance may support women's rights, but the primary purpose is to meet a goal of medicine. The prevention of disease and death is met with contraception and abortion; it is not met with providing MR to fertile people. Outside of subsidized healthcare, the first objection also confuses the negative right to procreation with the positive right to procreation. In many countries, the right not to be pregnant has been upheld through laws that have decriminalized abortion and contraception.[55] However, there has not been a corresponding law that gives anyone a right to be pregnant; therefore mandating subsidized access to MR cannot be legally demonstrated.

Second, subsidized MR for people with a past history of abortion is an affront to MR itself. Ostensibly, MR is used for creating a pregnancy. In cases of past pregnancies, the goal of MR is insensible. Therefore, singles and couples who have already had a pregnancy would be seeking MR not for pregnancy but for the scientific and technical aspects of fertilization and implantation. This clearly moves the purpose of MR from pregnancy to reproductive experience, which would require a new set of ethical criteria. It would have to be argued that subsidized healthcare should provide for not only the spectrum of prenatal and antenatal care for naturally conceived children but also the entire spectrum of medicalized pregnancy from artificial fertilization to artificially made pregnancy, to expulsion of the fetus either through childbirth or abortion. MR for fertile people assumes the good of simply creating a pregnancy through medical means—the technical aspects of gamete retrieval, fertilization, and implantation—independent of conception and gestation,[56]

POLICIES FOR SUBSIDIZED MEDICAL REPRODUCTION   141

which fertile people have already had. Since the experiences of natural and medicalized reproduction are parallel, women with a past pregnancy have already experienced the outcomes of MR, although using different methods. A person may find these technical aspects of MR desirable in as much as they might also want to defy the bounds of human limitation through transhumanism,[57] but this would not be an acceptable use of subsidized healthcare.[58] It is neither a medical need nor a goal of medicine.

Third, subsidized healthcare is a limited resource and should be used parsimoniously. Singles and couples who have used healthcare for abortions have already taken a share of their owed healthcare resources. In Germany, a panel on medical prioritization and rationing "developed criteria for prioritization and identified problematic areas such as . . . individual responsibility."[59] Arguing that subsidized MR should not be offered to fertile people with past pregnancy is not a punitive action toward those who have been pregnant or toward those who have had abortions.[60] Rather, it is an appropriate response for cost containment and resource conservation.

In sum, from an environmental ethics perspective, using MR after a past pregnancy is an unnecessary carbon expenditure in its technical requirements. From a sexual/parental ethics perspective, using MR after a past pregnancy is misdirected, as MR can only provide medicalized procreation and does not include parenting experiences after birth. Parenting experiences after birth are obtained through biological parenting, adoption, fostering, and co-parenting. From a medical perspective, using MR after a past pregnancy is unnecessary as the purpose of facilitating conception for the possibility of live birth has already occurred. Use of fertility ought to exclude access to subsidized MR. While there might be some exceptions, such as abortion after rape or abortion prior to the age of 22 (for example), subsidized MR for the fertile cannot be ethically justified.

Voluntary Sterilization

In some cases, men or women who have had biological children will voluntarily terminate their fertility through contraceptive sterilization and later seek MR to provide more children to their family.[61] These singles and couples already utilized their fertility, have children, and are not infertile. There is very little reason to justify provision of subsidized MR for people in this category.

142   ENVIRONMENTAL ETHICS AND MEDICAL REPRODUCTION

Contraceptive sterilization—either through vasectomy, tubal ligation, or new developments like Essure—is one of the most common forms of birth control in many countries, due to its effectiveness, permanency, and minimal side effects.[62] Most often, contraceptive sterilization is offered to those who have biological children and consider their family "complete"; that is, they do not want more children and are so convinced about their decision that they seek permanent contraception.[63] Indeed, it is sometimes difficult for the childfree to obtain sterilization as a form of birth control, despite its being legal in a number of countries.[64] However, as with any medical decision, sterilization may be regretted. Regret is less often associated with the childfree and more often seen in those who are parents.[65] Regret does not imply that one will pursue MR, of course. But it need not be a qualifying factor for subsidized MR, either, particularly when it is singles and couples with children—a constitutively different category from the childfree—who may use subsidized MR.

Regret over voluntary sterilization after procreation may come from a variety of circumstances, like death or divorce from one's partner, and is associated with many well-documented factors related to younger age, less education, and higher number of children already born.[66] However, regret must also be contextualized within the boundaries of informed consent: when one makes a medical decision, particularly one that is meant to be permanent, the informed consent process ensures that the person understands the irreversibility of their decision.[67] The use of subsidized healthcare to obtain sterilization may, in particular patient profiles, be an unwise allocation of resources. That does not mean that sterilization should not be given to younger, undereducated singles and couples who already have children, but, rather, that an informed choice is the obligation of the person seeking sterilization and that medical correction of regrets—when possible—is not the obligation of the healthcare provider.

Nonetheless, certain healthcare plans, for instance, the Massachusetts Blue Cross Blue Shield Elect Preferred PPO plan, does not cover reversal of voluntary sterilization but does provide unlimited MR.[68] Thus, there is an internal contradiction in the way some healthcare policies are currently written. This can be addressed through the exclusionary criteria which includes those who are fertile who have had biological children. If not, the argument must be made that subsidized MR exists to create a child of choice, despite the presence of biological children, and, moreover, that healthcare insurance companies and governments that provide healthcare ought to be financially

POLICIES FOR SUBSIDIZED MEDICAL REPRODUCTION   143

liable and medically responsible for an individual's change of mind about a life choice.[69]

As with other categories of adults with biological children, providing subsidized MR to those who have chosen sterilization is in conflict with the goals of medicine and the purpose of MR, which would be to facilitate the ability to become a parent of a biological child. Since those who have chosen sterilization were fertile, had biological children, and then made an informed and autonomous choice to become functionally infertile, they should be excluded from subsidized MR. As with other categories of fertile adults, they may still have the option for further reproduction via unsubsidized MR or parenting the children they already have, in addition to parenting through other means.

Exclusionary Criteria—Social Infertility

MR was originally developed to provide couples with epidemiological infertility an alternative to natural reproduction. Although medical developments ought not be constrained to their original purpose—which would thwart new applications of innovative technologies—when given in the realm of subsidized healthcare, there is reason to evaluate any use which does not meet primary objectives of the goals of medicine, for financial, environmental, and biomedical reasons. Subsidized MR is, in some cases, provided to people who are not clinically infertile, based on their social circumstances.

Although their bodies are capable of becoming pregnant and carrying a child to term, or impregnating a woman, due to lifestyle choices such as abstinence from heterosexual intercourse, these individuals will not become pregnant or impregnate without changing their social circumstance or using medical assistance. People in this category may also be called "socially infertile" to indicate that their life circumstance makes it challenging to reproduce without medical assistance. Typically, the term is applied to adults of a certain age, which is circumscribed by social norms of "appropriate" life stage to reproduce: a single 20-year-old would not be considered "socially infertile," just "single." The term is also connected to desirability of procreation: a person who is childfree by choice would not identify as "socially infertile" as they are just "fertile."

The socially infertile/clinically fertile category encompasses fertile single women and men and fertile coupled women and men. Within these groups,

144 ENVIRONMENTAL ETHICS AND MEDICAL REPRODUCTION

individuals may be gay, straight, or another irrelevant sexual orientation. Sexual orientation is irrelevant because it does not correlate to biological infertility. People in the socially infertile category may have a partner who is dead. The capacity for utilizing one's fertility does not always correspond to one's sexual orientation or partner status. Fertility, if one has it, is a capacity that one may choose to exercise or not.

Another way to describe these people is "not clinically infertile." As such, MR treatments are not clinically indicated. Initially, healthcare plans followed these distinctions. In 2006, the UK NHS declared that subsidized MR was "for sub-fertility not to fund reproduction."[70] The terminology is important, as the former denotes a clinical indication and the latter a reproductive project.

However, in 2008 the NHS began to fund reproduction for people who are biologically fertile based on the Human Fertilisation and Embryology Authority removal of the provision that prevented "couples in same-sex relationships and single mothers"[71] from accessing subsidized MR, thus opening access to those who are fertile. Similarly, in America, as of 2023, "21 states plus DC have passed fertility insurance coverage laws, 15 of those laws include IVF coverage, and 17 cover fertility preservation for iatrogenic (medically-induced) infertility." Most states do not specify that the "infertile" person has to be partnered or married.[72]

When MR is given to the clinically fertile, medical resources are used unnecessarily and the carbon impact of healthcare is directed at elective treatments rather than clinical benefit. Provision of MR to the socially infertile might be acceptable when paid for out of pocket. However, biological fertility ought to be an exclusionary criterion for subsidized MR for numerous environmental and medical reasons. When social, rather than biological, factors determine provision of subsidized MR, which is underwritten by the public and coded under "infertility services," the purpose of health insurance and the goals of medicine are disregarded.

Single People

Most people of childbearing age are fertile, based on our best epidemiological information. Being single does not alter one's fertility status. Therefore, it may be assumed that a majority of single people who access MR are indeed fertile and using medical resources for personal preferences rather

POLICIES FOR SUBSIDIZED MEDICAL REPRODUCTION   145

than clinical indication. Although single men and women are less likely to have biological children in their current situation, their "infertility" is due to circumstances and not clinical conditions like blocked tubes, amenorrhea, or other factors leading to infertility. They are "socially infertile" but do not require technological intervention to procreate. As such, MR is redundant, does not meet a goal of medicine, and is an unjustifiable waste of carbon emissions.

It may be argued, however, that subsidized MR for single women is less resource-intensive than subsidized MR for single men and therefore ought to be included in healthcare plans. To be sure, when a single man or a single woman seeks MR, there are significant differences in the biological demands of reproduction and the technical requirements of MR.[73] Biologically, the woman's contributions to reproduction, that is, gestation, birth, and nursing, are much more demanding than the man's. Technically, what is required of women to use MR is also much more physically demanding, that is, fertility drugs, egg retrieval, artificial insemination or IVF, than what is required of men: fertility drugs (perhaps) and autoeroticism. However, single men who use MR must depend on a woman for gestation, whereas single women do not require—but may opt for—the use of another woman. Moreover, a single man who uses MR will need to employ a gestational surrogate, and surrogates are an additional category of fertile people who use MR. Thus, use of subsidized healthcare for fertile single men to reproduce requires an additional argument that justifies MR for fertile gestational partners who one is not socially or romantically attached to.[74] It may seem that MR is better environmentally for single women who may only require sperm than a single man who will rely on another person. However, reproduction depends on both sexes' genetic contributions, and the environmental impact of MR in all of its phases—from gamete retrieval to birth—must be taken in aggregate, regardless of who initiates the process.

While it can be argued that single men and women have the right to become parents as they wish, or even use MR services to fulfill their life choices,[75] these arguments are based on the negative right (non-interference) of reproduction, and there is not a corresponding right to access subsidized fertility treatments in order to do so, nor is there a clinical justification. Funded reproduction for fertile single men and women who choose not to have a partner produces unnecessary carbon emissions. These individuals are not medically infertile in a way that could justify medical treatment to address a somatic cause of infertility. Provision of subsidized MR then violates

146 ENVIRONMENTAL ETHICS AND MEDICAL REPRODUCTION

the goals of medicine and purpose of healthcare insurance, confirming that being fertile—regardless of partner status—ought to be an exclusionary criterion for subsidized MR.

Same-Sex Couples

Sexual attraction is the desire humans feel toward another person. Sexual action is directed at a person one is having sex with. Sexual orientation is how one identifies with regard to attraction and action. These may or may not align. For instance, a woman may be sexually attracted to men and women, but partnered with a man and identify as bisexual as a sexual orientation. A man may be attracted to women, have sex with men (e.g., as part of work), and identify as straight. Sexual orientation is non-binary; therefore it is more appropriate to discuss the "social infertility" of same-sex couples rather than "gay" couples.[76] People in a same-sex relationship may identify as gay, straight, asexual, bisexual, queer, polysexual, or many other terms. From a medical perspective, the sexual orientation of the person does not—and should not—be a factor in determining clinical indication for MR. Like single people (which includes gay and straight), couples in same-sex relationships (as in opposite-sex relationships) are statistically likely to be fertile. Anyone—gay or straight—can be sub-fertile and may require fertility treatments if biological reproduction is desired. About 10% of people may be infertile,[77] and there is no reason to think that it is higher in same-sex couples. In fact, infertility might be lower in same-sex female couples if the women have been abstaining from using hormonal contraception, which interferes with fertility for a period after discontinuing use.[78]

However, as with the choice to have a partner or not, the choice of the sex of one's partner does not correlate to fertility or infertility. Choosing a same-sex partner does not make one clinically infertile. While some may argue that sexual orientation is not a choice, it is more accurate to say sexual attraction is not a choice. Even then, regardless of whether sexual attraction is innate or developed, our actions are chosen. Choosing to engage in or refrain from heterosexual sex is a choice. The absence of heterosexual sexual activity controls, rather than eradicates, fertility.

Moreover, consensus about the relationship between sexual orientation and sexual action has not been uniform, even within the gay community. Michel Foucault argued that the invention of homosexuality as a social category was a recent phenomenon.[79] Furthermore, the lesbian feminist movement in the 1980s viewed same-sex intercourse between women as tangential to attraction and central to political action.[80] In the late 1990s and 2000s, the queer movement revived the possibility of homosexual activity in the absence of attraction,[81] tracing back to the Greek pederast-catamite relationship.[82]

Sexual orientation is irrelevant for diagnostic purposes, which might lead to provision of subsidized MR since the "infertility" would be social and not clinical. And if it were to be argued that sexual orientation could be used as a diagnostic category, there would be enormous logistical problems defining diagnostic criteria for sexual orientation and establishing evidence of sexual orientation. In some cases, asylum seekers have been subjected to humiliating interrogation and unnecessary invasions into their personal life in an attempt to verify their sexual orientation as a basis for fleeing their country.[83] An additional metaphysical hurdle would be the connection between sexual orientation and sexual activity. For instance, if a bisexual person has had a same-sex partner for 10 years, it is unclear if they would be considered "gay" or "bisexual" for diagnostic purposes. Similarly, clinical guidelines for the number or kind of interruptions in a sexual identity which would constitute a significant enough break to revise an identity would be arbitrary. For instance, if a self-identified gay man has sex with one woman in 15 years, or three times in the past month and then never again, he might not be able to establish himself as "gay." Suggesting that gay people do have a form of infertility—social infertility—ignores the historical understanding about the relationship between sexual orientation and sexual action and creates a new medical category.[84]

Importantly, due to the historical discrimination against gay people and people in same-sex couples, and the attempts to delegitimize their unions by, for instance, blocking access to marriage,[85] adoption,[86] or parental rights of biological children,[87] it is essential that infertility not be used as an excuse to further prevent same-sex couples from accessing MR. When clinical disease is present, it may be treated with medicine. Thus, access to subsidized MR must only use the criterion of clinical infertility and keep partner status as an irrelevant factor to protect those in same-sex relationships.

Indeed, it is discriminatory to deny an infertile gay person fertility treatments on the basis that they are gay. To this end, the United Kingdom's National Health Service has recommended that "same sex couples should be treated in the same way as mixed sex couples in accessing assisted conception

148 ENVIRONMENTAL ETHICS AND MEDICAL REPRODUCTION

treatments if a couple can demonstrate that either one or both partners are sub-fertile."[88] While this policy moves in the right direction of clinical indication, one concern is that it does not specify that the sub-fertile partner has to be the one receiving treatment, thus leaving the door open for funding of fertile reproduction.

It should also be reiterated that, as with fertile single men and opposite-sex coupled fertile men, fertile men in same-sex relationships will require the use of a surrogate.[89] Thus, all of the bioethical and environmental concerns with funded fertility treatments would be applied to the gestational surrogate, who is fertile. It does not follow that same-sex female MR or same-sex male MR is more sustainable than the other: the same configuration of gametes and uterus is required. However, demanding access to surrogates as part of subsidized MR would be an additional resource burden that could not be justified based on clinical need, since the surrogate—the one receiving the MR treatments—is fertile, having been selected for their ability to bear children.[90]

Fertile people do not require fertility treatments for biological reproduction. When there are no clinical indications, there are no correlative treatments. MR may be used as part of a lifestyle choice and paid for out of pocket, irrespective of social infertility.[91] But MR cannot be legitimately subsidized under the goals of medicine or recognized as a purpose of healthcare.

Even when MR is voluntarily chosen as a lifestyle procedure, it is still a pernicious commentary on the "undesirability" of childfree, single, and LGBT lifestyles and demonstrates complicity with heterosexism and homophobia, which seek to restrict adults to pronatalist, heteronormative family models. A choice to willingly submit to medical treatments when there is no underlying cause may give the illusion of autonomy. However, when medical choices are made because it facilitates assimilation into couple-centric societies, because it frees one from the stigma of being childfree, because it meets the culturally imposed "gold standard" of biological children[92] at any economic, medical, or personal cost, then moral agents must question to what extent choices are really self-governed.

Death

Posthumous reproduction is a form of social infertility, whereby instead of not having an inseminating/gestative partner, one's partner has died and is no longer available to fulfill this function. Posthumous reproduction may occur using gametes that have been stored prior to death—for instance, from ongoing MR treatments, employer or military plans, or as part of oncofertility—or retrieved shortly after death. The latter will be discussed.

Gamete retrieval after death includes postmortem sperm retrieval (PMSR) and postmortem egg retrieval. PMSR is more common. Both would result in posthumous reproduction using MR. There is no clinical indication for gamete retrieval of the dead, and MR on dead people is not clinically necessary, either for the dead person or the living person who is associated with the deceased. The facilitation of posthumous reproduction from postmortem retrieval of gametes is outside of the goals of medicine because once a person is dead, medicine cannot make them well or palliate their end of life. As such, it is a futile medical treatment which uses resources without benefit and violates standards of medicine. Death ought to be an exclusionary criterion for subsidized healthcare insurance of MR for multiple reasons.

Both laws and policies have addressed the many ethical issues with a partner's request for posthumous gamete retrieval.[93] One objection to subsidized MR for the dead is that dead people are not entitled to medical treatments because they are no longer people.[94] Just as it would be absurd to offer cosmetic or cardiac surgery to a corpse, so too would utilizing any form of medical reproduction after death be outside of healthcare. There is no right to reproduce once a person is dead, and many people view death as the terminus for possibilities of life activities, including reproduction.[95] While it may be argued that a dead person is "infertile," the etiology is lack of existence, which is not a medical complaint. Thus, an argument for PMSR under subsidized medicine could only be made on its benefit to another person.

There are a few examples of postmortem surgical techniques, such as tissue and organ donation,[96] that are well-accepted forms of medicine, permitted and typically covered under healthcare insurance.[97] While these do not in any way benefit the cadaver, they do sustain life or support physical functioning for another person or people. However, there are significant differences between postmortem gamete retrieval and organ and tissue donation from the dead. In terms of medical importance, clearly vital physical functioning is incommensurate with MR both in degree and kind. Reproduction is trivial, and vital function significant. Thus, PMSR could not be considered a technique that meets a goal of medicine.

Moreover, organs and tissues are allocated and distributed through a third party, such as United Network for Organ Sharing in the United States[98] or

150   ENVIRONMENTAL ETHICS AND MEDICAL REPRODUCTION

Euro-transplant, a consortium for organ donation in Europe.[99] After death, the organ may not be directed at a specific person,[100] and the recipient of the organ or tissue is the one whose subsidized healthcare covers the process.[101] With postmortem gamete retrieval, the sperm are taken on behalf of a specific person and "donated" directly to that person, usually a lover or a surrogate of the family's choosing.[102] Thus, subsidized healthcare could not legitimately code for PMSR on the basis of clinical benefit for another, nor is the situation parallel to organ or tissue donation.

Moreover, acceding to the request for postmortem gamete retrieval is a case of "treating the family," commonly seen in pediatrics.[103] In these scenarios, the doctor performs procedures that do not benefit the patient, such as keeping them on life support after the chance of meaningful recovery is gone or providing treatments that do not address the medical issue. There are several biomedical problems with treating the family. First, performing procedures on a human being without their consent is a breach of autonomy. If the dead have not consented to postmortem gamete retrieval, medical standards are violated. Second, treating the family contradicts the goals of medicine, which are to treat and heal an individual. Third, when treating the family, there is no clinical indication. Thus, postmortem gamete retrieval may be questioned on the basis of who the procedure benefits.

Moreover, requests for postmortem gamete retrieval can come from extended family—parents and siblings—and not the partner of the dead.[104] If a parent makes the request for postmortem gamete retrieval with the objective of posthumous grandparenthood, it is not even the "family" who is treated, but a surrogate who would receive the sperm or egg.[105] Again, since the surrogate is generally fertile, they would not have a clinical indication for insemination. If a sibling makes the request, with the objective of using the gametes in case of infertility, the first ethical issue is proximity of next of kin. In most cases, domestic partners, then parents, then siblings is the order of next of kin.[106] This request for postmortem gamete retrieval by the parents is further away from legal entitlements and also cannot be legitimized as a goal of medicine. In another variation, the parent could make the request for postmortem gamete retrieval on behalf of their other living children. But this would be a clear conflict of interest.[107] There is no clinical indication for a parent to request gametes from their dead adult child. The second ethical issue with sibling requests for postmortem gamete retrieval is that there is no compelling reason to think that a sibling is infertile, so there would be no clinical indication for requesting another's gametes. If a sibling did happen to be infertile, they would have to argue that they have a rightful claim to the gametes of their sibling. As in the case of "savior siblings" with HLA matching, this is ethically controversial for lifesaving requests.[108] MR should be much more controversial as it is only for elective pregnancy, which is non-lifesaving.

Postmortem gamete retrieval at the request of the family cannot be legitimately placed under subsidized MR, nor can requests from friends,[109] since there is no legal entitlement to gametes by friends. Even less persuasive is that the parents may request postmortem gamete retrieval for use by a friend of the dead child. As with retrieval with intended use for siblings, there is no compelling reason to think that a friend is infertile and thus no clinical need for PMSR.

Finally, although postmortem gamete retrieval is not clinically indicated and does not meet a goal of medicine, even the legal argument of entitlement to the body does not legitimize subsidized MR for the dead. That is, after death the law permits family members to have access to the body of the dead for the purpose of mourning and burial.[110] However, this legal parameter cannot be extended to the use of the dead body for any reason, including PMSR.

Subsidized healthcare is for the living individual. Death terminates the medical and therapeutic relationship. Postmortem gamete retrieval has no clinical indication as dead people do not require medical treatments. Healthcare is not available for people who are dead. And partners (married or not), family members, and friends are not legally entitled to a person's physical material, nor would there be a clinical indication for such retrieval.

Climate change demands that medical procedures are evaluated for clinical efficacy. Carbon emissions ought not be expended on that which is not clinically necessary. Sustainable healthcare must first meet the goals of medicine. Ethically, subsidized MR for the fertile—either clinically fertile or socially infertile—cannot be maintained.

Exclusionary Criterion—Non-Infertility-Related MR

There are a growing number of MR procedures that do not address clinical infertility and therefore may be excluded from subsidized healthcare. The focus here is the MR offerings that are used by both fertile and infertile singles and couples. While both fertile and infertile people may avail themselves of these techniques, assuming the above exclusionary criteria of fertility is

152 ENVIRONMENTAL ETHICS AND MEDICAL REPRODUCTION

met, these recommendations would only be applied to the clinically infertile accessing MR through subsidized healthcare insurance. However, if some group of fertile people were still accessing subsidized MR, this set of exclusionary criteria would also be applicable.

Many social and medical ethical issues may be raised in the use of non-infertility-related MR, such as the instrumentalization of children and the limits of parental sovereignty. However, the amount of resources used and carbon emissions expended are rarely considered ethical factors. Additionally, these forms of non-infertility-related MR, since they may be used by the infertile, are sometimes associated with subsidized healthcare but do not have a clinical benefit. The conflation of non-infertility-related MR with infertility-related treatments financially burdens the healthcare system and policyholders. There are compelling reasons to exclude elective procedures from subsidized healthcare, so much more so excluding procedures which do not support the health of the person seeking the treatments.

Non-infertility-related MR does not treat the individual, but rather brings a new person with a specific type of genetics into being. These services do not cure, treat, or prevent either biological or social infertility. The objective of the procedures is to create a child of choice by using technologies to alter genetic makeup or attempt to ensure a certain kind of child. As such, these procedures are unrelated to the goals of medicine and thus the purpose of healthcare insurance. These policy suggestions would not foreclose the possibility of individuals and couples using unsubsidized healthcare for non-infertility-related MR. Even then, the use would still need to be within the ethical parameters of medicine, sustainability, and parental responsibility.

Pre-implantation Genetic Diagnosis and Genetic Disease

Pre-implantation genetic diagnosis, or PGD, is a technique that falls under the umbrella of MR. PGD does not exist for the benefit of the patient, as a person first has to be created. PGD also does not cure, treat, or prevent infertility. PGD, as a form of non-infertility-related MR, must be contextualized within the goals of medicine and the purpose of healthcare—to cure, treat, and prevent disease. While many healthcare insurance programs do not cover PGD,[111] they are increasingly being lobbied for, and covered under, subsidized healthcare insurance.[112]

POLICIES FOR SUBSIDIZED MEDICAL REPRODUCTION   153

Even when PGD is used as a workaround for possible, or known, genetic diseases of the parents, it is not a requirement of medicine to create embryos. Creating embryos treats neither infertility nor any other disease or condition. If one wanted to place PGD under the goals of medicine, a rather circular argument would have to be made that healthcare may create beings who may possibly have a disease so that they may cure them. Healthcare, of course, ought to try to cure people who are alive and in existence. Healthcare does not need to create the sick only to make them well.

Highlighting that PGD does not meet a goal of medicine does not imply that people who may have a genetic disease should be prevented from reproducing, which would violate the negative right to reproduce. Indeed, many bioethicists have argued that PGD itself is a destructive social commentary on disability,[113] which increases—rather than decreases—hostility and fear of the disabled, stating that the medical model of disease and disability is a "covertly discriminatory stance toward disability and disabled people that reduces the embryo, fetus, or child to her or his condition."[114] These critiques ought to be seriously considered alongside additional environmental and bioethical concerns.

PGD contributes to MR carbon by producing children in excess of what would occur if only natural reproduction were an option, as both the phases of MR, from gamete retrieval to IVF, are used—and the children themselves contribute to carbon. There is certainly value in progress, ingenuity, health, and flourishing, but the distance between PGD and the goals of medicine—remembering that it is a treatment developed for those who must be called into being and do not actually exist, and that PGD is not related to infertility—cannot be justified with the emissions it produces. There is no clinical benefit to the user of PGD [the parents] and it is outside of the purpose of subsidized healthcare.

It could be argued that, although PGD does not meet a goal of medicine, it may be environmentally advantageous, as it would save resources due to using fewer medical interventions of those with genetic conditions.[115] Yet, this argument assumes that PGD embryos would exist in any scenario, that fertile people with genetic disease would reproduce in any circumstance. This may not be the case, as those with genetic disease may choose to limit the number of biological children they have.[116] Even if those embryos did exist without PGD and did require medical treatments, the environmental cost would have to account for the carbon of MR to produce a PGD infant that may be genetically healthy—remembering that PGD is not perfect, and

154 ENVIRONMENTAL ETHICS AND MEDICAL REPRODUCTION

even when used it does not prevent disability later in life—versus medical resources used to treat the possible genetic condition after natural conception and birth. To be sure, the carbon emissions that occur from preventive health are often beneficial for the environment in the short term as they reduce health care burdens. Preventive health care is also beneficial for the person who can avoid medical treatments.[117] (However, preventive health care may be worse for the environment long-term as individuals may live longer lives.)[118] But, carbon emissions that are used to create an embryo to "prevent" a potential medical problem neither benefit the environment by avoiding extra healthcare carbon emissions nor the potential person by keeping them well, because these embryos do not exist until created and therefore have no health problems. PGD is not a medical treatment. The procedure is outside the goals of medicine and cannot be legitimized through subsidized health insurance.

Pre-implantation Genetic Diagnosis and HLA Compatibility

Some conditions, such as organ failure,[119] leukemia or lymphoma,[120] or Fanconi anemia,[121] which cannot be treated through conventional methods, may instead be cured or treated through "savior siblings." Here, pre-implantation genetic diagnosis is used to select for human leukocyte antigen compatibility in an embryo that will be gestated using in-vitro fertilization.[122] Once born, biological material will be taken from the infant and given to a sick sibling with the intention of cure or treatment. PGD-HLA does not cure, treat, or prevent illness in a person who already exists. Nor does it treat the embryo, who is not sick, nor the woman who is gestating the embryo. PGD-HLA may cure or treat the disease of another person, but only through the creation of a new person.

Biomedicine has commented on the ethics of this instrumentalization of humans.[123] But ethical concern has failed to identify the environmental implications, which are several-fold: first, that fertile people use PGD-HLA; second, that these fertile people already have at least one biological child; third, that fertile people with a history of genetic disease may naturally have a healthy child that would be HLA-compatible with the older child. In all these cases there are unnecessary emissions from the MR process itself. There will be additional emissions from the birth of the new MR child and the elective medical procedures of a donation nature. PGD-HLA is incompatible with the goals of medicine as it does not cure, treat, or prevent infertility or genetic disease. Having a terminally ill child is devastating. But subsidized health-care cannot be said to exist for ever more complicated permutations of MR such as PGD with HLA matching.

Pre-implantation Genetic Diagnosis and Selecting for Disability

Pre-implantation genetic diagnosis was initially intended to lessen the chances of passing genetic disease to a child. This in itself has been controversial, as disability rights advocates have rejected the medical model of disability that "suggests that even the hint of embodied differences from idealized norms that arise with a disabling condition ought to be corrected or eliminated."[124] There have been many social gains from disability advocacy, such as the Americans with Disabilities Act.[125] The ethical concerns of ableism have been explored in recent decades.[126] These social advances have also brought new opportunities for using PGD to select for an embryo with a "disability" such as achondroplasia (dwarfism) or deafness.

While these "disabilities" should not be seen as disvaluing the person, at the same time, using PGD to select for a disability does not cure, treat, or prevent disease and is not a goal of medicine. PGD for selection of disability also does not cure, treat, or prevent infertility. It is an elective manner of procreation which is akin to "designer babies," in that a parent or parents desire a particular type of child and use MR. As such, a disability becomes a cosmetic characteristic selected in pursuit of creating a child of choice and should not be offered under subsidized healthcare insurance.

Environmentally, there are concerns not only with the resources used for this form of MR, which is clinically unnecessary, but also the creation of a new child [regardless of disability]. It may also be observed that there may be additional environmental concerns about creating disabilities which may need to be treated with more medical resources, but this line of thought is unpersuasive: first, because these children are being created as disabled without the intention of correcting the disability—thus medical resources would not be used—and second, because of the eugenic implications that this line of reasoning would imply. To invoke the concern that there will be *more* resources used by disabled people leads to a dangerous and toxic conception

156 ENVIRONMENTAL ETHICS AND MEDICAL REPRODUCTION

of health that cannot be tolerated. To be sure, the child may eventually seek medical care for their imposed disability, but this would be within the goals of medicine and the purpose of healthcare.

Pre-implantation Genetic Diagnosis and Sex Selection

Unlike "regular" fertility treatments for those who are infertile, which is a workaround for the clinical condition of infertility, pre-implantation genetic diagnosis and sex selection is an elective part of MR. While it may be offered to the infertile in the course of subsidized medical treatments, or to the fertile at risk for genetic disease, PGD and sex selection must be considered a separate and additional offering of MR unrelated to clinical infertility. Both sex selection for "family balancing" and sex selection to avoid X-linked genes are medically unnecessary. The former indicates a superficial trait that is unrelated to the goals of medicine. Moreover, since these singles and couples already have one or more children, they would not need sex selection as an adjunctive to fertility treatments. The latter, much like PGD for genetic health, does not cure, treat, or prevent diseases in the individual, but rather creates many new embryos and then discards the sick. These embryos did not need to be created medically. That is, the creation of embryos serves no medical purpose.

There may be the environmental concern that if PGD and sex selection for family balancing were not available, then parents would reproduce until they have a child of a preferred sex, thus impacting population growth and resource consumption excessively. Yet, this concern does not align with best information on how adults decide the number of children to have.[127] Similarly, the idea that PGD and sex selection against chromosomal disease would lead to sick children being born, which would require more medical resources than preventing their disease, is also spurious reasoning. First, adults may simply abstain from reproducing. Second, even if they did reproduce naturally they would not necessarily have a sick child. Third, if they did have a sick child, medical resources would be clinically necessary and therefore well spent, environmentally.

Both PGD and sex selection for family balancing and sex selection for X-linked disease ought to be exclusionary criteria for subsidized healthcare, as they do not meet a goal of medicine. As with other forms of PGD, the option to purchase these services outside of healthcare may still exist.

But environmentally, their use as part of the carbon footprint of healthcare cannot be ethically justified.

Pre-implantation Genetic Diagnosis and Designer Babies

Finally, pre-implantation genetic diagnosis may be used for selection of purely superficial traits. Also known as "designer babies," there is a growing trend to use PGD to select for eye color, disposition of height, and other cosmetic features unrelated to health. Similarly, these PGD designer babies are also distinct from fertility treatments. This form of MR has not typically been covered under healthcare insurance[128] as it clearly does not meet a goal of medicine. However, with more evidence that accidental properties of humans may cause "social disabilities," like disadvantages in the workplace,[129] there may be a movement to cover this form of PGD in the future. Designer babies do, of course, use the medical industry and contribute to the carbon footprint of healthcare. However, the technique offers no concomitant medical benefit and ought to be excluded from any form of subsidized healthcare going forward.

MR Outside of Subsidized Healthcare

While ARTs for the fertile and non-infertility-related MR do not fit within the goals of medicine and therefore ought not to be given under subsidized healthcare insurance, they may still be available as a non-curative form of healthcare for those who would pay out of pocket. A negative right to reproduction or even a positive right to access reproductive technologies would not prohibit this, since presumably, these fertile singles and couples would not be turned away from using MR, assuming their reproductive project was ethical within broader biomedical principles, such as safety of the procedure,[130] health of the mother, and the "right to an open future."[131] Likewise, if they met other environmental standards and fit within parental ethics, unsubsidized MR for the fertile and for non-infertility-related procedures may be available.

One objection to failing to finance all forms of MR with subsidized healthcare insurance is that of fairness. Due to the cost of MR, and low success rates, it may be argued that if they are not covered under healthcare insurance, the

158   ENVIRONMENTAL ETHICS AND MEDICAL REPRODUCTION

poor would be disadvantaged. Since reproductive technologies "come at a considerable cost, some may not be able to afford them. (Therefore) merely establishing a negative right appears insufficient."[132] However, Jurgen De Wispelaere and Daniel Weinstock note the "negative right to reproductive technologies, even if cost prohibitive, may imply a form of inequality, but not objectionable injustice or unfairness provided 1) each person has a real opportunity to secure the core interest of becoming a parent; 2) those who prefer to parent their own child are not actively prevented from doing so; 3) and those unable to reproduce naturally or via ART because of its expense are given access to a perfectly reasonable alternative, adoption."[133] These three measures at once mitigate potential economic unfairness and also address the bioethical, environmental, and parental concerns that have been raised throughout the debates on medicalized reproduction.

Furthermore, it should be remembered that there are a great number of services that are out of reach financially for people—cars, single-family houses, a good bottle of wine, even, indeed, basic healthcare.[134] Society has an interest, and even an obligation, to ensure that basic rights are financially accessible.[135] And if one cannot pay for the object of the right independently, then government assistance would be appropriate.[136] But "the claim that there exists a positive right to reproduction [through technologies] by demanding that the state offer full or partial subsidy of the associated costs" goes beyond a basic claim to healthcare as it provides "every citizen *effective* access to the means for ART"[137] regardless of fertility status or use of MR. With limited financial and natural resources, this claim is very hard to support. Instead, subsidized healthcare should exclude clinical fertility and non-fertility-related MR from coverage in order to direct resources toward clinical benefit and the goals of medicine and in order to reduce carbon emissions of MR and the medical industry.

Inclusionary Criteria

There are numerous reasons to limit MR, just as there are numerous reasons to limit procreation and resource-intensive medical procedures. Additional justification for supporting any form of procreation—particularly when it utilizes external sources, such as the medical industry, must be seriously evaluated for social and environmental effects. The prevalence of MR exacerbates the ecological challenges of the modern world. Beyond merely accepting procreation as a negative right, "any attempt to assess the limits of obligation to promote fertility must begin with a critique of prevailing, highly individualistic accounts of procreative liberty."[138] Subsidizing MR encourages procreation and promotes fertility.

In light of the biomedical and environmental implications of MR, this chapter has outlined comprehensive—but not complete—exclusionary criteria for subsidized MR, based primarily on clinical indication of infertility, which points to the goals of medicine, and therefore the purpose of healthcare insurance. It does not follow that inclusionary criteria for subsidized MR would be anything outside of what has been discussed here. Nor should inclusionary criteria be conceptualized as a floor, with policymakers rushing to find as many ways as possible to subsidize MR within clinical indication. Rather, inclusionary criteria should be seen as a ceiling which ought to be lowered and ought to assume clinical infertility.

At the same time, inclusionary criteria will be contested, particularly since "reproductive freedom is such a widely accepted norm in Western society that some even assume it to be an individual's absolute or inalienable right."[139] However, objections should not stymie serious ethical reflection on ways to make MR more aligned with international environmental values.

Policies on subsidized MR for clinical infertility should not be regarded as a move toward the elimination of reproduction, but rather reduction of MR *at this time of urgency* must occur in order to meet the ethical requirements of ecology. The approach could be made toward natural reproduction, as well. Population degrowth must happen now. Yet, even if the ecological crisis was resolved, subsidized MR could still be contested in biomedical ethics for a number of reasons, including lack of clinical indication, prioritization, and economic burden. Natural and medicalized procreation would still be ethically objectionable based on the social, feminist, economic, and justice concerns that have been amply outlined elsewhere.

Nonetheless, in keeping with the foundational commitments of medicine and healthcare insurance, and the liberal Western values of the industrialized world, inclusionary criteria will suppose clinical infertility and advise how to proceed on that basis. The debatable—but nevertheless strong—sentiment that healthcare insurance entitles one to a positive right for treatments for clinical infertility will be acceded to, for the purpose of moving toward environmental sustainability.

160   ENVIRONMENTAL ETHICS AND MEDICAL REPRODUCTION

A Male-First Approach to Infertility

Testing men for infertility first, and developing more treatments for male-factor infertility, make up the first set of inclusionary criteria for subsidized MR. The prevalence of infertility is the same in both men and women (about 1 in 10),[140] and the Mayo Clinic reports that incidences of infertility can be traced to female factors in one-third of the cases, to male factors in one-third of the cases, and "in the remaining cases, the cause of infertility involves both the male and female, or no cause can be identified."[141] However, when infertility does arise, the social burden is on the woman first and foremost to arrange fertility treatments.[142] This is problematic not only from a perspective of diagnostic elegance,[143] whereby the quickest, easiest, and most economical approach to diagnosis is pursued, but also from an environmental perspective, as it wastes resources.

Testing for female factor infertility can be extensive and use a variety of medical and natural resources. These diagnostic tests range from low-tech, such as tracking menstrual cycles, incidence of intercourse, and basal body temperature,[144] to more invasive egg reserve tests, which require minor surgical procedures.[145] In contrast, testing for male infertility only requires a sperm sample, which can be taken after masturbation or intercourse.[146] Clinically, what is required of women for infertility testing is less efficient, more costly, and more resource-intensive.[147] Since the etiological cause of infertility may just as likely be the man as the woman, there are disproportionately burdensome risks of side effects when testing for female infertility,[148] whereas there are little known medical side effects of male auto-eroticism.

Thus, a male-first approach to infertility testing using subsidized healthcare ought to be the standard, not the exception. Primary objections to this can only come from patriarchal viewpoints which suppose that the woman has the primary burden not only for managing procreation (whether through contraception, abortion, or MR),[149] but also managing family matters, where "family" is a fallacious term for biological children.[150] Indeed, the "patriarchy survives in and through the social mediation of biological reproduction, especially by enlarging reproduction and attendant duties into women's virtually exclusive function."[151] In the medicalized, masculinist mindset, the "problem" of infertility is just as much a clinical matter for the woman as it is a metaphysical issue rooted in gender dissatisfaction, in not being a real woman, that is, a mother.[152] The gendering of infertility as a woman's "disease" or "problem" puts the medically unnecessary and environmentally significant burden on women not only to seek infertility testing first, but also use MR technologies even when they are fertile.

Instead, if biomedicine and society recognized the equal distribution of infertility in the sexes, male infertility would be more likely to be prevented on the front end of healthcare and better treatments for male infertility could be pursued on the back end. Some medical developments for male-factor infertility may include a sperm jet pack, sperm in an artificial penis,[153] or implantable penile hydraulics for impotent men.[154] Objections to these male alternatives may only come from the seeming absurdity of proposing that men have their bodies manipulated, especially with techniques as "humiliating" as those that compromise and alter their reproductive organs. This reaction uncovers how deeply the medical industry believes that it is the woman's obligation to seek reproductive treatments, and that the male body is sacrosanct. Today, and since the medicalization of reproduction, "the wombs of women—whether already pregnant or not—are containers to be captured by the ideologies and practices"[155] of healthcare. In addition to this being highly sexist, it is neither medically justifiable nor environmentally sustainable.

The reluctance of society, the medical industry, and healthcare insurance to address male infertility—independent of the concept of virility—must be resolved. The medical industry, the healthcare system, and the singles and couples who seek MR ought not to be beholden to antiquated and biologically unsound notions of infertility.

Divest from Pornography

When men are tested for infertility—regardless of whether they are tested first or second—pornography is often used to procure a sperm sample through masturbation. There is a significant, but often overlooked, partnership of pornography and MR. In 2010, it was disclosed that the UK's National Institute of Health had been purchasing and distributing pornographic materials to fertility clinics.[156] Based on lack of clinical indication and unnecessary carbon emissions, a further inclusionary criteria for subsidized MR ought to be fertility testing without pornography.

Pornographic viewing at fertility clinics is justified under the excuse that "men may benefit from using pornographic materials to provide a semen sample under stressful conditions in a clinic."[157] Yet, these explicit materials

162 ENVIRONMENTAL ETHICS AND MEDICAL REPRODUCTION

are not a medical tool, nor are they necessary for masturbation. Furthermore, masturbation is not necessary for obtaining sperm samples. Both surgical sperm collection and electroejaculation techniques can produce semen samples without self-stimulation, as well as partnered assistance and sexual intercourse with a perforated condom. Pornography is not clinically indicated for masturbation or obtaining a sperm sample. Even when considered a "medical supply," like a scalpel or personal protective equipment, pornography does not support a medical development, technique, or procedure which contributes to a goal of medicine as masturbation is not a medical procedure.

Moreover, the carbon impact of the pornography industry contributes to MR emissions. Consider the vast infrastructure necessary for print and visual pornography. Prior to arriving at a fertility clinic, carbon emissions come from adult film actors and actresses, cinematographers, and photographers traveling to and from locations, the production and dissemination of print and digital pornographic magazines and videos, and, in the modern era, the immense carbon of internet-based pornographic viewing, in addition to other supportive structure in the filming and shooting of pornography, such as costuming, catering, lighting, water, heat, and buildings. Once it is available for purchase by the medical industry, there are additional carbon emissions from purchasing and distributing materials to fertility clinics. Moreover, additional technological purchases so one can view pornography—a television player, internet access, and private "'masturbatoriums,' small rooms with erotic pictures on the walls and flat-screen televisions for watching pornographic movies,"[158] all use resources. None of these supports healthcare; they are simply preferences for how to obtain sperm. In 2010, about one-third of fertility centers in the UK provided pornography to clients, spending an estimated £700 per year.[159] However, some clinics "spent more than £7,000 of public money on a media suite and DVD unit" that allowed men to view pornography in a high-tech environment.[160]

Furthermore, pornographic purchases and viewing in fertility clinics are not one-time carbon expenses, as men undergoing sperm testing and men donating sperm for insemination regularly use fertility clinics and clinically necessary services. Indeed, in order to ensure quality and quantity, most sperm donors sign a contract agreeing to make "donations" every week for 12 months,[161] while men being tested for sperm motility and mobility will have follow-up testing done after, for instance, fertility drugs are given.

For the purpose of sustainable healthcare, pornography is objectionable as a non-medically necessary carbon expenditure. To be sure, there are other ethical concerns with pornography from a social perspective. Notably, Andrea Dworkin[162] and other feminists "use the word violence to describe pornography that would normally be classified as nonviolent . . . because they define as violent the power relation that they see inscribed in the sex acts pornography represents."[163] These objections to pornography are compounded when a government uses taxpayers' money to purchase and supply explicit materials.

MR and the healthcare industry must reduce its carbon emissions. The use of pornography as an "aid" for fertility testing is not clinically indicated, nor is it a diagnostic tool. As such, it may be excluded from the current high-impact offerings of MR when testing is done for clinical infertility and, by extension, sperm donation. Subsidized MR must eliminate that which does not support the goals of medicine and the purposes of healthcare insurance by divesting from pornography.

Singleton Births

Twins conceived using in-vitro fertilization have longer birth admissions to NICUs in their first year of life. These infants are also 60% more likely to be admitted to a NICU and have higher incidents of hospital admission later in life.[164] In these cases, NICUs become one of the final stages of medicalized reproduction and add to the environmental burden of MR. Hansen et al. frankly conclude, "[E]stimations of the cost of an ART twin delivery should include the extra 4 days on average spent in hospital at birth, the almost 4-fold increased risk of admission to a NICU and the increased risk of hospital admission in the first three years of life."[165] Thus, singleton births—either through single embryo transfer or through selective reduction—ought to be an inclusionary criterion for subsidized MR, when offered.

Indeed, since the 2010s there has been increased awareness of the disadvantage of twin pregnancies and clinical advocacy for singleton pregnancies primarily for reasons of health and cost.[166] Both are connected with environmental resource use. Following the carbon-intensive steps of MR prior to birth, including emissions from gamete retrieval, storage, testing, and fertilization, the resources used for twin and higher-order multiples include care of the mother and care of the infants. The health of the mother is jeopardized when she carries more than one fetus, which risks excess emissions from monitoring and control of high-risk pregnancy and high-risk birth.

164   ENVIRONMENTAL ETHICS AND MEDICAL REPRODUCTION

Despite the preference for singleton MR pregnancies, there is resistance by singles and couples using MR, for several reasons: the chances of pregnancy from MR are already low, there may be limited access to MR through subsidized health insurance, and many reproductive projects include desire for more than one child, particularly within a specific timeframe. The emissions from care of the premature infants, not only during gestation but also after birth and later in life, are also significant.

The obvious resource burden of birthing two or more infants, instead of one at a time, should not be overlooked. Two new lives will take more basic natural resources, such as food, clothing, and healthcare resources, than one new life born in the same place. Surely, some resources can be utilized without additional need for expansion for each child—such as living in one big house. Yet, as the twins grow and eventually reach adulthood, the resources used, like housing, will no longer be split with a new family unit. Moreover, these children usually go on to reproduce, thus absorbing more resources and emitting more carbon across a lifetime. This is doubled for the average twin pregnancy. Of course, an MR infant could die in childhood, or may not reproduce, or may make lower-carbon decisions. Even then, the resources for the medicalization of reproduction will have been expended.

Singleton births are better for the mother and the infant. Other stakeholders have a vested interest in limiting premature delivery from twins and higher-order multiples, as well. These include economic payers of MR—whether it is a health insurance company or a hospital that is financially responsible for care of infants—policyholders of healthcare insurance, and nations which care for the sick. Some subsidized MR policies are trying to address this concern.[167] However, multiple embryo transfer and multiple gestations remain within the scope of patient choice that doctors are hesitant to remove, thus creating unnecessary carbon emissions. Singleton pregnancies are clinically preferable and can conserve carbon emissions. If subsidized healthcare covers artificial fertilization, only one embryo ought to be transferred or one fetus gestated at a time.

Summary

Ethicists, healthcare workers, policymakers, and civil servants must create policies that reduce medical carbon emissions. Yet, it is not only the ethical responsibility of those who oversee healthcare resources to minimize carbon emissions from MR. Singles and couples have a responsibility to only use clinically necessary healthcare, as "attempts to institutionalize procreation as [a] natural right divest the person procreating of moral responsibility, so that anything a man or woman does to reproduce is treated as an instinctive response beyond the control of human will and human relations."[168] But those considering MR as part of a reproductive project—as well as a way to address clinical infertility—are obligated, as is every other person who uses healthcare or reproduces, to consider the carbon impact.

The under-regulated MR business can no longer be endorsed and the medical industry ought not operate in an environmental vacuum. Temporarily or permanently restricting all forms of medical reproduction—subsidized and unsubsidized—is the most environmentally sensible path, but this is highly unlikely even though global climate is changing at an unsustainable pace. While all major scientific organizations warn that human resource consumption must be attenuated,[169] MR proceeds with little regard for sustainability. Although it is neither as dramatic nor as publicized, climate change is a public health threat. Thus, governments and healthcare providers are well within their ethical obligations in limiting subsidized MR at this time of environmental urgency. By using the medical industry, MR demands resource use without clinical connection. Thus, there is ample room to object to subsidized coverage and overhaul healthcare insurance policies to fit the goals of medicine and the imperative of environmental ethics.

8

Rights and the Ethics of Sex and Procreation

Prior to widespread, effective, and decriminalized use of contraception,[1] procreative ethics were based in religion. In Judaism, there is the *mitzvah* (command) to reproduce and hence to enter into a sexually active opposite-sex marriage.[2] In Christianity, celibacy is the standard, both from the example of Jesus but also from the scriptures, where St. Paul endorses singleness without sex and hence being non-reproductive.[3] It was only centuries after Christ when marriage and procreation were legitimized to compensate for the failure of celibacy.[4] Islamic tradition, much like Judaism, is bound to reproduction.[5] Prior to secularization, Western religions advanced procreation not necessarily as a good itself, but tacitly due to the unacceptability of contraception,[6] abortion, and infanticide.[7] As sexual intercourse and procreation were intertwined, the ethics of reproduction have historically hinged on the ethics of sexual intercourse, which placed intercourse within marriage and the obligations to care for children that are born in the family.[8]

Modern, secular procreative ethics has divorced sexual intercourse from reproductive ethics due to the advent of effective, available contraception. Since sexual intercourse need not lead to procreation, the fields of sexual ethics and procreative ethics have distinct trajectories, with intersections at the point of reproductive sexuality. The birth control revolution provided the options of limiting the number of children born and of being childfree. With these options, procreation morphed from an inevitability to something within one's control and children moved from being an obligation that must be accepted to being a managed commodity. As such, procreation became a matter of applied—and not merely theoretical—ethics.

Environmental Ethics and Medical Reproduction. Cristina Richie, Oxford University Press.
© Oxford University Press 2024. DOI: 10.1093/oso/9780197745182.003.0009

Ethical Arguments against Procreation

Historically, both literature and philosophy are replete with ethical arguments against procreation. Some leitmotifs have included the tragedy of life and therefore the wrong done to the new person being born. Both ancient philosophers like Petrarch, who says that "a thousand pleasures are not worth one pain,"[9] and existential philosophers like Friedrich Nietzsche[10] underscored the intrinsic wrong of procreation. The Albigensians—a religious sect in the 12th and 13th centuries, condemned procreation for similar reasons.[11] Major religious figures, like the Catholic Pope Innocent III[12] and the Muslim Ibrahim ibn Adham,[13] highlighted the tragedy of birth for the newborn. These arguments have focused on the wrongfulness of life, which have reemerged in multiple recent lawsuits.[14]

Ethical arguments against procreation have also had some loose connections to environmental ethics in the past two centuries, emerging in full force in the past half-century. For instance, social movements in the 19th century which highlighted the effects of pollution on communities or the environmental hazards of certain jobs—such as chimney sweep and coal miner—examined the environmental effects on the health of those in lower classes jobs. However, the effects of the environment on humans were rarely invoked as a reason against having children, particularly given the social acceptability of procreation and the biological inevitability of conception. Thus, it would be anachronistic to posit these early environmental ethics as a form of sexual ethics. Ethical literature which discussed population growth, like Thomas Malthus's *An Essay on the Principle of Population*[15] and Margaret Sanger's "Too Many People,"[16] were concerned with the environmental impacts of unchecked reproduction at the local and global level, respectively, but were not against all procreation. The recent environmental movement has taken a more individualistic approach to reproduction and focused on two areas: first, the harms of new people on the environment and, second, the ethics of bringing a child into a world that is ecologically damaged.

The GINK movement (Green Inclinations, No Kids),[17] and those within it, cite both the impact on the natural environment and the irresponsibility of bringing a child into a toxic world as reasons not to procreate. Public health is well situated to comment on the latter. However, biomedical ethics more broadly ignores the responsibility to the child themselves.

Within a decade of the first baby born from IVF, the Ethics Committee of the American Fertility Society (ECAFS) issued a statement on assisted reproduction and population growth. Their 1986 report opined, "[T]he infertile couple should not be held responsible for the population problems of the world."[18] Even if this statement was ethically solid then, today it is irrelevant for several reasons. First, at the time, the world population was around 5 billion people. Thirty-five years later population has grown to over 7.5 billion.[19] Second, it is not only the infertile who use IVF; fertile people use it as well. Third, the ECAFS did not consider the resource use of procreation, only the arithmetic impact on population numbers. Fourth, data on carbon emissions—both of healthcare and of individuals—was under-available then; now it is widely publicized and indicates overuse of resources. Fifth, at the time, the atmospheric concentration of carbon dioxide was at a safe level; that is not the case anymore.[20]

In addition to the environmental movement, numerous other stakeholders have forwarded arguments against procreation in the modern era. Some feminists have illuminated the toxic institution of motherhood and petitioned women to drop out of the motherhood race.[21] Black liberationists have highlighted the political tactic of refusing to reproduce as a response to a racist society.[22] A new generation of conservative Christians who wish to revive the original biblical teachings on celibacy have appeared.[23] Queer people—much like anti-natalist Christians—have rejected procreation as what Lee Edelman terms "the prop of secular religion."[24]

Concretely, ethical arguments against procreation encourage simple steps to avoid reproduction. Negative actions (actions which take no extra initiative) include abstaining from procreative sex by engaging in celibacy, self-satisfaction, opposite-sex intercourse outside of fertile periods, and same-sex intercourse. Positive actions (actions which take extra initiative) would include use of contraception or abortion for opposite-sex couples who are having sexual intercourse during fertile times.

Ethical Arguments in Favor of Procreation

Instead of the pre-modern view of unlimited procreation as a benefit to family life—mostly for reasons of industry—in recent centuries, limited procreation has become a personal good, if not a social obligation. From Thomas Malthus[25] to the Chinese government,[26] to the Catholic Church,[27] arguments against having an unlimited number of children have appeared as means toward better prosperity, a more stable life, or even a religious

RIGHTS AND THE ETHICS OF SEX AND PROCREATION   169

obligation. With advances in biomedicine and genetic technology, a certain type of Social Darwinism has also appeared in favor of engineering a better society through selective or limited procreation.[28]

Historically, arguments in favor of procreation deem a certain level of reproduction—rather than too much or too little—as desirable. Economists have pointed to the need for continual population growth to sustain countries[29] and stimulate the economy with new consumers.[30] Children are justified because they will effect positive economic conditions for capitalistic systems. Closely tied to economics is national security. Before the modern era "the wealth of the nation and the adequacy of its military preparedness depended completely on the quantity of her people."[31] The practice of abortion and infanticide "deprive the nation of potential soldiers and farm workers" and was a paramount consideration in the morality of contraception. If children belong to the state then the fetus has value as a "potential producer and soldier."[32] It has therefore in the interest of the state to limit access to contraception or endorse procreation through propaganda[33] or financial incentives.[34]

Other arguments in favor of procreation are also jingoistic. Aging populations require caregivers, and some countries have argued that a replacement generation[35] or, in their absence, robots[36] ought to fulfill the ethical obligation to care for the elderly.[37] As migrant caregivers are undesirable, the "moral obligation" to procreate[38] remains. However, the implementation of pronatalist policies, which actually result in procreation, are morally problematic and incredibly difficult to orchestrate without violating human rights.[39] Thus, governmental and national influence on reproductive ethics has fallen into disfavor, with the choice of the couple taking the supreme place in reproductive ethics.

Aside from religion and nationalism, ethical arguments for parenthood remain specious. For insurance, the argument that one should adopt rather than procreate is prevalent, but this is an unfounded dichotomy: people can do both.[40] Other aspects of parental ethics, such as the value of birthing disabled children, offer debates on both sides.[41] Some theologians appeal to the morally transformative effect of having children as a moral good.[42] While there may be a great deal of emotion attached to having biological children, as well as epistemic ignorance which fails to evaluate widely accepted social practices like reproduction,[43] there are few arguments put forth in favor of producing biological children as an ethical goal in itself, that is, aside from its incidental moral goods.

Rights and Procreation

Indeed, most ethical arguments in favor of procreation hinge on the tacit assumption that procreation should be limited in, but not eliminated from, adult life. Children are seen as a conditional good. Many propositions that offer a reason for having children are descriptive rather than prescriptive. People cite love, fulfillment, and a sense of genetic kinship as reasons they wanted to—or did—have biological children.[44] These statements are not intended to compel others to have children, although they certainly feed into pro-natalist societies which are buttressed by myopic interpretations of religion, peer pressure, and anti–birth control healthcare practices.[45] Simply, most people do not believe that they need an *ethical* reason to procreate. Since procreation is so widespread, critical ethical assessment on an individual level is underdeveloped. Arguments advancing the elimination of procreation are often responded to with immediate rejection since reproduction is viewed as a discretionary morally neutral choice, if it is reflected on at all. Globally, in 2012, "eighty-five million pregnancies, representing 40 percent of all pregnancies, were unintended. Of these, 50 percent ended in abortion, 13 percent ended in miscarriage, and 38 percent resulted in an unplanned birth."[46]

Given that procreation is fraught with ethical concerns and is a biological inevitability, reproductive intercourse requires a defense. Yet, there is not a compelling ethical rationale for having biological children—while there are numerous ethical frameworks which render procreation unethical.[47] Thus, defending procreation moves from ethics to entitlement, specifically that one has the right to reproduce. Concretely, ethical arguments for procreation rely on a laissez-faire attitude, often invoking the language of rights to justify reproductive choices. Yet the concept of rights is nuanced and must be interrogated as a concept before evaluating the "right" to reproduce.

The Scope of Human Rights

Conceptually, the idea of human rights is relatively new. In 1948, following World War II and the Nuremburg trials, member states in the United Nations signed the *Universal Declaration of Human Rights*.[48] Prior to this, rights such as "life, liberty, and happiness," were bourgeois constructions inaccessible to the masses. Today, rights language proliferates in a variety of settings, often

RIGHTS AND THE ETHICS OF SEX AND PROCREATION   171

oriented toward women, LGBT communities, racial minorities, and even animals.[49] The readily familiar language of human rights, therefore, allows a large number of people to assent to, protect, and implement the manifestation of rights. Given its widespread usage and historical importance, human rights may be "the most successful universal moral project"[50] of the modern era. However, a thin conception of rights hinders accurate evaluation of many social practices which are swept under the rug of rights.

Rights are neither a handout nor a claim that can be made without context. Meghan Clark summarizes the concept of rights by stating, "[A] right begins with a person who is bearer of the right (subject) and includes a particular substance (object) that is claimed against another individual or group who has a correlative duty to respect this right."[51] She describes three components. First is the agent who can claim a right. The modern, Western understanding of an agent entitled to rights is a *Homo sapiens* outside the womb. Once born, humans become the subject, or the bearer of the right.

Second is the substance or object—what the agent is claiming a right to. Some purported rights are intangible, such as happiness. Other rights are physical, such as food and shelter. However, physical objects are limited by availability. In the case of food and non-renewable energy, there is only a set amount in the world that ought to be distributed equitably. John Locke argued that natural goods must be used in "keeping within the bounds, set by reason," namely "1. how much one can use before it spoils and 2. whatever one has mixed their own labor with, in order to claim it as property."[52] Significantly, this means that one should not take more than what one needs, because it may violate the rights of others. Thus, in a society, the rights of the person, their obligations to other rights-bearers, and the preservation of natural goods that sustain everyone vacillate, ideally creating an equilibrium where all people can thrive.

Third, after the object of the right is clarified, the nature of the claim must be adjudicated. Clark says that once a subject makes a claim to a right there is a "correlative duty to respect this right."[53] The manifestation of respect for a right depends on what type of right is being claimed. Rights may be negative or positive. A "negative" right is one that should not be interfered with. A "positive" right is one that requires assistance and demands that others (a person or government) facilitate the acquisition of this right.[54] Negative rights have a stronger moral claim because they are easier to respect. For instance, the right to free speech is upheld by institutions and organizations abstaining from restrictions. Positive rights are more difficult to claim since

172 ENVIRONMENTAL ETHICS AND MEDICAL REPRODUCTION

they require action. Creating outlets for free speech, such as news sources, requires resources that may not be available or may be costly to create. A number of positive rights—such as food, clean water, medicine, shelter, and safety—have solid ethical grounds and can be easily claimed as legitimate. However, other positive rights are more difficult to claim.

Contested Rights

While negative rights are generally uncontested, as the object of the claim may be obtained without demands on other moral agents, positive rights may be objected to for a number of reasons. For instance, a claim to something trivial, like federally funded cosmetics[55] or access to certain foods,[56] undermines the significance of rights language and can be challenged on two bases. The first challenge is that the object is not a right, and the second challenge is that the government ought not be obligated to provide this object. This claim to a positive right may be reframed to be more widely accepted as a right, such as "I have a right to purchase cosmetics if they are available" or "The government ought to provide food for people." But even in these cases, the right is not absolute.

Human rights necessarily entail corresponding duties or responsibilities of people who exercise their rights. This prevents individuals from making unilateral demands to entitlements that could jeopardize the rights of others. James Nash explains that "rights and responsibilities are not commensurate . . . but they are correlative: strict responsibilities to other beings exist because the others have just claims."[57] If my purchase of cosmetics hinges on unfair working conditions, or tortures sentient animals, or produces so much carbon as to threaten the health of others on the planet, then the claim to that object as a right must be reevaluated. Human rights, therefore, demonstrate give and take and must benefit the individual moral agent without neglecting the rights of others.

Moreover, a "right" might also be contested on the basis that it is too difficult to provide, for example, the "right to good health," where health is defined as "complete physical, social and mental well being, and not merely the absence of disease or infirmity,"[58] could not be orchestrated for every person. This definition may be an aspirational ideal, but it is not a right, since it cannot be guaranteed. The object of the right—in this case health—could be reframed as "Every person has the right to pursue health." This could be

RIGHTS AND THE ETHICS OF SEX AND PROCREATION   173

easily assented to, since it is a negative right that does not make a claim on another. Respecting this right would simply rely on non-interference.

Finally, rights can exist without being used. The right to own a gun or the right to vote does not compel one to engage in these activities. While the former may be supported by law and the latter only reaches the level of civic duty, neither are compulsory. Rights can also be temporarily abdicated as a result of actions, for instance as part of social rehabilitation during a prison term. Individual rights may also be suspended for the benefit of the common good. The COVID-19 pandemic highlighted this in a concrete way as basic rights to assemble, freedom of movement, and choice of clothing (i.e., compulsory masks) were removed from individuals in both private and public spheres.

Since society is the context for all of human life—including rights claims—it must be the arena in which human rights take shape and are employed. Human rights are situated in a larger community where rights become intelligible only in the company of others. As the essence of the human community is humans themselves, the manner in which humans conduct their lives is also a point of discussion.

Reproductive Rights

In the modern era, with the possibility of controlling pregnancy and the global acceptance of human rights, reproductive rights have centered on the duty of non-interference with biological reproduction and are underpinned by the sentiment that reproduction is generally desirable. "Liberal societies typically insist that we should respect people's (notably women's) reproductive freedom. . . . This right implies that individuals themselves get to decide whether, when and with whom to have a child through natural means."[59] Thus, the basic claim of the reproductive rights movement is that fertility should not be eliminated unless it is desired by the fertile person. Similarly, the term "reproductive freedom" accounts for both the desirability of procreation and also the desire that many people have in limiting or avoiding biological children. Both reproductive rights and reproductive freedom center on access to abortion and contraception, although one can avoid reproduction without use of medical intervention. As with other rights, reproductive rights may be claimed on negative or positive grounds.

174   ENVIRONMENTAL ETHICS AND MEDICAL REPRODUCTION

The negative right to reproduce is that of non-interference. There are two sub-rights which may be argued. First, that contraception or abortion should not be imposed on a person—this is the right to reproduce naturally. Second, that individuals should not be hindered from accessing contraception or abortion—this is the right not to reproduce. Both depend on medical inventions. In contrast, and harder to defend, is the positive right to reproduction, which states that biological reproduction ought to be facilitated by healthcare—this is the right to reproduce through medical means. This right also depends on medical developments, such as MR. The type of reproductive right being claimed—either negative or positive—is an important part of sexual, social, and medical ethics.

Negative Reproductive Rights: Non-interference with Natural Procreation

The negative right to reproduction emerges from a historical context which was only made possible through the development of artificial contraception and sterilization. Once developed, medical interference in the lives of socially or genetically "undesirable" individuals manifested in national eugenics programs. While the most notorious eugenics movement was the genocide and forced abortions and sterilizations in Nazi Germany, forced sterilizations have been a worldwide stain. These include programs of sterilization of indigenous women in Canada,[60] women with HIV in Latin America[61] and Africa,[62] women in Europe[63] and Asia,[64] women and girls with disabilities in Australia[65] and the United States.[66] Men have also been subjected to compulsory sterilization, but on a smaller scale. This includes men in India[67] and males who are transgender (transwomen).[68] The historical "treatment" of male homosexuality through chemical castration would have blocked reproduction, but as reproduction would have been indicative of "successful" treatment (i.e., heterosexual sex), that was not the intention of the drugs.[69] The drugs were rather to reorient the desire toward heterosexual attraction, regardless of reproduction.

Contraceptive eugenics violated both human rights and the negative right to reproduce. Restitution has been slow in coming, but it has been recognized internationally after the end of World War II and the signing of the UN *Declaration of Human Rights*. Individual nations have also recognized the right to bodily autonomy and non-interference in procreation, and the

US Supreme Court argued "that the right to procreate was fundamental, requiring a compelling state interest to justify interfering with it."[70] Despite this, forced sterilizations are still reported in the United States as recently as 2020.[71]

The negative right to reproduction is conditional. It assumes that fertility is present as a necessary, but not sufficient, condition of reproduction. A child who has not yet reached sexual maturity cannot claim that they have a right to reproduce. They may have a right in the future, but not until then.[72] If society believes that reproduction is a negative right, that only entitles one to non-interference. Making the argument that negative reproductive rights include access to contraception and, possibly, abortion requires another step. Many countries do recognize that the negative right to reproduction includes both the freedom to reproduce and the freedom to not reproduce. The latter has backing from law, healthcare, and national policy.

Negative Reproductive Rights: Access to Contraception and Subsidized Health

Internationally, contraception is widely available, decriminalized, and, in some cases, free to citizens. The manifestation of this right has evolved with the landscape of medical developments, healthcare insurance, and changing social norms. In the United States, for instance, the 1965 case *Griswold v. Connecticut* concluded that the Constitution protected a right to privacy, which included the use of contraception.[73] *Eisenstadt v. Baird* (1972) declared that unmarried people had the right to possess contraception on the same basis as married couples.[74] One year later the US Supreme Court decriminalized abortion and gave women the right not to be pregnant in *Roe v. Wade* (1973).[75] In a conjunctive suit of the same year, *Doe v. Bolton* asserted that a state may not unduly burden a woman's fundamental right to abortion by "prohibiting or substantially limiting access to the means of effectuating her decision."[76] The Voluntary Sterilization Act of 1974 reiterated both men's and women's right to avoid parenthood, pregnancy, fertilization, and conception by permitting single and married women and men of legal age to access contraceptive sterilization.[77]

This legal recognition of the right not to be pregnant can be regarded as a negative right—non-interference with procurement of unsubsidized healthcare services—or a positive right, which might facilitate access to contraception and abortion either through establishing family planning clinics or financial subsidization. Financial subsidization of contraception is a hallmark of the modern state. For instance, the US Affordable Care Act (ACA) of 2010 mandated that employers "offer insurance coverage of certain 'essential' health benefits," including coverage of "preventative services" and Food and Drug Administration–approved contraception (but not abortion).[78] Of course, many healthcare insurance policies in the US had been covering contraception and abortion prior to 2010.

Domestically and internationally, there is broad social assent that women have a compelling interest not to be pregnant due to medical, social, economic, and personal reasons.[79] Access to contraception thus follows from the negative right to be free from pregnancy and the recognition that prevention of pregnancy is a medical need. Medically, contraception is a form of preventive medicine and is effective in preventing maternal mortality[80] and morbidity, as well as domestic violence,[81] homicides,[82] suicides,[83] and accidental death associated with pregnancy.[84] As a medical need it is appropriately covered under healthcare, particularly as a majority of people use it to limit procreating,[85] often for the majority of their adult life.[86] In addition to contraception being widely used,[87] subsidized contraception is further supported by the relative inexpensive production of contraception[88] (especially when compared to pregnancy care),[89] the wide availability of various methods which are easy to disseminate,[90] and the high clinical efficacy when used correctly.[91]

Strikingly, the medical, economic, and social factors in support of negative reproductive rights are absent in arguments for positive reproductive rights. Moreover, if reproduction is a positive right, it is more difficult to argue as it makes a claim not only for an object (contraception) but also for a person or their genetic material.

Positive Reproductive Rights

Rights language has evolved with technology. Just as it was difficult to make an intelligible claim to the negative right to procreation before birth control, it was difficult to make an intelligible claim to a positive right to procreation without artificial reproductive technologies. To be sure, both claims are related to sexual intercourse: the former claim included the right to avoid sex and the latter the right to sex.

RIGHTS AND THE ETHICS OF SEX AND PROCREATION   177

Opining that there is a right to sexual interactions is particularly unethical. In some cases, it has been thought that men (specifically) ought to have access to women (specifically) for sexual release, perhaps not as a right, but as a basic need.[92] This claim would be made on the basis of sexism and stereotypes of male sexuality, only in contexts where women are sex objects. Perhaps the claim could be broadened to be a human need, along with a conjunctive notion, like "capabilities." For instance, Martha Nussbaum claims that "having opportunities for sexual satisfaction" is a basic capability related to embodiment[93] which should be supported somehow. While not as strong as a right, even the capability is morally suspect as it would demand social supports—such as supplying a spouse or sexual partner. Since this would violate the rights of other humans—although certainly someone may elect to do this, either through prostitution or a matchmaking service—it is not a common claim. Similarly, the claim or right to positive reproduction might hinge on either a component of entitlement—to a fertile sexual partner, their gametes, and reproductive technologies—or a component of non-interference in obtaining these objects. Since sexual intercourse is no longer a requirement of biological reproduction and infertility no longer prevents one from reproducing, the alleged positive right to reproduce is not only a matter of sexual ethics, but also one of medical ethics.

However, in the words of Jurgen De Wispelaere and Daniel Weinstock, claiming a right to reproductive technologies "does not necessarily follow from endorsing the right to reproductive freedom more generally. To the extent that the freedom to reproduce (naturally) is typically grounded in principles of bodily integrity, a state that refuses to establish ART facilities may not be interfering with a person's reproductive freedom in a strict sense. Such a person is free to do as she pleases with her body."[94] For this reason, interference in obtaining reproductive technologies by single women,[95] unmarried heterosexual couples,[96] homosexual couples[97] and transgender individuals[98] has been seen as violating the positive right to reproduce. However, these debates did not focus on the medical morality of such access—such as clinical necessity or financial subsidization—but rather the social acceptability of single, gay, or transgender parents.[99] At present, the only compelling reasons to deny access to MR in most Western countries are the health of the mother,[100] the possibility for success,[101] or the best interests of the child.[102] Thus, a person seeking unsubsidized MR would not be impeded simply because of their lifestyle.

178   ENVIRONMENTAL ETHICS AND MEDICAL REPRODUCTION

However, the positive right to reproduction with reproductive technologies hinges on the technology being available and an infrastructure of technological devices, distribution, clinics, and clinicians to provide the treatment.[103] Since positive human rights are more difficult to claim when they are connected to economics or human services, Jurgen De Wispelaere and Daniel Weinstock maintain that "while the state is wrong to interfere with individuals seeking ART (or professionals offering ART), no strict requirement to subsidize such services exists."[104] Establishing MR facilities— with attendant cryopreservation units and aftercare assistance—would be an insurmountable task in many countries; thus the argument that there is a positive right to reproduction is very difficult to make.[105]

While the inability to produce an object that a right-bearer has a claim to may not necessarily negate the right itself (for instance, there is still a human right to food even in a famine), it does call into question under which circumstances it could correctly be called a right.[106] For this reason, Martha Nussbaum writes, "if A has a right to S, then does this mean that there is always someone who has a duty to provide S, and how shall we decide who that someone is?"[107] One answer to this question is that the positive right to reproduce ought to be provided through medical assistance, and if that assistance is too expensive, then it ought to be subsidized. This requires an additional argument.

Positive Reproductive Rights: Reproductive Technologies and Subsidized Healthcare

The claim to subsidized reproductive technologies may rest on at least two different entitlements or rights. The first would be a right to medical care on the basis of an infertility diagnosis and the second would be the right to create a child in the way an adult sees fit. As most of this book makes clear, if one wants to put forth the supposition that there is a right to subsidized access to healthcare, it must be within the domain of medical ethics, the goals of medicine, the purpose of healthcare, and clinical necessity.

Remembering that many forms of MR do not cure, treat, or prevent infertility, and even when infertility is present MR does not meet the goals of medicine or the purpose of healthcare insurance, then entitlement to MR as a form of medical care is not applicable as a positive right to subsidized reproduction.

RIGHTS AND THE ETHICS OF SEX AND PROCREATION   179

Thus, a second rhetorical move is to cede that a positive right to reproduction through subsidized healthcare (if it exists) is unrelated to clinical necessity or health. Thus, the argument becomes that a positive right to reproduction entails subsidized healthcare for some existential project or lifestyle. For instance, there may be value in creating a child in the way one sees fit,[108] such as happiness, or the pursuit of happiness, or a genetic bond, or national support.[109] Like cosmetic surgery and other elective treatments, this argument is hard to support as a positive right which also requires subsidization.

In the absence of this, the claim might be made that reproduction, like housing, education, and public transportation,[110] is not a necessity but it should be subsidized—as these other goods are. This changes the ethical analysis from one of individual ethics—biomedical ethics or sexual ethics—to social ethics, and from rights of individual people to rights of individuals in general. With these rights come obligations. Subsidized housing implies proper conduct and upkeep of the home by the tenants.[111] Education may be intrinsically valuable, or for the enrichment of society.[112] Public transportation must be used without creating unsafe or unsanitary conditions for others.

Once it is recognized that there is not a right to subsidized reproductive technologies as a matter of clinical need or treating a health condition, and that the social value of reproduction is the right being sought, the discussion becomes muddled since it is not actually the "right" to reproductive technologies that is the object, but rather the successful outcome of MR. Put another way, the positive right to reproduction is essentially the right to become a parent.

Summary

The right to subsidized MR and the right to be a parent are two discrete claims, as one can use MR without reproducing due to low success rates and one can also become a parent in a number of ways: adoption, fostering, stepparenting, and co-parenting, to name a few.[113] Ostensibly, individuals and couples seek MR primarily because they want a biological child, arguing "that intimate parental relations represent the core interest motivating a right to ART, for instance by insisting that there is something special about the biological connection between parent and child."[114] However, in a number of cases, the MR child may not be genetically related to either or both parents. When using donor sperm, eggs, or embryos and in the case of three-person IVF the child being created is not of one's own lineage. This begs the question of advantage in using MR over parenting without procreation.

Even then, the right to be a parent, when framed as a positive entitlement, is a tremendous instrumentalization of another human being, as the correlative object of the desire—a child—is not an object but a person. As such, no country to my knowledge regards parenthood as a positive right, although once one becomes a parent there are a number of associated duties. Indeed, scores of laws and regulations attempt to ensure the well-being of children who are adopted or fostered,[115] thus thwarting free access to children. While biological parenthood is defended as a negative right, it follows from the right to do as one wishes with one's body, that is, have procreative intercourse, not on the basis of the child as object.

Procreative ethics needs to move beyond parenthood as a stand-alone right and examine other, relevant rights. These include the right to a clean planet, justice, and equality. Rights also entail obligations, namely the obligation that individuals have to reduce their carbon impact and engage in ethical parenting, when applicable. As it stands, MR is indeed seen as just another means to acquire children. As both an elective choice, outside of rights claims, and as a parenting preference, MR is then subject to the standards of sexual, biomedical, and environmental ethics.

9

Supporting Childwishes

Despite the detrimental effects of climate change on the environment and human health, there has been little effective progress in recognizing that biological reproduction is—in many countries—antithetical to sustainability. When this fact is recognized, it is dismissed or downplayed by relevant stakeholders, including governments, potential parents, and children themselves. Sometimes solutions to the environmental problem, as it is related to procreation, are proposed: couples limiting the number of children they have[1] or playing a more active role in climate change mitigation.[2] On the most sophisticated level of parental ethics, partners assess the current ecological climate and evaluate if it is the most ideal time to have children. If they determine that it is ethical and desirable to have children, they plan and prepare accordingly.[3] Beyond this, there is the occasional call for a childfree life.[4] These appeals rely on the goodwill and moral sensitivity of individuals, but are neither enforceable nor enforced.

Of course, limiting or reducing population is only one part of the environmental solution, with resource reduction and carbon limitation being the other. Reducing population may not ensure a minimally dignified existence if earth cannot produce enough resources or the climate continues to change. Moreover, a world in which population is lowered so that the standard of living could be satisfactory may not account for the other externalities of resource use which threatens the biodiversity, habitats, and ecosystems of other creatures on earth.[5] Reducing consumption in all forms is essential to survival of the planet and the creatures that inhabit it. This is the environmental challenge facing all humans, with urgent relevance for those who feel inclined to have children.

To be sure, the desire for children, or reproduction, is not pure and therefore is not a matter of balancing one good—a sustainable planet—with another. Reproduction is ethically dubious and, as Christine E. Gudorf notes, "the very language we use to describe many of the reasons for having children are revealing, to say little of respect for the dignity and identity of the child him/herself: to insure our mortality, to succeed more than I did; to be

Environmental Ethics and Medical Reproduction. Cristina Richie, Oxford University Press.
© Oxford University Press 2024. DOI: 10.1093/oso/9780197745182.003.0010

182   ENVIRONMENTAL ETHICS AND MEDICAL REPRODUCTION

the ___ I never got to be; for company and security in our old age; to see my-self in another person; to have someone who will love me; to have someone I can pour my love out on; to be a real woman (man)."[6] Even so, moral culpa-bility for having children is on a scale, like other evaluative forms of ethics, from unintended to intentional.[7] In this way, the "planned pregnancy" is more environmentally objectionable than the unplanned pregnancy, and the medically assisted pregnancy even more objectionable than the planned, natural pregnancy. Within this latter bracket, those who are fertile using MR are more responsible for environmental waste than those who are infertile. Since successful MR "implies the creation of a new person, which entails a higher degree of responsibility on the part of those involved because of the ability to cause extensive harm"[8]—not only environmental harm, but also harm to the child who is brought into this deteriorating planet, and a world of war, pandemics, ubiquitous racism and structural sexism—any defense of MR must be very strong indeed.

As the manifold reasons to avoid motherhood,[9] fatherhood,[10] preg-nancy,[11] and procreation[12] have been detailed elsewhere, it shall be expe-dient to leave these arguments aside and develop places of consensus within parenting ethics which support adults who wish to be parents while also acknowledging the larger supportive structures necessary to enable sustain-able parenthood. While this approach neither addresses the core objections to reproduction, whereby "the offspring as a particular child is not treated as an end in himself or herself, but as the means to a goal (a fulfilling parenting experience),"[13] the discussion ought to be a propaedeutic for those consid-ering children. The relevance for other stakeholders is broadly social, with sector-specific attention to the healthcare system, adults considering chil-dren, and places of business that employ parents.

Ultimately, non-procreative parenting and non-medical forms of repro-duction must be viable options for adults. Reproductive decisions affect not only the individual parent and the planet, but indeed the children who are born. Anca Gheaus argues that "no generation is morally permitted to procreate at a rate so high that at least some members of the next genera-tion will have to waive their right to parent on pain of endangering envi-ronmental sustainability."[14] Arguably, the human collective is past this point and has been for some time.[15] Sustainability is indeed endangered and the "freedom" to reproduce has been called into question many times over the past 150 years.[16] As such, the desire for parenthood and the reality that both biological and medically intensive reproduction is an egregious burden on the already over-taxed ecosystem must default toward corporate survival rather than individual preference. Through a two-fold approach to removing medical intervention in biological reproduction and advocating for non-biological parenting, sustainability can be prioritized. Before this can occur, recognition of the deeply embedded social and psychological reasons for reproduction must be addressed.

Social and Psychological Aspects of Reproduction

Procreation and the pursuit of medically assisted reproduction are not simply biological phenomena. Neither are they true options in that there are significant social and psychological reasons for reproduction which are often not counterbalanced by the economic and environmental reasons for abstaining from reproduction. Opening the space for intellectually honest conversations about reproductive ethics will encourage a societal move toward carbon reduction, as the desire for children—and pursuit thereof—are seen as morally complex. Both as social capital and as a palliative to anxiety over individual mortality, reproduction must be assessed frankly, thus creating true and concerted options in parenting choices by adults.

Children as Social Capital

Procreation is a synecdoche for conformity to a great number of social norms and expectations, forced and reinforced through a variety of subtle and overt religious, economic, and political tactics.[17] These tactics are internalized and externalized through ubiquitous societal cues.[18] Some of the associated norms of procreation are heterosexuality, sexual activity, long-term pairing, economic stability, and permanent residency. In short, the aspiration of procreation is indicated by a certain type of "maturity," the absence of which may disrupt expectations in a number of different social areas.

For instance, in the United States and other traditional countries, one of the first questions broached in a new social setting—after name and vocation—is marital status and children. This script is rehearsed at family reunions, at work, and in places of worship. Amy Laura Hall notes that "in American mainline Protestantism this culturally loaded conception of

184   ENVIRONMENTAL ETHICS AND MEDICAL REPRODUCTION

kinship subtly distinguished *us* from *them*. The relatively self-sufficient, middle-class, white, Protestant nuclear family of two parents and two or perhaps three aptly gender-balanced children came to be the model by which all other configurations . . . were viewed as, at best, unusual."[19] These exclusionary tactics place pressure on individuals to reproduce while also rewarding those who do so and punishing those who do not.

Reproductive expectations are reinforced by portrayals of happy families in media and advertising: the "perfect" family of one man, one woman, and two or three children (all spaced about three years apart), all white, getting into the minivan for their two-week vacation that year. Ostensibly, these manufactured fantasies about having children appeal to emotions and are underpinned by aspirational wealth. A couple must be financially stable to pay for education, housing, and vacation. By some calculations, it will take about a million dollars to raise the requisite 2.6 children to maturity, if the parents have healthy children who are generated naturally.[20]

Since pro-natalist images bombard consumers from birth, when it comes time to make a "decision" to be a parent, social pressure and expectations conspire to make procreation seem like *the* one superior, if not exclusive, life path. The drive for children is cultivated through societal expectations and benefits and reinforced through the healthcare industry, which guides patients to medicalized "solutions" for social failures, which are often a proxy for conformity to approved social scripts, namely those of production, capitalism, and heterosexuality. MR is not merely a medical tool; it is a statement about the value of certain lifestyles above others.

Children as Immortality

Social aspects of procreation go beyond pronatalism. Bonnie Miller-McLemore "argues that the generative impulse is rooted, among other places, in the human developmental need to come to terms with death and finitude."[21] Humans attempt to make meaning of our own mortality through extending biological lineage. That is, the desire for procreation is often a misplaced desire for immortality.

Sexual intercourse and death are related in a number of ways that are beyond the scope of this book. Relevant here is the internalization of mortality[22] and the desire, or compulsion, to ignore human finitude through means of reproduction.[23] In some ways, the inability or refusal to reproduce puts one's own mortality into sharp relief, while also, in some cases, making one feel as if one has died early since there is not an heir to continue one's lineage.[24] These very primitive reactions to something as natural as death are postponed through the use of modern medicine, including MR, but this is a double-edged sword, at best. Marco Luchetti and Giuseppe A. Marraro recount, "[H]uman beings have always been searching for immortality. Today's medicine appears to be a willing instrument in tackling this type of issue by making promises that will be hard not to break. The mythicisation of medicine and the endless expansion of its purview should be impugned with a critical mindset and a wide-ranging response capability in the cultural arena, so that the individual and society become aware of the actual and potential efficiency of health care services, without heeding the sirens of 'mythical expectations' without corollary in scientific evidence."[25] MR has consistently been one of the disappointments and over-sold promises of modern medicine. With low success rates[26] and a variety of physical,[27] financial,[28] and social[29] consequences of creating children through MR, the promise of circumventing infertility—or prolonging fertility—has led many adults to the treadmill of medical treatments that are costly,[30] painful,[31] and emotionally devastating[32] without concomitantly meeting the expectations of live birth.

The impulse to control sex and death through the medical industry has produced a tenuous veil of control that now controls the medical consumer. "While men [sic] have for ages been the masters of our reproductive capacity, the danger is now not imaginary that in an excessive technological application of science they may once again make themselves the masters of the woman's womb, see the procreation of children as a medical matter (hence 'culture') and set the tone once again"[33] for dominance over women just as sexual equality was beginning to take hold. MR children, then subsumed under the auspices of technological domination, become subjected to quality control standards. And any flaws in generation require accountability to healthcare, instead of humble acceptance that humans are neither omnipotent nor immortal. The inadvertent production of mosaic cells while using CRISPR-Cas9 in human embryos is a case in point,[34] as are the numerous lawsuits against the fertility industry for wrongful birth.[35] A number of lawsuits where women were inseminated with the wrong sperm or had the wrong embryos implanted[36] reinforce both the illusion of control over life and death and the commodification of MR, which is unsurprising since it is indeed a commodified service.

186 ENVIRONMENTAL ETHICS AND MEDICAL REPRODUCTION

As a way to purchase temporary existential relief, there are "important moral differences between the mature, considered desire to raise and even bear a child and the 'desperation' that so often passes as evidence for a desire (for a biological child)."[37] Both social and psychological factors that prompt pro-natalism have influenced the biomedical view of infertility. Thus, the anthropological discussion of infertility as a "hindrance" to reproduction has developed alongside healthcare options and perspectives on the ability to reproduce. That is, reproduction is distinctly neither a medical nor a physiological need, yet the medical industry has aggressively developed numerous ways to treat infertility, when possible, and circumvent it when treatment is not possible. Had the social and psychological aspects of reproduction not been present, the modern age would see little reason to offer a medical solution to a personal disappointment. However, the personal dissatisfaction of being unable to produce biological children has led to excessive resource use—like so many other aspects of life dissatisfaction that leads one to consume. While a personal revolution may not lead to the drastic reduction in resource use required to stabilize the planet, other tactics can. Infertility must be interrogated as both a social and a medical phenomenon, instead of exclusively the latter.

Infertility Awareness, Prevention, and Acceptance

While not all MR is used by infertile people, in some cases it is. Preventing infertility therefore has the potential to prevent reliance on some forms of MR. In some cases, this may also prevent births. MR providers prefer women to carry multiple embryos, so a person who might be inclined to only have one child, or one child at a time, often becomes the parent of multiple children if MR is successful. "Studies have shown that assisted reproductive technologies have contributed to an increase in multiple births."[38] While there have been some initiatives to modify insemination policies, trends are slow to change and multiples are still the standard for MR.[39]

Even if preventing infertility does not result in population degrowth or resource conservation after birth, preventing infertility and the reliance on MR would reduce the natural and structural resources used in the pursuit of MR, including the time, energy, and intellectual and physical labor of scientists and clinicians, as well as the governmental and healthcare expenditures on reproductive technologies. BBC News frankly reports that "IVF multiple births 'drain NHS.'[40] The environmental savings from not procuring a pregnancy through the MR industry—and the externalities of associated resource use—would be significant, particularly because of the acceleration of medical reproduction[41] and the medicalization of reproduction,[42] which over-relies on healthcare for natural functions. Thus, prevention of infertility is suggested, not to endorse biological, non-medical reproduction, but rather in an attempt to reduce the carbon of the medical industry. Public health and other social policies may attempt to, first, build awareness of infertility, second, attempt measures to prevent infertility, and third, support acceptance of infertility.

Infertility Awareness

A reframing of the concepts of infertility, procreation, and medically assisted reproduction is an *a priori* requirement of parenting ethics in a technological age. This "consciousness raising" is the first step toward awareness of infertility, not merely in the sense of being aware of the physical aspects of infertility the way one may be aware of sexual reproduction or heart disease, but rather, a critical awareness of how the language of infertility is constructed and deployed, both in healthcare and in the general vernacular.

It is not only the clinical definition of infertility that is relevant for infertility awareness, but also the social understanding of infertility.[43] Like other healthcare conditions or diseases, the public perception is different from the biological experience. The clinical diagnosis of infertility is filtered through social and print media,[44] which views it as undesirable, and reinforced through a variety of social cues, including pro-natalism,[45] consumeristic markets for motherhood,[46] and social pressure.[47] These social interpretations affect other healthcare conditions, for example, terminal diseases like cancer,[48] stigmatized conditions like being intersex,[49] natural parts of life like having arthritis,[50] or welcomed diagnostic relief like menopause.[51] Moreover, the individual's or couple's perception of a particular condition is highly inflected. While a couple who has a sister with Down syndrome might welcome a Down's infant, the couple who has never been close with a Down's person might lean toward terminating the pregnancy.[52]

The social view of infertility, or the inability to procreate naturally, is highly undesirable in most cultures, and in some societies being unable to conceive (or deliver a male child) can jeopardize one's livelihood.[53] This social view

188   ENVIRONMENTAL ETHICS AND MEDICAL REPRODUCTION

of infertility has a variety of mechanisms underpinning it, from suspicions of "deviant" (read: non-procreative) lifestyles,[54] to keeping women in traditional roles.[55] "The very description of women in the traditional family as necessarily mothers—and the long millennia that barren women have been despised or pitied—encourages women, in particular, to see children as fulfilling a basic need for women."[56] Pressure to procreate is also tied to larger social issues, including economic stimulus[57] and national defense.[58] Other social aspects of infertility include misconceptions like the naturalistic fallacy, or the idea that because procreation is natural it is also morally good.[59] There is great social pressure to reproduce, and when a woman cannot or will not, she can be unfairly targeted as a pariah.[60] Thus, "fertility and infertility alike are obvious flash points for explosive, unresolved questions about life goals, social purpose, and society's hidden influence over individuals' desires, and they are frequently made to bear the weight of all of these confusions."[61]

To this point, the social view of infertility does not necessarily correlate to an individual's or a couple's own desires for children. Certainly, many boy children are never socialized to want to be a father, given dolls to practice their fathering skills with, or encouraged to take a caregiver role with younger siblings.[62] In these cases, the thought of infertility is very far from their young minds and might not appear until they are married. On the other hand, a young girl in a conservative society who wants to be educated and have a career might see infertility, or religious celibacy, as one way to create a desirable life plan.[63] Because of this gendering of the performance of parenthood, which is socialized into young boys and girls (and intersex children, though in different ways), how an adult is "supposed" to react to the inability to become pregnant or successfully inseminate necessarily follows a script. This script hinges on the construction of desperation[64] which simultaneously justifies—and is offered as a rationale for—medical reproduction. The ability to distinguish between the social and clinical aspects of infertility must underscore any social or medical policies that attempt to prevent or treat infertility, as de-medicalization will not only support better adjusted adults, but also carbon reduction.

Infertility Prevention

Although some infertility is unavoidable, like that which results from chemotherapy,[65] other causes of infertility are preventable. When infertility is prevented and natural conception occurs, both the resources from MR use and, in many cases, the resources necessary to support multiple simultaneous births are reduced. This, of course, is only the case where women and men have access to MR. Infertility that is neither preventable nor in a population that has access to MR treatments also prevents environmental resource use. However, the latter also tends to be in places with lower levels of healthcare access, income, and infrastructure,[66] like the Global South, which points to a lower-carbon lifestyle[67] not necessarily indicative of a high quality of life. Thus, the healthcare and social system of the Global South must be improved in tandem with infertility prevention. In contrast, those in the Global North, with ample resource-intensive healthcare, will only need to focus on prevention of infertility, which is tied to a variety of factors and often related to one's lifestyle.

In high-income countries, or the Global North, "fertility is compromised by delayed childbearing, damage to reproductive organs from hormonal contraceptives and intra-uterine devices, and environmental and workplace toxins."[68] Taken in tandem with other risks of increasingly common geriatric pregnancies, such as higher rates of intellectual disabilities in children[69] and high risk of maternal mortality, it is advantageous—both medically and physically—to reproduce in one's late teens and twenties. Of course, the postponement of marriage in lieu of education or career, the use of reliable birth control, and the desire to avoid children until financially stable are conventions of the middle and upper classes[70] which lead to "infertility" when one is 30 or older. Even though declines in fertility are a predictable, expected, and natural part of aging,[71] reactionary steps—such as MR—are not often clinically necessary, or successful, thus pointing back to the responsibility of individuals to proactively take control of their fertile years. In this way, infertility prevention can take the form of public health campaigns, similar to advertisements about HIV, heart disease, and cancer.[72]

As with other diseases, in "the individualistic ideology of the medical-model health care . . . prevention rather than cure is the only rational strategy."[73] However, with infertility in particular, numerous social factors make "early" reproduction difficult or undesirable in the industrialized world. "Women's most fertile years are in their early and mid 20s, this is a time in their lives when they often wish—and are socially expected—to invest in education, career building, and financial stability . . . putting the socially ideal timing to start a family out of synch with the biologically ideal

190 ENVIRONMENTAL ETHICS AND MEDICAL REPRODUCTION

timing to do so."[74] At the same time, delayed reproduction which leads to natural infertility is not only a female problem.

Male sperm motility and mobility decline with age,[75] and older ages of fathers are associated with schizophrenia and autism in children.[76] But until men take an equal share of the burden of raising children,[77] women will likely continue to delay childbearing until they are established in their careers or finished with their education. Equal responsibility for raising children would, perhaps, make natural childbearing earlier more appealing for women,[78] which would reduce the reliance on MR. To be sure, gender (*sic*) justice must be present in society regardless of environmental impact or other justifications.[79] Women's liberation from patriarchal standards is a good in itself.[80] This ought to be remembered when discussing prevention of infertility across the Global North and Global South.

While women who are not well off enough to obtain higher education are more likely to have children younger[81] and thus avoid age-related infertility, they may still be harmed by a number of external factors which compromise fertility. Anne Dochin writes, "[E]verywhere the fertility of poor women is at risk from nutritional deficiencies, exposure to hazardous work situations, and damaging medical and environmental conditions."[82] Many of the health hazards facing poor women across the globe—also called social determinants of health—parallel healthcare disparities of poor women in the developed world. Josef Fuchs links the plight of the worldwide poor in terms of the "Fourth World" or "the situations of injustice in individual groups or states, in both the First and the Third Worlds."[83] This highlights the structural economic and racial components which are necessary to address in the prevention of infertility. In America, for instance, "high rates of infertility among black women may be linked to untreated chlamydia and gonorrhea, STDs that can lead to pelvic inflammatory disease; nutrition deficiencies; complications of childbirth and abortion; and environmental workplace hazards."[84] The common thread in the poor in both the Global South and the Global North is noxious environments.

In an ecologically grounded policy, the health of the body and the health of the planet are addressed as an interrelated social concern, whereby "more effort would be put into identifying and controlling the environmental and iatrogenic causes of infertility."[85] Through this public health approach to prevention of infertility, natural resources are conserved while the medical resources associated with MR use are minimized. Anne Dochin notes that "reduction of environmental pollutants and establishment of screening programs for the more common infectious agents could be accomplished at far less cost than treatment to alleviate the consequences of diminished fertility."[86] Thus, while preventing infertility may not reduce birth rates or resource use after birth, it can reduce carbon of MR through bypassing the demand for fertility treatments.

Accepting Infertility

If infertility cannot be prevented or treated, it can be reframed conceptually as a positive outcome, which allows freedom.[87] Accepting infertility on one's own terms, for example by using the term "childfree" instead of "childless," is a lexically appropriate starting point. The suffix "-free" has positive connotations, as in "home free," and "fancy free" whereas "-less" has negative connotations, as in "homeless," "jobless," and "penniless."[88] Making a concerted effort to speak in a way that upholds ethical values of environmental conservation could be a cornerstone of accepting infertility. Additional terminological work on "family" may also be considered.

In America, and many other individualistic societies, the term "family" has become a colloquialism, meaning "biological children."[89] Yet, expanding the conception of family to include grandparents, mothers, fathers, aunts, uncles, cousins, friends, religious communities, and social networks reinforces the value of kinship and a non-heteronormative, non-reproductive vision of family.[90] Indeed, "a healthy family is the product of mutual love and commitment, whether or not a genetic link between (parents and child) exist."[91] So too is a healthy family the product of love and trust between people. When confronted with the question "Do you want to have a family?" the infertile, pre-reproductive, and childfree can affirm they "already have a family."[92] This response places the burden on the interrogator to clarify the meaning of family, while also casting light on alternative, more linguistically accurate notions of family.

Infertility will not be accepted unless the stigma and fear surrounding childfree life is lifted. According to Erving Goffman, a person becomes stigmatized through "(1) abominations of the body; (or) (2) blemishes of individual character."[93] Infertility as a bodily stigma comes from the often erroneous link to disease, particularly for heterosexual individuals.[94] Infertility as a social stigma originates from the myth that people who do not procreate are selfish, thus improperly imputing a stigma of character.[95] Both need to be

192   ENVIRONMENTAL ETHICS AND MEDICAL REPRODUCTION

upended and rejected as constructs for infertility to be accepted. Acceptance will both prevent MR and resource use while also benefiting the social and emotional lives of those who are not reproductive.

Parenting without Procreation

There are many ways that adults can parent without procreation. These include adoption, fostering, and co-parenting, as well as mentoring, spiritual parenting, caring for step-children, and teaching. To be sure, both fertile and infertile can parent without procreation, and it ought to be underscored that acceptance of infertility does not necessarily lead one to parent without procreation. Nor should it be thought that the ability to procreate absolves one from considering parenting without procreation. Indeed, one of the reasons parenting without procreation is unpersuasive as a solution to childwishes, in addition to the ingrained social scripts, is that MR and non-reproductive parenting are treated "as either-or answers to infertility.... [T]he call to adoption is almost always selectively applied"[96] to those who are infertile, while the fertile are discouraged from considering adoption. For both the infertile and the fertile, understanding the wider ethical implications of MR is mandatory prior to entering into a discussion of how or why parenting without procreation is a viable option, that is also, perhaps, a *prima facie* duty.

Indeed, article 20 of the United Nations Convention on the Rights of the Child states, "[A] child temporarily or permanently deprived of his or her family environment, or in whose own best interests cannot be allowed to remain in that environment, shall be entitled to special protection and assistance provided by the State."[97] These children may be wards of the state if they cannot be placed with extended family and still require a nurturing environment. Through parenting without procreation parents "embark on the work of hospitality."[98] But alternative forms of parenting are more than just hospitality. They are a matter of justice.

Where there is a child in need, and a family that wants a child, combining the two needs produces a beneficial situation for all. According to Lisa Sowel Cahill, "ensuring that children have families is always a greater priority than ensuring that childless couples have children"[99] because children who actually exist have a stronger entitlement to emotional and physical resources than a potential child who does not have needs and cannot feel pain or suffering. *De Rerum Natura* is evocative in this regard. Lucretius writes:

> [W]hat loss were ours, if we had not known birth
> Let living men to longer life aspire
> While fond affections binds their hearts to the earth:
> But who never hath tasted life's desire,
> Unborn, impersonal, can feel no death.[100]

Parenting without procreation demonstrates solidarity and justice toward children who have insufficient or non-existent parenting support.

To be sure, all people, regardless of whether they are considering parenting, have an obligation to existing children, much as they have obligations toward other vulnerable groups in the world. And while it may be argued that they can discharge their duty to children in other ways, such as financially supporting an adoption agency, there is a special obligation for those who have the potential to most directly impact the lives of children waiting for homes—those who are inclined to parenting. By parenting without procreation, the ethical duty to others is partially fulfilled. Even more so when the duty to others includes the obligation to reduce resources and minimize population. For those individuals and couples considering medical reproduction, parenting without procreation removes the self from the matrix of high-carbon medical treatments and healthcare. Moreover, as all people are affected by carbon emissions, those who parent without procreation prevent further harm to people currently alive and children being born. Reproduction and MR damages the health of all living people, including new humans; avoiding MR does not cause any environmental harm, but rather minimizes resource use. Between the duties to others, the obligation to reduce carbon emissions, and the robust theories dedicated to parenting ethics, there is indeed a very strong case for parenting without procreation.

Adoption

Indeed, numerous philosophers and ethicists have argued that adoption, in particular, is preferable to medicalized reproduction,[101] clearly highlighting that "whereas 'adoptive children' can be harmed by promoting ART, 'ART children' cannot be similarly harmed by promoting adoption."[102] While a child taken into a new home in the developed world—regardless of birth country—will still face the disconcerting consumptive patterns so common to wealthy countries,[103] it might be justified by the principle of

194   ENVIRONMENTAL ETHICS AND MEDICAL REPRODUCTION

proportionality.[104] This principle allows "harm to otherkind only if the ecological and social values of the end outweigh the values lost in the use of means."[105] Raising any child in a developed country will harm the environment, but if the alternative is creating a new child and neglecting the child in need, it is better to practice non-procreative parenting. At the same time, efforts to reduce resource use must also be pursued.

Of course, adoption and alternative ways of parenting must be desirable options for those considering MR and non-medicalized parenthood.[106] Genetic fetishism[107] must be replaced with a more sophisticated morality that considers all options before embarking on parenthood, recognizing that "parents might also value adoption for other (moral) reasons independent of the intimate relationship with the future child."[108] These include more egalitarian parenthood duties between partners, ecological conservation, and the matter of social justice. These ethical considerations do not minimize the logistical challenges to adoption, which also need to be addressed.

In many countries, adoption laws are overly restrictive and discriminatory toward gay couples and single people.[109] The adoption process may be prolonged and costly.[110] Policymakers must lobby governments and private adoption agencies for efficient, affordable adoption procedures,[111] so the ethical choice is also the simple choice. Even with a straightforward process, adoption "continues to be perceived as a 'risky thing'"[112] and concerns about adjustment to a new family and emotional problems of new children are at the forefront of resistance to adoption. Yet, Gregory E. Kaebnick argues that while "behavioral problems are more likely to be diagnosed in adopted children than in children who are genetically related to their parents . . . the lack of genetic parental relationship may not be the cause of the gap. Perhaps more behavioral problems are diagnosed in adopted children simply because rearing parents and others are looking harder for problems."[113]

The ethical obligations to others may translate into policies that make adoption easier and may also be compelling reasons to make MR more difficult, according to some ethicists. "The asymmetry between assisted reproduction, where no child's interests plays a role before actual conception (or even birth) has taken place, and adoption, where children's interests are affected by any policy diminishing their chances at being adopted, clearly favors restricting access to ART."[114] More restrictive MR would need to be part of a comprehensive paradigm that supports alternative means of acquiring progeny. This change is plausible, as Cora A. Du Bois notes: "man's [*sic*] ego mechanisms are both expressive and defensive, but they are also adaptive. He will change his opportunities as his environment change. He will adopt family planning if he sees it as adaptive."[115] Family planning—here inclusive of parenting without procreation—is an ethical way to adapt to the challenges of climate change and reduce resources.

Fostering Children

It may be that adults with very strong childwishes would want to raise a child over the course of their lifespan and therefore adoption would be enthusiastically pursued. But there are other couples who value caring for more children on a less permanent basis through foster parenting. In the same way that adoption in lieu of reproduction would result in fewer children and less environmental impact, so too does fostering provide for the desire some couples have to raise children, and the desire that all children have for a family. Nicole Petrowski, Claudia Cappa, and Peter Gross evaluated "data on children living in residential and foster care from some 142 countries covering more than 80 per cent of the world's children" and "estimated that approximately 2.7 million children between the ages of 0 and 17 years could be living in institutional care worldwide."[116] Just as orphans require a stable place to thrive, so also do foster children need the support of a loving home.

Fostering children, of course, is not only the responsibility of those considering MR or natural reproduction. Yet, there is a specific inclination that drives one to have children which makes those who want children more suited for fostering above, say, those who have a strong antipathy toward parenting and would therefore be ill suited to foster.[117] "People who would make adequate parents have a powerful moral interest in raising at least a child," argues Anca Gheaus.[118] This interest is not only self-motivated; it is also directed at the benefit of the child.

Children in foster care are in a difficult and liminal place; they have parents, but the parents are temporarily or currently unequipped to raise their children. It may, in fact, be the case that children who end up in foster care are there because adults have unreflectively followed their reproductive script without actually evaluating the demands of parenthood.[119] There are many situations that can lead a child to be put into foster care. Many pregnancies are unwanted and unplanned, and "people have children for many different reasons (to save a marriage or relationship, to have something to hold, to

196 ENVIRONMENTAL ETHICS AND MEDICAL REPRODUCTION

placate potential grandparents etc.) and often for no particular reason at all."[120] Adults who reproduce are first and foremost responsible for the creation of their own children. But society as a whole—which is comprised of many different mature adults—is also obligated to take care of those children who have been abandoned through no fault of their own.

Parenting without procreation brings into highlights that "ethics is in need of a shift from an emphasis on the acquisition of children to an emphasis on the care of children."[121] This is a good in itself, just as adoption discharges the duty to others. With the additional environmental benefit of opening a home to those in need instead of bringing individuals into the world who would otherwise not exist, fostering can support childwishes.[122]

Co-parenting

While adoption and fostering have been "conventional" ways of parenting without procreation,[123] in recent decades, the proposal for co-parenting has appeared as one possibility to meet the moral requirement of reducing population and achieving social justice.[124] The most compelling arguments for co-parenting have been put forth by Anca Gheaus, who argues that co-parenting, or "multiparenting—that is, three, four, or possibly more adults co-raising the same child or children—is a desirable solution. Moreover, in cases where each individual or couple parenting one child would not result in sufficiently steep downsizing, multiparenting may be morally required."[125] Multiparents or co-parents would not necessarily link children and parents by birth, marriage, or adoption. This is in contrast to other important forms of co-parenting such as step-parenting.

Step-parenting ought to be more recognized as a valuable contribution to raising other children.[126] Whether the step-parent is taking a primary parenting role, in the case of the death of the biological parent, or the step-parent is taking a more secondary role in the new family configuration, raising the child that already exists does indeed fulfill the obligation to others and has the potential to reduce population growth instead of insisting on creating a new child in joining the family.

What has been said above about reducing MR resource use would also apply in the case of co-parenting, multiparenting, and step-parenting, particularly when the potential parents are of advanced age and may have declining fertility. As with other forms of parenting without procreation, social and institutional support are required. From a variety of perspectives, the value of procreation hinges on "acceptance of a socially supplied script. It is for this reason that responses to infertility that offer only another way to fulfill the role of parent (such as through adoption) or that focus only on altering the significance of the roles (such as challenging social expectations about women; role in reproduction) are unsatisfying as those that suppose reproductive technologies are the answer."[127] Fundamentally, adoption, fostering, and co-parenting have to be viewed as both an immediate and enduring lifestyle in response to population growth, resource use, climate change, and duties to others.

Work Policies That Do Not Incentivize Reproduction

Larger social structures that support childwishes will need to be created and maintained. These include work policies that either disincentivize reproduction or incentivize parenting without procreation. For instance, the internet company Trip Advisor offers adoption assistance as part of their benefits package. All full-time employees are eligible for legal and financial help in finding a child regardless of fertility status.[128] Similarly, other places of employment can encourage those who are not procreating by replacing discriminatory "parent-leave" policies with "family-leave" policies. There is no reason, it is said, that people should get time off work just because they have children, when the childfree, who may have obligations to extended family members, do not get the same consideration. Thus, the Family and Medical Leave Act of 1993 (FMLA) "allows an employee to take unpaid leave from work to care for family or take medical leave when he or she is unable to work. It also grants leave for adoption or foster care. An employee has up to 12 weeks FMLA leave in any 12-month period." This could be expanded for other forms of parenting without procreation such as familiarization of stepchildren and co-parenting.

The FMLA did not guarantee paid leave; it only ensured that the employee's job (or one similar to it) would be available when they return. However, some FMLA companies—like the American Civil Liberties Union (ACLU)—offer paid leave,[129] as well as most companies in Europe. While the United States has been lagging in this regard, there is some progress. In 2010, the ACLU Foundation of Massachusetts decided to "replace its 'parental leave' policy with a 'family leave' policy that provides for as much as 12 weeks of leave not

198 ENVIRONMENTAL ETHICS AND MEDICAL REPRODUCTION

only for new parents, but also for employees who need to care for a spouse, child, or parent with a serious health condition."[130]

Instituting benefits—both explicitly and implicitly—for workers without biological children is a pragmatic policy that is also beneficial to the environment. The director of the ACLU Foundation of Massachusetts remarked, "[W]e wanted a policy that took into account the fact that even employees who do not have children have family obligations."[131] These remarks point to a wider scope of social support for non-procreative lifestyles, while also having the felicitous benefit of making the decision not to reproduce easier.

Summary

There are myriad ways to support childwishes which do not require MR or natural reproduction. While preventing infertility may lead to a reduction in MR use, this is not always the case, as some MR use is by fertile people. And while parenting without procreating may also reduce the number of children born, there are logistical and emotional barriers. MR cannot be viewed in its proper light until concepts of infertility, procreation, and parenthood are deconstructed. Yet this alone will leave a gap in emotional and intellectual satisfaction. Thus, it is clear that MR will not be seen as ethically unappealing unless satisfying forms of adoption, fostering, and multiparenting exist. These must be straightforward and economical. As long as MR is more appealing, easier, and faster than going through the many steps to parenting without procreation or accepting infertility as a path to a childfree life, it will be the default. Society is enamored with technology, particularly as a means of confronting existential crises and avoiding reflection on one's own death. Despite the tidal wave of pro-natalism and egocentrism that drives reproduction, the associated biomedical, ecological, and reproductive ethical issues must be considered in evaluating MR. Indeed, the outstanding social issues of sexism, racism, migration, violence, and economic inequality are all compounded by—and connected to—climate change.[132] The dissemination, development, and use of MR cannot conscionably continue as is.

Conclusion

Environmental Sustainability beyond Medical Reproduction

Medicalized reproduction is an anthropogenic source of carbon emissions which contributes to climate change. While MR is used worldwide, it has the most environmental impact in the developed world since these countries have more resource-intensive infrastructures. However, the environmental impact of naturally made children cannot be ignored. The carbon emissions of many children born in the developed world is more resource-intensive than in the developing world, although the birth rate is lower. In a similar vein, the use of the medical industry in the developed world is more carbon-intensive than in the developing world, regardless of the procedure. While MR, the carbon of children in the developing world, and the carbon of the medical industry have been the target of environmental scrutiny here, there is an obvious need to reduce carbon emissions in all areas of life. Moreover, the world's highest-emitting nations have a proportionate obligation to reduce carbon as a matter of climate, social, and medical justice.

Climate Justice

Climate justice recognizes that carbon must be emitted in the course of life, but that all people should benefit from the emissions and none should be disproportionately burdened by it. Carbon emissions can be economically beneficial but biologically destructive, in as much as they contribute to climate change health hazards. By some estimates, "about 80% of the world's wealth benefits only 20% of its people, the vast majority have very little. Poverty is one of the main factors contributing to poor health, and it reduces the ability of populations to cope with environmental decline."[1] Such comments on wealth, which is often tied to resource use, highlight the current climate injustice of benefit and burden. In order to remedy this injustice, global carbon

---

Environmental Ethics and Medical Reproduction. Cristina Richie, Oxford University Press.
© Oxford University Press 2024. DOI: 10.1093/oso/9780197745182.003.0011

200 ENVIRONMENTAL ETHICS AND MEDICAL REPRODUCTION

emissions must shift; they must be reallocated across international and generational lines.

Internationally, climate justice examines the distribution of resource use per person. In order to be sustainable, "when the population grows the ecological footprint that each person may have shrinks, resulting in more demanding requirements for what counts as sustainable."[2] Concretely, more people must live with less. Or fewer people can live with more. This configuration is relevant both in the present and in the future, that is, with generational carbon allocations. There are significant climate justice concerns about the amount of resources being used by the current generation and those that will be available to future generations.[3] Willis Jenkins argues that "one way to conceptualize (carbon) allotments over time is to consider a total amount of GHGs (greenhouse gases) humanity can emit over time and still stay within an upper bounds of temperature rise. If that amount were one trillion tons over a 200 year period (as one study calculates), then a great deal has been spent by previous generations, leaving a limited amount to allot among today's peoples and future generation."[4] Of course, this is only a "problem" for a reproductive society. It may be that people decide they would rather continue their consumptive lifestyle and forgo having children. Since this is unlikely, for some of the reasons described in this book, resistance to climate justice must be examined so it can be overcome.

Effecting change in carbon allocation through resource conservation is very difficult, in part because of the "identifiable versus statistical victims" phenomenon.[5] Norman Daniels summarizes that "'identifiable victims' [are] people that we can actually see pictures of—or imagine as a person like ourselves... [and] 'statistical victims'... [are] the faceless number of people who die from unmemorable causes each day."[6] Whereas the former appear to be within "our" realm of concerns, the latter are excluded. Thus, consumer purchases and high-carbon lifestyles are more often changed when the impact is in front of the moral agent, whether that is because of national impacts or because of the thought of harm done to *their* children, whereas the people most affected by climate change—those in the developing world and the future generations who do not yet exist—are not considered. They are too far away, conceptually. This paucity in both moral sensitivity and imagination produces a "bias in favor of identified victims (which) also makes environmental law harder to use to protect the health and safety of statistical victims"[7] and also explains why carbon reallocation is so difficult to achieve.

CONCLUSION 201

To be sure, there are some movements which do address climate change justice. However, they tend to belligerently ignore current injustices in resource allocation and prefer to rely on future innovations, which do not address climate justice, only climate change. For instance, "serious discussion about climate engineering is starting to escalate"[8] and is part of many environmental policy discussions. It is presumed that climate engineering will solve the current carbon overload and that the next generation will be able to avail themselves of the full measure of carbon use. However, this neglects the reality that even if carbon emissions are attenuated, resources will still need to be allocated fairly. A lower-carbon world cannot account for the impacts of climate change thus far, nor can it ensure that carbon is allocated justly per person. The UK National Health Service's Sustainable Development Unit baldly states, "[T]he rapidly increasing risk of adverse effects on health from climate change is happening on this generation's watch—it will be this generation's legacy."[9] Carbon reduction is a requirement of climate justice.

Social Justice

Whereas climate justice requires carbon reduction to mitigate the impacts of climate change and the effects on humans, social justice also calls individuals to work toward sustainability through solidarity,[10] in particular, the solidarity found in low-carbon living, just responses to healthcare carbon, and proper parenting ethics. Indeed, a robust identity as an individual within larger networks of social groups is a key conceptual point of social justice. Jessica Pierce and Andrew Jameton contend, "[P]art of our sense of personal identity and integrity depends on our ability to assume responsibilities to others . . . to fulfill more completely the humanness of individuals."[11] In order to cultivate an identity as an ethical agent in solidarity with others, one must understand the self as part of the human community, with equal value to others.

Equal value does not dismiss close attachments to immediate kinship groups, yet it does recognize that all people must respect duties to others. Immanuel Kant recognized this in the categorical imperative. He writes, "[F]or in wishing I can be equally benevolent to everyone, whereas in acting I can, without violating the universal maxim, vary the degree greatly in accordance with the different objects of my love (one of whom concerns me more closely than another)."[12] Simultaneously, obligations to others as a

202 ENVIRONMENTAL ETHICS AND MEDICAL REPRODUCTION

matter of justice, and not mere preference, are met through this dictum. In an interdependent society, "justice does not require indifference to one's location; on the contrary, it should take shape within the global social relations that already connect agents."[13]

Recognizing these various social connections will lead to acceptance of duties of carbon reduction, sustainability, and not taking more than one's share of resources as one envisions the larger global community. Social justice is a broad concept. It includes—rather than excludes—other forms of justice. Racial, feminist, economic, and, in fact, medical justice are all within its purview.

Medical Justice

Nancy Kass persuasively argues that "social justice is highly correlated with better health outcomes, and social justice is a recurring theme of public health."[14] Thus, the medical aspects of carbon reduction, which have been stressed in this book, are also tied to larger imperatives of justice. Medical justice requires multiple tasks. Medical resources—including personnel, facilities, and healthcare services—should be allocated equitably. Medical solidarity between countries, through shared funding of healthcare services, will be essential in building a sustainable and just healthcare system. While "resources allocated to disease treatment are often seen as competing with resources available for disease prevention,"[15] this either/or fallacy obscures the underlying issue of misdistribution of resources. Ethicists should "remain suspicious, moreover, of the continued large budgeting expense of scarce human and funding resources"[16] that serve the well-off in countries that already have ample medical resources when so many people in other countries are dying without their most fundamental needs being met.

Concretely, this means that more international funding and attention need to be put into basic healthcare, public health efforts like subsidizing nutrient-dense food, access to green spaces, and a clean atmosphere, and preventative healthcare. Past efforts at allocation of medical resources have considered these aspects as policymakers "argue[d] that preventive and primary care services should be privileged in resource allocation decisions. Mainstays of public health care delivery—prenatal care and immunizations—often were cited as among the least controversial services to be included in a basic, minimum package of service"[17] in healthcare plans. As these efforts have appealed to the limits of medicine and justice as rationales for reallocation of resources, so too do the limits of the planet need to be factored into allocation and distribution of resources.

The concern that those with sophisticated levels of healthcare in the developed world will suffer from fewer resources is unfounded. Medical resources do not need to disappear from those in the developed world in order to meet the needs in the developing. Rather, medical needs must be prioritized as healthcare is streamlined. For instance, curtailing elective procedures and proceeding with caution before more non-clinically beneficial treatments are developed must become part of the fabric of healthcare delivery. The lust to implement one's personal medical projects cannot trump the need for healthcare worldwide.

Challenges to achieving medical justice are numerous, but equitable access to healthcare must be folded into the environmental obligations of high-emitting countries. Awareness of medical discrepancies is the starting point; those in privileged positions who overlook misdistribution of resources are called to realize that the lifestyles of the affluent and the death of people in poor countries exist in "a mutual cause-and-effect relationship."[18] Each individual is responsible for their actions, and the effects thereof.

Climate justice, social justice, and medical justice are intertwined. All need to be present in society, and none absolves the healthcare industry, users of MR, or biological parents from considering the ethical demands of the global environmental crisis. This is not, as it were, adding the supposed "injustice" of healthcare limitation, which will mostly affect the well-off, to the injustice of climate change, which affects all people. Robert Nozick expresses this well: "Perhaps one thinks of the possibility that a whole social structure is just, even though none of its parts are, because the injustice in each part somehow balances out or counteracts another one, and the total injustice ends up being balanced out or nullified. But can a part satisfy the most fundamental principle of justice yet still clearly be unjust, apart from its failure to perform any supposed task of counterbalancing another existing injustice?"[19] The supposed "injustice" of resource limitation is not created by the environmental crisis, but rather a response to it. Climate change is the prime injustice, which indeed hinges on a regressive set of climate, social, and medical injustices. It is frankly arrogant to think otherwise. Addressing MR as part of the nexus of medical, sexual and reproductive ethics, and viewing it as the carbon emitter that it is, will only address a small part of climate change. The ethical imperative for environmental conservation must be ubiquitous and immediate.

Notes

Introduction

1. Climate change can also be a neutral description, which describes the way weather and temperature differ throughout time. Periods of natural climate change have little moral value assigned to them. However, meteorological records which indicate historical differences in global temperature sometimes correspond to periods of mass animal and plant extinction. When humans contribute to impoverishing the earth of creatures, there are reasons for ethical concern. David A. King, "Climate Change Science: Adapt, Mitigate, or Ignore?," *Science* 303, no. 5655 (2004): 176–177.

2. Environmental Protection Agency, "Climate Change Indicators in the United States," 2010, http://www.epa.gov/climatechange/indicators.html, accessed July 18, 2012.

3. International Energy Agency, "CO_2 Emissions from Fuel Combustion—2011 Highlights," http://www.iea.org/co2highlights/co2highlights.pdf, accessed July 18, 2012.

4. NOAA, "Climate Change: Atmospheric Carbon Dioxide," August 14, 2020, https://www.climate.gov/news-features/understanding-climate/climate-change-atmospheric-carbon-dioxide.

5. John E. N. Veron, Ove Hoegh-Guldberg, Timothy M. Lenton, Janice M. Lough, David O. Obura, Paul Pearce-Kelly, Charles R. C. Sheppard, Marianne Spalding, Mary Gillian Stafford-Smith, and Alex David Rogers, "The Coral Reef Crisis: The Critical Importance of < 350 ppm CO_2," *Marine Pollution Bulletin* 58, no. 10 (2009): 1428–1436.

6. Camilo Mora, Daniele Spirandelli, Erik C. Franklin, John Lynham, Michael B. Kantar, Wendy Miles, Charlotte Z. Smith, et al. "Broad Threat to Humanity from Cumulative Climate Hazards Intensified by Greenhouse Gas Emissions," *Nature Climate Change* 8, no. 12 (2018): 1062–1071.

7. C. Zimring, *Clean and White: A History of Environmental Racism in the United States* (New York: NYU Press, 2017).

8. Charles J. Moseley, ed., *The Official World Wildlife Fund Guide to Endangered Species of North America: Species Listed August 1989 to December 1991,* vol. 3 (Beacham, 1992).

9. James Justus, Mark Colyvan, Helen Regan, and Lynn Maguire, "Buying into Conservation: Intrinsic versus Instrumental Value," *Trends in Ecology & Evolution* 24, no. 4 (2009): 187–191.

10. Friedrich Lohmann, "Climate Justice and the Intrinsic Value of Creation: The Christian Understanding of Creation and Its Holistic Implications," *Religion in Environmental and Climate Change: Suffering, Values, Lifestyles* (2012): 85–106.

11. K. McShane, "Why Environmental Ethics Shouldn't Give Up on Intrinsic Value," *Environmental Ethics* 29, no. 1 (2007): 43–61.

206 NOTES

12. Marcello Di Paola and Mirko Daniel Garasic, "The Dark Side of Sustainability: On Avoiding, Engineering, and Shortening Human Lives in the Anthropocene," *Rivista di Studi sulla Sostenibilità* 3, no. 2 (2013): 59–81.

13. Wesley J. Smith, "Babies Are Children, Not 'Carbon Legacies!,'" *National Review*, August 5, 2014, http://www.nationalreview.com/human-exceptionalism/384676/bab ies-are-children-not-carbon-legacies-wesley-j-smith.

14. Garret Hardin, "The Tragedy of the Commons," *Science* 162, no. 3859 (1968): 1245.

15. Alan D. Lopez, Colin D. Mathers, Majid Ezzati, Dean T. Jamison, and Christopher J. L. Murray, "Global and Regional Burden of Disease and Risk Factors, 2001: Systematic Analysis of Population Health Data," *The Lancet* 367, no. 9524 (2006): 1747–1757.

16. Ting Shi, Angeline Denouel, Anna K. Tietjen, Iain Campbell, Emily Moran, Xue Li, Harry Campbell, et al., "Global Disease Burden Estimates of Respiratory Syncytial Virus–Associated Acute Respiratory Infection in Older Adults in 2015: A Systematic Review and Meta-analysis," *Journal of Infectious Diseases* (2019).

17. World Health Organization, *Global Health Risks: Mortality and Burden of Diseases Attributable to Selected Major Risks* (Geneva: WHO Press, 2009), 24.

18. https://www.who.int/heli/risks/climate/climatechange/en/.

19. https://www.who.int/news-room/fact-sheets/detail/climate-change-and-health.

20. A. Prüss-Ustün, J. Wolf, C. Corvalán, T. Neville, R. Bos, and M. Neira, "Diseases Due to Unhealthy Environments: An Updated Estimate of the Global Burden of Disease Attributable to Environmental Determinants of Health," *Journal of Public Health* 39, no. 3 (2017): 464–475.

21. United Church of Christ Commission on Racial Justice, *Toxic Wastes and Race in the United States: A National Report on the Racial and Socio-Economic Characteristics of Communities with Hazardous Waste Sites* (United Church of Christ Commission on Racial Justice, Public Data Access, 1987).

22. Nancy Kass, "Public Health Ethics: From Foundations and Frameworks to Justice and Global Public Health," *Journal of Law, Medicine and Ethics* 32, no. 2 (2004): 236.

23. B. Luppi, F. Parisi, and S. Rajagopalan, "The Rise and Fall of the Polluter-Pays Principle in Developing Countries," *International Review of Law and Economics* 32, no. 1 (2012): 135–144.

24. John Clarke, "Consumers, Clients or Citizens? Politics, Policy and Practice in the Reform of Social Care," *European Societies* 8, no. 3 (2006): 423–442.

25. D. Asin and M Parker, "Covering Climate: What's Population Got to Do with It?," Woodrow Wilson International Center for Scholars, October 14, 2009.

26. Jane Dalton, "Humans Have Used a Year's Worth of Earth's Resources in Just Seven Months," *Independent UK*, July 24, 2018, https://www.independent.co.uk/news/ earth-overshoot-day-natural-resources-humans-planet-nature-damage-global- footprint-a8460756.html.

27. Global Footprint Network, "How Big Is the Human Footprint on Earth?," 2010, http:// www.footprintnetwork.org/en/index.php/GFN/page/2010_living_planet_report/, accessed November 29, 2012.

28. P. Murtaugh and M. Schla, "Reproduction and the Carbon Legacies of Individuals," *Global Environmental Change* 19, no. 1 (2009):14–20.

NOTES   207

29. U.S. Census Bureau, "U.S. Population Projections," 2009, http://www.census.gov/pop ulation/www/projections/2009projections.html, accessed November 15, 2011.

30. Corey J. A. Bradshaw and Barry W. Brook, "Human Population Reduction Is Not a Quick Fix for Environmental Problems," *PNAS* 111, no. 46 (2014): 16610–16615.

31. Daniel Callahan, *What Kind of Life? The Limits of Medical Progress* (Washington, DC: Georgetown University Press, 1995).

32. Daniel Callahan, *Setting Limits: Medical Goals in an Aging Society* (New York: Touchstone Books, 1988).

33. Paul R. Ehrlich, Dennis R. Parnell, and Al Silbowitz, *The Population Bomb* (New York: Ballantine Books, 1971).

34. Barbara Entwisle and William M. Mason, "Multilevel Effects of Socioeconomic Development and Family Planning Programs on Children Ever Born," *American Journal of Sociology* 91, no. 3 (1985): 616–649.

35. Martha C. Nussbaum, "Human Functioning and Social Justice," *Political Theory* 20, no. 2 (1992): 202–246.

36. Union of Concerned Scientists, "Each Country's Share of CO_2 Emissions," July 16, 2008, updated 2020, https://www.ucsusa.org/resources/each-countrys-share-co2-emissions.

37. Maura Ryan, *The Ethics and Economics of ART: The Cost of Longing* (Washington, DC: Georgetown University Press, 2001), 35.

38. Gro Harlem Brundtland, *Report of the World Commission on Environment and Development: "Our Common Future"* (New York: United Nations, 1987).

39. S. E. Vollset, E. Goren, C. W. Yuan, J. Cao, A. E. Smith, T. Hsiao, C. Bisignano, G. S. Azhar, E. Castro, J. Chalek, and A. J. Dolgert, "Fertility, Mortality, Migration, and Population Scenarios for 195 Countries and Territories from 2017 to 2100: A Forecasting Analysis for the Global Burden of Disease Study," *The Lancet* 396, no. 10258 (2020): 1285–1306.

40. Oleg Smirnov, Minghua Zhang, Tingyin Xiao, John Orbell, Amy Lobben, and Josef Gordon, "The Relative Importance of Climate Change and Population Growth for Exposure to Future Extreme Droughts," *Climatic Change* 138, nos. 1–2 (2016): 41–53.

41. James Hansen, Pushker Kharecha, Makiko Sato, Valerie Masson-Delmotte, Frank Ackerman, David J. Beerling, Paul J. Hearty, et al., "Assessing 'Dangerous Climate Change': Required Reduction of Carbon Emissions to Protect Young People, Future Generations and Nature," *PLoS One* 8, no. 12 (2013): e81648.

42. R. B. Mitchell, "Technology Is Not Enough: Climate Change, Population, Affluence, and Consumption," *Journal of Environment & Development* 21, no. 1 (2012): 24–27; Bala Govindasamy and Ken Caldeira, "Geoengineering Earth's Radiation Balance to Mitigate CO_2-Induced Climate Change," *Geophysical Research Letters* 27, no. 14 (2000): 2141–2144.

43. J. Craig, "Replacement Level Fertility and Future Population Growth," *Population Trends* 78 (1994): 20–22.

44. Vollset et al., "Fertility, Mortality, Migration."

45. Vladimíra Kantorová, Mark C. Wheldon, Philipp Ueffing, and Aisha N. Z. Dasgupta, "Estimating Progress towards Meeting Women's Contraceptive Needs in 185

208 NOTES

Countries: A Bayesian Hierarchical Modelling Study," *PLoS Medicine* 17, no. 2 (2020): e1003026.

46. Joint United Nations Programme on HIV/AIDS, *Gap Report* (Geneva: UNAIDS, 2014), 234.

47. Cristina Richie, "Voluntary Sterilization for Childfree Women: Understanding Patient Profiles, Evaluating Accessibility, Examining Legislation," *Hastings Center Report* 43, no. 6 (2013): 36–44.

48. United Nations General Assembly, "Sustainable Development Goals," *SDGs, Transforming Our World: The* 2030 (2015): 338–350.

49. Murtaugh and Schla, "Reproduction and the Carbon Legacies of Individuals."

50. Union of Concerned Scientists, "Each Country's Share of CO_2 Emissions."

51. Vollset et al., "Fertility, Mortality, Migration."

52. Union of Concerned Scientists, "Each Country's Share of CO_2 Emissions."

53. World Population Review, "Birth Rate by Country 2020 by Population 2020," 2002, https://worldpopulationreview.com/country-rankings/birth-rate-by-country#dataTable.

54. United Nations, Department of Economic and Social Affairs, Population Division, "Data Query: Net Migration Rate (per 1,000 Population)," https://population.un.org/wpp/DataQuery/.

55. Forty-seven percent of women in America ages 15–44 are currently without children and 20% of all women in America will never have a biological child. G. Livingston and D'V. Cohn, "More Women without Children," Pew Research Center, June 25, 2010.

56. Hilary Greaves, "Climate Change and Optimum Population," *The Monist* 102, no. 1 (2019): 42–65.

57. "ARTs in a Warming World," *Blog, Journal of Medical Ethics*, July 25, 2014, https://blogs.bmj.com/medical-ethics/2014/07/25/arts-in-a-warming-world/.

58. Dominic Wilkinson, "Gaia Doesn't Care Where Your Baby Comes From," *Blog, Journal of Medical Ethics*, July 25, 2014, https://blogs.bmj.com/medical-ethics/2014/07/25/gaia-doesnt-care-where-your-baby-comes-from/.

59. Kyung Ae Cho, "Korea's Low Birth Rate Issue and Policy Directions," *Korean Journal of Women's Health Nursing* 27, no. 1 (2021): 6–9; Shixiong Cao and Xiuqing Wang, "Unsustainably Low Birth Rates: A Potential Crisis Leading to Loss of Racial and Cultural Diversity in China," *Journal of Policy Modeling* 32, no. 1 (2010): 159–162; Mariya Aleksandrovna Shishkina and Larisa Alekseevna Popova, "Impact of Modern Pro-Family Demographic Policy on Birth Rate Intensity in the Northern Regions of Russia," *Economic and Social Changes: Facts, Trends, Forecast* 10, no. 1 (2017): 161–177.

60. Loren Lutzenhiser and Sylvia Bender, "The 'Average American' Unmasked: Social Structure and Differences in Household Energy Use and Carbon Emissions," (2008): 191–204.

61. Jonas Nordström, Jason F. Shogren, and Linda Thunström, "Do Parents Counter-balance the Carbon Emissions of Their Children?," *PLoS One* 15, no. 4 (2020): e0231105.

NOTES 209

62. Alan Thein Durning, "The Environmental Costs of Consumption," in *Contemporary Moral Problems*, 9th ed., ed. J. E. White (Belmont, CA: Thomas Wadsworth, 2009), 377–383.

63. Grant McCracken, "Diderot Unities and the Diderot Effect," *Culture and Consumption: New Approaches to the Symbolic Character of Consumer Goods and Activities* (1988): 118–129.

64. Murtaugh and Schla, "Reproduction and the Carbon Legacies of Individuals."

65. David Lazarevic and Michael Martin, "Life Cycle Assessments, Carbon Footprints and Carbon Visions: Analysing Environmental Systems Analyses of Transportation Biofuels in Sweden," *Journal of Cleaner Production* 137 (2016): 249–257.

66. P. Scarborough et al., "Dietary Greenhouse Gas Emissions of Meat-Eaters, Fish-Eaters, Vegetarians and Vegans in the UK," *Climatic Change* 125, no. 2 (2014): 179–192.

67. R. Hersher, "U.S. Formally Begins to Leave the Paris Climate Agreement," NPR, November 4, 2019, https://www.npr.org/2019/11/04/773474657/u-s-formally-beg ins-to-leave-the-paris-climate-agreement, accessed August 11, 2020.

68. A. Stirling, "Deliberate Futures: Precaution and Progress in Social Choice of Sustainable Technology," *Sustainable Development* 15, no. 5 (2007): 286–295.

69. Katherine White, Rishad Habib, and David J. Hardisty, "How to SHIFT Consumer Behaviors to Be More Sustainable: A Literature Review and Guiding Framework," *Journal of Marketing* 83, no. 3 (2019): 22–49.

70. Remah Moustafa Kamel, "Assisted Reproductive Technology after the Birth of Louise Brown," *Journal of Reproduction & Infertility* 14, no. 3 (2013): 96.

71. Hawley Fogg-Davis, "Navigating Race in the Market for Human Gametes," in *Genetics: Science, Ethics, and Public Policy*, ed. Thomas A. Shannon (Lanham, MD: Rowman & Littlefield, 2005), 115.

72. Cristina Richie, "What Would an Environmentally Sustainable Reproductive Technology Industry Look Like?," *Journal of Medical Ethics* 41, no. 5 (2015): 383–387.

73. Olga van den Akker, "Psychological and Ethical Issues in Third Party Assisted Conception and Surrogate Motherhood," in *Pathways and Barriers to Parenthood* (Cham: Springer, 2019), 113–125.

74. Paula Galdino Cardin de Carvalho, Cristiane da Silva Cabral, Laura Ferguson, Sofia Gruskin, and Carmen Simone Grilo Diniz, "'We Are Not Infertile': Challenges and Limitations Faced by Women in Same-Sex Relationships When Seeking Conception Services in São Paulo, Brazil," *Culture, Health & Sexuality* 21, no. 11 (2019): 1257–1272.

75. Mélodie Vander Borght and Christine Wyns, "Fertility and Infertility: Definition and Epidemiology," *Clinical Biochemistry* 62 (2018): 2–10.

76. Trevor Hedberg, "The Duty to Reduce Greenhouse Gas Emissions and the Limits of Permissible Procreation," *Essays in Philosophy* 20, no. 1 (2019): 1–24.

77. Fernando Zegers-Hochschild, Javier A. Crosby, and Juan Enrique Schwarze, "ART Surveillance in Latin America," in *Assisted Reproductive Technology Surveillance*, ed. Dmitry M. Kissin, G. David Adamson, Georgina Chambers, and Christian De Geyter (Cambridge: Cambridge University Press, 2019), 182.

210   NOTES

78. "More Than 250,000 UK Babies Born through IVF," *The Guardian*, November 4, 2016.

79. J. Bryner, "5 Million Babies Born from IVF, Other Reproductive Technologies," *Live Science*, July 3, 2012.

80. S. Sunderam, D. M. Kissin, S. B. Crawford, S. G. Folger, S. L. Boulet, L. Warner, and W. D. Barfield, "Reproductive Technology Surveillance—United States, 2015," 2018.

81. Daphna Birenbaum-Carmeli, "Thirty-Five Years of Assisted Reproductive Technologies in Israel," *Reproductive Biomedicine & Society Online* 2 (2016): 16–23.

82. Birenbaum-Carmeli, "Thirty-Five Years."

83. Malcolm J. Faddy, Matthew D. Gosden, and Roger G. Gosden, "A Demographic Projection of the Contribution of Assisted Reproductive Technologies to World Population Growth," *Reproductive Biomedicine Online* 36, no. 4 (2018): 455–458.

84. Faddy, Gosden, and Gosden, "A Demographic Projection."

85. Murtaugh and Schla, "Reproduction and the Carbon Legacies of Individuals."

86. Murtaugh and Schla, "Reproduction and the Carbon Legacies of Individuals."

87. Murtaugh and Schla, "Reproduction and the Carbon Legacies of Individuals."

88. Amos Hawley, "Ecology," in *International Encyclopedia of Population*, vol. 1, ed. John Ross (New York: Free Press, 1982), 159–163.

89. Mats Brännström et al., "Livebirth after Uterus Transplantation," *The Lancet*, October 5, 2014, 1–10.

90. Ewen Callaway, "World Hails UK Vote on Three-Person Embryos," *Nature News* 518, no. 7538 (2015): 145.

91. The World Health Organizations defines epidemiological infertility as "women of reproductive age (15–49 years) at risk of becoming pregnant (not pregnant, sexually active, not using contraception and not lactating) who report trying unsuccessfully for a pregnancy for two years or more." World Health Organization, "Infertility Definitions and Terminology," 2020, https://www.who.int/reproductivehealth/topics/infertility/definitions/en/; G. Bahadur, R. Homburg, A. Muneer, P. Racich, T. Alangaden, A. Al-Habib, and S. Okolo, "First Line Fertility Treatment Strategies regarding IUI and IVF Require Clinical Evidence," *Human Reproduction* 31, no. 6 (2016): 1141–1146.

92. K. Peterson- Iyer, *Designer Children: Reconciling Genetic Technology, Feminism, and Christian Ethics* (Cleveland, OH: Pilgrim Press, 2004), 187.

93. M. Hargreave, A. Jensen, M. K. Hansen, C. Dehlendorff, J. F. Winther, K. Schmiegelow, and S. K. Kjær, "Association between Fertility Treatment and Cancer Risk in Children," *JAMA* 322, no. 22 (2019): 2203–2210.

94. Yinusa Ademola Adediran and A. Abdulkarim, "Challenges of Electronic Waste Management in Nigeria," *International Journal of Advances in Engineering & Technology* 4, no. 1 (2012): 640.

95. Katheryn D. Katz, "Parenthood from the Grave: Protocols for Retrieving and Utilizing Gametes from the Dead or Dying," *University of Chicago Legal Forum* (2006): 289.

96. R. Grundy, V. Larcher, R. G. Gosden, M. Hewitt, A. Leiper, H. A. Spoudeas, D. Walker, and W. H. B. Wallace, "Fertility Preservation for Children Treated for

Cancer (2): Ethics of Consent for Gamete Storage and Experimentation," *Archives of Disease in Childhood* 84, no. 4 (2001): 360–362.

97. Susan Golombok, Fiona MacCallum, and Emma Goodman, "The 'Test-Tube' Generation: Parent-Child Relationships and the Psychological Well-Being of in Vitro Fertilization Children at Adolescence," *Child Development* 72, no. 2 (2001): 599–608.

98. Giancarlo Tamanza, Federica Facchin, Federica Francini, Silvia Ravani, Marialuisa Gennari, and Giuseppe Mannino, "'Doubly Mother': Heterologous Artificial Insemination between Biological and Social Parenthood: A Single Case Study," *World Futures* 75, no. 7 (2019): 480–501.

99. J. Harper et al., "Adjuncts in the IVF Laboratory: Where Is the Evidence for 'Add-On' Interventions?," *Human Reproduction* 32, no. 3 (2017): 485–491.

100. Holly Jones, "Contracts for Children: Constitutional Challenges to Surrogacy Contracts and Selective Reduction Clauses," *Hastings Legal Journal* 70 (2018): 595.

101. Puyu Yang, Yang Wang, Zhangxin Wu, Ningning Pan, Liying Yan, and Caihong Ma, "Risk of Miscarriage in Women with Endometriosis Undergoing IVF Fresh Cycles: A Retrospective Cohort Study," *Reproductive Biology and Endocrinology* 17, no. 1 (2019): 21.

102. Luisa Masciullo, Luciano Petruzziello, Giuseppina Perrone, Francesco Pecorini, Caterina Remiddi, Paola Galoppi, and Roberto Brunelli, "Caesarean Section on Maternal Request: An Italian Comparative Study on Patients' Characteristics, Pregnancy Outcomes and Guidelines Overview," *International Journal of Environmental Research and Public Health* 17, no. 13 (2020): 4665.

103. Anna Barbuscia, Pekka Martikainen, Mikko Myrskylä, Hanna Remes, Edgardo Somigliana, Reija Klemetti, and Alice Goisis, "Maternal Age and Risk of Low Birth Weight and Premature Birth in Children Conceived through Medically Assisted Reproduction: Evidence from Finnish Population Registers," *Human Reproduction* 35, no. 1 (2020): 212–220.

104. Mona Mohamed Aboulghar, Yahia El-Faissal, Ahmed Kamel, Ragaa Mansour, Gamal Serour, Mohamed Aboulghar, and Yomna Islam, "The Effect of Early Administration of Rectal Progesterone in IVF/ICSI Twin Pregnancies on the Preterm Birth Rate: A Randomized Trial," *BMC Pregnancy and Childbirth* 20, no. 1 (2020): 1–8.

105. Ahmed Al-Badr and Waleed H. Alkhamis, "Laser Vaginal Tightening Complications: Report of Three Cases," *Lasers in Surgery and Medicine* 51, no. 9 (2019): 757–759.

106. L. Sundheimer et al., "Adverse Perinatal Outcomes Associated with Fertility Treatment in Late Preterm Infants," *Fertility and Sterility* 106, no. 3 (2016): e175.

107. H. Tabuchi, "'Worse Than Anyone Expected': Air Travel Emissions Vastly Outpace Predictions," *New York Times,* 2019.

108. T. Vidalis, "Surrogacy 'Tourism,'" *Culture and Research* 5(2016): 113–118.

109. Jingjing Zeng, Yonglin Wen, Chao Bi, and Richard Feiock, "Effect of Tourism Development on Urban Air Pollution in China: The Moderating Role of Tourism Infrastructure," *Journal of Cleaner Production* 280 (2020): 124397.

212 NOTES

110. Pablo de Lora, "Reproductive Rights in Spain: From 'Abortion Tourism' to 'Reproduction Destination,'" *Ethics of Life: Contemporary Iberian Debates* (2016): 163.

111. Nicole Campion, Cassandra L. Thiel, Justin DeBlois, Noe C. Woods, Amy E. Landis, and Melissa M. Bilec, "Life Cycle Assessment Perspectives on Delivering an Infant in the US," *Science of the Total Environment* 425 (2012): 191–198.

112. P. E. Bailey, J. van Roosmalen, G. Mola, C. Evans, L. de Bernis, and B. Dao, "Assisted Vaginal Delivery in Low and Middle Income Countries: An Overview," *BJOG: An International Journal of Obstetrics & Gynaecology* 124, no. 9 (2017): 1335–1344.

113. Ushma D. Upadhyay, Nicole E. Johns, Rebecca Barron, Alice F. Cartwright, Chantal Tapé, Alyssa Mierjeski, and Alyson J. McGregor, "Abortion-Related Emergency Department Visits in the United States: An Analysis of a National Emergency Department Sample," *BMC Medicine* 16, no. 1 (2018): 88.

114. Nichole Wyndham, Paula Gabriela Marin Figueira, and Pasquale Patrizio, "A Persistent Misperception: Assisted Reproductive Technology Can Reverse the 'Aged Biological Clock,'" *Fertility and Sterility* 97, no. 5 (2012): 1044–1047.

115. Cardin de Carvalho et al., "'We Are Not Infertile.'"

116. M. Said Yildiz and M. Mahmud Khan, "Opportunities for Reproductive Tourism: Cost and Quality Advantages of Turkey in the Provision of in-Vitro Fertilization (IVF) Services," *BMC Health Services Research* 16, no. 1 (2016): 1–8.

117. Faddy, Gosden, and Gosden, "A Demographic Projection."

118. U. Outka, "Fairness in the Low-Carbon Shift: Learning from Environmental Justice," In *Energy Justice* (Edward Elgar, 2018).

119. Elicia Grilley Green, Robert Truog, and J. Wesley Boyd, "How Ought Health Care Be Allocated? Two Proposals," *Perspectives in Biology and Medicine* 62, no. 4 (2019): 765–777.

120. Bill McKibben, *The End of Nature,* quoted in William R. LaFleur, *Liquid Life: Abortion and Buddhism in Japan* (Princeton, NJ: Princeton University Press, 1992), 191.

121. "Nobel Prize in Physiology or Medicine 2010 Was Awarded to Robert G. Edwards for IVF Fertilization," *ScienceDaily*, October 4, 2010, www.sciencedaily.com/relea ses/2010/10/101004101447.htm.

Chapter 1

1. L. Belkhir and A. Elmeligi, "Carbon Footprint of the Global Pharmaceutical Industry and Relative Impact of Its Major Players," *Journal of Cleaner Production* 214, no. 5 (2019): 185–194.

2. J. Pierce and A. Jameton, "Sustainable Health Care and Emerging Ethical Responsibilities," *Canadian Medical Association Journal* 164 (2001): 365.

3. I. Roberts, "The NHS Carbon Reduction Strategy," *BMJ* 38 (2009): 248–49, at 248.

4. NHS Sustainable Development Unit, *Saving Carbon, Improving Health: NHS Carbon Reduction Strategy for England* (London: NHS Sustainable Development Unit, 2009), 31.

NOTES 213

5. Sustainable Development Unit for NHS England and Public Health England. *Reducing the Use of Natural Resources in Health and Social Care: 2018 Report* (Cambridge: Victoria House, 2018), figure 4.

6. J. Chung and D. Meltzer, "Estimate of the Carbon Footprint of the US Health Care Sector," *JAMA* 302 (2009): 1970–1972.

7. Matthew Eckelman and Jodi Sherman, "Environmental Impacts of the U.S. Health Care System and Effects on Public Health," *PLoS ONE* 1 (2016): e0157014.

8. Carnegie Mellon University, Green Design Institute, "Economic Input-Output Life Cycle Assessment (EIO-LCA) US 2002 (428 Sectors) Producer Model," 2021, http://www.eiolca.net/.

9. N. Hawkes, "Cutting Emissions by Drug Industry Is Crucial to Reducing NHS's Carbon Footprint," *BMJ* 345 (2012), doi:https://doi.org/10.1136/bmj.e8243.

10. NHS Sustainable Development Unit, *Saving Carbon, Improving Health*, 34.

11. Sustainable Development Unit for NHS England and Public Health England, *Reducing the Use of Natural Resources in Health and Social Care: 2018 Report,* 2018, https://www.sduhealth.org.uk/documents/Policy%20and%20strategy/20180912_Health_and_Social_Care_NRF_web.pdf.

12. Cristina Richie, "Environmental Sustainability and the Carbon Emissions of Pharmaceuticals," *Journal of Medical Ethics* 48, no. 5 (2022): 334–337.

13. One exception is the carbon footprint of 200mg of Lithium Carbonate is estimated to be 215.2 gCO2e. Daniel Lawrence Maughan, "Determining an Approach to Estimating the Carbon Footprint of Mental Health Care That Is Fit for Purpose" (PhD dissertation, Warwick Medical School, University of Warwick, November 2015), 123, table 20.

14. Penelope M. Webb, "Fertility Drugs and Ovarian Cancer," *BMJ* 338 (2009): a3075.

15. M. Semet, M. Paci, J. Saïas-Magnan, C. Metzler-Guillemain, R. Boissier, H. Lejeune, and J. Perrin, "The Impact of Drugs on Male Fertility: A Review," *Andrology* 5, no. 4 (2017): 640–663.

16. J. Whitty, "Diagnosing Health Care's Carbon Footprint," *Mother Jones,* November 10, 2009, http://www.motherjones.com/blue-marble/2009/11/diagnosing-health-cares-carbon-footprint.

17. Willis Jenkins, *The Future of Ethics: Sustainability, Social Justice, and Religious Creativity* (Washington, DC: Georgetown University Press, 2013), 219.

18. National Center for Health Statistics National Health and Nutrition Examination Survey, table 38, 2018, https://www.cdc.gov/nchs/data/hus/2018/038.pdf; R. Beau-Lejdstrom, Ian Douglas, Stephen JW Evans, and Liam Smeeth, "Latest Trends in ADHD Drug Prescribing Patterns in Children in the UK: Prevalence, Incidence and Persistence," *BMJ Open* 6, no. 6 (2016): e010508; B. Mars et al., "Influences on Antidepressant Prescribing Trends in the UK: 1995–2011," *Social Psychiatry and Psychiatric Epidemiology* 52 (2017): 193–200; E. D. Kantor et al., "Trends in Prescription Drug Use among Adults in the United States from 1999–2012," *JAMA* 314 (2015): 1818–1830; P. Rui and T. Okeyode, "National Ambulatory Medical Care Survey: 2016 National Summary Tables," https://www.cdc.gov/nchs/data/ahcd/namcs_summary/2016_namcs_web_tables.pdf.

214   NOTES

19. J. Tauber et al. "Quantification of the Cost and Potential Environmental Effects of Unused Pharmaceutical Products in Cataract Surgery," *JAMA Ophthalmology* 137 (2019): 1156–1163.

20. T. H. Dellit et al., "Infectious Diseases Society of America and the Society for Healthcare Epidemiology of America Guidelines for Developing an Institutional Program to Enhance Antimicrobial Stewardship," *Clinical Infectious Diseases* 44 (2007): 159–177.

21. D. Mendelson, Rajeev Ramchand, Richard Abramson, and Anne Tumlinson. "Prescription Drugs in Nursing Homes: Managing Costs and Quality in a Complex Environment," no. 784 (2002): 1–18, at 3.

22. World Health Organization, "Adherence to Long Term Therapies: Evidence for Action," 2003, https://apps.who.int/iris/bitstream/handle/10665/42682/9241545992.pdf.

23. M. J. Green, "Medication Nonadherence: There's an App for That!," *Mayo Clinic Proceedings* 93 (2018): 1346–1350.

24. Centers for Disease Control and Prevention, National Center for Injury Prevention and Control, and Division of Unintentional Injury Prevention, "Understanding the Epidemic," 2017, https://www.cdc.gov/drugoverdose/epidemic/index.html.

25. U. Bauer et al., "Prevention of Chronic Disease in the 21st Century: Elimination of the Leading Preventable Causes of Premature Death and Disability in the USA," *Lancet* 384 (2014): 45–52.

26. A. Dunlop and L. Newman, "ADHD and Psychostimulants—Overdiagnosis and Overprescription," *Medical Journal of Australia* 204 (2016): 139.

27. Elizabeth R. Bertone-Johnson et al., "Anti-Müllerian Hormone Levels and Incidence of Early Natural Menopause in a Prospective Study," *Human Reproduction* 33, no. 6 (2018): 1175–1182.

28. Sofia Gameiro et al., "Why Do Patients Discontinue Fertility Treatment? A Systematic Review of Reasons and Predictors of Discontinuation in Fertility Treatment," *Human Reproduction Update* 18, no. 6 (2012): 652–669.

29. Danielle G. Tsevat et al., "Sexually Transmitted Diseases and Infertility," *American Journal of Obstetrics and Gynecology* 216, no. 1 (2017): 1–9.

30. Paraskevi Matsota, Eva Kaminioti, and Georgia Kostopanagiotou, "Anesthesia Related Toxic Effects on in Vitro Fertilization Outcome: Burden of Proof," *BioMed Research International* 2015 (2015): 1–9.

31. Jessica Selter, Timothy Wen, Katherine L. Palmerola, Alexander M. Friedman, Zev Williams, and Eric J. Forman, "Life-Threatening Complications among Women with Severe Ovarian Hyperstimulation Syndrome," *American Journal of Obstetrics and Gynecology* 220, no. 6 (2019): 575–e1.

32. So-Hyun Choi et al., "Psychological Side-Effects of Clomiphene Citrate and Human Menopausal Gonadotrophin," *Journal of Psychosomatic Obstetrics & Gynecology* 26, no. 2 (2005): 93–100.

33. Frutos Carlos Marhuenda-Egea et al., "Improving Human Embryos Selection in IVF: Non-invasive Metabolomic and Chemometric Approach," *Metabolomics* 7, no. 2 (2011): 247–256.

34. J. Avorn, "The $2.6 Billion Pill—Methodologic and Policy Considerations," *New England Journal of Medicine* 372 (2015): 1877–1879.

35. J. Tucker and M. Faul, "Industrial Research: Drug Companies Must Adopt Green Chemistry," *Nature News* 534 (2016): 27.

36. M. Angell, "Excess in the Pharmaceutical Industry," *Canadian Medical Association Journal* 171 (2004): 1451–1453.

37. G. Gomez and F. Stanford, "US Health Policy and Prescription Drug Coverage of FDA-Approved Medications for the Treatment of Obesity," *International Journal of Obesity* 42 (2018): 495–500.

38. Wei Yang, "How Does the Pharmaceutical Industry Influence Prescription? A Qualitative Study of Provider Payment Incentives and Drug Remunerations in Hospitals in Shanghai," *Health Economics, Policy and Law* 11, no. 4 (2016): 379–395.

39. Chris Morris, "Things Are Looking Up in America's Porn Industry," NBC News, January 20, 2015, http://www.nbcnews.com/business/business-news/things-are-looking-americas-porn-industry-n289431.

40. Other ethical concerns are highlighted and addressed in Chapter 5.

41. Maik Birnbach, Annekatrin Lehmann, Elisa Naranjo, and Matthias Finkbeiner, "A Condom's Footprint—Life Cycle Assessment of a Natural Rubber Condom," *International Journal of Life Cycle Assessment* 25 (2020): 1–16.

42. M. F. Townsend, J. R. Richard, and M. A. Witt, "Artificially Stimulated Ejaculation in the Brain-Dead Patient: A Case Report," *Urology* 47, no. 5 (1996): 760–762.

43. Nils H. Nilsson, Bjørn Malmgren-Hansen, Nils Bernth, Eva Pedersen, and Kirsten Pommer, "Survey and Health Assessment of Chemicals Substances in Sex Toys," *Survey of Chemical Substances in Consumer Products* 77 (2006): 1–85.

44. N. K.Tumram, R. V. Bardale, and V. N. Ambade, "Sperm Motility and Viability Extracted from Penile Tract of Corpses: A Preliminary Study," *Medico-Legal Journal* 84, no. 3 (2016): 132–134; S. Shefi et al., "Posthumous Sperm Retrieval: Analysis of Time Interval to Harvest Sperm," *Human Reproduction* 21, no. 11 (2006): 2890–2893.

45. Shefi et al., "Posthumous Sperm Retrieval," 2890–2893.

46. Tumram, Bardale, and Ambade, "Sperm Motility and Viability Extracted from Penile Tract of Corpses," 132–134.

47. Andrzej Pastwa, "Responsible Procreation—Co-responsibility of Spouses: From Adequate Anthropology to the Legal Anthropology of Matrimony," *Philosophy and Canon Law* 6 (2020): 37–55.

48. Siavash Vaziri, Farya Fakouri, Maryam Mirzaei, Mandana Afsharian, Mohsen Azizi, and Morteza Arab-Zozani, "Prevalence of Medical Errors in Iran: A Systematic Review and Meta-analysis," *BMC Health Services Research* 19, no. 1 (2019): 1–11.

49. John M. Smoot, "Why Sperm 'Donation' Is Bad for Dads and Kids," *Public Discourse*, February 27, 2013, http://www.thepublicdiscourse.com/2013/02/7571/.

50. Smoot, "Why Sperm 'Donation' Is Bad for Dads and Kids.

51. Alessandra Babore, Liborio Stuppia, Carmen Trumello, Carla Candelori, and Ivana Antonucci, "Male Factor Infertility and Lack of Openness about Infertility as Risk

216 NOTES

Factors for Depressive Symptoms in Males Undergoing Assisted Reproductive Technology Treatment in Italy," *Fertility and Sterility* 107, no. 4 (2017): 1041–1047.

52. J. Gerris, "Methods of Semen Collection Not Based on Masturbation or Surgical Sperm Retrieval," *Human Reproduction Update* 5, no. 3 (1999): 211–215.

53. Alison Chapple, Maria Salinas, Sue Ziebland, Ann McPherson, and Aidan Macfarlane, "Fertility Issues: The Perceptions and Experiences of Young Men Recently Diagnosed and Treated for Cancer," *Journal of Adolescent Health* 40, no. 1 (2007): 69–75.

54. Laura Benaglia, Andrea Busnelli, Rossella Biancardi, Walter Vegetti, Marco Reschini, Paolo Vercellini, and Edgardo Somigliana, "Oocyte Retrieval Difficulties in Women with Ovarian Endometriomas," *Reproductive Biomedicine Online* 37, no. 1 (2018): 77–84.

55. Catheryne Chiang, Sharada Mahalingam, and Jodi A. Flaws, "Environmental Contaminants Affecting Fertility and Somatic Health," *Seminars in Reproductive Medicine* 35, no. 3 (2017): 241 (NIH Public Access).

56. Cassandra L. Thiel, Matthew Eckelman, Richard Guido, Matthew Huddleston, Amy E. Landis, Jodi Sherman, Scott O. Shrake, Noe Copley-Woods, and Melissa M. Bilec, "Environmental Impacts of Surgical Procedures: Life Cycle Assessment of Hysterectomy in the United States," *Environmental Science & Technology* 49, no. 3 (2015): 1779–1786.

57. Abhijeet G. Parvatker, Huseyin Tunceroglu, Jodi D. Sherman, Philip Coish, Paul Anastas, Julie B. Zimmerman, and Matthew J. Eckelman, "Cradle-to-Gate Greenhouse Gas Emissions for Twenty Anesthetic Active Pharmaceutical Ingredients Based on Process Scale-Up and Process Design Calculations," *ACS Sustainable Chemistry & Engineering* 7, no. 7 (2019): 6580–6591.

58. Farnaz Sohrabvand, Fedyeh Haghollahi, Masoomeh Maasomi, and Mamak Shariat, "Effect of Piroxicam on ART Outcome: A Pilot Study," *International Journal of Fertility & Sterility* 8, no. 3 (2014): 243.

59. Irene Kwan, Rui Wang, Emily Pearce, and Siladitya Bhattacharya, "Pain Relief for Women Undergoing Oocyte Retrieval for Assisted Reproduction," *Cochrane Database of Systematic Reviews* 5 (2018): 1–92.

60. Paolo Emanuele Levi-Setti, Federico Cirillo, Valeria Scolaro, Emanuela Morenghi, Francesca Heilbron, Donatella Girardello, Elena Zannoni, and Pasquale Patrizio, "Appraisal of Clinical Complications after 23,827 Oocyte Retrievals in a Large Assisted Reproductive Technology Program," *Fertility and Sterility* 109, no. 6 (2018): 1038–1043.

61. Janice Raymond, *Women as Wombs* (San Francisco: Harper Collins, 1993), 134.

62. Rebecca Sundhagen, "Breastfeeding and Child Spacing," in *Childbirth across Cultures* ed. Helaine Selin (Dordrecht: Springer, 2009), 23–32.

63. J. Habbema et al., "The Effect of in Vitro Fertilization on Birth Rates in Western Countries," *Human Reproduction* 24, no. 6 (2009): 1414–1419.

64. E. A. DeFranco, L. M. Seske, J. M. Greenberg, and L. J. Muglia, "Influence of Interpregnancy Interval on Neonatal Morbidity," *American Journal of Obstetrics and Gynecology* 212, no 3 (March 2015): 386.e1–386.e9.

65. Ray Miller and Mahesh Karra, "Birth Spacing and Child Health Trajectories," *Population and Development Review* 46, no. 2 (2020): 347–371.
66. Susan E. Lanzendorf, Catherine A. Boyd, Diane L. Wright, Suheil Muasher, Sergio Oehninger, and Gary D. Hodgen, "Use of Human Gametes Obtained from Anonymous Donors for the Production of Human Embryonic Stem Cell Lines," *Fertility and Sterility* 76, no. 1 (2001): 132–137.
67. Marjan Omidi, Azita Faramarzi, Azam Agharahimi, and Mohammad Ali Khalili, "Noninvasive Imaging Systems for Gametes and Embryo Selection in IVF Programs: A Review," *Journal of Microscopy* 267, no. 3 (2017): 253–264.
68. Elizabeth S. Ginsburg, Valerie L. Baker, Catherine Racowsky, Ethan Wantman, James Goldfarb, and Judy E. Stern, "Use of Preimplantation Genetic Diagnosis and Preimplantation Genetic Screening in the United States: A Society for Assisted Reproductive Technology Writing Group Paper," *Fertility and Sterility* 96, no. 4 (2011): 865–868.
69. Kevin N. Keane, Peter M. Hinchliffe, Philip K. Rowlands, Gayatri Borude, Shanti Srinivasan, Satvinder S. Dhaliwal, and John L. Yovich, "DHEA Supplementation Confers No Additional Benefit to That of Growth Hormone on Pregnancy and Live Birth Rates in IVF Patients Categorized as Poor Prognosis," *Frontiers in Endocrinology* 9 (2018): 14.
70. Jianghui Li, Mingru Yin, Bian Wang, Jiaying Lin, Qiuju Chen, Ningling Wang, Qifeng Lyu, Yun Wang, Yanping Kuang, and Qianqian Zhu, "The Effect of Storage Time after Vitrification on Pregnancy and Neonatal Outcomes among 24,698 Patients Following the First Embryo Transfer Cycles," *Human Reproduction* 35, no. 7 (2020): 1675–1684.
71. Yan-Ting Wu, Cheng Li, Yi-Min Zhu, Shu-Hua Zou, Qiong-Fang Wu, Li-Ping Wang, Yan Wu, et al., "Outcomes of Neonates Born Following Transfers of Frozen-Thawed Cleavage-Stage Embryos with Blastomere Loss: A Prospective, Multicenter, Cohort Study," *BMC Medicine* 16, no. 1 (2018): 1–13.
72. Heather Silber Mohamed, "Embryonic Politics: Attitudes about Abortion, Stem Cell Research, and IVF," *Politics and Religion* 11, no. 3 (2018): 459–497.
73. Laurie Zoloth and Alyssa Henning, "Bioethics and Oncofertility: Arguments and Insights from Religious Traditions," in *Oncofertility: Ethical, Legal, Social, and Medical Perspectives*, ed. Teresa Woodruff, Laurie Zoloth, Lisa Campo-Engelstein, Sarah Rodriguez (New York: Springer, 2010), 266.
74. Kathryn Macapagal, Ramona Bhatia, and George J. Greene, "Differences in Healthcare Access, Use, and Experiences within a Community Sample of Racially Diverse Lesbian, Gay, Bisexual, Transgender, and Questioning Emerging Adults," *LGBT Health* 3, no. 6 (2016): 434–442.
75. Obiajulu Nnamuchi, "Nigeria's Same Sex Marriage (Prohibition) Act and Threat of Sanctions by Western Countries: A Legitimate Case of Human Rights Advancement or What," *Sw. J. Int'l L.* 25 (2019): 120–154; Elaine Jeffreys and Pan Wang, "Pathways to Legalizing Same-Sex Marriage in China and Taiwan: Globalization and 'Chinese Values,'" in *Global Perspectives on Same-Sex Marriage*, ed. Bronwyn Winter, Maxime Forest, Réjane Sénac (Cham: Palgrave Macmillan, 2018), 197–219.

218 NOTES

76. Camisha Russell, "Rights-Holders or Refugees? Do Gay Men Need Reproductive Justice?," *Reproductive Biomedicine & Society Online* 7 (2018): 131–140; Weei Lo and Lisa Campo-Engelstein, "Expanding the Clinical Definition of Infertility to Include Socially Infertile Individuals and Couples," in *Reproductive Ethics II*, EditorsLisa Campo-Engelstein and Paul Burcher (Cham: Springer, 2018), 71–83.

77. Irina A. Sukhareva, Shanmugaraj Kulanthaivel, and Keerthanaa Balasundaram, "Characteristics of Surrogacy Procedure in the View of Surrogates, Infertile Couples, Doctors and Society," *International Medical Journal* 27, no. 4 (2020): 415–418.

78. Karen Busby and Delaney Vun, "Revisiting the Handmaid's Tale: Feminist Theory Meets Empirical Research on Surrogate Mothers," *Can. J. Fam. L.* 26 (2010): 13–93.

79. Kenneth Lee Raby and Mary Dozier, "Attachment across the Lifespan: Insights from Adoptive Families," *Current Opinion in Psychology* 25 (2019): 81–85.

80. NHS Birmingham and Solihull Clinical Commissioning Group and NHS Sandwell and West Birmingham Clinical Commissioning Group, "Policy for the Provision of NHS Funded Gamete Retrieval and Cryopreservation for the Preservation of Fertility," final version 7, approved December 11, 2018, section 3: "Timescales for NHS Funding for Storage of Gametes," https://www.birminghamandsolihullccg.nhs. uk/about-us/publications/policies/2409-provision-of-nhs-funded-gamete-retrieval-and-cryopreservation-for-the-preservation-of-fertility/file.

81. Lindsay P. Cohn and Nathan W. Toronto, "Markets and Manpower: The Political Economy of Compulsory Military Service," *Armed Forces & Society* 43, no. 3 (2017): 436–458.

82. Anne E. Martini and Joseph O. Doyle, "Fertility Preservation Before Deployment: Oocyte and Sperm Freezing in Members of the Active Duty Military," *Seminars in Reproductive Medicine* 37, no. 05/06 (2019): 232–238.

83. Felicia L. Balzano and Steven J. Hudak, "Military Genitourinary Injuries: Past, Present, and Future," *Translational Andrology and Urology* 7, no. 4 (2018): 646.

84. Balzano and Hudak, "Military Genitourinary Injuries," 646.

85. D. Even, "Dead Woman's Ova Harvested after Court Okays Family Request," *Haaretz*, August 8, 2011, https://www.haaretz.com/dead-woman-s-ova-harvested-after-court-okays-family-request-1.377495.

86. A. Raziel et al., "Nationwide Use of Postmortem Retrieved Sperm in Israel: A Follow-up Report," *Fertility and Sterility* 95, no. 8 (June 2011): 2694.

87. Teri Weaver, "U.S. Personnel in Iraq Could Face Court-Martial for Getting Pregnant," *Stars and Stripes*, December 19, 2009, http://www.stripes.com/news/u-s-personnel-in-iraq-could-face-court-martial-for-getting-pregnant-1.97533.

88. Kayla Williams, "Veterans' Access to Reproductive Healthcare: Enhance Equity Now," testimony before House Veterans Affairs Committee Subcommittee on Health, July 1, 2020, https://www.jstor.org/stable/pdf/resrep28748.pdf.

89. Oliver Belcher, Patrick Bigger, Ben Neimark, and Cara Kennelly, "Hidden Carbon Costs of the 'Everywhere War': Logistics, Geopolitical Ecology, and the Carbon Boot-print of the US Military," *Transactions of the Institute of British Geographers* 45, no. 1 (2020): 65–80.

NOTES 219

90. Vasileios Bozoudis and Ioannis Sebos, "The Carbon Footprint of Transport Activities of the 401 Military General Hospital of Athens," *Environmental Modeling & Assessment* 26, no. 2 (2021): 155–162.

91. A local Boston magazine aimed at professionals in their 30s and 40s regularly features advertisement as such. See *Improper Bostonian,* http://www.improper.com.

92. Dominic Stoop, Ana Cobo, and Sherman Silber, "Fertility Preservation for Age-Related Fertility Decline," *Lancet* 384, no. 9950 (2014): 1311–1319.

93. Karin Hammarberg, Maggie Kirkman, Natasha Pritchard, Martha Hickey, Michelle Peate, John McBain, Franca Agresta, Chris Bayly, and Jane Fisher, "Reproductive Experiences of Women Who Cryopreserved Oocytes for Non-medical Reasons," *Human Reproduction* 32, no. 3 (2017): 575–581.

94. Margi Murphy, "Why Facebook and Google Offer Egg Freezing as a Perk of the Job," *The Telegraph,* May 3, 2019, https://www.telegraph.co.uk/technology/2019/05/03/facebook-google-offer-egg-freezing-perk-job/.

95. Petra Bueskens, *Modern Motherhood and Women's Dual Identities: Rewriting the Sexual Contract* (Milton Park: Routledge, 2018).

96. Margaret Gough, "Birth Spacing, Human Capital, and the Motherhood Penalty at Midlife in the United States," *Demographic Research* 37 (2017): 363–416.

97. Monica Owoko, "Student Pregnancy and Maternity: Implications for Teacher Training Colleges," *Journal of African Studies in Educational Management and Leadership* 8, no. 1 (2017): 36–57.

98. Jay L. Zagorsky, "Divergent Trends in US Maternity and Paternity Leave, 1994–2015," *American Journal of Public Health* 107, no. 3 (2017): 460–465.

99. Shulamith Firestone observes that a feminist revolution requires the revolt of women and the "seizure of control of reproduction: not only the full restoration to women of ownership of their own bodies" (which has been accomplished through contraception, abortion, and, some would maintain, medicalized reproduction) but also "all the social institutions of childbearing and childrearing." The latter have not been accomplished. Shulamith Firestone, *The Dialectic of Sex: The Case for Feminist Revolution* (New York: Bantam, 1970), 11.

100. Adam H. Boyette, Sheina Lew-Levy, Mallika S. Sarma, and Lee T. Gettler, "Testosterone, Fathers as Providers and Caregivers, and Child Health: Evidence from Fisher-Farmers in the Republic of the Congo," *Hormones and Behavior* 107 (2019): 35–45.

101. Bruno Schoumaker, "Male Fertility around the World and over Time: How Different Is It from Female Fertility," *Population and Development Review* 45, no. 3 (2019): 459.

102. Hilde de Kluiver, Jacobine E. Buizer-Voskamp, Conor V. Dolan, and Dorret I. Boomsma, "Paternal Age and Psychiatric Disorders: A Review," *American Journal of Medical Genetics Part B: Neuropsychiatric Genetics* 174, no. 3 (2017): 202–213.

103. Line Elmerdahl Frederiksen, Andreas Ernst, Nis Brix, Lea Lykke Braskhøj Lauridsen, Laura Roos, Cecilia Høst Ramlau-Hansen, and Charlotte Kvist Ekelund, "Risk of Adverse Pregnancy Outcomes at Advanced Maternal Age," *Obstetrics & Gynecology* 131, no. 3 (2018): 457–463.

220 NOTES

104. Geneviève Horwood, Charles Opondo, Saswati Sanyal Choudhury, Anjali Rani, and Manisha Nair, "Risk Factors for Maternal Mortality among 1.9 Million Women in Nine Empowered Action Group States in India: Secondary Analysis of Annual Health Survey Data," *BMJ Open* 10, no. 8 (2020): e038910.

105. Sarah Knapton, "Delaying Motherhood by Freezing Eggs Could Harm Birth Chances," *Telegraph*, August 11, 2015, https://www.telegraph.co.uk/news/health/news/11796 942/Delaying-motherhood-by-freezing-eggs-could-harm-birth-chances.html.

106. Sumer Allensworth Wallace, Kiara L. Blough, and Laxmi A. Kondapalli, "Fertility Preservation in the Transgender Patient: Expanding Oncofertility Care beyond Cancer," *Gynecological Endocrinology* 30, no. 12 (2014): 868–871.

107. Anna Smajdor, "Should IVF Guidelines Be Relaxed in the UK?," *Expert Review of Obstetrics & Gynecology* 4, no. 5 (2009): 501–508.

108. Teresa Woodruff and Karrie Ann Snyder, eds., *Oncofertility: Fertility Preservation for Cancer Survivors.* vol. 138 (Berlin: Springer Science & Business Media, 2007).

109. Angela Dauti, Brigitte Gerstl, Serena Chong, Orin Chisholm, and Antoinette Anazodo, "Improvements in Clinical Trials Information Will Improve the Reproductive Health and Fertility of Cancer Patients," *Journal of Adolescent and Young Adult Oncology* 6, no. 2 (2017): 235–269.

110. Landon Trost and Robert Brannigan, "Oncofertility and the Male Cancer Patient," *Current Treatment Options in Oncology* 13, no. 2 (2012): 146–160.

111. Stoop, Cobo, and Silber, "Fertility Preservation for Age-Related Fertility Decline," 1311–1319.

112. Pascale Jadoul, Apolline Guilmain, J. Squifflet, Mathieu Luyckx, Raffaella Votino, Christine Wyns, and Marie-Madeleine Dolmans, "Efficacy of Ovarian Tissue Cryopreservation for Fertility Preservation: Lessons Learned from 545 Cases," *Human Reproduction* 32, no. 5 (2017): 1046–1054.

113. Gwendolyn P. Quinn et al., "Preserving the Right to Future Children: An Ethical Case Analysis," *American Journal of Bioethics* 12, no. 6 (2012): 38–43.

114. R. Ronn and H. E. G. Holzer, "Oncofertility in Canada: Cryopreservation and Alternative Options for Future Parenthood," *Current Oncology* 21, no. 1 (2014): e137.

115. Clarisa R. Gracia, Jorge J. E. Gracia, and Shasha Chen, "Ethical Dilemmas in Oncofertility: An Exploration of Three Clinical Scenarios," in *Oncofertility: Ethical, Legal, Social, and Medical Perspectives*, ed. Teresa Woodrufff et al. (New York: Springer, 2010), 198.

116. Mindy S. Christianson, Judy E. Stern, Fangbai Sun, Heping Zhang, Aaron K. Styer, Wendy Vitek, and Alex J. Polotsky, "Embryo Cryopreservation and Utilization in the United States from 2004–2013," *F&S Reports* 1, no. 2 (2020): 71–77.

117. Robert D. Nachtigall, Gay Becker, Carrie Friese, Anneliese Butler, and Kirstin MacDougall, "Parents' Conceptualization of Their Frozen Embryos Complicates the Disposition Decision," *Fertility and Sterility* 84, no. 2 (2005): 431–434.

118. Antoinette Anazodo, Lauren Ataman-Millhouse, Yasmin Jayasinghe, and Teresa K. Woodruff, "Oncofertility—An Emerging Discipline Rather Than a Special Consideration," *Pediatric Blood & Cancer* 65, no. 11 (2018): e27297.

NOTES 221

119. Sénat de Belgique, "La loi du 6 juillet 2007 relative à la procréation médicalement assistée et à la destination des embryons surnuméraires et des gametes," *Moniteur belge* 38575 (2007): art. 15.

120. Joseph A. Raho, "In Whose Best Interests? Critiquing the 'Family-as-Unit' Myth in Pediatric Ethics," in *Bioethics: Medical, Ethical and Legal Perspectives,* ed. Peter A. Clark (London: IntechOpen, 2016), 145–160.

121. Laurie Zoloth and Alyssa Henning, "Bioethics and Oncofertility: Arguments and Insights from Religious Traditions," in *Oncofertility: Ethical, Legal, Social, and Medical Perspectives,* ed. Teresa Woodrufff et al. (New York: Springer, 2010), 264.

122. American Pregnancy Association, "In Vitro Fertilization: IVF," accessed August 30, 2023, http:// americanpregnancy.org.

123. Jadoul et al., "Efficacy of Ovarian Tissue Cryopreservation for Fertility Preservation," 1046–1054.

124. Teresa K. Woodruff, "The Oncofertility Consortium—Addressing Fertility in Young People with Cancer," *Nature Reviews Clinical Oncology* 7, no. 8 (2010): 466.

125. Maughan, "Determining an Approach to Estimating the Carbon Footprint of Mental Health Care That Is Fit for Purpose," 187, table 32. The total difference in carbon footprint between groups according to the different assumptions for how the carbon footprint of therapy sessions equates to appointments.

126. Y. Wang, Shanna Logan, K. Stern, C. E. Wakefield, R. J. Cohn, F. Agresta, Y. Jayasinghe, et al., "Supportive Oncofertility Care, Psychological Health and Reproductive Concerns: A Qualitative Study," *Supportive Care in Cancer* 28, no. 2 (2020): 809–817.

127. Glen A. Lau and Anthony J. Schaeffer, "Current Standing and Future Directions in Pediatric Oncofertility: A Narrative Review," *Translational Andrology and Urology* 7, no. suppl. 3 (2018): S276.

128. Karina Kubicius and Monika Michałowska, "Shaping the Body of a Child: Invasive Medical Procedures on Incompetent Patients—Some Ethical and Medical Remarks on Ashley's Case 1," *Analiza i Egzystencja* 49 (2020): 5–29.

129. Evelyn Verbeke, Jeroen Luyten, and Thomas D'Hooghe, "The Economics of IVF: Evaluating the Necessity and Value of Public Funding," in *Patient-Centered Assisted Reproduction: How to Integrate Exceptional Care with Cutting-Edge Technology,* ed. Alice D. Domar, Denny Sakkas, Thomas L. Toth (Cambridge: Cambridge University Press, 2020): 106–134.

130. Emily Jackson, "'Social' Egg Freezing and the UK's Statutory Storage Time Limits," *Journal of Medical Ethics* 42, no. 11 (2016): 738–741.

131. Gerard Letterie and Dov Fox, "Lawsuit Frequency and Claims Basis over Lost, Damaged, and Destroyed Frozen Embryos over a 10-Year Period," *F&S Reports* 1, no. 2 (2020): 78–82.

132. Sharon T. Mortimer and David Mortimer, *Quality and Risk Management in the IVF Laboratory* (Cambridge: Cambridge University Press, 2015).

133. E. M. E. Balkenende, W. Dondorp, M. C. Ploem, C. B. Lambalk, M. Goddijn, and F. Mol, "A Mother's Gift of Life: Exploring the Concerns and Ethical Aspects of Fertility

222 NOTES

Preservation for Mother-to-Daughter Oocyte Donation," *Human Reproduction* 32, no. 1 (2017): 2–6.

134. K. Baum, "Golden Eggs: Toward the Rational Regulation of Oocyte Donation," Brigham Young University Law Review 107 (2001): 107–166.

135. Nancy Li, Yasmin Jayasinghe, Matthew A. Kemertzis, Paddy Moore, and Michelle Peate, "Fertility Preservation in Pediatric and Adolescent Oncology Patients: The Decision-Making Process of Parents," *Journal of Adolescent and Young Adult Oncology* 6, no. 2 (2017): 213–222.

136. Monica M. Rivera-Franco and Eucario Leon-Rodriguez, "Delays in Breast Cancer Detection and Treatment in Developing Countries," *Breast Cancer: Basic and Clinical Research* 12 (2018): 1178223417752677.

137. Ellen Warner, Karen Glass, Shu Foong, and Emily Sandwith, "Update on Fertility Preservation for Younger Women with Breast Cancer," *CMAJ* 192, no. 35 (2020): E1003–E1009.

138. Tineke Vandenbroucke, Magali Verheecke, Monica Fumagalli, Christianne Lok, and Frédéric Amant, "Effects of Cancer Treatment during Pregnancy on Fetal and Child Development," *Lancet Child & Adolescent Health* 1, no. 4 (2017): 302–310.

139. Chehin Nelson, Annie Janvier, Pamela G. Nathanson, and Chris Feudtner, "Ethics and the Importance of Good Clinical Practices," *American Journal of Bioethics* 20, no. 1 (2020): 67–70.

140. Mauricio B. Chehin, Tatiana C. S. Bonetti, Paulo C. Serafini, and Eduardo L. A. Motta, "Knowledge regarding Fertility Preservation in Cancer Patients: A Population-Based Survey among Brazilian People during the Pink October Awareness Event," *JBRA Assisted Reproduction* 21, no. 2 (2017): 84.

141. Rebecca A. Ferrer and Wendy Berry Mendes, "Emotion, Health Decision Making, and Health Behaviour," *Psychology & Health* 33, no. 1 (2018): 1–16.

142. Chloe Parton, Jane M. Ussher, and Janette Perz, "Hope, Burden or Risk: A Discourse Analytic Study of the Construction and Experience of Fertility Preservation in the Context of Cancer," *Psychology & Health* 34, no. 4 (2019): 456–477.

143. Daniela Cutas and Kristien Hens, "Preserving Children's Fertility: Two Tales about Children's Right to an Open Future and the Margins of Parental Obligations," *Medicine, Health Care and Philosophy* 18, no. 2 (2015): 253–260.

144. M. Reigstad et al., "Cancer Risk among Parous Women Following Assisted Reproductive Technology," *Human Reproduction* 30, no. 8 (2015): 1952–1963.

145. National Health Services Sustainable Development Unit, *Saving Carbon, Improving Health*, 67.

146. Ellen J. Hoekman, Dan Knoester, Alexander A. W. Peters, Frank W. Jansen, Cornelis D. de Kroon, and Carina G. J. M. Hilders, "Ovarian Survival after Pelvic Radiation: Transposition until the Age of 35 Years," *Archives of Gynecology and Obstetrics* 298, no. 5 (2018): 1001–1007.

147. Jacqueline Clarke, "Dying to Be Mommy: Using Intentional Parenthood as a Proxy for Consent in Posthumous Egg Retrieval Cases," *Michigan State Law Review* no. 4 (2012): 1331–1373.

148. Bethany Bruno and Kavita Shah Arora, "Uterus Transplantation: The Ethics of Using Deceased versus Living Donors," *American Journal of Bioethics* 18, no. 7 (2018): 6–15.

149. R v. Human Fertilisation & Embryology Auth. ex parte Blood (1997), 2 W.L.R. 806 (Eng. C.A.); "Blood Lines," *The Guardian*, October 18, 2004, https://www.theguard ian.com/science/2004/oct/18/medicineandhealth.lifeandhealth.

150. BBC News, "On This Day: 6 February 1997: Widow Allowed Dead Husband's Baby," 2008, http://news.bbc.co.uk/onthisday/hi/dates/stories/february/6/new sid_2536000/2536119.stm.

151. BBC News, "On This Day."

152. BBC News, "On This Day."

153. UK Public General Acts, Human Fertilisation and Embryology (Deceased Fathers) Act 2003, Chapter 24, https://www.legislation.gov.uk/ukpga/2003/24.

154. B. Lewis, *The Ethical and Legal Consequences of Posthumous Reproduction: Arrogance, Avarice and Anguish* (Milton Park: Routledge, 2016), 30.

155. J. R. Dostal, R. Utrata, S. Loyka, J. Brezinova, M. Svobodova, and F. Shenfield, "Postmortem Sperm Retrieval in New European Union Countries: Case Report," *Human Reproduction* 20, no. 8 (2005): 2359–2361.

156. R. Dostal, R. Utrata, S. Loyka, J. Brezinova, M. Svobodova, and F. Shenfield, "Postmortem Sperm Retrieval in New European Union Countries," 2359–2361.

157. A. K. Sikary, O. P. Murty, and R. V. Bardale, "Postmortem Sperm Retrieval in Context of Developing Countries of Indian Subcontinent," *Journal of Human Reproductive Sciences* 9, no. 2 (2016): 82.

158. B. Kroon, Frederick Kroon, Saul Holt, Brittany Wong, and Anusch Yazdani, "Postmortem Sperm Retrieval in Australasia," *Australian and New Zealand Journal of Obstetrics and Gynaecology* 52, no. 5 (2012): 489.

159. Jennifer A. Tash, Linda D. Applegarth, Susan M. Kerr, Joseph J. Fins, Zev Rosenwaks, and Peter N. Schlegel, "Postmortem Sperm Retrieval: The Effect of Instituting Guidelines," *Journal of Urology* 170, no. 5 (2003): 1922–1925.

160. Ethics Committee of the American Society for Reproductive Medicine, "Posthumous Collection and Use of Reproductive Tissue: A Committee Opinion," *Fertility and Sterility* 99, no. 7 (2013): 1842–1845.

161. Ethics Committee of the American Society for Reproductive Medicine, "Posthumous Collection and Use of Reproductive Tissue," 1842–1845.

162. Only 14 of the 50 centers reported. N. Waler and R. Ramasamy, "Policy on Posthumous Sperm Retrieval: Survey of 50 Major Academic Medical Centers," *Fertility and Sterility* 106, no. 3 (2016): e44.

163. Ethics Committee of the American Society for Reproductive Medicine, "Posthumous Collection and Use of Reproductive Tissue," 1842–1845.

164. Ethics Committee of the American Society for Reproductive Medicine, "Posthumous Collection and Use of Reproductive Tissue," 1842–1845.

165. E. Rubinstein, "Postmortem Sperm Retrieval and Its Use," *Israel Attorney General Guidelines* 1, no. 2202 (2003): 1–13.

224 NOTES

166. M. Halperin, "Post-mortem Sperm Retrieval," *Jewish Medical Ethics* 4, no. 1 (2001): 9–13.

167. A. Raziel, Shevach Friedler, Deborah Strassburger, Sarit Kaufman, Ana Umansky, and Raphael Ron-El, "Using Sperm Posthumously: National Guidelines versus Practice," *Fertility and Sterility* 94, no. 3 (2010): 1155.

168. Y. Hashiloni-Dolev and S. Schicktanz, "A Cross-Cultural Analysis of Posthumous Reproduction: The Significance of the Gender and Margins-of-Life Perspectives," *Reproductive Biomedicine & Society Online* 4 (2017): 26.

169. Y. Hashiloni-Dolev, "Posthumous Reproduction (PHR) in Israel: Policy Rationales versus Lay People's Concerns, a Preliminary Study," *Culture, Medicine, and Psychiatry* 39, no. 4 (2015): 645.

170. Nathan Hodson and Joshua Parker, "The Ethical Case for Non-directed Postmortem Sperm Donation," *Journal of Medical Ethics* 46, no. 7 (2020): 489–492.

171. Dena Towner and Roberta Springer Loewy, "Ethics of PGD for a Woman Destined to Develop Early-Onset Alzheimer Disease," in *Genetics: Science, Ethics, and Public Policy,* ed. T. A. Shannon (Lanham, MD: Rowman & Littlefield, 2005), 78.

Chapter 2

1. For instance, "embodied emissions in the manufacture and transportation of purchased goods and services account for over half (60%) of the emissions attributable to NHS England." Sustainable Development Commission, "NHS England Carbon Emissions Carbon Footprinting Report," (UK: NHS, 2009): 1–90, at 5.

2. D. E. Pegg, "Principles of Cryopreservation," in *Methods in Molecular Biology*, ed. John Day and Glyn Stacey (New York: Springer, 2007), 39–57.

3. Chun-jing Shang, Cheng-long Chu, and Zhi-hui Zhang, "Quantitative Assessment on Carbon Emission of Different Structures in Building Life Cycle," *Building Science* 27, no. 12 (2011): 66–70.

4. Alexander M. Quaas and Guido Pennings, "The Current Status of Oocyte Banks: Domestic and International Perspectives," *Fertility and Sterility* 110, no. 7 (2018): 1203–1208.

5. World Health Organization, "Infertility Definitions and Terminology," 2020, https://www.who.int/reproductivehealth/topics/infertility/definitions/en/; American Society of Reproductive Medicine, "Infertility," 2020, https://www.asrm.org/topics/topics index/infertility/.

6. A. Lenzi, F. Lombardo, P. Salacone, L. Gandini, and E. A. Jannini, "Stress, Sexual Dysfunctions, and Male Infertility," *Journal of Endocrinological Investigation* 26, no. 3 suppl. (2003): 72–76.

7. Talat Naz, Lubna Hassan, Nighat F. Gulmeen, and Shahida Sultan, "Laparoscopic Evaluation in Infertility," Journal of the College of Physicians and Surgeons Pakistan 19, no. 11 (2009): 704–707.

8. T. G. Cooper, E. Noonan, S. Von Eckardstein, J. Auger, H. G. Baker, H. M. Behre, T. B. Haugen, T. Kruger, C. Wang, M. T. Mbizvo, and K. M. Vogelsong, "World

Health Organization Reference Values for Human Semen Characteristics," *Human Reproduction Update* 16, no. 3 (2010): 231–245.

9. S. M. Curi, J. I. Ariagno, P. H. Chenlo, Gabriela R. Mendeluk, M. N. Pugliese, L. M. Sardi Segovia, H. E. H. Repetto, and A. M. Blanco, "Asthenozoospermia: Analysis of a Large Population," *Archives of Andrology* 49, no. 5 (2003): 343–349.

10. ESHRE Task Force on Ethics and Law, including W. Dondorp, G. de Wert, G. Pennings, F. Shenfield, P. Devroey, B. Tarlatzis, P. Barri, and K. Diedrich, "Oocyte Cryopreservation for Age-Related Fertility Loss," *Human Reproduction* 27, no. 5 (2012): 1231–1237.

11. Hayden Anthony Homer, "The Role of Oocyte Quality in Explaining 'Unexplained' Infertility," *Seminars in Reproductive Medicine* 38, no. 1 (2020): 21–28.

12. Ewelina Bolcun-Filas, Vera D. Rinaldi, Michelle E. White, and John C. Schimenti, "Reversal of Female Infertility by Chk2 Ablation Reveals the Oocyte DNA Damage Checkpoint Pathway," *Science* 343, no. 6170 (2014): 533–536, at 533.

13. Joe Leigh Simpson, Anver Kuliev, and Svetlana Rechitsky, "Overview of Preimplantation Genetic Diagnosis (PGD): Historical Perspective and Future Direction," *Prenatal Diagnosis* (2019): 23–43.

14. S. Rechitsky and A. Kuliev, "I23 PGD for Genetic Predisposition to Common Disorders," *Reproductive BioMedicine Online* 26 (2013): S9.

15. Anne Donchin, "In Whose Interest? Policy and Politics in Assisted Reproduction," *Bioethics* 25, no. 2 (2011): 94.

16. D. J. Weatherall and John B. Clegg, "Inherited Haemoglobin Disorders: An Increasing Global Health Problem," *Bulletin of the World Health Organization* 79 (2001): 704–712.

17. S. Kahraman, C. Beyazyurek, M. A. Yesilipek, G. Ozturk, M. Ertem, S. Anak, S. Kansoy, S. Aksoylar, B. Kuşkonmaz, H. Oniz, and S. Slavin, "Successful Haematopoietic Stem Cell Transplantation in 44 Children from Healthy Siblings Conceived after Preimplantation HLA Matching," *Reproductive Biomedicine Online* 29, no. 3 (2014): 340–351.

18. Amy Laura Hall, *Conceiving Parenthood: American Protestantism and the Spirit of Reproduction* (Grand Rapids, MI: Eerdmans, 2008), 27.

19. S. Hyatt, "A Shared History of Shame: Sweden's Four-Decade Policy of Forced Sterilization and the Eugenics Movement in the United States," Indiana International & Comparative Law Review 8 (1997): 475–504.

20. Claudia Paz Bailey, "Guatemala: Gender and Reparations for Human Rights Violations," in *What Happened to the Women? Gender and Reparations for Human Rights Violations*, ed. Ruth Rubio-Marín, Pablo De Greiff, and Alexander Mayer-Rieckh (New York: Social Science Research Council, 2006), 92–135.

21. Paul A. Lombardo, *Three Generations, No Imbeciles: Eugenics, the Supreme Court, and* Buck v. Bell (Baltimore: Johns Hopkins University Press, 2008).

22. Janet Smith, "The Introduction to the Vatican Instruction," in *Reproductive Technologies, Marriage and the Church*, ed. Donald G. McCarthy (Braintree, MA: Pope John XXIII Center, 1998), 13–28.

23. Amy Laura Hall, *Conceiving Parenthood: American Protestantism and the Spirit of Reproduction* (Grand Rapids, MI: Eerdmans, 2008), 283.

226 NOTES

24. Hall, *Conceiving Parenthood*, 219.
25. Armand Marie Leroi, "The Future of Neo-eugenics: Now That Many People Approve the Elimination of Certain Genetically Defective Fetuses, Is Society Closer to Screening All Fetuses for All Known Mutations?," *EMBO Reports* 7, no. 12 (2006): 1184–1187.
26. Angelina P. Olesen, Siti Nurani Mohd Nor, Latifah Amin, and Anisah Che Ngah, "Public Perceptions of Ethical, Legal and Social Implications of Pre-implantation Genetic Diagnosis (PGD) in Malaysia," *Science and Engineering Ethics* 23, no. 6 (2017): 1563–1580.
27. Elisabeth Hildt, "Autonomy and Freedom of Choice in Prenatal Genetic Diagnosis," *Medicine, Health Care and Philosophy* 5, no. 1 (2002): 65–72.
28. M. Spriggs, "Commodification of Children Again and Non-disclosure Preimplantation Genetic Diagnosis for Huntington's Disease," *Journal of Medical Ethics* 30, no. 6 (2004): 538–538.
29. Karín Lesnik-Oberstein, ed., *Rethinking Disability Theory and Practice: Challenging Essentialism* (New York: Palgrave MacMillan, 2015).
30. Erik Parens and Adrienne Asch, "The Disability Rights Critique of Prenatal Genetic Testing: Reflections and Recommendations," *Hastings Center Report* 29, no. 5, suppl. (1999): S6.
31. Mathana Amaris Fiona Sivaraman, "Ethical Guiding Principles of 'Do No Harm' and the 'Intention to Save Lives' in Relation to Human Embryonic Stem Cell Research: Finding Common Ground between Religious Views and Principles of Medical Ethics," *Asian Bioethics Review* 11, no. 4 (2019): 409–435.
32. National Institutes for Health Research, "Carbon Reduction Guidelines," October 2010, 1–20, www.nihr.ac.uk/files/NIHR_Carbon_Reduction_Guidelines.pdf.
33. Lichun Tang, Yanting Zeng, Hongzi Du, Mengmeng Gong, Jin Peng, Buxi Zhang, Ming Lei, F. Zhao, W. Wang, X. Li, and J. Liu, "CRISPR/Cas9-Mediated Gene Editing in Human Zygotes Using Cas9 Protein," *Molecular Genetics and Genomics* 292, no. 3 (2017): 525–533.
34. Patrick D. Hsu, Eric S. Lander, and Feng Zhang, "Development and Applications of CRISPR-Cas9 for Genome Engineering," *Cell* 157, no. 6 (2014): 1262–1278.
35. Xiang Jin Kang, Chiong Isabella Noelle Caparas, Boon Seng Soh, and Yong Fan, "Addressing Challenges in the Clinical Applications Associated with CRISPR/Cas9 Technology and Ethical Questions to Prevent Its Misuse," *Protein & Cell* 8, no. 11 (2017): 791–795.
36. H. Bi, "Technique Discussion of CRISPR Babies—A Comment to Jiankui He's Research," *Journal of Medical Discovery* 3, no. 4 (2018): md18047.
37. Jing-ru Li, Simon Walker, Jing-bao Nie, and Xin-qing Zhang, "Experiments That Led to the First Gene-Edited Babies: The Ethical Failings and the Urgent Need for Better Governance," *Journal of Zhejiang University SCIENCE B* 20, no. 1 (2019): 32–38.
38. Tetsuya Ishii, "Reproductive Medicine Involving Genome Editing: Clinical Uncertainties and Embryological Needs," *Reproductive Biomedicine Online* 34, no. 1 (2017): 27–31.

NOTES   227

39. K. S. Bosley, M. Botchan, A. L. Bredenoord, D. Carroll, R. A. Charo, E. Charpentier, R. Cohen, J. Corn, J. Doudna, G. Feng, and H. T. Greely, "CRISPR Germline Engineering—The Community Speaks," *Nature Biotechnology* 33, no. 5 (2015): 478–486.

40. K. S. Bosley, M. Botchan, A. L. Bredenoord, D. Carroll, R. A. Charo, E. Charpentier, R. Cohen, J. Corn, J. Doudna, G. Feng, and H. T. Greely, 2015. "CRISPR Germline Engineering," 478–486.

41. Jennifer M. Gumer, "The Wisdom of Germline Editing: An Ethical Analysis of the Use of CRISPR-Cas9 to Edit Human Embryos," *New Bioethics* 25, no. 2 (2019): 137–152.

42. Matthew Liao, Anders Sandberg, and Rebecca Roache, "Human Engineering and Climate Change," *Ethics, Policy and the Environment* 15, no. 2 (2012): 206–221.

43. Anna Smajdor, Daniela Cutas, and Tuija Takala, "Artificial Gametes, the Unnatural and the Artefactual," *Journal of Medical Ethics* 44, no. 6 (2018): 404–408.

44. Angel Petropanagos, "Pronatalism, Geneticism, and ART," *IJFAB: International Journal of Feminist Approaches to Bioethics* 10, no. 1 (2017): 119–147.

45. Thomas Dietz and Eugene A. Rosa, "Rethinking the Environmental Impacts of Population, Affluence and Technology," *Human Ecology Review* 1, no. 2 (1994): 277–300.

46. Yao Song, Zhenzhen Qin, Tao Kang, and Yang Jin, "Robot Helps When Robot Fits: Examining the Role of Baby Robots in Fertility Promotion," *Healthcare* 7, no. 4 (2019): 147.

47. Brock E. Barry and Joseph R. Herkert, "Engineering Ethics," in *Cambridge Handbook of Engineering Education Research*, ed. Aditya Johri and Barbara M. Olds (Cambridge: Cambridge University Press, 2015), 673–692.

48. G. Opelz, T. Wujciak, B. Döhler, S. Scherer, and J. Mytilineos, "HLA Compatibility and Organ Transplant Survival: Collaborative Transplant Study," *Reviews in Immunogenetics* 1, no. 3 (1999): 334–342.

49. Yasuo Morishima, Takehiko Sasazuki, Hidetoshi Inoko, Takeo Juji, Tatsuya Akaza, Ken Yamamoto, Yoshihide Ishikawa, S. Kato, H. Sao, H. Sakamaki, and K. Kawa, "The Clinical Significance of Human Leukocyte Antigen (HLA) Allele Compatibility in Patients Receiving a Marrow Transplant from Serologically HLA-A, HLA-B, and HLA-DR Matched Unrelated Donors," *Blood: The Journal of the American Society of Hematology* 99, no. 11 (2002): 4200–4206.

50. Margaret L. MacMillan and John E. Wagner, "Haematopoeitic Cell Transplantation for Fanconi Anaemia—When and How?," *British Journal of Haematology* 149, no. 1 (2010): 14–21.

51. Willem Verpoest, "PGD and HLA Matching: Not a Quick Fix," *Reproductive Biomedicine Online* 23, no. 3 (2011): 271–273.

52. U. Shankarkumar, "The Human Leukocyte Antigen (HLA) System," *International Journal of Human Genetics* 4, no. 2 (2004): 91–103.

53. Svetlana Rechitsky, Anver Kuliev, Illan Tur-Kaspa, Randy Morris, and Yury Verlinsky, "Preimplantation Genetic Diagnosis with HLA Matching," *Reproductive Biomedicine Online* 9, no. 2 (2004): 210–221.

228 NOTES

54. Georgia Kakourou, Christina Vrettou, Maria Moutafi, and Joanne Traeger-Synodinos, "Pre-implantation HLA Matching: The Production of a Saviour Child," *Best Practice & Research Clinical Obstetrics & Gynaecology* 44 (2017): 76–89.

55. Susannah Baruch, David Kaufman, and Kathy L. Hudson, "Genetic Testing of Embryos: Practices and Perspectives of US in Vitro Fertilization Clinics," *Fertility and Sterility* 89, no. 5 (2008): 1053–1058.

56. Shachar Zuckerman, David A. Zeevi, Sigal Gooldin, and Gheona Altarescu, "Acceptable Applications of Preimplantation Genetic Diagnosis (PGD) among Israeli PGD Users," *European Journal of Human Genetics* 25, no. 10 (2017): 1113–1117.

57. BBC News, "NHS to Fund 'Designer Baby' Bid," updated March 22, 2004, http://news.bbc.co.uk/1/hi/health/3557989.stm.

58. S. Sheldon and S. Wilkinson, "Should Selecting Saviour Siblings Be Banned?," *Journal of Medical Ethics* 30 (2004): 533–537.

59. Immanuel Kant and Jerome B. Schneewind, *Groundwork for the Metaphysics of Morals* (New Haven, CT: Yale University Press, 2002).

60. J. Mills, "Understanding the Position of the Savior Sibling: How Can We Save Lives and Protect Savior Siblings?" (PhD dissertation, Wake Forest University, 2013).

61. Muna Qayed, Tao Wang, Michael T. Hemmer, Stephen Spellman, Mukta Arora, Daniel Couriel, Amin Alousi, M. Qayed, T. Wang, M. T. Hemmer, S. Spellman, M. Arora, D. Couriel, A. Alousi, J. Pidala, H. Abdel-Azim, M. Aljurf, and M. Ayas, "Influence of Age on Acute and Chronic GVHD in Children Undergoing HLA-Identical Sibling Bone Marrow Transplantation for Acute Leukemia: Implications for Prophylaxis," *Biology of Blood and Marrow Transplantation* 24, no. 3 (2018): 521–528.

62. Ephraim J. Fuchs, Paul V. O'Donnell, Mary Eapen, Brent Logan, Joseph H. Antin, Peter Dawson, Steven Devine, M. M. Horowitz, M. E. Horwitz, C. Karanes, and E. Leifer, "Double Unrelated Umbilical Cord Blood vs HLA-Haploidentical Bone Marrow Transplantation: The BMT CTN 1101 Trial," *Blood* 137, no. 3 (2021): 420–428.

63. Kelly M., East, Meagan Cochran, Whitley V. Kelley, Veronica Greve, Kristina Emmerson, Grace Raines, Jesse Nicholas Cochran, Adam M. Hott, and David Bick, "Understanding the Present and Preparing for the Future: Exploring the Needs of Diagnostic and Elective Genomic Medicine Patients," *Journal of Genetic Counseling* 28, no. 2 (2019): 438–448.

64. Fergus Walsh, "First Successful Saviour Sibling Treatment for UK," BBC News, December 21, 2010.

65. Amy T. Y. Lai, "To Be or Not to Be My Sister's Keeper? A Revised Legal Framework Safeguarding Savior Siblings' Welfare," *Journal of Legal Medicine* 32, no. 3 (2011): 261–293.

66. Tom L. Beauchamp, "Autonomy and Consent," in *The Ethics of Consent: Theory and Practice,* ed. Franklin Miller and Alan Wertheimer (Oxford: Oxford: 2010): 55–78.

67. Anne Mette Maria Lebech, "Anonymity and Informed Consent in Artificial Procreation," *Bioethics* 11, nos. 3–4 (1997): 336–340.

68. Erica K. Salter, "Deciding for a Child: A Comprehensive Analysis of the Best Interest Standard," *Theoretical Medicine and Bioethics* 33, no. 3 (2012): 179–198.

69. Kimberly Strong, Ian Kerridge, and Miles Little, "Savior Siblings, Parenting and the Moral Valorization of Children," *Bioethics* 28, no. 4 (2014): 187–193.

NOTES 229

70. Mary K. Shenk, "Our Children: Parental Decisions—How Much to Invest in Your Offspring," in *Essential Building Blocks of Human Nature*, ed. U. J. Frey, C. Störmer, K. P. Willführ (Berlin, Heidelberg: Springer, 2011): 17–38.

71. Marley McClean, "Children's Anatomy v. Children's Autonomy: A Precarious Balancing Act with Preimplantation Genetic Diagnosis and the Creation of Savior Siblings," *Pepperdine Law Review* 43 (2015): 837–880.

72. Kalena R. Kettering, "'Is Down Always Out?': The Right of Icelandic Parents to Use Preimplantation Genetic Diagnosis to Select for a Disability," *George Washington International Law Review* 51, no. 4 (2019): 1–29.

73. S. Baruch, D. Kaufman and K. L. Hudson, "Genetic Testing of Embryos: Practices and Perspectives of US IVF Clinics," *Fertility and Sterility* 89 (2008): 1053–1058, at 1055.

74. Fredrik Svenaeus, "Phenomenology and Embryo Ethics," *Topos: Journal for Philosophy and Cultural Studies* 2 (2020): 11–26.

75. S. Baruch, D. Kaufman, and K. L. Hudson, "Genetic Testing of Embryos: Practices and Perspectives of US In Vitro Fertilization Clinics," *Fertility and sterility*, 89, no. 5 (2008): 1053–1058, at 1055.

76. Bonnie Poitras Tucker, "Deaf Culture, Cochlear Implants, and Elective Disability," *Hastings Center Report* 28, no. 4 (1998): 6–14.

77. Ilaria Cortinovis, Eugenia Luraschi, Sara Intini, Marco Sessa, and Antonella Delle Fave, "The Daily Experience of People with Achondroplasia," *Applied Psychology: Health and Well-Being* 3, no. 2 (2011): 207–227.

78. Julian Savulescu, "Deaf Lesbians, 'Designer Disability,' and the Future of Medicine," *BMJ* 325, no. 7367 (2002): 771–773.

79. Jacqueline Mae Wallis, "Is It Ever Morally Permissible to Select for Deafness in One's Child?," *Medicine, Health Care and Philosophy* 23, no. 1 (2020): 3–15.

80. Elizabeth A. Yonko, Jillian S. Emanuel, Erin M. Carter, and Cathleen L. Raggio, "Quality of Life in Adults with Achondroplasia in the United States," *American Journal of Medical Genetics Part A* 185, no. 3 (2021): 695–701.

81. Josephine Johnston, "Judging Octomom," *Hasting Center Report* 39 (2009): 24.

82. Donald M. Berwick, and Andrew D. Hackbarth, "Eliminating Waste in US Health Care," *JAMA* 307, no. 14 (2012): 1513–1516.

83. Limor Meoded Danon, "Time Matters for Intersex Bodies: Between Socio-medical Time and Somatic Time," *Social Science & Medicine* 208 (2018): 89–97; Robert Sparrow, "Gender Eugenics? The Ethics of PGD for Intersex Conditions," *American Journal of Bioethics* 13, no. 10 (2013): 29–38.

84. Sarah M. Capelouto, Sydney R. Archer, Jerrine R. Morris, Jennifer F. Kawwass, and Heather S. Hipp, "Sex Selection for Non-medical Indications: A Survey of Current Pre-implantation Genetic Screening Practices among US ART Clinics," *Journal of Assisted Reproduction and Genetics* 35, no. 3 (2018): 409–416.

85. J. Sidhu, "Gender Selection Has Become a Multimillion-Dollar Industry," *Slate*, September 17, 2012, https://slate.com/technology/2012/09/sex-selection-in-bab ies-through-pgd-americans-are-paying-to-have-daughters-rather-than-sons. html#pagebreak_anchor_3.

86. Tasnim Eghbal Eftekhaari, Abdol Azim Nejatizadeh, Minoo Rajaei, Saeede Soleimanian, Soghra Fallahi, Rahman Ghaffarzadegan, and Forough Mahmoudi,

230 NOTES

"Ethical Considerations in Sex Selection," *Journal of Education and Health Promotion* 4 (2015): 1–5.

87. Annelien L. Bredenoord, Wybo Dondorp, Guido Pennings, and Guido De Wert, "Avoiding Transgenerational Risks of Mitochondrial DNA Disorders: A Morally Acceptable Reason for Sex Selection?," *Human Reproduction* 25, no. 6 (2010): 1354–1360, at 1354.

88. Arianne Shahvisi, "Engendering Harm: A Critique of Sex Selection for 'Family Balancing,'" *Journal of Bioethical Inquiry* 15, no. 1 (2018): 123–137.

89. Z. Kilani and L. Haj Hassan, "Sex Selection and Preimplantation Genetic Diagnosis at the Farah Hospital," *Reproductive Biomedicine Online* 4, no. 1 (2002): 68–70.

90. Aniruddha Malpani, Anjali Malpani, and Deepak Modi, "Preimplantation Sex Selection for Family Balancing in India," *Human Reproduction* 17, no. 1 (2002): 11–12.

91. Sarah M. Capelouto, Sydney R. Archer, Jerrine R. Morris, Jennifer F. Kawwass, and Heather S. Hipp, "Sex Selection for Non-medical Indications: A Survey of Current Pre-implantation Genetic Screening Practices among US ART Clinics," *Journal of Assisted Reproduction and Genetics* 35, no. 3 (2018): 409–416, at 409.

92. Erik Parens and Adrienne Asch, "Special Supplement: The Disability Rights Critique of Prenatal Genetic Testing Reflections and Recommendations," *Hastings Center Report* 29, no. 5 (1999): S1–S22.

93. Calum MacKellar and Christopher Bechtel, eds., *The Ethics of the New Eugenics* (New York: Berghahn Books, 2014).

94. Stephanie Lee, Jeremy Dwyer, Eldho Paul, David Clarke, Sophie Treleaven, and Robert Roseby, "Differences by Age and Sex in Adolescent Suicide," *Australian and New Zealand Journal of Public Health* 43, no. 3 (2019): 248–253.

95. Margaret Farley, *Just Love: A Framework for Christian Sexual Ethics* (New York: Continuum, 2006), 230; Tereza Hendl, "A Feminist Critique of Justifications for Sex Selection," *Journal of Bioethical Inquiry* 14, no. 3 (2017): 427–438.

96. N. Qian, "Missing Women and the Price of Tea in China: The Effect of Sex-Specific Earnings on Sex Imbalance," *Quarterly Journal of Economics* 123, no. 3 (2008): 1251–1285.

97. Judith Butler, "Performative Acts and Gender Constitution: An Essay in Phenomenology and Feminist Theory," *Theatre Journal* 40, no. 4 (1988): 519–531.

98. Logan S. Casey, Sari L. Reisner, Mary G. Findling, Robert J. Blendon, John M. Benson, Justin M. Sayde, and Carolyn Miller, "Discrimination in the United States: Experiences of Lesbian, Gay, Bisexual, Transgender, and Queer Americans," *Health Services Research* 54 (2019): 1454–1466.

99. Bennett Singer and David Deschamps, *LGBTQ Stats: Lesbian, Gay, Bisexual, Transgender, and Queer People by the Numbers* (New York: New Press, 2017).

100. Maura Priest, "Transgender Children and the Right to Transition: Medical Ethics When Parents Mean Well but Cause Harm," *American Journal of Bioethics* 19, no. 2 (2019): 45–59.

101. Annemiek Nelis and Danielle Posthuma, "Genetic Enhancement of Human Beings: Reality or Fiction?," in *Engineering the Human*, ed. B. Koops, C. Lüthy, A. Nelis, C. Sieburgh, J. Jansen, M. Schmid (Berlin: Springer, 2013), 63–70.

NOTES 231

102. Robert Klitzman, Paul S. Appelbaum, Wendy Chung, and Mark Sauer, "Anticipating Issues Related to Increasing Preimplantation Genetic Diagnosis Use: A Research Agenda," *Reproductive Biomedicine Online* 17 (2008): 33–42.

103. Maura A. Ryan, "The Argument for Unlimited Procreative Liberty: A Feminist Critique," *Hastings Center Report* 20, no. 4 (1990): 8.

104. H. Kauffman, "Designer Babies Ethical?," CBS News, March 3, 2009; S. Baruch, D. Kaufman, and K. L. Hudson, "Genetic Testing of Embryos: Practices and Perspectives of U.S. IVF Clinics," *Fertility and Sterility* 89 (2008): 1053–1058.

105. Anne Donchin, "In Whose Interest? Policy and Politics in Assisted Reproduction," *Bioethics* 25, no. 2 (2011): 99.

106. Jennifer I. Manuel, "Racial/Ethnic and Gender Disparities in Health Care Use and Access," *Health Services Research* 53, no. 3 (2018): 1407–1429.

107. James Anderson, "The Semen of Animals and Its Use for Artificial Insemination," technical communication, Imperial Bureau of Animal Breeding and Genetics, Edinburgh, 1945.

108. R. Vishwanath, "Artificial Insemination: The State of the Art," *Theriogenology* 59, no. 2 (2003): 571–584.

109. International Congress on the Breeding of Sheep and Goats, "Sheep and Goat Breeding and Husbandry: Potentials under Socio-Economic Conditions," *Genetic Resources* 2, no. S1 (2021): 1–114.

110. Sarah Knapton, "Coronavirus Sees Women in 40s Denied IVF Treatment," *Telegraph*, January 9, 2021, https://www.telegraph.co.uk/news/2021/01/09/coronavirus-sees-women-40s-denied-ivf-treatment/.

111. *Kate Plus 8*, a television series about a woman and her eight children from in-vitro fertilization, ran from 2010 to 2017. See https://www.imdb.com/title/tt5209238/.

112. Mayo Clinic, "Infertility: Causes of Infertility," http://www.mayoclinic.com/health/infertility/DS00310/DSECTION=causes, accessed August 18, 2023.

113. Centers for Disease Control, "Sexually Transmitted Diseases in the United States, 2008," http://www.cdc.gov/std/stats08/trends.htm#f3.

114. Teresa Iglesias, *IVF and Moral Justice: Moral, Social, and Legal Issues Related to Human in Vitro Fertilization* (London: Linacre Centre, 1990), 105.

115. J. Harper, E. Jackson, K. Sermon, R. J. Aitken, S. Harbottle, E. Mocanu, T. Hardarson, R. Mathur, S. Viville, A. Vail, and K. Lundin, "Adjuncts in the IVF Laboratory: Where Is the Evidence for 'Add-on' Interventions?," *Human Reproduction* 32, no. 3 (2017): 485–491.

116. Human Fertilisation and Embryology Authority, "Fertility Treatment 'Add ons,'" paper 823 presented at a meeting of HFEA, January 18, 2017, 1–11.

117. Willem Ombelet and Johan Van Robays, "Artificial Insemination History: Hurdles and Milestones," *Facts, Views & Vision in ObGyn* 7, no. 2 (2015): 137–143.

118. P. S. C. Stephenson and M. G. Wagner, "Turkey-Baster Babies: A View from Europe," *Milbank Quarterly* 69, no. 1 (1991): 45–50.

119. Joseph B. Doyle, "The Cervical Spoon . . . an Aid to Spermigration and Semen Sampling," *Linacre Quarterly* 16, no. 1 (1949): 41–47.

120. L. Lemmens, S. Kos, C. Beijer, D. D. M. Braat, W. L. D. M. Nelen, A. M. M. Wetzels, for the Section Semen of the Dutch Foundation for Quality Assessment in Medical

232 NOTES

Laboratories, "Techniques Used for IUI: Is It Time for a Change?," *Human Reproduction* 32, no. 9 (2017): 1835–1845.

121. Imogen Tennison and NHS England, "Indicative Carbon Emissions per Unit of Healthcare Activity," Eastern Region Public Health Observatory, Briefing No. 23, April 9, 2010.

122. G. Bahadur, R. Homburg, J. E. Bosmans, J. A. Huirne, P. Hinstridge, K. Jayaprakasan, P. Racich, R. Alam, I. Karapanos, A. Illahibuccus, and A. Al-Habib, "Observational Retrospective Study of UK National Success, Risks and Costs for 319,105 IVF/ICSI and 30,669 IUI Treatment Cycles," *BMJ Open* 10, no. 3 (2020): e034566.

123. Remah Moustafa Kamel, "Assisted Reproductive Technology after the Birth of Louise Brown," *Journal of Reproduction & Infertility* 14, no. 3 (2013): 96.

124. G. Bahadur, R. Homburg, J. E. Bosmans, J. A. Huirne, P. Hinstridge, K. Jayaprakasan, P. Racich, R. Alam, I. Karapanos, A. Illahibuccus, and A. Al-Habib, "Observational Retrospective Study of UK National Success, Risks and Costs for 319,105 IVF/ICSI and 30,669 IUI Treatment Cycles," *BMJ Open* 10, no. 3 (2020): e034566.

125. Michael Bebbington, "Selective Reduction in Multiple Gestations," *Best Practice & Research Clinical Obstetrics & Gynaecology* 28, no. 2 (2014): 239–247.

126. Yan Ouyang, Pei Cai, Fei Gong, Ge Lin, Jiabi Qin, and Xihong Li, "The Risk of Twin Pregnancies Should Be Minimized in Patients with a Unicornuate Uterus Undergoing IVF-ET," *Scientific Reports* 10, no. 1 (2020): 1–8.

127. Janice Raymond, *Women as Wombs* (San Francisco: Harper Collins, 1993), xxx.

128. Cristina Richie, "Lessons from Queer Bioethics: A Response to Timothy F. Murphy," *Bioethics* 30, no. 5 (2016): 365–371.

129. Diksha Munjal-Shankar, "Identifying the 'Real Mother' in Commercial Surrogacy in India," *Gender, Technology and Development* 18, no. 3 (2014): 387–405.

130. Margaret A. Farley, "Feminist Theology and Bioethics," in *Theology and Bioethics*, ed. Earl E. Shelp (Dordrecht: Springer, 1985), 163–185.

131. Edward G., Hughes and Mita Giacomini, "Funding in Vitro Fertilization Treatment for Persistent Subfertility: The Pain and the Politics," *Fertility and Sterility* 76, no. 3 (2001): 431–442.

132. Cristina Richie, "What Would an Environmentally Sustainable Reproductive Technology Industry Look Like?," *Journal of Medical Ethics* 41, no. 5 (2015): 383–387.

133. James W. Catt and Sally L. Rhodes, "Comparative Intracytoplasmic Sperm Injection (ICSI) in Human and Domestic Species," *Reproduction, Fertility and Development* 7, no. 2 (1995): 161–166.

134. Deborah L. Forman, "Abortion Clauses in Surrogacy Contracts: Insights from a Case Study," *Family Law Quarterly* 49 (2015): 2–53.

135. A. L. Allen, "Privacy, Surrogacy, and the Baby M Case," *Georgetown law Journal* 76, no. 5 (1988): 1759–1792.

136. Kiran M. Perkins, Sheree L. Boulet, Aaron D. Levine, Denise J. Jamieson, and Dmitry M. Kissin, "Differences in the Utilization of Gestational Surrogacy between States in the US," *Reproductive Biomedicine & Society Online* 5 (2018): 1–4.

137. Stephanie Saul, "21st-Century Babies: Building a Baby, with Few Ground Rules," *New York Times*, December 12, 2009, http://www.nytimes.com/2009/12/13/us/13su rrogacy.html?pagewanted=1&_r=1&th&emc=th.

138. Sophia Fantus and Peter A. Newman, "Motivations to Pursue Surrogacy for Gay Fathers in Canada: A Qualitative Investigation," *Journal of GLBT Family Studies* 15, no. 4 (2019): 342–356.

139. Kate Swanson, Joseph M. Letourneau, Miriam Kuppermann, and Brett D. Einerson, "Obstetric Morbidity in Gestational Carrier Pregnancies: A Population-Based Study," *Journal of Assisted Reproduction and Genetics* 38, no. 1 (2021): 177–183.

140. Teresa Baron, "Nobody Puts Baby in the Container: The Foetal Container Model at Work in Medicine and Commercial Surrogacy," *Journal of Applied Philosophy* 36, no. 3 (2019): 491–505.

141. Anastasia Paraskou and Babu P. George, "The Market for Reproductive Tourism: An Analysis with Special Reference to Greece," *Global Health Research and Policy* 2, no. 1 (2017): 1–12.

142. A. Clark, A. Adegunsoye, K. Capuzzi, and D. Gatta. "Medical Tourism: Winners and Losers," *Internet Journal of Health* 14, no. 1 (2013). http://ispub.com/IJH/14/1/2962.

143. Eleni Zervogianni, "Lessons Drawn from the Regulation of Surrogacy in Greece, Cyprus, and Portugal, or a Plea for the Regulation of Commercial Gestational Surrogacy," *International Journal of Law, Policy and the Family* 33, no. 2 (2019): 160–180.

144. Aaron Tham, "Sand, Surgery and Stakeholders: A Multi-stakeholder Involvement Model of Domestic Medical Tourism for Australia's Sunshine Coast," *Tourism Management Perspectives* 25 (2018): 29–40.

145. M. Brännström, L. Johannesson, H. Bokström, N. Kvarnström, J. Mölne, P. Dahm-Kähler, A. Enskog, M. Milenkovic, J. Ekberg, C. Diaz-Garcia, and M. Gäbel, "Livebirth after Uterus Transplantation," *The Lancet* 385, no. 9968 (2015): 607–616.

146. M. Arora, "Mom Donates Womb to Daughter in India's First Uterus Transplant," CNN, May 19, 2017, https://edition.cnn.com/2017/05/19/health/india-uterus-womb-transplant/index.html.

147. Lars Sandman, "The Importance of Being Pregnant: On the Healthcare Need for Uterus Transplantation," *Bioethics* 32, no. 8 (2018): 519–526.

148. Cristina Richie, "Not Sick: Liberal, Trans, and CripFeminist Critiques of Medicalization," *Journal of Bioethical Inquiry* 16, no. 3 (2019): 375–387.

149. Sawsan As-Sanie, Sara R. Till, Erika L. Mowers, Courtney S. Lim, Bethany D. Skinner, Laura Fritsch, Alex Tsodikov, Vanessa K. Dalton, Daniel J. Clauw, and Chad M. Brummett, "Opioid Prescribing Patterns, Patient Use, and Postoperative Pain after Benign Hysterectomy," *Obstetrics and Gynecology* 130, no. 6 (2017): 1261–1268.

150. Oscar Raúl Muñoz Angel, "New Hysterectomy Technique with Correction of Stress Urinary Incontinence, and Mixed Urinary Incontinence," *Journal of Gynecology and Obstetrics* 9, no. 3 (2021): 75–78.

151. Eman Alshawish, Shurouq Qadous, and Miss Ala Yamani, "Experience of Palestinian Women after Hysterectomy Using a Descriptive Phenomenological Study," *Open Nursing Journal* 14, no. 1 (2020): 74–79.

152. S. Zaami, A. Di Luca, and E. Marinelli, "Advancements in Uterus Transplant: New Scenarios and Future Implications," *European Review for Medical and Pharmacological Sciences* 23, no. 2 (2019): 892–902.

234 NOTES

153. Sarah E. Andiman, Xiao Xu, John M. Boyce, Elizabeth M. Ludwig, Heidi R. W. Rillstone, Vrunda B. Desai, and Linda L. Fan, "Decreased Surgical Site Infection Rate in Hysterectomy: Effect of a Gynecology-Specific Bundle," *Obstetrics & Gynecology* 131, no. 6 (2018): 991–999.

154. L. Johannesson, G. Testa, R. Flyckt, R. Farrell, C. Quintini, A. Wall, K. O'Neill, A. Tzakis, E. G. Richards, S. M. Gordon, and P. M. Porrett, "Guidelines for Standardized Nomenclature and Reporting in Uterus Transplantation: An Opinion from the United States Uterus Transplant Consortium," *American Journal of Transplantation* 20, no. 12 (2020): 3319–3325.

155. G. Testa, E. C. Koon, and L. Johannesson, "Living Donor Uterus Transplant and Surrogacy: Ethical Analysis According to the Principle of Equipoise," *American Journal of Transplantation* 17, no. 4 (2017): 912–916.

156. M. Arora, "Mom Donates Womb to Daughter in India's First Uterus Transplant," CNN, May 19, 2017, https://edition.cnn.com/2017/05/19/health/india-uterus-womb-transplant/index.html.

157. Jan Kilicaslan and Melissa Petrakis, "Heteronormative Models of Health-care Delivery: Investigating Staff Knowledge and Confidence to Meet the Needs of LGBTIQ+ People," *Social Work in Health Care* 58, no. 6 (2019): 612–632.

158. A. Hirshberg and S. K. Srinivas, "Epidemiology of Maternal Morbidity and Mortality," *Seminars in Perinatology* 41, no. 6 (2017): 332–337.

159. M. Holmes, "Mind the Gaps: Intersex and (Re-productive) Spaces in Disability Studies and Bioethics," *Journal of Bioethical Inquiry* 5, nos. 2–3 (2008): 169–181.

160. "Angelina Jolie 'Conceived Twins by IVF' in Race for More Babies," *Daily Mail,* July 26, 2008, https://www.dailymail.co.uk/tvshowbiz/article-1038578/Angelina-Jolie-conceived-twins-IVF-race-babies.html.

161. Personal communication to the author from a co-worker.

162. BCC Research Market Forecasting, "Human Reproductive Technologies: Products and Global Markets," 2013, http://www.bccresearch.com/market-research/healthc are/human-reproductive-technologies-hlc017d.html.

163. Statistics for 2010. Note this does not include non-reporting clinics. Centers for Disease Control, "Assisted Reproductive Technology (ART): What Is Assisted Reproductive Technology?," https://www.cdc.gov/art/whatis.html Last Reviewed: October 8, 2019.

164. A. Asch and R. Marmor, "Assisted Reproduction," in *From Birth to Death and Bench to Clinic: The Hastings Center Bioethics Briefing Book for Journalists, Policymakers, and Campaigns,* ed. Mary Crowley (Garrison, NY: Hastings Center, 2008), 5–10.

165. Viveca Söderström-Anttila, Ulla-Britt Wennerholm, Anne Loft, Anja Pinborg, Kristiina Aittomäki, Liv Bente Romundstad, and Christina Bergh, "Surrogacy: Outcomes for Surrogate Mothers, Children and the Resulting Families—A Systematic Review," *Human Reproduction Update* 22, no. 2 (2016): 260–276.

166. Kiran M. Perkins, Sheree L. Boulet, Denise J. Jamieson, Dmitry M. Kissin, and National Assisted Reproductive Technology Surveillance System, "Trends and

Outcomes of Gestational Surrogacy in the United States," *Fertility and Sterility* 106, no. 2 (2016): 435–442; Henrike E. Peters, Roel Schats, Marieke O. Verhoeven, Velja Mijatovic, Christianne J. M. de Groot, Joanna L. Sandberg, Immelie P. Peeters, and Cornelis B. Lambalk, "Gestational Surrogacy: Results of 10 Years of Experience in the Netherlands," *Reproductive Biomedicine Online* 37, no. 6 (2018): 725–731.

167. Kristine Schanbacher, "India's Gestational Surrogacy Market: An Exploitation of Poor, Uneducated Women," Hastings Women's Law Journal 25 (2014): 201–220.

168. Vasanti Jadva, Natalie Gamble, Helen Prosser, and Susan Imrie, "Parents' Relationship with Their Surrogate in Cross-border and Domestic Surrogacy Arrangements: Comparisons by Sexual Orientation and Location," *Fertility and Sterility* 111, no. 3 (2019): 562–570.

169. Niraj Vyas, Kanan Gamit, and Manan Raval, "Male Infertility: A Major Problem Worldwide and Its Management in Ayurveda," *Pharma Science Monitor* 9, no. 1 (2018): 446–469.

170. National Conference of State Legislatures, "State Laws Related to Insurance Coverage for Infertility Treatment," March 2012, http://www.ncsl.org/issues-resea rch/health/insurance-coverage-for-infertility-laws.aspx.

171. Deborah Dempsey, Jennifer Power, and Fiona Kelly, "A Perfect Storm of Intervention? Lesbian and Cisgender Queer Women Conceiving through Australian Fertility Clinics," *Critical Public Health* 32, no. 2 (2020): 1–11.

172. Shannon L. Corbett, Helena M. Frecker, Heather M. Shapiro, and Mark H. Yudin, "Access to Fertility Services for Lesbian Women in Canada," *Fertility and Sterility* 100, no. 4 (2013): 1077–1080.

173. Fiona K. Bloomer and Danielle Mackle, "Access to Fertility Treatment for Lesbian/ Bisexual Women in Northern Ireland," Reproductive Health Law and Policy Advisory Group Briefing Paper, 2017, https://pure.ulster.ac.uk/en/publications/acc ess-to-fertility-treatment-for-lesbianbisexual-women-in-northe.

174. Josephine Johnston, "Judging Octomom," *Hastings Center Report* 39, no. 3 (2009): 23–25.

175. J. Sidhu, "Gender Selection Has Become a Multimillion-Dollar Industry," *Slate,* September 17, 2012.

176. S. O. Akande, I. O. Dipeolu, and A. J. Ajuwon, "Attitude and Willingness of Infertile Persons towards the Uptake of Assisted Reproductive Technologies in Ibadan, Nigeria," *Annals of Ibadan Postgraduate Medicine* 17, no. 1 (2019): 51–58.

177. L. Cooke and S. M. Nelson, "Reproductive Ageing and Fertility in an Ageing Population," *Obstetrician and Gynaecologist* 13 (2011): 161–168; S. Borland, "Career Women 'Fuel a Surge in Abortions': Over-30s Relying on IVF Show Biggest Rise in Terminations," *Daily Mail*, May 29, 2012.

178. The take-home rate of live children born through IVF is 23–86% based on age and six cycles of IVF B. A. Malizia, M. R. Hacker, and A. S. Penzias, "Cumulative Live-Birth Rates after in Vitro Fertilization," *New England Journal of Medicine* 360 (2009): 236–243.

236 NOTES

Chapter 3

1. Ann Oakley, *The Captured Womb: A History of the Medical Care of Pregnant Women* (Oxford: Basil Blackwell, 1984), 2.
2. Mark Evans, Doina Ciorica, David W. Britt, and John C. Fletcher, "Update on Selective Reduction," *Prenatal Diagnosis* 25, no. 9 (2005): 807–813.
3. R. C. Wimalasundera, "Selective Reduction and Termination of Multiple Pregnancies," *Seminars in Fetal and Neonatal Medicine*, 15, no. 6 (2010): 327–335.
4. Marie-Victoire Senat, Pierre-Yves Ancel, Marie-Helene Bouvier-Colle, and Gerard Bréart, "How Does Multiple Pregnancy Affect Maternal Mortality and Morbidity?," *Clinical Obstetrics and Gynecology* 41, no. 1 (1998): 79–83.
5. Ulli Weisz, Peter-Paul Pichler, Ingram S. Jaccard, Willi Haas, Sarah Matej, Florian Bachner, Peter Nowak, and Helga Weisz, "Carbon Emission Trends and Sustainability Options in Austrian Health Care," *Resources, Conservation and Recycling* 160 (2020): 104862; Arunima Malik, Manfred Lenzen, Scott McAlister, and Forbes McGain, "The Carbon Footprint of Australian Health Care," *Lancet Planetary Health* 2, no. 1 (2018): e27–e35.
6. Isabel De La Fuente Fonnest, Finn Søndergaard, Gert Fonnest, and Agnete Vedsted-Jacobsen, "Attitudes among Health Care Professionals on the Ethics of Assisted Reproductive Technologies and Legal Abortion," *Acta Obstetricia et Gynecologica Scandinavica* 79, no. 1 (2000): 49–53.
7. Joachim W. Dudenhausen, and Rolf F. Maier, "Perinatal Problems in Multiple Births," *Deutsches Ärzteblatt International* 107, no. 38 (2010): 663–668.
8. I. K. Warriner and I. H. Shah, eds., *Preventing Unsafe Abortion and Its Consequences: Priorities for Research and Action* (New York: Guttmacher Institute, 2006).
9. Oakley, *The Captured Womb*, 98.
10. Oakley, *The Captured Womb*, 166.
11. Cristina Richie, *Principles of Green Bioethics: Sustainability in Health Care* (East Lansing: Michigan State University Press, 2019).
12. Elpida Fragouli and Dagan Wells, "Human Embryonic Aneuploidy," *eLS*, August 15, 2014, https://doi.org/10.1002/9780470015902.a0025706.
13. Judy Slome Cohain, Rina E. Buxbaum, and David Mankuta, "Spontaneous First Trimester Miscarriage Rates per Woman among Parous Women with 1 or More Pregnancies of 24 Weeks or More," *BMC Pregnancy and Childbirth* 17, no. 1 (2017): 1–7.
14. Eli Y. Adashi and Rajiv C. McCoy, "Technology versus Biology: The Limits of Pre-implantation Genetic Screening: Better Methods to Detect the Origin of Aneuploidy in Pre-implantation Embryos Could Improve the Success Rate of Artificial Reproduction," *EMBO Reports* 18, no. 5 (2017): 670–672.
15. Corinna Pallacks, Jens Hirchenhain, Jan-Steffen Krüssel, Tanja N. Fehm, and Daniel Fehr, "Endometriosis Doubles Odds for Miscarriage in Patients Undergoing IVF or ICSI," *European Journal of Obstetrics & Gynecology and Reproductive Biology* 213 (2017): 33–38.
16. Zhiqin Bu, Linli Hu, Yingchun Su, Yihong Guo, Jun Zhai, and Ying-Pu Sun, "Factors Related to Early Spontaneous Miscarriage during IVF/ICSI Treatment: An

NOTES 237

Analysis of 21,485 Clinical Pregnancies," *Reproductive Biomedicine Online* 40, no. 2 (2020): 201–206.

17. Tjitske Zaat, Miriam Zagers, Femke Mol, Mariëtte Goddijn, Madelon Wely, and Sebastiaan Mastenbroek, "Fresh versus Frozen Embryo Transfers in Assisted Reproduction," *Cochrane Database of Systematic Reviews* 2 (2021): 1–53.

18. Z. J. Chen, Y. Shi, Y. Sun, B. Zhang, X. Liang, Y. Cao, J. Yang, J. Liu, D. Wei, N. Weng, and L. Tian, "Fresh versus Frozen Embryos for Infertility in the Polycystic Ovary Syndrome," *New England Journal of Medicine* 375 (2016): 523–533.

19. L. Xia, S. Zhao, H. Xu, X. Wu, A. Zhang, and Z. Niu, "Miscarriage Rate Is High with Frozen-Thawed Blastocysts Arising from Poor-Quality Cleavage Stage Embryos," *Frontiers in Endocrinology* 11 (2020): doi.10.3389/fendo.2020.561085

20. Chen et al., "Fresh versus Frozen Embryos for Infertility in the Polycystic Ovary Syndrome."

21. Zdravka Veleva, Aila Tiitinen, Sirpa Vilska, Christel Hydén-Granskog, Candido Tomás, Hannu Martikainen, and Juha S. Tapanainen, "High and Low BMI Increase the Risk of Miscarriage after IVF/ICSI and FET," *Human Reproduction* 23, no. 4 (2008): 878–884.

22. Slome Cohain, Buxbaum, and Mankuta, "Spontaneous First Trimester Miscarriage Rates per Woman among Parous Women with 1 or More Pregnancies of 24 Weeks or More."

23. Carmen Rubio, Tugce Pehlivan, Lorena Rodrigo, Carlos Simón, Jose Remohí, and Antonio Pellicer, "Embryo Aneuploidy Screening for Unexplained Recurrent Miscarriage: A Minireview," *American Journal of Reproductive Immunology* 53, no. 4 (2005): 159–165.

24. Kathankumar A. Chaudhari and Manthankumar N. Kapadiya, "A Study to Assess the Level of Depression among Women Who Are Attending Infertility Clinic in Selected Hospital of Ahmedabad District with View to Providing of Information Booklet," *Asian Journal of Nursing Education and Research* 11, no. 1 (2021): 7–10.

25. François Olivennes, "Avoiding Multiple Pregnancies in ART Double Trouble: Yes a Twin Pregnancy Is an Adverse Outcome," *Human Reproduction* 15, no. 8 (2000): 1661–1663.

26. Natasa Tul, Miha Lucovnik, Ivan Verdenik, Mirjam Druskovic, Ziva Novak, and Isaac Blickstein, "The Contribution of Twins Conceived by Assisted Reproduction Technology to the Very Preterm Birth Rate: A Population-Based Study," *European Journal of Obstetrics & Gynecology and Reproductive Biology* 171, no. 2 (2013): 311–313.

27. ESHRE Capri Workshop Group, "Multiple Gestation Pregnancy," *Human Reproduction* 15, no. 8 (2000): 1856–1864.

28. Judith F. Daar, "Selective Reduction of Multiple Pregnancy: Lifeboat Ethics in the Womb," *UC Davis Law Review* 25 (1991): 773–844.

29. Joyce Martin, Brady Hamilton, Michelle Osterman, Sally Curtin, and T. J. Mathews, "Births: Final Data for 2013," *National Vital Statistics Reports* 64, no. 1 (2015): 3.

30. Megan K. Tracy and Sara K. Berkelhamer, "Bronchopulmonary Dysplasia and Pulmonary Outcomes of Prematurity," *Pediatric Annals* 48, no. 4 (2019): e148–e153.

238 NOTES

31. ESHRE Capri Workshop Group, "Multiple Gestation Pregnancy."

32. Noviyani Leksomono, Retno Sutomo, and Ekawaty Lutfia Haksari, "Predictors of Early Growth Failure in Preterm, Very Low Birth Weight Infants during Hospitalization," *Paediatrica Indonesiana* 59, no. 1 (2019): 44–50.

33. Hugo Madar, François Goffinet, Aurélien Seco, Patrick Rozenberg, Corinne Dupont, and Catherine Deneux-Tharaux, "Severe Acute Maternal Morbidity in Twin Compared with Singleton Pregnancies," *Obstetrics & Gynecology* 133, no. 6 (2019): 1141–1150.

34. Katariina Laine, Gulim Murzakanova, Kristina Baker Sole, Aase Devold Pay, Siri Heradstveit, and Sari Räisänen, "Prevalence and Risk of Pre-eclampsia and Gestational Hypertension in Twin Pregnancies: A Population-Based Register Study," *BMJ Open* 9, no. 7 (2019): e029908.

35. Jodie Dodd and Caroline Crowther, "Multifetal Pregnancy Reduction of Triplet and Higher-Order Multiple Pregnancies to Twins," *Fertility and Sterility* 81, no. 5 (2004): 1420–1422.

36. Georgina M. Chambers and William Ledger, "The Economic Implications of Multiple Pregnancy Following ART," *Seminars in Fetal and Neonatal Medicine* 19, no. 4 (2014): 254–261.

37. Georgina Chambers, Evelyn Lee, Michele Hansen, Elizabeth Sullivan, Carol Bower, and Michael Chapman, "Hospital Costs of Multiple-Birth and Singleton-Birth Children during the First 5 Years of Life and the Role of Assisted Reproductive Technology," *JAMA Pediatrics* 168, no. 11 (2014): 1045–1053.

38. H. H. Chang, J. Larson, H. Blencowe, C. Y. Spong, C. P. Howson, S. Cairns-Smith, E. M. Lackritz, S. K. Lee, E. Mason, A. C. Serazin, and S. Walani, "Preventing Preterm Births: Analysis of Trends and Potential Reductions with Interventions in 39 Countries with Very High Human Development Index," *The Lancet* 381, no. 9862 (2013): 223–234.

39. March of Dimes, "Premature Birth: The Financial Impact on Businesses," December 2013, at 1. https://onprem.marchofdimes.org/materials/premature-birth-the-financ ial-impact-on-business.pdf.

40. Karissa M. Johnston, Katherine Gooch, Ellen Korol, Pamela Vo, Oghenowede Eyawo, Pamela Bradt, and Adrian Levy, "The Economic Burden of Prematurity in Canada," *BMC Pediatrics* 14, no. 1 (2014): 1–10.

41. John B. C. Tan, Danilo S. Boskovic, and Danilyn M. Angeles, "The Energy Costs of Prematurity and the Neonatal Intensive Care Unit (NICU) Experience," *Antioxidants* 7, no. 3 (2018): 37.

42. Wenda R. Trevathan, "The Evolutionary History of Childbirth," *Human Nature* 4, no. 4 (1993): 337–350; Richard W. Wertz and Dorothy C. Wertz, *Lying-in: A History of Childbirth in America* (New Haven, CT: Yale University Press, 1989).

43. Edwin R. Van Teijlingen, George W. Lowis, Peter McCaffery, and Maureen Porter, eds., *Midwifery and the Medicalization of Childbirth: Comparative Perspectives* (New York: Nova, 2004).

44. Dena Goffman, Robert C. Madden, Ellen A. Harrison, Irwin R. Merkatz, and Cynthia Chazotte, "Predictors of Maternal Mortality and Near-Miss Maternal Morbidity," *Journal of Perinatology* 27, no. 10 (2007): 597–601.

NOTES 239

45. Oakley, *The Captured Womb*, 142.
46. David W. Crippen, "United States—Academic Medicine: Where Have We Been?," in *ICU Resource Allocation in the New Millennium: Will We Say "No"?*, ed. David Crippen (New York: Springer, 2013), 101.
47. Jennifer Meierhans, "Agoraphobic Mum-to-Be Can Be Forced to Hospital for Birth, Court Rules," BBC News, May 13, 2021, https://www.bbc.co.uk/news/uk-57108649.
    Renée Ann Cramer, "The Limits of Law in Securing Reproductive Freedoms: Midwife-Assisted Homebirth in the United States," *Global Discourse* 8, no. 3 (2018): 493–509.
48. Victoria Pitts, *In the Flesh: The Cultural Politics of Body Modification* (New York: Palgrave Macmillan, 2003), 18.
49. Oakley, *The Captured Womb*, 214.
50. Oakley, *The Captured Womb*, 213.
51. Oakley, *The Captured Womb*, 145.
52. Barbara Harper, *Gentle Birth Choices* (New York: Simon and Schuster, 2005).
53. Susan Mayor, "NHS Should Bring in Measures to Reduce Its Carbon Footprint, BMA Says," *BMJ* 336 (2008): 740–740.
54. Nicole Campion, Cassandra L. Thiel, Noe C. Woods, Leah Swanzy, Amy E. Landis, and Melissa M. Bilec, "Sustainable Healthcare and Environmental Life-cycle Impacts of Disposable Supplies: A Focus on Disposable Custom Packs," *Journal of Cleaner Production* 94 (2015): 47.
55. My calculation: 19.8, 12.3, 7.8, 10.8, 10.4, 6.7, 5.8, 6.0, 6.0, 10.3, 5.8, 2.8 = (104.5/ 12) = 8.7.
56. Packs contained content list plastic wrapper, towels, gowns (under buttocks/drape), leggings, lap sponges, gauze, packing sponge, OB pad, bulb syringe, umbilical cord clamp, needle counter, placenta basin, placenta foam lid, baby blanket, abdominal sheet, cover sheet. Nicole Campion, Cassandra L. Thiel, Justin DeBlois, Noe C. Woods, Amy E. Landis, and Melissa M. Bilec, "Life Cycle Assessment Perspectives on Delivering an Infant in the US," *Science of the Total Environment* 425 (2012): 191–198.
57. "Births: Final Data for 2019," *National Vital Statistics Reports* 70, no. 2 (March 23, 2021): 1:50, 37, table 18.
58. Airplanes emit much more CO_2 than cars, but they also carry more people. A 3,000-mile round-trip flight (like one from Boston to London and back) emits approximately one ton of CO_2 per passenger. Kathryn Tso, "How Much Is a Ton of Carbon Dioxide?," Ask MIT Climate, December 2, 2020, https://climate.mit.edu/ask-mit/how-much-ton-carbon-dioxide.
59. Hayley Tsukayama, "How Bad Is Email for the Environment?," *Washington Post*, January 25, 2017, https://www.washingtonpost.com/news/the-switch/wp/2017/01/25/how-bad-is-email-for-the-environment/?wpisrc=nl_draw2&wpmm=1, cited by Phil Riebel, "The Carbon Footprint of Email (Is Quite Large!)," *Printing Impressions*, February 1, 2017, https://www.piworld.com/post/the-carbon-footprint-of-email-is-quite-large/#_edn.
60. Imogen Tennison and NHS England, "Indicative Carbon Emissions per Unit of Healthcare Activity," Eastern Region Public Health Observatory Briefing No. 23, April 9, 2010.

240 NOTES

61. National Audit Office, "Maternity Services in England," 2013, http://www.nao.org.uk/wp-content/uploads/2013/11/10259-001-Maternity-Services-Book-1.pdf.

62. John Bowers and Helen Cheyne, "Reducing the Length of Postnatal Hospital Stay: Implications for Cost and Quality of Care," *BMC Health Services Research* 16, no. 1 (2015): 1–12.

63. Eileen K. Hutton, Angela Reitsma, Julia Simioni, Ginny Brunton, and Karyn Kaufman, "Perinatal or Neonatal Mortality among Women Who Intend at the Onset of Labour to Give Birth at Home Compared to Women of Low Obstetrical Risk Who Intend to Give Birth in Hospital: A Systematic Review and Meta-analyses," *EClinicalMedicine* 14 (2019): 59–70; Judith Lothian, "Making Home Birth Even Safer for Mothers and Babies," *Journal of Perinatal Education* 26, no. 1 (2017): 3–6.

64. Joseph J. Apuzzio, Leslie Iffy, and Gerson Weiss, "Mode of Delivery in Breach Presentation," *Acta Obstetricia et Gynecologica Scandinavica* 81, no. 11 (2002): 1091–1091.

65. Darios Getahun, Daniel Strickland, Jean M. Lawrence, Michael J. Fassett, Corinna Koebnick, and Steven J. Jacobsen, "Racial and Ethnic Disparities in the Trends in Primary Cesarean Delivery Based on Indications," *American Journal of Obstetrics and Gynecology* 201, no. 4 (2009): 422.e1–422.e7.

66. Jennifer S. Read and Marie-Louise Newell, "Efficacy and Safety of Cesarean Delivery for Prevention of Mother-to-Child Transmission of HIV-1," *Cochrane Database of Systematic Reviews* 4 (2005): 1–13.

67. Theresa Morris and Joan H. Robinson, "Forced and Coerced Cesarean Sections in the United States," *Contexts* 16, no. 2 (2017): 24–29.

68. Sylvia Burrow, "On the Cutting Edge: Ethical Responsiveness to Cesarean Rates," *American Journal of Bioethics* 12, no. 7 (2012): 44–52.

69. Erika Werner, presentation to the Society for Maternal-Fetal Medicine annual meeting, Dallas, February 9, 2012, cited in Karen N. Peart, "C-Sections Linked to Breathing Problems in Preterm Infants," *Yale News*, February 10, 2010, http://news.yale.edu/2012/02/10/c-sections-linked-breathing-problems-preterm-infants.

70. Lucky Jain and Golde G. Dudell, "Respiratory Transition in Infants Delivered by Cesarean Section," *Seminars in Perinatology* 30, no. 5 (2006): 296–304.

71. Iwona Szymusik, Katarzyna Kosinska-Kaczynska, Dorota Bomba-Opon, and Miroslaw Wielgos, "IVF versus Spontaneous Twin Pregnancies—Which Are at Higher Risk of Complications?," *Journal of Maternal-Fetal & Neonatal Medicine* 25, no. 12 (2012): 2725–2728.

72. Richard K. Silver, Elaine I. Haney, William A. Grobman, Scott N. MacGregor, Holly L. Casele, and Mark G. Neerhof, "Comparison of Active Phase Labor between Triplet, Twin, and Singleton Gestations," *Journal of the Society for Gynecologic Investigation* 7, no. 5 (2000): 297–300.

73. Published in Andrea Dworkin, *Pornography: Men Possessing Women* (New York: Plume, 1981), 217–218.

74. Jaclyn Cappell and Caroline F. Pukall, "Perceptions of the Effects of Childbirth on Sexuality among Nulliparous Individuals," *Birth* 45, no. 1 (2018): 55–63.

75. Viv Groskop, "Do You Really Need a 'Mommy Makeover'?," *The Guardian*, August 4, 2008, http://www.theguardian.com/lifeandstyle/2008/aug/05/women.healthandwellbeing.

NOTES   241

76. Kuang-Hung Hsu, Pei-Ju Liao, and Chorng-Jer Hwang, "Factors Affecting Taiwanese Women's Choice of Cesarean Section," *Social Science & Medicine* 66, no. 1 (2008): 201–209.

77. Douglas Almond, Christine Pal Chee, Maria Micaela Sviatschi, and Nan Zhong, "Auspicious Birth Dates among Chinese in California," *Economics & Human Biology* 18 (2015): 153–159.

78. "Births: Final Data for 2019," 2.

79. Oakley, *The Captured Womb*, 88.

80. Luz Gibbons, José M. Belizán, Jeremy A. Lauer, Ana P. Betrán, Mario Merialdi and Fernando Althabe, *The Global Numbers and Costs of Additionally Needed and Unnecessary Caesarean Sections Performed per Year: Overuse as a Barrier to Universal Coverage: World Health Report* (Geneva: World Health Organization, 2010), table 3.

81. Campion et al., "Life Cycle Assessment Perspectives on Delivering an Infant in the US," 194.

82. Campion et al., "Life Cycle Assessment Perspectives on Delivering an Infant in the US," 196, figure 3.

83. K. V. Meriwether, D. D. Antosh, C. K. Olivera, S. Kim-Fine, E. M. Balk, M. Murphy, C. L. Grimes, A. Sleemi, R. Singh, A. A. Dieter, and C. C. Crisp, "Uterine Preservation vs. Hysterectomy in Pelvic Organ Prolapse Surgery: A Systematic Review with Meta-analysis and Clinical Practice Guidelines," *American Journal of Obstetrics and Gynecology* 219, no. 2 (2018): 129–146.

84. Daniel Altman, Åsa Ekström, Catharina Gustafsson, Annika López, Christian Falconer, and Jan Zetterström, "Risk of Urinary Incontinence after Childbirth: A 10-Year Prospective Cohort Study," *Obstetrics & Gynecology* 108, no. 4 (2006): 873–878.

85. Kim Keltie, Sohier Elneil, Ashwani Monga, Hannah Patrick, John Powell, Bruce Campbell, and Andrew J. Sims, "Complications Following Vaginal Mesh Procedures for Stress Urinary Incontinence: An 8 Year Study of 92,246 Women," *Scientific Reports* 7, no. 1 (2017): 1–9.

86. A. M. El Ayadi, J. K. Barageine, S. Miller, J. Byamugisha, H. Nalubwama, S. Obore, A. Korn, S. Sukumar, O. Kakaire, H. Mwanje, and F. Lester, "Women's Experiences of Fistula-Related Stigma in Uganda: A Conceptual Framework to Inform Stigma-Reduction Interventions," *Culture, Health & Sexuality* 22, no. 3 (2020): 352–367.

87. Rondi K. Walker, "After the Birth of Your Baby," Walker Plastic Surgery, accessed September 1, 2023, http://www.walkerplasticsurgery.com/procedures/surgical-pro cedures/after-the-birth-of-your-baby/.

88. Naveen Rao and Neha Sharma, "Current Trends in Female Genital Cosmetic Surgery," *Apollo Medicine* 9, no. 3 (2012): 219–223.

89. Sally Sheldon and Stephen Wilkinson, "Female Genital Mutilation and Cosmetic Surgery: Regulating Non-therapeutic Body Modification," *Bioethics* 12, no. 4 (1998): 263–285.

90. Carla Fernanda Voese, William Vinicius Kleinpaul, and Analidia Rodolpho Petry, "Esthetic Plastic Surgery: Experiences concerning Corporal (Re)Constructions and Implications for Nursing," *Revista da Rede de Enfermagem do Nordeste* 16, no. 2 (2015): 185–193.

242 NOTES

91. Mitchel P. Goldman, Richard E. Fitzpatrick, and Richard G. Bennett, "Instrumentation for Cosmetic Surgery," *Clinics in Dermatology* 6, no. 3 (1988): 108–121.

92. Andrea J. MacNeill, Robert Lillywhite, and Carl J. Brown, "The Impact of Surgery on Global Climate: A Carbon Footprinting Study of Operating Theatres in Three Health Systems," *Lancet Planetary Health* 1, no. 9 (2017): e381–e388.

93. Oakley, *The Captured Womb*, 263.

94. Blue Cross Massachusetts, "Breast Pump Savings," 2020, http://www.bluecrossma.com/breast-pump/.

95. Catherine Pearson, "Breast Pumps Now Covered by Insurance, but Does It Help?," *Huffington Post*, updated January 23, 2014, http://www.huffingtonpost.com/2013/01/08/breast-pumps-insurance-free_n_2432777.html.

96. Bijoy Krishna Banik, "A Sociological Analysis of the Medicalization Process of Pregnancy and Child Birth in Bangladesh," *Bangladesh e-Journal of Sociology* 16, no. 2 (2019): 78–96; Zehra Zeynep Sadıkoğlu, "The Medicalization of Pregnancy and Childbirth in Contemporary Turkey: The Effect of Risk Discourses for Turkish Women's Experiences," in *Childbearing and the Changing Nature of Parenthood: The Contexts, Actors, and Experiences of Having Children*, ed. R. P. Costa and S. L. Blair, Contemporary Perspectives in Family Research, vol. 14 (Bingley, UK: Emerald, 2019), 121–142.

97. Shulamith Firestone, *The Dialectic of Sex: The Case for Feminist Revolution* (New York: Bantam, 1970).

98. Rory E. Kraft Jr., "Pregnancy as a Harm?," *Perspectives in Biology and Medicine* 55 no. 2, (2012): 216.

99. United States v. Yankton, 986 F.2d 1225, 1230 (8th Cir. 1993), https://www.casemine.com/judgement/us/5914e7b6add7b04934918e64.

100. Fenelon v. State, 629 So.2d 955, 956 (Fla.App. 1993), https://scholar.google.com/scholar_case?case=11355401221982509614&hl=en&as_sdt=40000006&as_vis=1.

101. People v. Sargent, 86 Cal.App.3d 148, 150 Cal.Rptr. 113 (1978), https://scholar.google.com/scholar_case?case=14715508829362436103&hl=en&as_sdt=40000006&as_vis=1.

102. United States of America v. Defabian C. Shannon, 110 F.3d 382 (1997) No. 95-2367; argued January 3, 1996; decided September 3, 1996; reargued December 18, 1996; decided April 1, 1997; rehearing denied May 23, 1997, http://scholar.google.com/scholar_case?case=3306858869539759428&hl=en&as_sdt=40000006&as_vis=1.

103. Kraft, "Pregnancy as a Harm?," 216.

104. Emily McTernan, "Should Fertility Treatment Be State Funded?," *Journal of Applied Philosophy* 32, no. 3 (2015): 227–240.

Chapter 4

1. Ismail Jatoi and Sunita Sah, "Clinical Practice Guidelines and the Overuse of Health Care Services: Need for Reform," *Canadian Medical Association Journal* 191, no. 11 (2019): E297–E298.

NOTES   243

2. Josh Karliner, Scott Slotterback, Richard Boyd, Ben Ashby, Kristian Steele, and Jennifer Wang. "Health Care's Climate Footprint: The Health Sector Contribution and Opportunities for Action." *European Journal of Public Health* 30, no. 5 (2020): 165–843.

3. P.-P. Pichler, et al., "International Comparison of Health Care Carbon Footprints," *Environmental Research Letters* 14, no. 6 (2019): 064004.

4. Forbes McGain and Chris Naylor, "Environmental Sustainability in Hospitals— A Systematic Review and Research Agenda," *Journal of Health Services Research & Policy* 19, no. 4 (2014): 245–252.

5. Charlie Tomson, "Reducing the Carbon Footprint of Hospital-Based Care," *Future Hospital Journal* 2, no. 1 (2015): 57–62; Cristina Richie, "Environmental Sustainability and the Carbon Emissions of Pharmaceuticals," *Journal of Medical Ethics* 48, no. 5 (2022): 334–337.

6. Pichler et al., "International Comparison of Health Care Carbon Footprints."

7. Barbara Starfield, "Is US Health Really the Best in the World?," *JAMA* 284, no. 4 (2000): 483–485.

8. Donald M. Berwick and Andrew D. Hackbarth, "Eliminating Waste in US Health Care," *JAMA* 307, no. 14 (2012): 1513–1516.

9. Samuel L. Dickman, David U. Himmelstein, and Steffie Woolhandler, "Inequality and the Health-Care System in the USA," *The Lancet* 389, no. 10077 (2017): 1431–1441.

10. Ajay Tandon, Christopher J. L. Murray, Jeremy A. Lauer, and David B. Evans, "Measuring Overall Health System Performance for 191 Countries," *Geneva: World Health Organization* (2000): 18–20.

11. Cristina Richie, *Principles of Green Bioethics: Sustainability in Health Care* (East Lansing: Michigan State University Press, 2019).

12. David M. Driesen, "Capping Carbon," *Environmental Law* 40 (2010): 1–51.

13. John Leach, Rosalind Driver, Philip Scott, and Colin Wood-Robinson, "Children's Ideas about Ecology 2: Ideas Found in Children Aged 5–16 about the Cycling of Matter," *International Journal of science education* 18, no. 1 (1996): 19–34.

14. Jeff Tollefson and Kenneth R. Weiss, "Nations Approve Historic Global Climate Accord," *Nature News* 528, no. 7582 (2015): 315.

15. Sebastian Oberthür and Hermann E. Ott, *The Kyoto Protocol: International Climate Policy for the 21st Century* (Berlin: Springer Science & Business Media, 1999).

16. Michael Hoel, "Should a Carbon Tax Be Differentiated across Sectors?," *Journal of Public Economics* 59, no. 1 (1996): 17–32; James M. Poterba, *Tax Policy to Combat Global Warming: On Designing a Carbon Tax*. No. w3649 (Cambridge, MA: National Bureau of Economic Research, 1991).

17. Pichler et al., "International Comparison of Health Care Carbon Footprints"; National Health Services Sustainable Development Unit, *Saving Carbon, Improving Health: NHS Carbon Reduction Strategy for England* (London: NHS Sustainable Development Unit, 2009).

18. National Health Services Sustainable Development Unit, *Saving Carbon, Improving Health*; Sustainable Development Unit for NHS England and Public Health England, "Reducing the Use of Natural Resources in Health and Social Care: 2018 Report,"

244 NOTES

https://www.sduhealth.org.uk/documents/Policy%20and%20strategy/20180912_
Health_and_Social_Care_NRF_web.pdf.

19. Zelda J. Ghersin, Michael R. Flaherty, Phoebe Yager, and Brian M. Cummings, "Going
Green: Decreasing Medical Waste in a Paediatric Intensive Care Unit in the United
States," *New Bioethics* 26, no. 2 (2020): 98–110.

20. Trevor Hedberg, "Climate Change, Moral Integrity, and Obligations to Reduce
Individual Greenhouse Gas Emissions," *Ethics, Policy & Environment* 21, no. 1
(2018): 64–80.

21. D. S. Morris, T. Wright, J. E. A. Somner, and A. Connor, "The Carbon Footprint of
Cataract Surgery," *Eye* 27, no. 4 (2013): 495–501.

22. Mike Berners-Lee, *How Bad Are Bananas? The Carbon Footprint of Everything*
(London: Profile Book, 2010), 131–132.

23. A. E. Lim, A. Perkins, and J. W. Agar, "The Carbon Footprint of an Australian Satellite
Haemodialysis Unit," *Australian Health Review* 37 (2013): 369–374.

24. N. Campion, Cassandra L. Thiel, Justin DeBlois, Noe C. Woods, Amy E. Landis, and
Melissa M. Bilec, "Life Cycle Assessment Perspectives on Delivering an Infant in the
US," *Science of the Total Environment* 425 (2012): 191–198.

25. P. Murtaugh and M. G. Schla, "Reproduction and the Carbon Legacies of Individuals,"
Global Environmental Change 19 (2009): 14–20.

26. D. Woods, S. Isani, T. McAndrew, N. Nevadunsky, J. Hou, G. Goldberg, and D. Kuo,
"Comparison of the Environmental Impact of Commonly Used Surgical Approaches
to Hysterectomy," *Gynecologic Oncology* 1, no. 130 (2013): e143.

27. A. S. Pollard, J. J. Paddle, T. J. Taylor, and A. Tillyard, "The Carbon Footprint of
Acute Care: How Energy Intensive Is Critical Care?," *Public Health* 128, no. 9
(2014): 771–776.

28. K. Lyle, Louise Dent, Sally Bailey, Lynn Kerridge, Ian Roberts, and Ruairidh Milne,
"Carbon Cost of Pragmatic Randomised Controlled Trials: Retrospective Analysis of
Sample of Trials," *British Medical Journal* 339 (2009): b4187.

29. B. Duane, M. Berners Lee, S. White, R. Stancliffe, and I. Steinbach, "An Estimated
Carbon Footprint of NHS Primary Dental Care within England: How Can Dentistry
Be More Environmentally Sustainable?," *British Dental Journal* 223, no. 8 (2017): 589.

30. D. L. Maugha, "Determining an Approach to Estimating the Carbon Footprint of
Mental Health Care That Is Fit for Purpose" (PhD diss., University of Warwick, 2016).

31. Nicole Campion, Cassandra L. Thiel, Noe C. Woods, Leah Swanzy, Amy E. Landis,
and Melissa M. Bilec, "Sustainable Healthcare and Environmental Life-Cycle Impacts
of Disposable Supplies: A Focus on Disposable Custom Packs," *Journal of Cleaner
Production* 94 (2015): 46–55.

32. Cristina Richie, "What Would an Environmentally Sustainable Reproductive
Technology Industry Look Like?," *Journal of Medical Ethics* 41, no. 5 (2015): 383–387.

33. Richie, "What Would An Environmentally Sustainable Reproductive Technology
Industry Look Like?"

34. Joseph H. Howell and William Frederick Sale, "Specifying the Goals of Medicine," in
Life Choices: A Hastings Center Introduction to Bioethics, 2nd ed., ed. Joseph H. Howell
and William Frederick Sale (Washington, DC: Georgetown, 2000), 62.

Chapter 5

1. Health Care Without Harm, https://noharm.org/.
2. Practice Greenhealth, "History," 2014, https://practicegreenhealth.org/about/history
3. Healthier Hospitals Initiative, "Participating Hospital," 2023, http://healthierhospit als.org/about-hhi/participating-hospitals.
4. Catholic Health Association and Practice Greenhealth, *Environmental Sustainability: Getting Started Guide* (St. Louis, MO: Catholic Health Association of the United States, 2010); Catholic Health Association, Catholic Healthcare Ministry, "Environmental Responsibility," https://www.chausa.org/docs/default-source/gene ral-files/catholic-healthcare-ministry-environmental-responsibility.pdf?sfvrsn= 6; Laura Anderko, Stephanie Chalupka, and Brenda M. Afzal, *Climate Change and Health: Is There a Role for the Health Care Sector?* (St. Louis, MO: Catholic Health Association of the United States, 2012); Catholic Health Initiatives, "Environmental Stewardship," 2014, http://catholichealthinit.org/environmental-stewardship; Catholic Health Association of the United States, *Faithfully Healing the Earth: Catholic Health Care and Climate Change* (Washington, DC: Catholic Health Association, 2009), http://build7.medseek.com/websitefiles/chinational58533/documents_pub lic/Advocacy/climatechangebrochure.pdf.
5. Health Care Climate Council, "Climate Action: A Playbook for Hospitals," revised July 2020, https://climatecouncil.noharm.org/.
6. Cristina Richie, "What Would an Environmentally Sustainable Reproductive Technology Industry Look Like?," *Journal of Medical Ethics* 41, no. 5 (2015): 383–387.
7. Lisa M. Lee, "A Bridge Back to the Future: Public Health Ethics, Bioethics, and Environmental Ethics," *American Journal of Bioethics* 17, no. 9 (2017): 5–12.
8. Joseph H. Howell and William Frederick Sale, "Specifying the Goals of Medicine," in *Life Choices: A Hastings Center Introduction to Bioethics*, 2nd ed., ed. Joseph H. Howell and William Frederick Sale (Washington, DC: Georgetown University Press, 2000), 62–73.
9. Adrian Diaz, Benjamin A. Sarac, Anna R. Schoenbrunner, Jeffrey E. Janis, and Timothy M. Pawlik, "Elective Surgery in the Time of COVID-19," *American Journal of Surgery* 219, no. 6 (2020): 900–902.
10. Kjell Asplund, "Use of in Vitro Fertilization—Ethical Issues," *Upsala Journal of Medical Sciences* 125, no. 2 (2020): 192–199.
11. P. Murtaugh and M. Schla, "Reproduction and the Carbon Legacies of Individuals," *Global Environmental Change* 19, no. 1 (2009): 14–20.
12. Bruno Schuller, "Direct Killing/Indirect Killing," in *Readings in Moral Theology*, No 1, ed. R. McCormick and C. Curran (New York: Paulist Press, 1979), 138–157; B. Schuller, "The Double Effect in Catholic Thought: A Reevaluation," in *Doing Evil to Achieve Good*, ed. R. McCormick and P. Ramsey (Chicago: Loyola University, 1978), 165–92; William McClelland and Ewan C. Goligher, "Withholding or Withdrawing Life Support versus Physician-Assisted Death: A Distinction with a Difference?," *Current Opinion in Anesthesiology* 32, no. 2 (2019): 184–189.
13. O. Schachter, *International Law in Theory and Practice* (Leiden: Brill Nijhoff, 1991).

246 NOTES

14. Patricia W. Birnie and Alan E. Boyle, *International Law and the Environment* (Oxford: Clarendon Press, 1992).

15. Geoff Herbert, "Buffalo Teachers Still Get Free Plastic Surgery Courtesy of Taxpayers," *Syracuse.com*, January 19, 2012, http://www.syracuse.com/news/index.ssf/2012/01/buffalo_teachers_get_free_plas.html.

16. B. Duane, M. Berners Lee, S. White, R. Stancliffe, and I. Steinbach, "An Estimated Carbon Footprint of NHS Primary Dental Care within England: How Can Dentistry Be More Environmentally Sustainable?," *British Dental Journal* 223, no. 8 (2017): 589–593.

17. Pope John Paul II, *Centesimus Annus Encyclical Letter: On the Hundredth Anniversary of Rerum Novarum,* May 1, 1991, 48, https://www.vatican.va/content/john-paul-ii/en/encyclicals/documents/hf_jp-ii_enc_01051991_centesimus-annus.html.

18. William J. Byron, "Ten Building Blocks of Catholic Social Teaching," *America,* October 31, 1998, 11.

19. Cf. Constance McDermott, Benjamin Cashore, and Peter Kanowski, *Global Environmental Forest Policies: An International Comparison* (London: Earthscan, 2010).

20. Indur M. Goklany, "Meeting Global Food Needs: The Environmental Trade-offs between Increasing Land Conversion and Land Productivity," *Technology* 6, nos. 1–2 (1999): 107–130.

21. Paul A. Murtaugh and Michael G. Schlax, "Reproduction and the Carbon Legacies of Individuals," *Global Environmental Change* 19, no. 1 (2009): 14–20.

22. Larry Lohmann, Niclas Hällström, Robert Österbergh, and Olle Nordberg, *Carbon Trading: A Critical Conversation on Climate Change, Privatisation and Power* (Uppsala: Dag Hammarskjöld Centre, 2006).

23. Andrew A. Alola, "The Trilemma of Trade, Monetary and Immigration Policies in the United States: Accounting for Environmental Sustainability," *Science of The Total Environment* 658 (2019): 260–267.

24. Anqing Shi, "The Impact of Population Pressure on Global Carbon Dioxide Emissions, 1975–1996: Evidence from Pooled Cross-country Data," *Ecological Economics* 44, no. 1 (2003): 29–42.

25. Ramesh Thakur and Thomas G. Weiss, "United Nations 'Policy': An Argument with Three Illustrations," *International Studies Perspectives* 10, no. 1 (2009): 18–35.

26. Henry Shue, "Subsistence Emissions and Luxury Emissions," *Law & Policy* 15, no. 1 (1993): 39–60.

27. Dominic Wilkinson, "Gaia Doesn't Care where your Baby Comes From," *Blog, Journal of Medical Ethics,* 25 July 2014, https://blogs.bmj.com/medical-ethics/2014/07/25/gaia-doesnt-care-where-your-baby-comes-from/.

28. United Nations Framework Convention on Climate Change, Kyoto Climate Change Conference, third session, agenda item 5, December 10, 1997, https://unfccc.int/documents/2409.

29. United Nations Climate Change, "What Is the Kyoto Protocol?," 2020, https://unfccc.int/kyoto_protocol.

NOTES 247

30. Michael Grubb, Christiaan Vrolijk, and Duncan Brack, *Routledge Revivals: Kyoto Protocol (1999): A Guide and Assessment* (London: Routledge, 2018), foreword.

31. Richie, "What Would an Environmentally Sustainable Reproductive Technology Industry Look Like?"

32. Emma Strubell, Ananya Ganesh, and Andrew McCallum, "Energy and Policy Considerations for Deep Learning in NLP," *arXiv preprint arXiv:1906.02243* (2019).

33. D. S. Morris, T. Wright, J. E. A. Somner, and A. Connor, "The Carbon Footprint of Cataract Surgery," *Eye* 27, no. 4 (2013): 495–501.

34. James Hansen, Makiko Sato, Pushker Kharecha, David Beerling, Robert Berner, Valerie Masson-Delmotte, Mark Pagani, Maureen Raymo, Dana L. Royer, and James C. Zachos, "Target Atmospheric CO_2: Where Should Humanity Aim?," *Open Atmospheric Science Journal* 2 (2008): 217–231; U.S. Department of Commerce, National Oceanic and Atmospheric Administration, Earth System Research Laboratory, Global Monitoring Division, "Trends in Atmospheric Carbon Dioxide: Recent Monthly Average Mauna Loa CO_2," https://www.esrl.noaa.gov.

35. Union of Concerned Scientists, "Each Country's Share of CO_2 Emissions," updated August 12, 2020, https://www.ucsusa.org/resources/each-countrys-share-co2-emissions.

36. Michael S. Northcott, "The Concealments of Carbon Markets and the Publicity of Love in a Time of Climate Change," *International Journal of Public Theology* 4, no. 3 (2010): 303.

37. John Hamilton Bradford and Alexander M. Stoner, "The Treadmill of Destruction in Comparative Perspective: A Panel Study of Military Spending and Carbon Emissions, 1960–2014," *Journal of World-Systems Research* 23, no. 2 (2017): 298–325.

38. Mariana Conte Grand, "Carbon Emission Targets and Decoupling Indicators," *Ecological Indicators* 67 (2016): 649–656.

39. Wales, Labour Party, "One Wales: A Progressive Agenda for the Government of Wales: An Agreement between the Labour and Plaid Cymru Groups in the National Assembly," https://archive.hefcw.ac.uk/documents/policy_areas/widening_access/OneWales%20English.pdf.

40. United Kingdom, Climate Change Act 2008, ch. 27, http://www.legislation.gov.uk/ukpga/2008/27/pdfs/ukpga_20080027_en.pdf.

41. National Health Service Sustainable Development Unit, *Saving Carbon, Improving Health: NHS Carbon Reduction Strategy for England* (London: NHS Sustainable Development Unit, 2009).

42. National Health Services Sustainable Development Unit, *Saving Carbon, Improving Health*.

43. National Institutes for Health Research, "Carbon Reduction Guidelines," October 2010, 2, www.nihr.ac.uk/files/NIHR_Carbon_Reduction_Guidelines.pdf.

44. *Climate Change Strategy for Wales*, Summary Version, 2010, https://gweddill.gov.wales/docs/desh/publications/101006ccstratfinalen.pdf.

45. NHS Health Scotland, *A Fairer Healthier Scotland: A Strategic Framework for Action 2017–2022* (Edinburgh: NHS Health Scotland, 2017).

248 NOTES

46. A. Conacher, *SMaSH Workplan: To Be Read in Conjunction with the Work Programme 2017–20 Work Plan Activity 2019–20* (Edinburgh: Scottish Managed Sustainable Health Network, 2009).

47. Health and Social Care, 2020, http://online.hscni.net.

48. S. Courtney-Guy, "NHS Vows to Cut Single-Use Plastic by Up to Half," *The Metro*, October 12, 2019, https://metro.co.uk/2019/10/12/nhs-vows-cut-single-use-plastic-half-10905520/.

49. A. Bawden, "The NHS Produces 5.4% of the UK's Greenhouse Gases: How Can Hospitals Cut Their Emissions?," *The Guardian*, September 18, 2019, https://www.theguardian.com/society/2019/sep/18/hospitals-planet-health-anaesthetic-gases-electric-ambulances-dialysis-nhs-carbon-footprint.

50. Sustainable Development Unit for NHS England and Public Health England, *Reducing the Use of Natural Resources in Health and Social Care: 2018 Report*, https://www.sduhealth.org.uk/documents/Policy%20and%20strategy/20180912_Health_and_Social_Care_NRF_web.pdf.

51. S. Stillman, "What Is Carbon Credit?," *MoneyWatch*, February 5, 2008.

52. Clive L. Spash, "The Brave New World of Carbon Trading," *New Political Economy* 15, no. 2 (2010): 169–195.

53. Nathan Clark, "Chicago Climate Exchange, Inc.," December 2005, 1, https://62.225.2.61/files/meetings/cop_11/climate_talk_series/application/pdf/cop11_kiosk_clark.pdf.

54. Chicago Climate Exchange, "Members of CCX," 2007, https://web.archive.org/web/20100202014432/http://www.chicagoclimatex.com/content.jsf?id=64.

55. European Commission, "EU ETS Handbook," 2015, 4. https://ec.europa.eu/clima/sites/clima/files/docs/ets_handbook_en.pdf.

56. Southern Alliance for Clean Energy, "Carbon Tax, Cap and Trade or Cap and Dividend?," accessed April 26, 2013, http://www.cleanenergy.org/index.php?/Learn-About-Details.html?form_id=52&item_id=22#.UXsBirWkptE.

57. Jouni Paavola, "Health Impacts of Climate Change and Health and Social Inequalities in the UK," *Environmental Health* 16, no. 1 (2017): 61–68.

58. M. J. Eckelman and J. Sherman, "Environmental Impacts of the U.S. Health Care System and Effects on Public Health," *PLoS ONE* 11, no. 6 (2016): e0157014.

59. A. Cimprich, Jair Santillán-Saldivar, Cassandra L. Thiel, Guido Sonnemann, and Steven B. Young, "Potential for Industrial Ecology to Support Healthcare Sustainability: Scoping Review of a Fragmented Literature and Conceptual Framework for Future Research," *Journal of Industrial Ecology* 23, no. 6 (2019): 1344–1352.

60. F. McGain and Chris Naylor, "Environmental Sustainability in Hospitals—A Systematic Review and Research Agenda," *Journal of Health Services Research & Policy* 19, no. 4 (2014): 245–252.

61. Blue Cross Blue Shield, "About Us," 2020, https://www.bcbs.com/about-us.

62. Kaiser Permanente, "About," n.d., https://about.kaiserpermanente.org/. Accessed October 19, 2023.

63. Peter-Paul Pichler, Ingram S. Jaccard, Ulli Weisz, and Helga Weisz, "International Comparison of Health Care Carbon Footprints," *Environmental Research Letters* 14, no. 6 (2019): 064004.

64. Jeanette W. Chung and David O. Meltzer, "Estimate of the Carbon Footprint of the US Health Care Sector," *JAMA* 302, no. 18 (2009): 1970–1972.
65. June Carbone and Paige Gottheim, "Markets, Subsidies, Regulation, and Trust: Building Ethical Understandings into the Market for Fertility Services," *Journal of Gender, Race & Justice* 9 (2005): 509.
66. Business Wire, "Ferring Receives Acceptance of Marketing Authorisation Filing from EMA for Personalised Fertility Treatment with REKOVELLE® (Follitropin Delta)," October 30, 2015, https://www.businesswire.com/news/home/20151030005609/en/Ferring-receives-acceptance-Marketing-Authorisation-filing-EMA.
67. L. Hymas, "The GINK Manifesto: Say It Loud: I'm Childfree and I'm Proud," *Grist*, March 31, 2010, https://grist.org/article/2010-03-30-gink-manifesto-say-it-loud-im-childfree-and-im-proud/.
68. J. A. Castilla, E. Hernandez, Y. Cabello, J. L. Navarro, J. Hernandez, J. L. Gomez, N. Pajuelo, J. Marqueta, and B. Coroleu, "Assisted Reproductive Technologies in Public and Private Clinics," *Reproductive Biomedicine Online* 19, no. 6 (2009): 872–878.
69. Daniel R. DiLeo, "Faithful Citizenship in the Age of Climate Change: Why US Catholics Should Advocate for a National Carbon Tax," *Journal of Catholic Social Thought* 11, no. 2 (2014): 431–464.
70. G. P. Peters and E. G. Hertwich, "CO_2 Embodied in International Trade with Implications for Global Climate Policy," *Environmental Science & Technology* 42, no. 5 (2008): 1401–1407.
71. Jacques de Mouzon, Georgina M. Chambers, Fernando Zegers-Hochschild, Ragaa Mansour, Osamu Ishihara, Manish Banker, Silke Dyer, Markus Kupka, and G. David Adamson, "International Committee for Monitoring Assisted Reproductive Technologies World Report: Assisted Reproductive Technology 2012," *Human Reproduction* 35, no. 8 (2020): 1900–1913.
72. Ian Parry, "Increasing Carbon Pricing in the EU: Evaluating the Options," *European Economic Review* 121 (2020): 103341.
73. Shi-Ling Su, *The Case for a Carbon Tax: Getting Past Our Hang-ups to Effective Climate Policy* (Washington: Island Press, 2012), 15–16.
74. David Pearce, "The Role of Carbon Taxes in Adjusting to Global Warming," *Economic Journal* 101, no. 407 (1991): 938–948.
75. Arnaud Brohé, Nick Eyre, and Nicholas Howarth, *Carbon Markets: An International Business Guide* (London: Earthscan, 2012).
76. Jeremy Carl and David Fedor, "Tracking Global Carbon Revenues: A Survey of Carbon Taxes versus Cap-and-Trade in the Real World," *Energy Policy* 96 (2016): 50–77.
77. Wanting Chen and Zhi-Hua Hu, "Using Evolutionary Game Theory to Study Governments and Manufacturers' Behavioral Strategies under Various Carbon Taxes and Subsidies," *Journal of Cleaner Production* 201 (2018): 123–141.
78. Stefano Carattini, Maria Carvalho, and Sam Fankhauser, "Overcoming Public Resistance to Carbon Taxes," *Wiley Interdisciplinary Reviews: Climate Change* 9, no. 5 (2018): e531.
79. J. Petri, "Airline Carbon Plan Takes a Step Forward While Carriers Suffer," *Bloomberg*, March 15, 2020, https://www.bloomberg.com/news/articles/2020-03-16/airline-carbon-offset-plan-moves-forward-as-the-industry-suffers.

250 NOTES

80. DiLeo, "Faithful Citizenship in the Age of Climate Change."
81. Christopher A. Michaels, "Biotechnology and the Requirement for Utility in Patent Law," *Journal of the Patent & Trademark Office Society* 76 (1994): 247–260.
82. Jon Martin Denstadli and Knut Veisten, "The Flight Is Valuable Regardless of the Carbon Tax Scheme: A Case Study of Norwegian Leisure Air Travelers," *Tourism Management* 81 (2020): 104150.
83. Dale W. Jorgenson and Peter J. Wilcoxen, "Reducing US Carbon Dioxide Emissions: An Assessment of Different Instruments," *Journal of Policy Modeling* 15, nos. 5-6 (1993): 491–520.
84. Individual cars must follow emissions standards in the U.S. This is one way the products of the businesses are regulated, but there are not caps on the number of cars sold or how much they can emit corporately.
85. Environmental Protection Agency, "Regulatory Information by Sector: Automotive Sectors (NAICS 336, 4231, 8111)," updated August 7, 2020, https://www.epa.gov/regulatory-information-sector/automotive-sectors-naics-336-4231-8111.
86. Thomas C. Austin and Karl H. Hellman, "Passenger Car Fuel Economy—Trends and Influencing Factors," *SAE Transactions* vol. 82, SECTION 4: Papers 730669–730990 (1973): 2678–2701.
87. Hunt Allcott, Benjamin B. Lockwood, and Dmitry Taubinsky, "Should We Tax Sugar-Sweetened Beverages? An Overview of Theory and Evidence," *Journal of Economic Perspectives* 33, no. 3 (2019): 202–227.
88. Felipe Goncalves and Steven Mello, "Does the Punishment Fit the Crime? Speeding Fines and Recidivism," October 27, 2017, https://ssrn.com/abstract=3064406 or http://dx.doi.org/10.2139/ssrn.3064406.
89. James Hansen, Makiko Sato, Pushker Kharecha, David Beerling, Robert Berner, Valerie Masson-Delmotte, Mark Pagani, Maureen Raymo, Dana L. Royer, and James C. Zachos, "Target Atmospheric CO_2: Where Should Humanity Aim?," *Open Atmospheric Science Journal* 2 (2008): 217–231; U.S. Department of Commerce, National Oceanic and Atmospheric Administration, Earth System Research Laboratory, Global Monitoring Division, "Trends in Atmospheric Carbon Dioxide."
90. Kevin A. Hassett, Aparna Mathur, and Gilbert E. Metcalf, "The Incidence of a US Carbon Tax: A Lifetime and Regional Analysis," *Energy Journal* 30, no. 2 (2009): 1–40.
91. Diarmuid Martin, "Intervention by His Excellency Mons. Diarmuid Martin to the Plenary Council of the World Trade Organization on Trade-Related Aspects of Intellectual Property Rights," *L'Osservatore Romano*, weekly edition in English, June 20, 2001, 7.
92. A. S. Pollard, J. J. Paddle, T. J. Taylor, and A. Tillyard, "The Carbon Footprint of Acute Care: How Energy Intensive Is Critical Care?," *Public Health* 128, no. 9 (2014): 771–776.
93. Howard Bauchner, "Rationing of Health Care in the United States: An Inevitable Consequence of Increasing Health Care Costs," *JAMA* 321, no. 8 (2019): 751–752.
94. Shue, "Subsistence Emissions and Luxury Emissions."

NOTES   251

95. Tim Jackson, "Live Better by Consuming Less: Is There a 'Double Dividend' in Sustainable Consumption?," *Journal of Industrial Ecology* 9, nos. 1–2 (2005): 19–27.

96. William C. French, "On Knowing Oneself in an Age of Ecological Concern," in *Confronting the Climate Crisis: Catholic Theological Perspectives*, ed. James Schaefer (Milwaukee, WI: Marquette University Press, 2011), 152.

97. Murtaugh and Schlax, "Reproduction and the Carbon Legacies of Individuals."

98. Zhihua Ding, Xin Jiang, Zhenhua Liu, Ruyin Long, Zinan Xu, and Qingren Cao, "Factors Affecting Low-Carbon Consumption Behavior of Urban Residents: A Comprehensive Review," *Resources, Conservation and Recycling* 132 (2018): 3–15.

99. Katie Harris, Hugh Burley, Robert McLachlan, Mark Bowman, Alan Macaldowie, Kate Taylor, Michael Chapman, and Georgina Mary Chambers, "Socio-economic Disparities in Access to Assisted Reproductive Technologies in Australia," *Reproductive Biomedicine Online* 33, no. 5 (2016): 575–584.

100. Mohammed Harith, Yusri Yusup, and Sofri Bin Yahya, "The Optimal Progressive Tax Policy to Reduce Vehicles Externalities," *Journal of Asian Scientific Research* 8, no. 8 (2018): 265–276.

101. John Larsen, Noah Kaufman, Peter Marsters, Whitney Herndon, Hannah Kolus, and Ben King, "Expanding the Reach of a Carbon Tax," Columbia University, Center on Global Energy Policy, 2020, 1–51.

102. Garry Egger, "Personal Carbon Trading: A Potential 'Stealth Intervention' for Obesity Reduction?," *Medical Journal of Australia* 187, no. 3 (2007): 185–187.

103. Egger, "Personal Carbon Trading."

104. T. Fawcett and Y. Parag, "An Introduction to Personal Carbon Trading," *Climate Policy* 10, no. 4 (2010): 329–338.

105. Thereza R. S. De Aguiar, Anne Fearfull, and María V. Sanagustín Fons, "Calculating the Carbon Footprint: Implications for Governing Emissions and Gender Relations," *Accounting Forum* 40, no. 2 (2016): 63–77.

106. Shue, "Subsistence Emissions and Luxury Emissions."

107. Alice Rosi, Pedro Mena, Nicoletta Pellegrini, Silvia Turroni, Erasmo Neviani, Ilario Ferrocino, Raffaella Di Cagno, Luca Ruini, Roberto Ciati, Donato Angelino, Jane Maddock, Marco Gobbetti, Furio Brighenti, Daniele Del Rio and Francesca Scazzina, "Environmental Impact of Omnivorous, Ovo-lacto-vegetarian, and Vegan Diet," *Scientific Reports* 7, no. 1 (2017): 1–9.

108. Shreya Dave, "Life Cycle Assessment of Transportation Options for Commuters," Massachusetts Institute of Technology, 2010, http://www.seeds4green.org/sites/default/files/Pietzo_LCAwhitepaper.pdf.

109. Anne Schwenkenbecher, "Is There an Obligation to Reduce One's Individual Carbon Footprint?," *Critical Review of International Social and Political Philosophy* 17, no. 2 (2014): 172.

110. Jeffrey D. Moss, "Solar Panels, Tax Incentives, and Your House," *Probate and Property* 24 (2010): 17–21.

111. Rachel A. Howell, "Living with a Carbon Allowance: The Experiences of Carbon Rationing Action Groups and Implications for Policy," *Energy Policy* 41 (2012): 250–258.

252 NOTES

112. Egger, "Personal Carbon Trading," 185.

113. Steve Vanderheiden, "Personal Carbon Trading and Individual Mitigation Accountability," in *Transformative Climates and Accountable Governance*, ed. Beth Edmondson and Stuart Levy (Cham: Palgrave Macmillan, 2019), 273–299.

114. Etienne Terrenoire, D. A. Hauglustaine, Thomas Gasser, and Olivier Penanhoat, "The Contribution of Carbon Dioxide Emissions from the Aviation Sector to Future Climate Change," *Environmental Research Letters* 14, no. 8 (2019): 084019.

115. Barry Walters, "Personal Carbon Trading: A Potential 'Stealth Intervention' for Obesity Reduction?," *Medical Journal of Australia* 189 no. 3 (2008): 181.

116. Niek Stadhouders, Florien Kruse, Marit Tanke, Xander Koolman, and Patrick Jeurissen, "Effective Healthcare Cost-Containment Policies: A Systematic Review," *Health Policy* 123, no. 1 (2019): 71–79.

117. Rosemary Morgan, Moses Tetui, Ronald Muhumuza Kananura, Elizabeth Ekirapa-Kiracho, and A. S. George, "Gender Dynamics Affecting Maternal Health and Health Care Access and Use in Uganda," *Health Policy and Planning* 32, suppl. 5 (2017): v13–v21.

118. K. Arges, T. Assimes, V. Bajaj, S. Balu, M. R. Bashir, L. Beskow, R. Blanco, R. Califf, P. Campbell, L. Carin, and V. Christian, "The Project Baseline Health Study: A Step towards a Broader Mission to Map Human Health," *NPJ Digital Medicine* 3, no. 1 (2020): 1–10.

119. Angela Donkin, Peter Goldblatt, Jessica Allen, Vivienne Nathanson, and Michael Marmot, "Global Action on the Social Determinants of Health," *BMJ Global Health* 3, suppl. 1 (2018): 1–7.

120. Daniel Callahan, *Setting Limits: Medical Goals in an Aging Society* (New York: Touchstone Books, 1988); Daniel Callahan, *What Kind of Life: The Limits of Medical Progress* (Washington, DC: Georgetown University Press, 1995).

121. Alena Buyx and Barbara Prainsack, "Lifestyle-Related Diseases and Individual Responsibility through the Prism of Solidarity," *Clinical Ethics* 7, no. 2 (2012): 79–85.

122. Jeffrey L. Goldhagen, Sherry Shenoda, Charles Oberg, Raúl Mercer, Ayesha Kadir, Shanti Raman, Tony Waterston, and Nicholas J. Spencer, "Rights, Justice, and Equity: A Global Agenda for Child Health and Wellbeing," *Lancet Child & Adolescent Health* 4, no. 1 (2020): 80–90.

123. Amarty Sen, *Inequality Reexamined* (Oxford: Clarendon Press, 1995).

124. S. I. Okafor, "Inequalities in the Distribution of Health Care Facilities in Nigeria," in *Health and Disease in Tropical Africa*, ed. R. Akhar (London: Gordon and Breach, 1987), 383–401.

125. Earth Overshoot Day, 2020, https://www.overshootday.org/; Dan Tong, Qiang Zhang, Yixuan Zheng, Ken Caldeira, Christine Shearer, Chaopeng Hong, Yue Qin, and Steven J. Davis, "Committed Emissions from Existing Energy Infrastructure Jeopardize 1.5 C Climate Target," *Nature* 572, no. 7769 (2019): 373–377.

126. In the UK it is up to £545 per year per child. Danielle Richardson, "Child Tax Credit: Calculate How Much Child Tax Credit You Are Entitled to Receive in the 2021–22 Tax Year," *Which.co.uk*, May 2021, https://www.which.co.uk/money/tax/tax-cred its-and-benefits/tax-credits/child-tax-credits-atxv75s3q5gc#headline_5.

NOTES   253

127. Katie Teague, "When Is the Next Child Tax Credit Payment Coming? Dates to Know, Unenroll Deadline," CNet, October 4, 2021, https://www.cnet.com/personal-fina nce/taxes/when-is-the-next-child-tax-credit-payment-coming-dates-to-know-unenroll-deadline/.

128. US Department of Agriculture, Center for Nutrition Policy and Promotion, "Expenditures on Children by Families, 2015," January 9, 2017, 1–37, https://www.fns.usda.gov/resource/2015-expenditures-children-families.

129. Associated Press, "Australia Should Introduce a Baby Tax 'to Save the Planet,'" *Daily Mail UK*, December 10, 2007, http://www.dailymail.co.uk/news/article-501059/Australia-introduce-baby-tax-save-planet.html.

130. Walters, "Personal Carbon Trading," 181.

131. Oscar Erixson and Sebastian Escobar, "Deathbed Tax Planning," *Journal of Public Economics* 185 (2020): 104170.

132. Carbon Tax Center, "Supporters," accessed March 27, 2013, http://www.carbon tax.org/who-supports/; Alex Bowen and Duncan Clark, "What Is a Carbon Price and Why Do We Need One?," *The Guardian*, July 16, 2012, http://www.guard ian.co.uk/environment/2012/jul/16/carbon-price-tax-cap; Howard Schneider, "IMF: Governments Need to End Energy Subsidies," *Washington Post*, March 27, 2013, http://www.washingtonpost.com/business/economy/imf-citing-trillions-in-government-subsidies-calls-for-end-to-mispricing-of-energy/2013/03/27/09957 d6e-96e1-11e2-814b-063623d80a60_story.html?hpid=z2.

133. Congressional Budget Office, "Effects of a Carbon Tax on the Economy and the Environment," accessed August 17, 2013, http://www.cbo.gov/sites/default/files/cbofiles/attachments/44223_Carbon_0.pdf.

134. Walter Rauschenbusch, *A Theology for the Social Gospel* (New York: Abingdon, 1945), 111.

135. Murtaugh and Schla, "Reproduction and the Carbon Legacies of Individuals."

136. D. Chandler, "Leaving Our Mark," *MIT Tech Talk* 52, no. 1 (2008): 4–5.

137. DiLeo, "Faithful Citizenship in the Age of Climate Change."

138. Martha C. Nussbaum, "Human Functioning and Social Justice," *Political Theory* 20, no. 2 (1992): 231.

Chapter 6

1. Jacalyn Duffin, *History of Medicine: A Scandalously Short Introduction* (Toronto: University of Toronto Press, 2010).

2. J. S. Hacker, *The Divided Welfare State: The Battle over Public and Private Social Benefits in the United States* (Cambridge: Cambridge University Press, 2002).

3. D. Blumenthal, "Employer-Sponsored Health Insurance in the United States: Origins and Implications," *New England Journal of Medicine* 355, no. 1 (2006): 82–88.

4. Charles Webster, *The National Health Service: A Political History* (New York: Oxford University Press, 2002).

254 NOTES

5. Arthur Newsholme and John Adams Kingsbury, *Red Medicine: Socialized Health in Soviet Russia* (London: Willian Heinemann Ltd, 1934), 192.
6. Z. C. Brot-Goldberg, A. Chandra, B. R. Handel, and J. T. Kolstad, "What Does a Deductible Do? The Impact of Cost-Sharing on Health Care Prices, Quantities, and Spending Dynamics," *Quarterly Journal of Economics* 132, no. 3, (2017): 1261–1318.
7. Pitkin Derose, Kathryn, Benjamin W. Bahney, Nicole Lurie, and José J. Escarce, "Immigrants and Health Care Access, Quality, and Cost," *Medical Care Research and Review* 66, no. 4 (2009): 355–408.
8. Andrea S. Christopher, David U. Himmelstein, Steffie Woolhandler, and Danny McCormick, "The Effects of Household Medical Expenditures on Income Inequality in the United States," *American Journal of Public Health* 108, no. 3 (2018): 351–354.
9. Mir M. Ali, Judith L. Teich, and Ryan Mutter, "Characteristics of Individuals with Behavioral Health Conditions Who Remain Uninsured after Full Implementation of the ACA," *Psychiatric Services* 68, no. 7 (2017): 667–673.
10. W. Yip, H. Fu, A. T. Chen, T. Zhai, W. Jian, R. Xu, J. Pan, M. Hu, Z. Zhou, Q. Chen, and W. Mao, "10 Years of Health-care Reform in China: Progress and Gaps in Universal Health Coverage," *The Lancet* 394, no. 10204 (2019): 1192–1204.
11. Chul Y. Chung, Mark D. Alson, Richard Duszak, and Andrew J. Degnan, "From Imaging to Reimbursement: What the Pediatric Radiologist Needs to Know about Health Care Payers, Documentation, Coding and billing," *Pediatric Radiology* 48, no. 7 (2018): 904–914.
12. Elias Mossialos and Julian Le Grand, eds., *Health Care and Cost Containment in the European Union* (London: Routledge, 2019).
13. Aisha K. Lofters, Rahim Moineddin, Stephen W. Hwang, and Richard H. Glazier, "Predictors of Low Cervical Cancer Screening among Immigrant Women in Ontario, Canada," *BMC Women's Health* 11, no. 1 (2011): 1–11.
14. Oregon Health Plan, "Prioritized List of Health Services," January 1, 2015, http://www.oregon.gov/oha/herc/Pages/PrioritizedList.aspx.
15. Elias Mossialos, Anna Dixon, Josep Figueras, Joe Kutzin, and World Health Organization, *Funding Health Care: Options for Europe* (Geneva: WHO, 2002); Joseph Kutzin, "A Descriptive Framework for Country-Level Analysis of Health Care Financing Arrangements," *Health Policy* 56, no. 3 (2001): 171–204.
16. L. Fleck, *Just Caring: Health Care Rationing and Democratic Deliberation* (New York: Oxford University Press, 2009).
17. C. Tomson, "Reducing the Carbon Footprint of Hospital-Based Care," *Future Hospital Journal* 2, no. 1 (2015): 57–62.
18. Lori McMullen, "Patient Assistance Programs," *Clinical Journal of Oncology Nursing* 23, no. 5 (2019): 36–40.
19. Alan Lyles, "Direct Marketing of Pharmaceuticals to Consumers," *Annual Review of Public Health* 23, no. 1 (2002): 73–91.
20. Lisa M. Schwartz and Steven Woloshin, "Medical Marketing in the United States, 1997–2016," *JAMA* 321, no. 1 (2019): 80–96.
21. J. Folger, "How to Choose between Bronze, Silver, Gold and Platinum Health Insurance Plan," *Forbes*, October 1, 2013, https://www.forbes.com/sites/investope

dia/2013/10/01/how-to-choose-between-bronze-silver-gold-and-platinum-health-insurance-plans/#1fbcb1c22b2e.

22. Allen E. Buchanan, "The Right to a Decent Minimum of Health Care," *Philosophy & Public Affairs* (1984): 55–78.

23. G. Ooms, K. Derderian, and D. Melody, "Do We Need a World Health Insurance to Realise the Right to Health?," *PLoS Med*, 3 no. 2 (2006): 2171–2176.

24. Ross Hofmeyr, "South Africa: Where Are We Going?," in *ICU Resource Allocation in the New Millennium: Will We Say "No"?*, ed. David W. Crippen (New York: Springer, 2013), 172.

25. Jane Hall, Richard de Abreu Lourenco, and Rosalie Viney, "Carrots and Sticks—The Fall and Fall of Private Health Insurance in Australia," *Health Economics* 8, no. 8 (1999): 653–660.

26. T. Beauchamp and J. Childress, *Principles of Biomedical Ethics*, 4th ed. (New York: Oxford University Press, 1994), 16.

27. Christopher Ham, *Health Policy in Britain* (London: Macmillan International Higher Education, 2009).

28. Saeko Kikuzawa, Sigrun Olafsdottir, and Bernice A. Pescosolido, "Similar Pressures, Different Contexts: Public Attitudes toward Government Intervention for Health Care in 21 Nations," *Journal of Health and Social Behavior* 49, no. 4 (2008): 385–399.

29. Ronald Bayer and Amy L. Fairchild, "The Genesis of Public Health Ethics," *Bioethics* 18, no. 6 (2004): 489. Cf. Lawrence O. Gostin, "Public Health Law in an Age of Terrorism: Rethinking Individual Rights and Common Goods," *Health Affairs* 21, no. 6 (2002): 79–93.

30. Matthew J. Eckelman and Jodi Sherman, "Environmental Impacts of the US Health Care System and Effects on Public Health," *PloS One* 11, no. 6 (2016): e0157014.

31. Shota Hamada, Hideto Takahashi, Nobuo Sakata, Boyoung Jeon, Takahiro Mori, Katsuya Iijima, Satoru Yoshie, Tatsuro Ishizaki, and Nanako Tamiya, "Household Income Relationship with Health Services Utilization and Healthcare Expenditures in People Aged 75 Years or Older in Japan: A Population-Based Study Using Medical and Long-Term Care Insurance Claims Data," *Journal of Epidemiology* 29, no. 10 (2019): 377–383.

32. Michael K. Chapko, Jenifer L. Ehreth, and Susan Hedrick, "Methods of Determining the Cost of Health Care in the Department of Veterans Affairs Medical Centers and Other Nonpriced Settings," *Evaluation & the Health Professions* 14, no. 3 (1991): 282–303.

33. Geoff Herbert, "Buffalo Teachers Still Get Free Plastic Surgery Courtesy of Taxpayers," *Syracuse.com*, January 19, 2012, http://www.syracuse.com/news/index.ssf/2012/01/buffalo_teachers_get_free_plas.html.

34. Patient Protection and Affordable Care Act, H.R. 3590, 111th Congress (2009–2010), ratified March 23, 2010, https://www.congress.gov/bill/111th-congress/house-bill/3590/.

35. Nathan Ford, David Wilson, Paul Cawthorne, Aree Kumphitak, Siriras Kasi-Sedapan, Suntharaporn Kaetkaew, Saengsri Teemanka, Boripat Donmon, and Chalerm Preuanbuapan, "Challenge and Co-operation: Civil Society Activism for Access

256 NOTES

to HIV Treatment in Thailand," *Tropical Medicine & International Health* 14, no. 3 (2009): 258–266.

36. Thomas Kerz, "Germany: Where Are We Going?," in *ICU Resource Allocation in the New Millennium: Will We Say "No"?*, ed. D. W. Crippen (New York: Springer, 2013), 133.

37. Kerz, "Germany," 133.

38. Frank H. Bosch, "The Netherlands: Where Have We Been?," in *ICU Resource Allocation in the New Millennium: Will We Say "No"?*, ed. David W. Crippen (New York: Springer, 2013), 59.

39. National Health Services Sustainable Development Unit, *Saving Carbon, Improving Health: NHS Carbon Reduction Strategy for England* (London: NHS Sustainable Development Unit, 2009).

40. National Institutes for Health Research, "Carbon Reduction Guidelines," October 2010, 1–20, www.nihr.ac.uk/files/NIHR_Carbon_Reduction_Guidelines.pdf.

41. Mary Hanna and Gregory L. Bryson, "A Long Way to Go: Minimizing the Carbon Footprint from Anesthetic Gases," *Canadian Journal of Anesthesia* 66 (2019): 1–2.

42. Cassandra L. Thiel, Noe C. Woods, and Melissa M. Bilec, "Strategies to Reduce Greenhouse Gas Emissions from Laparoscopic Surgery," *American Journal of Public Health* 108, no. S2 (2018): S158–S164.

43. Sherri M. Cook, Bryan J. VanDuinen, Nancy G. Love, and Steven J. Skerlos, "Life Cycle Comparison of Environmental Emissions from Three Disposal Options for Unused Pharmaceuticals," *Environmental Science & Technology* 46, no. 10 (2012): 5535–5541.

44. Cristina Richie, "Environmental Sustainability and the Carbon Emissions of Pharmaceuticals," *Journal of Medical Ethics* 48, no. 5 (2022): 334–337.

45. Endang Sutrisno, Taty Sugiarti, and Novani Ambarsari Pratiwi, "Environmental Law Enforcement in Hazardous-Waste Management in West Java Indonesia: A Critical Trajectory of Green and Anthropogenic-Based Environmental Policy Orientations," *International Journal of Scientific & Technology Research* 8 no. 8 (2019): 429–434.

46. Ashkan Nabavi-Pelesaraei, Reza Bayat, Homa Hosseinzadeh-Bandbafha, Hadi Afrasyabi, and Kwok-wing Chau, "Modeling of Energy Consumption and Environmental Life Cycle Assessment for Incineration and Landfill Systems of Municipal Solid Waste Management: A Case Study in Tehran Metropolis of Iran," *Journal of Cleaner Production* 148 (2017): 427–440.

47. Zentrale Ethikommission bei der Bundesärztekammer, "Priorisierung medizinischer Leistungenm System der Gesetzlichen Krankenversicherung (GKV) Stellungnahme der Zentralen Kommission zur Wahrung ethischer Grundsätze in der Medizin und ihren Grenzgebieten (Zentrale Ethikkommission) bei der Bundesärztekammer," 2007, http://www.zentrale-ethikkommission.de/downloads/Stellungnahme_Priori sierung2007.pdf.

48. Pierre L. Yong, Robert S. Saunders, and LeighAnne Olsen, *The Healthcare Imperative: Lowering Costs and Improving Outcomes* (Washington, DC: National Academies Press, 2010).

49. Eugene Litvak and Maureen Bisognano, "More Patients, Less Payment: Increasing Hospital Efficiency in the Aftermath of Health Reform," *Health Affairs* 30, no. 1 (2011): 76–80.

50. Cristina Richie, "Can United States Healthcare Become Environmentally Sustainable? Towards Green Healthcare Reform," *Journal of Law, Medicine, and Ethics* 48, no. 4 (2020): 643–652.

51. Joseph H. Howell and William Frederick Sale, "Specifying the Goals of Medicine," in *Life Choices: A Hastings Center Introduction to Bioethics*, 2nd ed., ed. Joseph H. Howell and William Frederick Sale (Washington, DC: Georgetown University Press, 2000), 62–73.

52. Michael R. Bowers, John E. Swan, and William F. Koehler, "What Attributes Determine Quality and Satisfaction with Health Care Delivery?," *Health Care Management Review* 19, no. 4 (1994): 49–55.

53. Deborah Korenstein, Susan Chimonas, Brooke Barrow, Salomeh Keyhani, Aaron Troy, and Allison Lipitz-Snyderman, "Development of a Conceptual Map of Negative Consequences for Patients of Overuse of Medical Tests and Treatments," *JAMA Internal Medicine* 178, no. 10 (2018): 1401–1407.

54. Udo P. Pennell, U. P. Sechtem, C. B. Higgins, W. J. Manning, G. M. Pohost, F. E. Rademakers, A. C. van Rossum, L. J. Shaw, and E. K. Yucel, "Clinical Indications for Cardiovascular Magnetic Resonance (CMR): Consensus Panel Report," *European Heart Journal* 25, no. 21 (2004): 1940–1965.

55. Natalie Joseph-Williams, Amy Lloyd, Adrian Edwards, Lynne Stobbart, David Tomson, Sheila Macphail, Carole Dodd, Kate Brain, Glyn Elwyn, and Richard Thomson, "Implementing Shared Decision Making in the NHS: Lessons from the MAGIC Programme," *BMJ* 357 (2017): c5146–c5146.

56. Glyn Elwyn, M. A. Durand, J. Song, J. Aarts, P. J. Barr, Z. Berger, N. Cochran, D. Frosch, D. Galasiński, P. Gulbrandsen, and P. K. Han, "A Three-Talk Model for Shared Decision Making: Multistage Consultation Process," *BMJ* 359 (2017): j4891.

57. Katherine Baicker, Kasey S. Buckles, and Amitabh Chandra, "Geographic Variation in the Appropriate Use of Cesarean Delivery: Do Higher Usage Rates Reflect Medically Inappropriate Use of This Procedure?," *Health Affairs* 25, suppl. 1 (2006): W355–W367.

58. T. A. Caulfield, "Wishful Thinking: Defining 'Medically Necessary' in Canada," *Health Law Journal* 4 (1996): 63–85.

59. David C. Radley, Stan N. Finkelstein, and Randall S. Stafford, "Off-Label Prescribing among Office-Based Physicians," *Archives of Internal Medicine* 166, no. 9 (2006): 1021–1026.

60. World Health Organization, *WHO Best-Practice Statement on the Off-Label Use of Bedaquiline and Delamanid for the Treatment of Multidrug-Resistant Tuberculosis*, No. WHO/HTM/TB/2017.20 (Geneva: World Health Organization, 2017).

61. Grant S. Hamilton, Jeffrey S. Carrithers, and Lucy H. Karnell, "Public Perception of the Terms Cosmetic, Plastic, and Reconstructive Surgery," *Archives of Facial Plastic Surgery* 6, no. 5 (2004): 315–320.

258 NOTES

62. Josephine Johnston, "Judging Octomom," *Hasting Center Report* 39 (May–June 2009): 24.
63. Cristina Richie, "Reading between the Lines: Infertility and Current Health Insurance Policies in the United States," *Clinical Ethics* 9, no. 4 (2014): 127–134.
64. Marco Luchetti and Giuseppe A. Marraro, "Italy: Where Have We Been?," in *ICU Resource Allocation in the New Millennium: Will We Say "No"?*, ed. David W. Crippen (New York: Springer, 2013), 47.
65. Cristina Richie, "Applying Catholic Responsibility to In-Vitro Fertilization: Obligations to the Spouse, the Body, and the Common Good," *Christian Bioethics*, 18, no. 3 (2012): 281–283.
66. Maura A. Ryan, *The Ethics and Economics of Assisted Reproduction: The Cost of Longing* (Washington, DC: Georgetown University Press, 2001).
67. Teresa Iglesias, *IVF and Moral Justice: Moral, Social, and Legal Issues related to Human in vitro Fertilization* (London: Linacre Centre, 1990), 91.
68. James M. Dupree, Ryan M. Dickey, and Larry I. Lipshultz, "Inequity between Male and Female Coverage in State Infertility Laws," *Fertility and Sterility* 105, no. 6 (2016): 1519–1522.
69. R. Landau, "Posthumous Sperm Retrieval for the Purpose of Later Insemination or IVF in Israel: An Ethical and Psychosocial Critique," *Human Reproduction* 19, no. 9 (2004): 1956.
70. Dina Kraft, "Where Families Are Prized, Help Is Free," *New York Times,* July 17, 2011, http://www.nytimes.com/2011/07/18/world/middleeast/18israel.html?pagewan ted=all.
71. H. Rimon-Greenspan and V. Ravitsky, "New Frontiers in Posthumous Reproduction," *BioNews* 709 (June 17, 2013), http://www.bionews.org.uk/page_313450.asp.
72. Daphna Birenbaum-Carmeli, "Thirty-Five Years of Assisted Reproductive Technologies in Israel," *Reproductive Biomedicine & Society Online* 2 (2016): 16–23.
73. Birenbaum-Carmeli, "Thirty-Five Years of Assisted Reproductive Technologies in Israel."
74. Michèle Hansen, Lyn Colvin, Beverly Petterson, Jennifer J. Kurinczuk, Nicholas de Klerk, and Carol Bower, "Twins Born Following Assisted Reproductive Technology: Perinatal Outcome and Admission to Hospital," *Human Reproduction* 24, no. 9 (2009): 2321–2331.
75. Kirsten Riggan, "G12 Country Regulations of Assisted Reproductive Technologies," *Dignitas* 16, no. 4 (Winter 2009): 6–7.
76. Associated Press, "Report Finds IVF Provision Varies on the NHS," *NHS News,* June 7, 2011, http://www.nhs.uk/news/2011/06June/Pages/report-finds-ivf-provision-var ies-on-the-nhs.aspx.
77. Michelle Roberts, "IVF Multiple Births 'Drain NHS,'" BBC News, June 19, 2005, http://news.bbc.co.uk/1/hi/health/4120398.stm.
78. Human Fertility and Embryo Authority, "Fertility Treatment in 2013, Trends and Figures," https://www.hfea.gov.uk/media/2081/hfea-fertility-trends-2013.pdf.
79. Human Fertility and Embryo Authority, "Fertility Treatment 2019: Trends and Figures," May 2021, https://www.hfea.gov.uk/about-us/publications/research-and-data/fertility-treatment-2019-trends-and-figures/.

NOTES 259

80. Patient Protection and Affordable Care Act (P.L. 111-148), signed March 23, 2010.
81. Kraft, "Where Families Are Prized, Help Is Free."
82. Division of Health Care Finance and Policy, "Review and Evaluation of Proposed Legislation Entitled: An Act Relative to Increasing Coverage for Infertility Treatments," Senate Bill 485 Provided for the Joint Financial Services Committee, (Milwaukee: Oliver Wyman Actuarial Consulting August 2009), 1–19, at 9.
83. National Conference of State Legislatures and the American Society for Reproductive Medicine, "State Laws Related to Insurance Coverage for Infertility Treatment," March 2012, http://www.ncsl.org/issues-research/health/insurance-coverage-for-infertility-laws.aspx.
84. Richie, "Reading between the Lines."
85. Examples include B.U.M.P.S., Inc., Bringing U Maternal Paternal Success; the Tinina Q. Cade Foundation, which provides $10,000 for fertility treatment or adoption; Fertile Dreams—The Embracing Hope Grant, for women without IVF insurance; Pay it Forward Fertility Foundation, also for women without IVF insurance; and the International Council on Infertility Information Dissemination.
86. RESOLVE: The National Infertility Association, "Infertility Treatment Grants and Scholarships," 2023. https://resolve.org/learn/financial-resources-for-family-build ing/fertility-treatment-scholarships-and-grants/.
87. Luchetti and Marraro, "Italy," 51.
88. As of early 2010, this and much more are excluded by Blue Cross Blue Shield Blue Care Elect Preferred PPO. In vitro fertilization, however, is covered.
89. Dennis Hollinger, *The Meaning of Sex: Christian Ethics and the Moral Life* (Grand Rapids, MI: Baker, 2009).
90. Janice Raymond, *Women as Wombs* (San Francisco: Harper Collins, 1993).
91. Iva Skoch, "Should IVF Be Affordable to All?," *Newsweek*, July 21, 2010.

Chapter 7

1. G. Weston and B. Vollenhoven, "Is IVF Becoming a Band Aid for Social Infertility?," *Australian and New Zealand Journal of Obstetrics and Gynaecology* 42 (2002): 476–477.
2. Robin E. Jensen, Nicole Martins, and Melissa M. Parks, "Public Perception of Female Fertility: Initial Fertility, Peak Fertility, and Age-Related Infertility among US Adults," *Archives of Sexual Behavior* 47, no. 5 (2018): 1507–1516.
3. Brittany J. Harrison, Tara N. Hilton, Raphaël N. Rivière, Zachary M. Ferraro, Raywat Deonandan, and Mark C. Walker, "Advanced Maternal Age: Ethical and Medical Considerations for Assisted Reproductive Technology," *International Journal of Women's Health* 9 (2017): 561.
4. Centers for Disease Control, "National Survey of Family Growth: Childlessness," 2015, https://www.cdc.gov/nchs/nsfg/key_statistics/c.htm# childlessness.
5. Megan L. Kavanaugh and Jenna Jerman, "Contraceptive Method Use in the United States: Trends and Characteristics between 2008, 2012 and 2014," *Contraception* 97, no. 1 (2018): 14–21.

260 NOTES

6. World Health Organization. *Reproductive Health Indicators for Global Monitoring: Guidelines for their Generation, Interpretation and Analysis for Global Monitoring.* Geneva: World Health Organization, 2006, 1–63, at 49.

7. World Health Organization, *International Classification of Diseases*, 11th revision (Geneva: WHO, 2018).

8. F. Signore, C. Gulìa, R. Votino, V. De Leo, S. Zaami, L. Putignani, S. Gigli, E. Santini, L. Bertacca, A. Porrello, and R. Piergentili, "The role of number of copies, structure, behavior and copy number variations (CNV) of the Y chromosome in male infertility," *Genes*, 11, no. 1 (2019): 1–30 at 2.

9. American Society for Reproductive Medicine, Practice Committee Report, "Definition of Infertility and Recurrent Pregnancy Loss," *Fertility and Sterility* 90, suppl. 3 (2008): S60.

10. American Society of Reproductive Medicine, "Infertility," 2020, https://www.asrm.org/topics/topics index/infertility/.

11. Gareth Weston and Beverley Vollenhoven, "Is IVF Becoming a Band Aid for Social Infertility?," *Australian and New Zealand Journal of Obstetrics and Gynaecology* 42, no. 5 (2002): 476–477.

12. Govert Den Hartogh, "Suffering and Dying Well: On the Proper Aim of Palliative Care," *Medicine, Health Care and Philosophy* 20, no. 3 (2017): 413–424.

13. Elena Ricci, Paola Viganò, Sonia Cipriani, Francesca Chiaffarino, Stefano Bianchi, Giorgia Rebonato, and Fabio Parazzini, "Physical Activity and Endometriosis Risk in Women with Infertility or Pain: Systematic Review and Meta-analysis," *Medicine* 95, no. 40 (2016): 1–10.

14. C. Le Ray, L. Pelage, A. Seco, M. H. Bouvier-Colle, A. A. Chantry, C. Deneux-Tharaux, Epimoms Study Group, B. Langer, C. Dupont, R. C. Rudigoz, and F. Vendittelli, "Risk of Severe Maternal Morbidity Associated with in Vitro Fertilisation: A Population-Based Study," *BJOG: An International Journal of Obstetrics & Gynaecology* 126, no. 8 (2019): 1033–1041.

15. Reference within quote: R. J. Cook, B. M. Dickens and M. F. Fathalla, *Reproductive Health and Human Rights* (Oxford: Clarendon Press, 2003); E. G. Hughes and M. Giacomini, "Funding In Vitro Fertilization Treatment for Persistent Subfertility: The Pain and the Politics," *Fertility and Sterility*, 76, no. 3(2001): 431–442; P. Mladovsky and C. Sorensen, "Public Financing of IVF: A Review of Policy Rationales," *Health Care Analysis* 18 (2010): 113–128; P. J. Neumann, "Should Health Insurance Cover IVF? Issues and Options," *Journal of Health Politics, Policy, and Law*, 22, no. 5 (1997): 1215–1237.

16. Jurgen De Wispelaere and Daniel Weinstock, "State Regulation and Assisted Reproduction: Balancing the Interests of Parents and Children," in *Family-Making: Contemporary Ethical Challenges*, ed. Françoise Baylis and Carolyn MacLeod (Oxford: Oxford University Press, 2014), 131–150.

17. Rebecca Brown, "Irresponsibly Infertile? Obesity, Efficiency, and Exclusion from Treatment," *Health Care Analysis* 27, no. 2 (2019): 61–76; Trudie Gerrits, "Assisted Reproductive Technologies in Ghana: Transnational Undertakings, Local Practices and 'More Affordable' IVF," *Reproductive Biomedicine & Society Online* 2 (2016): 32–38.

NOTES   261

18. R. John Simes and Alan S. Coates, "Patient Preferences for Adjuvant Chemotherapy of Early Breast Cancer: How Much Benefit Is Needed?," *JNCI Monographs* 2001, no. 30 (2001): 146–152.

19. Gordon Ngo, Graham Trope, Yvonne Buys, and Ya-Ping Jin, "Significant Disparities in Eyeglass Insurance Coverage in Canada," *Canadian Journal of Ophthalmology* 53, no. 3 (2018): 260–265.

20. However, it does seem that health insurance companies are more willing to fund low-tech alternative and ancillary healthcare services such as acupuncture, massage therapy, nutritional counseling, personal training, Pilates, tai chi, and yoga. See Blue Cross of Massachusetts, "Perks," 2015, http://www.studentbluema.com/perks.php Accessed October 23, 2023, Blue Cross Blue Shield of Massachusetts, "Fitness Benefit," 2009, https://www.bluecrossma.com/common/en_US/pdfs/New_SOB/Fitness_Benefit_Form.pdf. Accessed October 23, 2023.

21. Renuka Tipirneni, Mary C. Politi, Jeffrey T. Kullgren, Edith C. Kieffer, Susan D. Goold, and Aaron M. Scherer, "Association between Health Insurance Literacy and Avoidance of Health Care Services Owing to Cost," *JAMA Network Open* 1, no. 7 (2018): e184796–e184796.

22. Michèle Hansen, Lyn Colvin, Beverly Petterson, Jennifer J. Kurinczuk, Nicholas de Klerk, and Carol Bower, "Twins Born Following Assisted Reproductive Technology: Perinatal Outcome and Admission to Hospital," *Human Reproduction* 24, no. 9 (2009): 2321–2331.

23. Blue Cross of Massachusetts, "Living Healthy Babies," n.d., http://www.bluecrossma.com/breast-pump/. Accessed October 23, 2023.

24. Geoff Herbert, "Buffalo Teachers Still Get Free Plastic Surgery Courtesy of Taxpayers," *Syracuse.com*, January 19, 2012, http://www.syracuse.com/news/index.ssf/2012/01/buffalo_teachers_get_free_plas.html.

25. Cristina Richie, "Not Sick: Liberal, Trans, and CripFeminist Critiques of Medicalization," *Journal of Bioethical Inquiry* 16, no. 3 (2019): 375–387.

26. Maurice Rickard, "Is It Medically Legitimate to Provide Assisted Reproductive Treatments to Fertile Lesbians and Single Women?," Maurice Rickard Social Policy Group 27, 2001, 1–35.

27. Mark S. Hochberg, Carolyn D. Seib, Russell S. Berman, Adina L. Kalet, Sondra R. Zabar, and H. Leon Pachter, "Perspective: Malpractice in an Academic Medical Center: A Frequently Overlooked Aspect of Professionalism Education," *Academic Medicine* 86, no. 3 (2011): 365–368.

28. Marco Luchetti and Giuseppe A. Marraro, "Italy: Where Have We Been?," in *ICU Resource Allocation in the New Millennium: Will We Say "No"?*, ed. David W. Crippen (New York: Springer, 2013), 51.

29. Zentrale Ethikommission bei der Bundesärztekammer, "Priorisierung medizinischer Leistungen m System der Gesetzlichen Krankenversicherung (GKV) Stellungnahme der Zentralen Kommission zur Wahrung ethischer Grundsätze in der Medizin und ihren Grenzgebieten (Zentrale Ethikkommission) bei der Bundesärztekammer," 2007, https://www.zentrale-ethikkommission.de/fileadmin/user_upload/_old-files/downloads/pdf-Ordner/Zeko/LangfassungPriorisierung.pdf

262 NOTES

30. Zentrale Ethikommission bei der Bundesärztekammer, Priorisierung medizinischer Leistungen m System der Gesetzlichen Krankenversicherung." https://www.zentr ale-ethikkommission.de/fileadmin/user_upload/_old-files/downloads/pdf-Ordner/ Zeko/LangfassungPriorisierung.pdf.

31. A. Cobo, J. García-Velasco, J. Domingo, A. Pellicer, and J. Remohí, "Elective and Onco-fertility Preservation: Factors related to IVF Outcomes," *Human Reproduction* 33, no. 12 (2018): 2222–2231.

32. Bagus Komang Satriyasa, "Botulinum Toxin (Botox) A for Reducing the Appearance of Facial Wrinkles: A Literature Review of Clinical Use and Pharmacological Aspect," *Clinical, Cosmetic and Investigational Dermatology* 12 (2019): 223.

33. Cristina Richie, "A Queer, Feminist Bioethics Critique of Facial Feminization Surgery," *American Journal of Bioethics* 18, no. 12 (2018): 33–35.

34. Cristina Richie, *Principles of Green Bioethics: Sustainability in Health Care* (East Lansing: Michigan State University Press, 2019).

35. Dena Towner and Roberta Springer Loewy, "Ethics of PGD for a Woman Destined to Develop Early-Onset Alzheimer Disease," in *Genetics: Science, Ethics, and Public Policy*, ed. T. A. Shannon (Lanham, MD: Rowman & Littlefield, 2005), 75.

36. Abdelhafid Benksim, Noureddine Elkhoudri, Rachid Ait Addi, Abdellatif Baali, and Mohamed Cherkaoui, "Difference between Primary and Secondary Infertility in Morocco: Frequencies and Associated Factors," *International Journal of Fertility & Sterility* 12, no. 2 (2018): 142–146.

37. Trevor Hedberg, "One Child: Do We Have a Right to Have More? by Sarah Conly," *Philosophy East and West* 67, no. 3 (2017): 934–938.

38. Hugh P. McDonald, "Chapter 7 Population: A Critical Evaluation of the 'Right' to Unlimited Procreation," *Environmental Philosophy* (Leiden: Brill 2014), 231–271.

39. Sarah Conly, "The Right to Procreation: Merits and Limits," *American Philosophical Quarterly* 42, no. 2 (2005): 105–115.

40. Zha Blong Xiong, Patricia A. Eliason, Daniel F. Detzner, and Michael J. Cleveland, "Southeast Asian Immigrants' Perceptions of Good Adolescents and Good Parents," *Journal of Psychology* 139, no. 2 (2005): 159–175.

41. Maria Rita Testa, "Childbearing Preferences and Family Issues in Europe: Evidence from the Eurobarometer 2006 Survey," *Vienna Yearbook of Population Research* (Vienna: Osterreichische Akademie der Wissenschaften, Verlag, 2007): 357–379; Kellie J. Hagewen and S. Philip Morgan, "Intended and Ideal Family Size in the United States, 1970–2002," *Population and Development Review* 31, no. 3 (2005): 507–527.

42. Adriean Mancillas, "Challenging the Stereotypes about Only Children: A Review of the Literature and Implications for Practice," *Journal of Counseling & Development* 84, no. 3 (2006): 268–275.

43. Naomi R. Cahn and Jennifer M. Collins, "Eight Is Enough," *Northwestern University Law Review Colloquy* 103 (2008): 501–513.

44. Theresa Miller-Sporrer, "The Octo Mom Meets Constitutional Law: Testing the Constitutionality of Restricting Fertility Treatments," *Pittsburgh Journal of Environmental and Public Health Law* 5 (2011): 81–102.

NOTES   263

45. Paul Bentley, "Octomum's Fertility Doctor Has His Licence Revoked—for Implanting Her with SIX TIMES the Normal Number of Embryos," *Daily Mail,* June 1, 2011, https://www.dailymail.co.uk/news/article-1393251/Octomum-Nadya-Sulemans-fertility-doctor-Michael-Kamrava-licence-revoked.html.

46. Associated Press, "Report Finds IVF Provision Varies on the NHS," *NHS News,* June 7, 2011.

47. Brooke A. Levandowski, Linda Kalilani-Phiri, Fannie Kachale, Paschal Awah, Godfrey Kangaude, and Chisale Mhango, "Investigating Social Consequences of Unwanted Pregnancy and Unsafe Abortion in Malawi: The Role of Stigma," *International Journal of Gynecology & Obstetrics* 118 (2012): S167–S171.

48. Marge Berer, "Abortion Law and Policy around the World: In Search of Decriminalization," *Health and Human Rights* 19, no. 1 (2017): 13–27.

49. Rachel K. Jones and Jenna Jerman, "Abortion Incidence and Service Availability in the United States, 2014," *Perspectives on Sexual and Reproductive Health* 49, no. 1 (2017): 17–27.

50. Patricia Beattie Jung "Abortion and Organ Donation: Christian Reflections on Bodily Life Support," *Journal of Religious Ethics* 16, no. 2 (1988): 297.

51. Sidney Callahan, "A Case for Pro-Life Feminism," *Commonweal* 113, no. 8 (1986): 232–238.

52. Marc Dhont, "History of Oral Contraception," *European Journal of Contraception & Reproductive Health Care* 15, suppl. 2 (2010): S12–S18.

53. Sophie Borland, "Career Women 'Fuel a Surge in Abortions': Over-30s Relying on IVF Show Biggest Rise in Terminations," *Daily Mail UK,* May 29, 2012.

54. L. Cooke and S. M. Nelson, "Reproductive Ageing and Fertility in an Ageing Population," *Obstetrician and Gynaecologist* 13 (2011): 161–168.

55. Berer, "Abortion Law and Policy around the World."

56. J. A. Robertson, "Is There a Right to Gestate?," *Journal of Law and the Biosciences,* no. 4 (2017): 630–636.

57. Julian Huxley, "Transhumanism," *Journal of Humanistic Psychology* 8, no. 1 (1968): 73–76.

58. Charles McConnel and Leigh Turner, "Medicine, Ageing and Human Longevity: The Economics and Ethics of Anti-ageing Interventions," *EMBO Reports* 6, no. S1 (2005): S59–S62.

59. Thomas Kerz, "Germany: Where Are We Going?," In *ICU Resource Allocation in the New Millennium: Will We Say "No"?,* ed. David W. Crippen (New York: Springer, 2013), 135.

60. Jane Harries, Kathryn Stinson, and Phyllis Orner, "Health Care Providers' Attitudes towards Termination of Pregnancy: A Qualitative Study in South Africa," *BMC Public Health* 9, no. 1 (2009): 296.

61. Victor Gomel, "Reversal of Tubal Sterilization versus IVF in the Era of Assisted Reproductive Technology: A Clinical Dilemma," *Reproductive Biomedicine Online* 15, no. 4 (2007): 403–407.

62. Kavanaugh and Jerman, "Contraceptive Method Use in the United States."

264 NOTES

63. Ernesto F. L. Amaral, "Profile of Female Sterilization in Brazil," *Social Sciences* 8, no. 10 (2019): 269.
64. Cristina Richie, "Voluntary Sterilization for Childfree Women: Understanding Patient Profiles, Evaluating Accessibility, Examining Legislation," *Hastings Center Report* 43, no. 6 (2013): 36–44.
65. Richie, "Voluntary Sterilization for Childfree Women."
66. Centers for Disease Control and National Center for Health Statistics, "Surgical Sterilization in the United States: Prevalence and Characteristics, 1965–95," *Vital and Health Statistics* 23, no. 20 (June 1998): 17, 26, 27.
67. Lika Nusbaum, Brenda Douglas, Karla Damus, Michael Paasche-Orlow, and Neenah Estrella-Luna, "Communicating Risks and Benefits in Informed Consent for Research: A Qualitative Study," *Global Qualitative Nursing Research* 4 (2017): doi:2333393617732017.
68. Cristina Richie, "Reading between the Lines: Infertility and Current Health Insurance Policies in the United States," *Clinical Ethics* 9, no. 4 (2014): 127–134.
69. Sonya B. Borrero, Matthew F. Reeves, Eleanor B. Schwarz, James E. Bost, Mitchell D. Creinin, and Said A. Ibrahim, "Race, Insurance Status, and Desire for Tubal Sterilization Reversal," *Fertility and Sterility* 90, no. 2 (2008): 272–277.
70. Anne Donchin, "In Whose Interest? Policy and Politics in Assisted Reproduction," *Bioethics* 25 no. 2 (2011): 96.
71. Donchin, "In Whose Interest?," 96.
72. Resolve, "Insurance Coverage by State," 2023, at https://resolve.org/learn/financial-resources-for-family-building/insurance-coverage/insurance-coverage-by-state/.
73. Cristina Richie, "Whose Interests Are Advanced by LGBT Bioethics?," *Ethics, Medicine and Public Health/Ethique, Médecine et Politiques Publiques* 13 (2020): 100467.
74. Henrike E. Peters, Roel Schats, Marieke O. Verhoeven, Velja Mijatovic, Christianne J. M. de Groot, Joanna L. Sandberg, Immelie P. Peeters, and Cornelis B. Lambalk, "Gestational Surrogacy: Results of 10 Years of Experience in the Netherlands," *Reproductive Biomedicine Online* 37, no. 6 (2018): 725–731.
75. Susanna Graham and Andrea Braverman, "Chapter 11 ARTs and the Single Parent," in *Reproductive Donation: Practice, Policy and Bioethics* ed. Martin Richards, Guido Pennings, John B. Appleby (Cambridge: Cambridge University Press, 2012), 189–210.
76. Alison Better and Brandy L. Simula, "How and for Whom Does Gender Matter? Rethinking the Concept of Sexual Orientation," *Sexualities* 18, nos. 5–6 (2015): 665–680.
77. Jacky Boivin, Laura Bunting, John Collins, and Karl G. Nygren, "International Estimates of Infertility Prevalence and Treatment-Seeking: Potential Need and Demand for Infertility Medical Care," *Human Reproduction* 22 no. 6 (2007): 1506–1512.
78. Tadele Girum and Abebaw Wasie, "Return of Fertility after Discontinuation of Contraception: A Systematic Review and Meta-analysis," *Contraception and Reproductive Medicine* 3, no. 1 (2018): 1–9.
79. Michel Foucault, *The History of Sexuality: An Introduction*, vol. 1, trans. Robert Hurley (New York: Vintage, 1990), 95.

NOTES 265

80. Sheila Jeffreys, *Unpacking Queer Politics* (Cambridge, UK: Polity Press, 2002), 34.

81. Valerie Solanas and Avital Ronell, *SCUM Manifesto* (London: Verso, 2004); Catriona Sandilands, "Lesbian Separatist Communities and the Experience of Nature: Toward a Queer Ecology," *Organization & Environment* 15, no. 2 (2002): 131–163.

82. John Thorp, "The Social Construction of Homosexuality," *Phoenix* 46, no. 1 (1992): 54–61.

83. Barry O'Leary, "'We Cannot Claim Any Particular Knowledge of the Ways of Homosexuals, Still Less of Iranian Homosexuals . . .': The Particular Problems Facing Those Who Seek Asylum on the Basis of Their Sexual Identity," *Feminist Legal Studies* 16, no. 1 (2008): 87–95.

84. Timothy F. Murphy, "LGBT People and the Work Ahead in Bioethics," *Bioethics* 29, no. 6 (2015): ii–iii; Timothy F. Murphy, "Pathways to Genetic Parenthood for Same-Sex Couples," *Journal of Medical Ethics* (2017): doi:10.1136 medethics-2017-104291, published online first.

85. Dawn Michelle Baunach, "Changing Same-Sex Marriage Attitudes in America from 1988 through 2010," *Public Opinion Quarterly* 76, no. 2 (2012): 364–378.

86. Annette R. Appell, "Chapter 3 Legal Issues in Lesbian and Gay Adoption," *Adoption by Lesbians and Gay Men: A New Dimension in Family Diversity* ed. David M. Brodzinsky, Adam Pertman (Oxford: Oxford University Press, 2011), 36–61.

87. Fiona Tasker, "Lesbian and Gay Parenting Post-heterosexual Divorce and Separation," in *LGBT-Parent Families* ed. Abbie E. Goldberg, Katherine R. Allen (New York: Springer, 2013), 3–20.

88. Associated Press, "Same-Sex Couples to Get IVF Help in Greater Manchester," BBC News, December 13, 2010, http://news.bbc.co.uk/local/manchester/hi/people_and_places/newsid_9282000/9282620.stm.

89. Dana Berkowitz, "Gay Men and Surrogacy," in *LGBTQ-Parent Families* ed. Abbie E. Goldberg and Katherine R. Allen (Cham: Springer, 2020), 143–160.

90. Samantha Yee, Shilini Hemalal, and Clifford L. Librach, "'Not My Child to Give Away': A Qualitative Analysis of Gestational Surrogates' Experiences," *Women and Birth* 33, no. 3 (2020): e256–e265.

91. Lauren W. Milman, Suneeta Senapati, Mary D. Sammel, Katherine D. Cameron, and Clarisa Gracia, "Assessing Reproductive Choices of Women and the Likelihood of Oocyte Cryopreservation in the Era of Elective Oocyte Freezing," *Fertility and Sterility* 107, no. 5 (2017): 1214–1222.

92. Murphy, "Pathways to Genetic Parenthood for Same-Sex Couples."

93. Miriam Hadj-Moussa, Kaitlyn DelBene, Carl Cohen, Dale L. Hebert, and Dana A. Ohl, "Postmortem Sperm Retrieval: Ethical, Legal, and Logistical Considerations," in *The Complete Guide to Male Fertility Preservation* ed. Ahmad Majzoub and Ashok Agarwal (Cham: Springer, 2018), 129–144.

94. K. Sodesaki, "The Legal Status of a Human Corpse," *Nihon hoigaku zasshi/Japanese Journal of Legal Medicine* 55, no. 2 (2001): 235–242.

95. Kirsten Rabe Smolensky, "Rights of the Dead," *Hofstra Law Review* 37, no. 3 (2009): 763–803.

96. M. J. Dos Santos, E. Leal de Moraes, M. Santini Martins, E. Carlos de Almeida, L. Borges de Barros e Silva, V. Urias, M. C. Silvano Corrêa Pacheco Furtado, Á. Brito Nunes, and S. El Hage, "Trend Analysis of Organ and Tissue Donation for Transplantation," *Transplantation Proceedings*, 50, no. 2 (2018): 391–393.

97. Marina Serper, Therese Bittermann, Michael Rossi, David S. Goldberg, Arwin M. Thomasson, Kim M. Olthoff, and Abraham Shaked, "Functional Status, Healthcare Utilization, and the Costs of Liver Transplantation," *American Journal of Transplantation* 18, no. 5 (2018): 1187–1196.

98. A. Briasoulis, E. Akintoye, and P. Alvarez, "Outcomes of Heart Re-Transplantation: Analysis of the United Network for Organ Sharing (UNOS)," *Journal of Heart and Lung Transplantation* 39, no. 4 (2020): S286–S287.

99. Euro-transplant, n.d., https://www.eurotransplant.org/

100. Muhammad H. Raza, Hassan Aziz, Navpreet Kaur, Mary Lo, Linda Sher, Yuri Genyk, and Juliet Emamaullee, "Global Experience and Perspective on Anonymous Nondirected Live Donation in Living Donor Liver Transplantation," *Clinical Transplantation* 34, no. 4 (2020): e13836.

101. See See, A. K. Bello, A. Levin, M. Lunney, M. A. Osman, F. Ye, G. E. Ashuntantang, E. Bellorin-Font, M. Benghanem Gharbi, S. Davison, and M. Ghnaimat, "Availability, coverage, and scope of health information systems for kidney care across world countries and regions," *Nephrology Dialysis Transplantation* 37, no. 1 (2022): 159–167.

102. Andrew R. Zinkel, Felix K. Ankel, Aaron J. Milbank, Colleen I. Casey, and Jeremy J. Sundheim, "Postmortem Sperm Retrieval in the Emergency Department: A Case Report and Review of Available Guidelines," *Clinical Practice and Cases in Emergency Medicine* 3, no. 4 (2019): 405–408.

103. J. Raho, "In Whose Best Interests? Critiquing the 'Family-as-Unit' Myth in Pediatric Ethics," in *Bioethics: Medical, Ethical and Legal Perspectives*, ed. P. A. Clark (Croatia: InTech, 2016), 145–160.

104. Laura W. Morgan and Hannah G. Morgan, "The Legal and Medical Ethics of Post-Mortem Sperm Retrieval on Behalf of Grandparents," *Journal of the American Academy of Matrimonial Law* 33 (2020): 67.

105. Yael Hashiloni-Dolev and Zvi Triger, "The Invention of the Extended Family of Choice: The Rise and Fall (to Date) of Posthumous Grandparenthood in Israel," *New Genetics and Society* 39, no. 3 (2020): 250–270.

106. Amanda M. Rosenblum, Lucy D. Horvat, Laura A. Siminoff, Versha Prakash, Janice Beitel, and Amit X. Garg, "The Authority of Next-of-Kin in Explicit and Presumed Consent Systems for Deceased Organ Donation: An Analysis of 54 Nations," *Nephrology Dialysis Transplantation* 27, no. 6 (2012): 2533–2546.

107. James Dwyer and Elizabeth Vig, "Rethinking Transplantation between Siblings," *Hastings Center Report* 25, no. 5 (1995): 7–12.

108. Robert Sheppard Nickel and Naynesh R. Kamani, "Ethical Challenges in Hematopoietic Cell Transplantation for Sickle Cell Disease," *Biology of Blood and Marrow Transplantation* 24, no. 2 (2018): 219–227.

109. Cristina Richie, "Postmortem Sperm Retrieval and Posthumous Grandparenthood in the United States and Internationally," *Global Bioethics Enquiry* 8, no. 1 (2020): 13–22.

NOTES 267

110. Lesley A. Sharp, "Commodified Kin: Death, Mourning, and Competing Claims on the Bodies of Organ Donors in the United States," *American Anthropologist* 103, no. 1 (2001): 112–133.

111. Andrea L. Kalfoglou, Joan Scott, and Kathy Hudson, "PGD Patients' and Providers' Attitudes to the Use and Regulation of Preimplantation Genetic Diagnosis," *Reproductive Biomedicine Online* 11, no. 4 (2005): 486–496.

112. Victoria Wehrmann, "To Fund or Not to Fund? Evaluating States' Current Funding of IVF and PGD, the Impact of the Lack of Funding, and Why One Round of Coverage Is Better than None" (South Orange, NJ: Seton Hall University, 2021).

113. See Chapter 2. Eric Parens and A. Asch, "The Disability Rights Critique of Prenatal Genetic Testing: Reflections and Recommendations," *Hastings Center Report* 29, suppl. (1999): S1–S22.

114. Mary Jo Iozzio, "Genetic Anomaly or Genetic Diversity: Thinking in the Key of Disability on the Human Genome," *Theological Studies* 66 no. 4 (2005): 872.

115. Ilana Löwy, "ART with PGD: Risky Heredity and Stratified Reproduction," *Reproductive Biomedicine & Society Online* 11 (2020): 48–55.

116. Susan E. Kelly, "Choosing Not to Choose: Reproductive Responses of Parents of Children with Genetic Conditions or Impairments," *Sociology of Health & Illness* 31, no. 1 (2009): 81–97.

117. Richard Birtwhistle, Neil R. Bell, Brett D. Thombs, Roland Grad, and James A. Dickinson, "Periodic Preventive Health Visits: A More Appropriate Approach to Delivering Preventive Services: From the Canadian Task Force on Preventive Health Care," *Canadian Family Physician* 63, no. 11 (2017): 824.

118. Berhanu Alemayehu and Kenneth E. Warner, "The Lifetime Distribution of Health Care Costs," *Health Services Research* 39, no. 3 (2004): 627–642.

119. G. Opelz, T. Wujciak, B. Döhler, S. Scherer, and J. Mytilineos, "HLA Compatibility and Organ Transplant Survival: Collaborative Transplant Study," *Reviews in Immunogenetics* 1, no. 3 (1999): 334–342.

120. Y. Morishima, T. Sasazuki, H. Inoko, T. Juji, T. Akaza, K. Yamamoto, Y. Ishikawa, S. Kato, H. Sao, H. Sakamaki, and K. Kawa, "The Clinical Significance of Human Leukocyte Antigen (HLA) Allele Compatibility in Patients Receiving a Marrow Transplant from Serologically HLA-A, HLA-B, and HLA-DR Matched Unrelated Donors," *Blood, the Journal of the American Society of Hematology* 99, no. 11 (2002): 4200–4206.

121. Margaret L. MacMillan and John E. Wagner, "Haematopoeitic Cell Transplantation for Fanconi Anaemia—When and How?," *British Journal of Haematology* 149, no. 1 (2010): 14–21.

122. Willem Verpoest, "PGD and HLA Matching: Not a Quick Fix," *Reproductive Biomedicine Online* 23, no. 3 (2011): 271–273.

123. Giovanni Rubeis and Florian Steger, "Saving Whom? The Ethical Challenges of Harvesting Tissue from Savior Siblings," *European Journal of Haematology* 103, no. 5 (2019): 478–482; Aviad Raz, Christina Schües, Nadja Wilhelm, and Christoph Rehmann-Sutter, "Saving or Subordinating Life? Popular Views in Israel and Germany of Donor Siblings Created through PGD," *Journal of Medical Humanities* 38, no. 2 (2017): 191–207.

268 NOTES

124. Iozzio, "Genetic Anomaly or Genetic Diversity," 872.
125. Samuel R. Bagenstos, "The ADA Amendments Act and the Projects of the American Disability Rights Movement," University of the District of Columbia Law Review 23 (2020): 139–150.
126. Fiona Campbell, *Contours of Ableism: The Production of Disability and Abledness* (London: Palgrave Macmillan, 2009).
127. Frank Heiland, Alexia Prskawetz, and Warren C. Sanderson, "Are Individuals' Desired Family Sizes Stable? Evidence from West German Panel Data," *European Journal of Population/Revue européenne de Démographie* 24, no. 2 (2008): 129–156.
128. Kalfoglou, Scott, and Hudson, "PGD Patients' and Providers' Attitudes to the Use and Regulation of Preimplantation Genetic Diagnosis."
129. Deborah L. Rhode, *The Beauty Bias: The Injustice of Appearance in Life and Law* (Oxford: Oxford University Press, 2010).
130. Michael Pineda, Ashley Lear, James P. Collins, and Samira Kiani, "Safe CRISPR: Challenges and Possible Solutions," *Trends in Biotechnology* 37, no. 4 (2019): 389–401.
131. J. Feinberg, *The Child's Right to an Open Future. Freedom and Fulfillment: Philosophical Essays* (Princeton, NJ: Princeton University Press, 1992).
132. Jurgen De Wispelaere and Daniel Weinstock, "Chapter 7 State Regulation and Assisted Reproduction: Balancing the Interests of Parents and Children," in *Family-Making: Contemporary Ethical Challenges*, ed. Françoise Baylis and Carolyn MacLeod (Oxford University Press, 2014), 131–150, at 134.
133. De Wispelaere and Weinstock, "State Regulation and Assisted Reproduction," Jurgen De Wispelaere and Daniel Weinstock, "Chapter 7 State Regulation and Assisted Reproduction: Balancing the Interests of Parents and Children," in *Family-Making: Contemporary Ethical Challenges*, ed. Françoise Baylis and Carolyn MacLeod (Oxford University Press, 2014): 131–150, at 134.
134. C. Ramraj and C. R. Quinonez, "Self-Reported Cost-Prohibitive Dental Care Needs among Canadians," *International Journal of Dental Hygiene* 11, no. 2 (2013): 115–120; Jennifer Cohn, "Prohibitive Cost of HIV/AIDS Therapy in the United States," *AMA Journal of Ethics* 11, no. 7 (2009): 492–497.
135. Stuart Gordon White, *The Civic Minimum: On the Rights and Obligations of Economic Citizenship* (Oxford: Oxford University Press, 2003).
136. K. Arambulo, *Strengthening the Supervision of the International Covenant on Economic, Social and Cultural Rights* (Utrecht: Intersentia-Hart, 1999).
137. De Wispelaere and Weinstock, "State Regulation and Assisted Reproduction," 133.
138. Maura Ryan, *The Ethics and Economics of ART: The Cost of Longing* (Washington, DC: Georgetown University Press 2001), 10.
139. Towner and Springer Loewy, "Ethics of PGD for a Woman Destined to Develop Early-Onset Alzheimer Disease," 75.
140. Anjani Chandra, Casey E. Copen, and Elizabeth H. Stephen. *Infertility and impaired fecundity in the United States, 1982–2010: Data from the National Survey of Family Growth.* No. 2013. US Department of Health and Human Services, Centers for Disease Control and Prevention, National Center for Health Statistics, 2013.

141. Mayo Clinic Staff, "Infertility: Causes," July 19, 2013, http://www.mayoclinic.com/health/infertility/DS00310/DSECTION=causes.

142. Samira Ebrahimzadeh Zagami, Robab Latifnejad Roudsari, Roksana Janghorban, Seyed Mojtaba Mousavi Bazaz, Maliheh Amirian, and Helen T. Allan, "Infertile Couples' Needs after Unsuccessful Fertility Treatment: A Qualitative Study," *Journal of Caring Sciences* 8, no. 2 (2019): 95–104.

143. George Khushf, "The Aesthetics of Clinical Judgment: Exploring the Link between Diagnostic Elegance and Effective Resource Utilization," *Medicine, Health Care and Philosophy* 2, no. 2 (1999): 141–159.

144. Maren Goeckenjan, Esther Schiwek, and Pauline Wimberger, "Continuous Body Temperature Monitoring to Improve the Diagnosis of Female Infertility," *Geburtshilfe und Frauenheilkunde* 80, no. 7 (2020): 702–712.

145. Chiara Perono Biacchiardi, Luisa Delle Piane, Marco Camanni, Francesco Deltetto, Elena Maria Delpiano, Gian Luigi Marchino, Gianluca Gennarelli, and Alberto Revelli, "Laparoscopic Stripping of Endometriomas Negatively Affects Ovarian Follicular Reserve Even If Performed by Experienced Surgeons," *Reproductive Biomedicine Online* 23, no. 6 (2011): 740–746.

146. Saad Elzanaty and Johan Malm, "Comparison of Semen Parameters in Samples Collected by Masturbation at a Clinic and at Home," *Fertility and Sterility* 89, no. 6 (2008): 1718–1722.

147. Sandro C. Esteves, Alaa Hamada, Victor Kondray, Aruna Pitchika, and Ashok Agarwal, "What Every Gynecologist Should Know about Male Infertility: An Update," *Archives of Gynecology and Obstetrics* 286, no. 1 (2012): 217–229.

148. Caroline Rusterholz, "English and French Women Doctors in International Debates on Birth Control (1920–1935)," *Social History of Medicine* 31, no. 2 (2018): 328–347.

149. Lynn M. Thomas, *Politics of the Womb: Women, Reproduction, and the State in Kenya* (Berkeley: University of California Press, 2003).

150. Satvinder Purewal and Olga van Den Akker, "The Socio-cultural and Biological Meaning of Parenthood," *Journal of Psychosomatic Obstetrics & Gynecology* 28, no. 2 (2007): 79–86.

151. Lisa Sowle Cahill, "Feminist Ethics, Differences, and Common Ground," in *Readings in Moral Theology No. 9: Feminist Ethics and the Catholic Moral Tradition*, ed. Charles E. Curran, Margaret A. Farley, and Richard A. McCormick (Mahwah, NJ: Paulist Press, 1996), 184–205, at 197.

152. Men can also be susceptible to this gender-essentialist mindset and report infertility affecting them as 'neutered' men who 'shoot blanks.'" Maura A. Ryan, "Particular Sorrows, Common Challenges: Specialized Infertility Treatment and the Common Good," *The Annual of the Society of Christian Ethics* 14 (1994): 187–206, at 197.

153. Andy Miah and Emma Rich, *The Medicalization of Cyberspace* (New York: Routledge, 2008), 87. See Philip Zhai, *Get Real: A Philosophical Adventure in Virtual Reality* (Lanham: Rowman & Littlefield, 1998).

154. Eric Chung, "Translating Penile Erectile Hydraulics to Clinical Application in Inflatable Penile Prosthesis Implant," *Current Sexual Health Reports* 9, no. 2 (2017): 84–89.

270 NOTES

155. Ann Oakley, *The Captured Womb: A History of the Medical Care of Pregnant Women* (Oxford: Basil Blackwell, 1984), 292.

156. Associated Press, "NHS Criticised for Supplying Pornography to IVF Couples," *The Independent*, September 8, 2010.

157. Alan Thornhill, "Porn in the NHS: A Matter of Perspective," *BioNews 576*, September 20, 2010.

158. John M. Smoot, "Why Sperm 'Donation' Is Bad for Dads and Kids," *Public Discourse*, February 27, 2013.

159. Associated Press, "NHS Criticised for Supplying Pornography to IVF Couples."

160. Emma Hill, "Who Said Pornography Was Acceptable in the Workplace?," *2020health. org*, August 9, 2010.

161. New England Cryogenic Center, "Become a Sperm Donor," accessed January 8, 2014, http://www.necryogenic.com/become-a-donor.php.

162. Andrea Dworkin, *Pornography: Men Possessing Women* (New York: Plume, 1981).

163. Leo Bersani, "Is the Rectum a Grave?," *AIDS: Cultural Analysis/Cultural Activism* 43 (1987): 197–222.

164. Hansen et al., "Twins Born Following Assisted Reproductive Technology."

165. Hansen et al., "Twins Born Following Assisted Reproductive Technology," 2330.

166. Abha Maheshwari, Siriol Griffiths, and Siladitya Bhattacharya, "Global Variations in the Uptake of Single Embryo Transfer," *Human Reproduction Update* 17, no. 1 (2011): 107–120.

167. Georgina M. Chambers, Yueping A. Wang, Michael G. Chapman, Van Phuong Hoang, Elizabeth A. Sullivan, Hossam I. Abdalla, and William Ledger, "What Can We Learn from a Decade of Promoting Safe Embryo Transfer Practices? A Comparative Analysis of Policies and Outcomes in the UK and Australia, 2001–2010," *Human Reproduction* 28, no. 6 (2013): 1679–1686.

168. Janice Raymond, *Women as Wombs* (San Francisco: Harper Collins, 1993), 189–190.

169. Christopher B. Field, ed., *Climate Change 2014—Impacts, Adaptation and Vulnerability: Regional Aspects* (Cambridge: Cambridge University Press, 2014).

Chapter 8

1. Griswold v. Connecticut, 381 U.S. 479 (1965).

2. Joseph G. Schenker, "Human Reproduction: Jewish Perspectives," *Gynecological Endocrinology* 29, no. 11 (2013): 945–948.

3. Cristina Richie, "The Augustinian Legacy of the Procreative Marriage: Contemporary Implications and Alternatives," *Feminist Theology* 23, no. 1 (2014): 18–36.

4. Augustine, *On the Excellence of Marriage*, in *Marriage and Virginity: Works of Saint Augustine: A Translation for the 21st Century*, ed. David G. Hunter (Hyde Park, NY: New City Press, 1997).

5. Zulie Sachedina, "Islam, Procreation and the Law," *International Family Planning Perspectives* 16, no. 3 (1990): 107–111.

NOTES 271

6. Paul VI, *Humanae Vitae* (Washington, DC: US Conference of Catholic Bishops, 1968).

7. Rashmi Dube Bhatnagar, Renu Dube, and Reena Dube, *Female Infanticide in India: A Feminist Cultural History* (Albany, NY: SUNY Press, 2012).

8. Pius XI, *On Christian Marriage: Casti Connubii* (Washington, DC: US Conference of Catholic Bishops, 1930).

9. In John Rawls, *Theory of Justice* (Cambridge, MA: Harvard University Press, 1971), 557.

10. Friedrich Nietzsche, *On the Genealogy of Morals*, trans. Walter Kaufmann (New York: Vintage Books, 1967), 2nd essay, section 7.

11. See Albert Jonsen, *Responsibility in Modern Religious Ethics* (Washington, DC: Corpus Books, 1968), 202.

12. Pope Innocent III, *On the Misery of the Human Condition*, vol. 132 (Indianapolis: Bobbs-Merrill, 1969).

13. "When a man marries he boards a ship, and when a child is born to him he suffers a shipwreck." Quoted in Annemarie Schimmel, "'I Take Off the Dress of the Body': Eros in Sufi Literature," in *Religion and the Body*, ed. Sarah Coakley (Cambridge: Cambridge University Press, 1997), 270.

14. Seana Valentine Shiffrin, "Wrongful Life, Procreative Responsibility, and the Significance of Harm," *Legal Theory* 5, no. 2 (1999): 117–148.

15. Thomas Malthus, *An Essay on the Principle of Population* (London: J. Johnson, 1798).

16. Margaret Sanger, "Too Many People," *Together*, September 1957, 16–17.

17. Lisa Hymas, "The GINK Manifesto: Say It Loud—I'm Childfree and I'm Proud," *Grist*, March 31, 2010, http://grist.org/article/2010-03-30-gink-manifesto-say-it-loud-im-childfree-and-im-proud/.

18. Ethics Committee of the American Fertility Society, "Ethical Consideration of in Vitro Fertilization," in *The Ethics of Reproductive Technology*, ed. K. Alpern (New York: Oxford University Press 1992), 302.

19. Barry Bogin, *Patterns of Human Growth*, vol. 88 (Cambridge: Cambridge University Press, 2020).

20. Tyler A. Jacobson, Jasdeep S. Kler, Michael T. Hernke, Rudolf K. Braun, Keith C. Meyer, and William E. Funk, "Direct Human Health Risks of Increased Atmospheric Carbon Dioxide," *Nature Sustainability* 2, no. 8 (2019): 691–701.

21. Adrienne Rich, *Of Woman Born: Motherhood as Experience and Institution* (New York: W. W. Norton, 1995).

22. Jamaica Kincaid, *The Autobiography of My Mother: A Novel* (New York: Farrar, Straus and Giroux, 1996).

23. Cristina Richie, "Disrupting the Meaning of Marriage? Childfree, Infertile and Gay Unions in Evangelical and Catholic Theologies of Marriage," *Theology & Sexuality* 19, no. 2 (2013): 123–142.

24. Lee Edelman, *No Future: Queer Theory and the Death Drive* (Durham, NC: Duke University Press, 2004), 12.

25. Malthus, *An Essay on the Principle of Population*.

26. ESHRE Capri Workshop Group, "Europe the Continent with the Lowest Fertility," *Human Reproduction Update* 16, no. 6 (2010): 590–602.

272 NOTES

27. Pontifical Commission on Birth Control, "Schema Documenti de Responsabili Paternitate," June 4–9, 1966, http://ldysinger.stjohnsem.edu/@magist/1963_paul6/068_hum_vitae/majority%20report.pdf.
28. Richard John Halliday, "Social Darwinism: A Definition," *Victorian Studies* 14, no. 4 (1971): 389–405.
29. "The Incredible Shrinking Country," *The Economist*, March 25, 2014, http://www.economist.com/blogs/banyan/2014/03/japans-demography.
30. Nicholas Eberstadt, "The Demographic Future: What Population Growth—and Decline—Means for the Global Economy," *Foreign Affairs* 89, no. 6, (2010): 54–64.
31. Ann Oakley, *The Captured Womb: A History of the Medical Care of Pregnant Women* (Oxford: Basil Blackwell, 1984), 108, quoting a text from the year 1849.
32. Oakley, *The Captured Womb*, 109.
33. Athalya Brenner, *The Intercourse of Knowledge* (Leiden: Brill, 1997), ch. 4.
34. Philip A. Neher, "Peasants, Procreation, and Pensions," *American Economic Review* 61, no. 3 (1971): 380–389.
35. Timothy M. Dall, Paul D. Gallo, Ritasree Chakrabarti, Terry West, April P. Semilla, and Michael V. Storm, "An Aging Population and Growing Disease Burden Will Require a Large and Specialized Health Care Workforce by 2025," *Health Affairs* 32, no. 11 (2013): 2013–2020.
36. Tom Sorell and Heather Draper, "Robot Carers, Ethics, and Older People," *Ethics and Information Technology* 16, no. 3 (2014): 183–195.
37. Florian Coulmas, *Population Decline and Ageing in Japan: The Social Consequences* (London: Routledge, 2007).
38. David Daube, *The Duty of Procreation* (Eugene: Wipf and Stock, 2011).
39. Glenn Cohen, "The Constitution and the Rights Not to Procreate," *Stanford Law Review* 60 (2007): 1135–1196.
40. Maura A. Ryan, *Ethics and Economics of Assisted Reproduction: The Cost of Longing* (Washington, DC: Georgetown University Press, 2003).
41. Dena S. Davis, "Genetic Dilemmas and the Child's Right to an Open Future," *Hastings Center Report* 27, no. 2 (1997): 7–15.
42. G. M. Brelsford, "Sanctification and Spiritual Disclosure in Parent-Child Relationships: Implications for Family Relationship Quality," *Journal of Family Psychology* 27, no. 4 (2013): 639–649
43. Gaile Pohlhaus, "Relational Knowing and Epistemic Injustice: Toward a Theory of Willful Hermeneutical Ignorance," *Hypatia* 27, no. 4 (2012): 715–735.
44. Darren Langdridge, Paschal Sheeran, and Kevin Connolly, "Understanding the Reasons for Parenthood," *Journal of Reproductive and Infant Psychology* 23, no. 2 (2005): 121–133.
45. Cristina Richie, "Voluntary Sterilization for Childfree Women: Understanding Patient Profiles, Evaluating Accessibility, Examining Legislation," *Hastings Center Report* 43, no. 6 (2013): 36–44.
46. Gilda Sedgh, Susheela Singh, and Rubina Hussain, "Intended and Unintended Pregnancies Worldwide in 2012 and Recent Trends," *Studies in Family Planning* 45, no. 3 (2014): 301–314.

NOTES 273

47. Christine Overall, *Why Have Children?: The Ethical Debate* (Cambridge, MA: MIT Press, 2012).

48. United Nations, *Universal Declaration of Human Rights* (Geneva: United Nations, 1948).

49. United Nations Educational, Scientific and Cultural Organization, *Universal Declaration of Animal Rights* (Paris: UNESCO, 1978).

50. Willis Jenkins, *The Future of Ethics: Sustainability, Social Justice, and Religious Creativity* (Washington, DC: Georgetown University Press, 2013), 120.

51. Meghan Clark, *The Vision of Catholic Social Thought: The Virtue of Solidarity and the Praxis of Human Rights* (Minneapolis, MN: Fortress, 2014), 2.

52. John Locke, *Second Treaties of Government* (Indianapolis, IN: Hackett, 1980), 20–21.

53. Clark, *The Vision of Catholic Social Thought*.

54. See Charles Fried, *Right and Wrong* (Cambridge, MA: Harvard University Press, 1978), 110.

55. Sarah Lamble, "Rethinking Gendered Prison Policies: Impacts on Transgender Prisoners," *ECAN Bulletin* 16 (2012): 7–12.

56. Avi Brisman, "Fair Fare: Food as Contested Terrain in US Prisons and Jails," *Georgetown Journal on Poverty Law and Policy* 15, no. 1 (2008): 49–94.

57. James A. Nash, "Biotic Rights and Human Ecological Responsibilities," in *The Annual of the Society of Christian Ethics*, ed. Harlan Beckley (Washington, DC: Georgetown University Press, 1993), 143.

58. Preamble to the Constitution of the World Health Organization as adopted by the International Health Conference, New York, June 19–22, 1946, signed on July 22, 1946, by the representatives of 61 states, Official Records of the World Health Organization, no. 2, p. 100, and entered into force on April 7, 1948.

59. Jurgen De Wispelaere and Daniel Weinstock, "State Regulation and Assisted Reproduction: Balancing the Interests of Parents and Children," in *Family-Making: Contemporary Ethical Challenges*, ed. Françoise Baylis and Carolyn MacLeod (Oxford: Oxford University Press, 2014), 131–150.

60. Christine Shawana, Chaneesa Ryan, and Abrar Ali, "Forced or Coerced Sterilization in Canada: An Overview of Recommendations for Moving Forward," *International Journal of Indigenous Health* 16, no. 1 (2021): 275–290.

61. Tamil Kendall and Claire Albert, "Experiences of Coercion to Sterilize and Forced Sterilization among Women Living with HIV in Latin America," *Journal of the International AIDS Society* 18, no. 1 (2015): 1–7.

62. Stephanie Bi and Tobin Klusty, "Forced Sterilizations of HIV-Positive Women: A Global Ethics and Policy Failure," *AMA Journal of Ethics* 17, no. 10 (2015): 952–957.

63. Christina Zampas and Adriana Lamačková, "Forced and Coerced Sterilization of Women in Europe," *International Journal of Gynecology & Obstetrics* 114, no. 2 (2011): 163–166.

64. Apoorva Jadhav and Emily Vala-Haynes, "Informed Choice and Female Sterilization in South Asia and Latin America." *Journal of Biosocial Science* 50, no. 6 (2018): 823–839.

274 NOTES

65. Sarah McInnes, "The Legality of Forced Sterilisation of Women and Girls with Disabilities," *Bulletin (Law Society of South Australia)* 42, no. 11 (2020): 24–27.

66. Michael G. Silver, "Eugenics and Compulsory Sterilization Laws: Providing Redress for the Victims of a Shameful Era in United States History," *George Washington Law Review* 72, no. 4 (2004): 862–892.

67. Carolyn Henning Brown, "The Forced Sterilization Program under the Indian Emergency: Results in One Settlement," *Human Organization* 43, no. 1 (1984): 49–54.

68. A. J. Lowik, "Reproducing Eugenics, Reproducing while Trans: The State Sterilization of Trans People," *Journal of GLBT Family Studies* 14, no. 5 (2018): 425–445.

69. Michael King and Annie Bartlett. "British Psychiatry and Homosexuality," *British Journal of Psychiatry* 175, no. 2 (1999): 106–113.

70. Skinner v. Oklahoma, (1942). 316 U.S. 535, 62 S. Ct. 1110, 86 L. Ed. 1655, 1942 U.S. 493. https://supreme.justia.com/cases/federal/us/316/535/. Douglas S. Diekema, "Involuntary Sterilization of Persons with Mental Retardation: An Ethical Analysis," *Mental Retardation and Developmental Disabilities Research Reviews* 9 (2003): 21–26.

71. Project South Georgia Detention Watch, Georgia Latino Alliance for Human Rights, and South Georgia Immigrant Support Network, "Re: Lack of Medical Care, Unsafe Work Practices, and Absence of Adequate Protection against COVID-19 for Detained Immigrants and Employees Alike at the Irwin County Detention Center," September 14, 2020, https://projectsouth.org/wp-content/uploads/2020/09/OIG-ICDC-Complaint-1.pdf.

72. This is now contested with advances in oncofertility.

73. Griswold v. Connecticut, 381 U.S. 479 (1965).

74. Eisenstadt v. Baird, 405 U.S. 438 (1972).

75. Roe v. Wade, 410 U.S. 113, argued December 13, 1971; decided January 22, 1973.

76. Doe v. Bolton, 410 U.S. 179, argued December 13, 1971; decided January 22, 1973.

77. Singapore, Voluntary Sterilization Act, 1974, Chapter 347 Section 3 (2) a–c, http://statutes.agc.gov.sg/non_version/cgi-bin/cgi_retrieve.pl?actno=REVED-347&docti tle=VOLUNTARY%20STERILIZATION%20ACT%0A&date=latest&method=part.

78. Patient Protection and Affordable Care Act, March 23, 2010, 42 U.S.C. 300gg-13. For a bioethical analysis of the case, see I. Glenn Cohen, Holly Fernandez Lynch, and Gregory D. Curfman, "When Religious Freedom Clashes with Access to Care," *New England Journal of Medicine* 371, no. 7 (2014): 596.

79. Olena Y. Nizalova, Tamara Sliusarenko, and Solomiya Shpak, "The Motherhood Wage Penalty in Times of Transition," *Journal of Comparative Economics* 44, no. 1 (2016): 56–75.

80. Central Intelligence Agency, "The World FactBook: Country Comparison: Maternal Mortality Rates," n.d., at https://www.cia.gov/the-world-factbook/field/maternal-mortality-ratio/country-comparison/Accessed 23 October 2023.

81. Douglas A. Brownridge, Tamara L. Taillieu, Kimberly A. Tyler, Agnes Tiwari, Ko Ling Chan, and Susy C. Santos, "Pregnancy and Intimate Partner Violence: Risk Factors, Severity, and Health Effects," *Violence Against Women* 17, no. 7 (2011): 858–881.

82. Christie Lancaster Palladino, Vijay Singh, Jacquelyn Campbell, Heather Flynn, and Katherine Gold, "Homicide and Suicide during the Perinatal Period: Findings from

the National Violent Death Reporting System," *Obstetrics and Gynecology* 118, no. 5 (2011): 1056–1063.

83. Georgia Health Sciences University, "Homicide, Suicide Outpace Traditional Causes of Death in Pregnant, Postpartum Women," *ScienceDaily*, October 20, 2011.

84. Donald A. Redelmeier, Sharon C. May, Deva Thiruchelvam, and Jon F. Barrett, "Pregnancy and the Risk of a Traffic Crash," *Canadian Medical Association Journal* 186, no. 10 (2014): 742–750.

85. Brady E. Hamilton, and Sharon E. Kirmeyer, "Trends and Variations in Reproduction and Intrinsic Rates: United States, 1990–2014," *National Vital Statistics Reports* 66, no. 2 (2017): 1–14.

86. Clara Lemani, Nenani Kamtuwanje, Billy Phiri, Ilene S. Speizer, Kavita Singh, Olive Mtema, Ndidza Chisanu, and Jennifer H. Tang, "Effect of Family Planning Interventions on Couple Years of Protection in Malawi," *International Journal of Gynecology & Obstetrics* 141, no. 1 (2018): 37–44.

87. Chelsea B. Polis and Rachel K. Jones, "Multiple Contraceptive Method Use and Prevalence of Fertility Awareness Based Method Use in the United States, 2013–2015," *Contraception* 98, no. 3 (2018): 188–192.

88. M. P. A. Kelly Cleland, Jeffrey F. Peipert, Carolyn Westhoff, Scott Spear, and James Trussell, "Family Planning as a Cost-Saving Preventive Health Service," *New England Journal of Medicine* 2011, no. 364 (2011): e37.

89. J. Trussell, "The Cost of Unintended Pregnancy in the United States," *Contraception* 75 no. 3 (2007): 168–170.

90. Jokin De Irala, Alfonso Osorio, Silvia Carlos, and Cristina Lopez-del Burgo, "Choice of Birth Control Methods among European Women and the Role of Partners and Providers," *Contraception* 84, no. 6 (2011): 558–564.

91. NHS, "How Effective Is Contraception at Preventing Pregnancy? Your Contraception Guide," April 17, 2020, https://www.nhs.uk/conditions/contraception/how-effective-contraception/.

92. Kazuko Watanabe, "Trafficking in Women's Bodies, Then and Now: The Issue of Military 'Comfort Women,'" *Peace & Change* 20, no. 4 (1995): 501–514.

93. Martha C. Nussbaum, "Human Functioning and Social Justice," *Political Theory* 20, no. 2 (1992): 217.

94. De Wispelaere and Weinstock, "State Regulation and Assisted Reproduction."

95. Susanna Graham and Andrea Braverman, "11 ARTs and the Single Parent," in *Reproductive Donation: Practice, Policy and Bioethics*, ed. Martin Richards, Guido Pennings, John B. Appleby (Cambridge: Cambridge University Press, 2012), 189.

96. Ethics Committee of the American Society for Reproductive Medicine, "Access to Fertility Treatment by Gays, Lesbians, and Unmarried Persons: A Committee Opinion," *Fertility and Sterility* 100, no. 6 (2013): 1524–1527.

97. Ethics Committee of the American Society for Reproductive Medicine, "Access to Fertility Treatment by Gays, Lesbians, and Unmarried Persons."

98. Timothy F. Murphy, "The Ethics of Helping Transgender Men and Women Have Children," *Perspectives in Biology and Medicine* 53, no. 1 (2010): 46–60.

276   NOTES

99. John A. Robertson, "Gay and Lesbian Access to Assisted Reproductive Technology," *Case Western Reserve Law Review* 55 (2004): 323–372.

100. Elisabetta Tosti, Adriana Fortunato, and Alessandro Settimi, "The Impact of in Vitro Fertilization on the Health of the Mother and the Offspring," *Current Women's Health Reviews* 2, no. 4 (2006): 239–247.

101. von Wolff, Michael, Alexandra Kohl Schwartz, Norman Bitterlich, Petra Stute, and Monika Fäh, "Only Women's Age and the Duration of Infertility Are the Prognostic Factors for the Success Rate of Natural Cycle IVF," *Archives of Gynecology and Obstetrics* 299, no. 3 (2019): 883–889.

102. Anne Melton Clark, "Ethics of IVF Treatment: Remember the Patient!," in *Organization and Management of IVF Units* ed. Steven D. Fleming and Alex C. Varghese (Cham: Springer, 2016), 269–286.

103. G. David Adamson, Jacques de Mouzon, Georgina M. Chambers, Fernando Zegers-Hochschild, Ragaa Mansour, Osamu Ishihara, Manish Banker, and Silke Dyer, "International Committee for Monitoring Assisted Reproductive Technology: World Report on Assisted Reproductive Technology, 2011," *Fertility and Sterility* 110, no. 6 (2018): 1067–1080.

104. De Wispelaere and Weinstock, "State Regulation and Assisted Reproduction."

105. N. J. Wikler, "Society's Response to the New Reproductive Technologies: The Feminist Perspectives," *Southern California Law Review* 59, no. 5 (1986): 1043–1057.

106. Mark Tushnet, "Essay on Rights," *Texas Law Review* 62, no. 8 (1983): 1363.

107. Martha Nussbaum, *Women and Human Development* (Cambridge: Cambridge University Press, 2000), 97.

108. Ann-Katrin Gembries, Theresia Theuke, and Isabel Heinemann, eds., *Children by Choice? Changing Values, Reproduction, and Family Planning in the 20th Century*, vol. 3 (Berlin: Walter de Gruyter, 2018).

109. Marina Štambuk, Marina Milković, and Antonija Maričić, "Motivation for Parenthood among LGBTIQ People in Croatia: Reasons for (Not) Becoming a Parent," *Revija za sociologiju* 49, no. 2 (2019): 149–173.

110. Avigail Ferdman and Margaret Kohn, "The Theory and Politics of Solidarity and Public Goods," *Critical Review of International Social and Political Philosophy* 21, no. 5 (2018): 545–553.

111. Anna M. Santiago, George C. Galster, and Peter Tatian, "Assessing the Property Value Impacts of the Dispersed Subsidy Housing Program in Denver," *Journal of Policy Analysis and Management: The Journal of the Association for Public Policy Analysis and Management* 20, no. 1 (2001): 65–88.

112. Shahid Javed Burki, *Education Reform in Pakistan: Educating the Pakistani Masses* (Washington, DC: Woodrow Wilson International Center for Scholars, 2005), 15–32; John Stuart Blackie, *Education in Scotland: An Appeal to the Scottish People on the Improvement of Their Scholastic and Academical Institutions* (Edinburgh: William Tait, 1846).

113. Anca Gheaus, "More Co-parents, Fewer Children: Multiparenting and Sustainable Population," *Essays in Philosophy* 20, no. 1 (2019): 2–21.

NOTES 277

114. De Wispelaere and Weinstock, "State Regulation and Assisted Reproduction."
115. Ashley J. Provencher, Nicholas E. Kahn, and Mary Eschelbach Hansen, "Adoption Policy and the Well-Being of Adopted Children in the United States," *Child Welfare* 95, no. 1 (2016): 27–56.

Chapter 9

1. Travis N. Rieder, *Toward a Small Family Ethic: How Overpopulation and Climate Change Are Affecting the Morality of Procreation* (Switzerland: Springer, 2016).
2. Elizabeth Cripps, "Do Parents Have a Special Duty to Mitigate Climate Change?," *Politics, Philosophy & Economics* 16, no. 3 (2017): 308–325.
3. Laura Cavalli and Alessandro Rosina, "An Analysis of Reproductive Intentions of Italian Couples," *Population Review* 50, no. 1 (2011): 21–39.
4. Cristina Richie, "'Green' Reproduction, Resource Conservation, and Ecological Responsibility," *Worldviews: Global Religions, Culture, and Ecology* 18, no. 2 (2014): 144–172.
5. David R. Smith, Nathan L. Allan, Conor P. McGowan, Jennifer A. Szymanski, Susan R. Oetker, and Heather M. Bell, "Development of a Species Status Assessment Process for Decisions under the US Endangered Species Act," *Journal of Fish and Wildlife Management* 9, no. 1 (2018): 302–320.
6. Christine E. Gudorf, "Western Religion and the Patriarchal Family," in *Feminist Ethics and the Catholic Moral Tradition*, ed. Charles E Curran, Margaret A. Farley. and Richard A. McCormick (New York: Paulist Press, 1996), 270
7. Joseph Shaw, "Intention in Ethics," *Canadian Journal of Philosophy* 36, no. 2 (2006): 187–223.
8. D. Benatar, *Better Never to Have Been: The Harm of Coming into Existence* (Oxford: Oxford University Press, 2006); S. Shiffrin, "Wrongful Life, Procreative Responsibility, and the Significance of Harm," *Legal Theory* 5 (1999): 117–148, quoted in Jurgen De Wispelaere and Daniel Weinstock, "State Regulation and Assisted Reproduction: Balancing the Interests of Parents and Children," in *Family-Making: Contemporary Ethical Challenges*, ed. Françoise Baylis and Carolyn MacLeod (Oxford: Oxford University Press, 2014), 131–150.
9. Lynda Ross, *Interrogating Motherhood* (Athabasca: Athabasca University Press, 2016).
10. Patricia Waldvogel and Ulrike Ehlert, "Testosterone Is Associated with Perceived Constraint in Early Fatherhood," *Adaptive Human Behavior and Physiology* 4, no. 1 (2018): 69–90.
11. Stacie E. Geller, Abigail R. Koch, Caitlin E. Garland, E. Jane MacDonald, Francesca Storey, and Beverley Lawton, "A Global View of Severe Maternal Morbidity: Moving beyond Maternal Mortality," *Reproductive Health* 15, no. 1 (2018): 31–43.
12. Minna Saavala, *Fertility and Familial Power Relations: Procreation in South India* (London: Routledge, 2013).

278 NOTES

13. Maura A. Ryan, "The Argument for Unlimited Procreative Liberty: A Feminist Critique," *Hastings Center Report* 20, no. 4 (1990): 6–12, at 11.
14. A. Gheaus, "The Right to Parent and Duties concerning Future Generations," *Journal of Political Philosophy* 24 (2016): 487–508.
15. Paul R. Ehrlich, Dennis R. Parnell, and Al Silbowitz, *The Population Bomb* (New York: Ballantine Books, 1971).
16. Hugh P. McDonald, *Environmental Philosophy* (Leiden: Brill Rodopi, 2014).
17. S. Joseph, "Gay and Lesbian Movement in India," *Economic and Political Weekly* 31, no. 33 (1996): 2228–2233.
18. M. E. Sanchez, "Antisocial Procreation," in *Queer Shakespeare: Desire and Sexuality*, ed. Goran Stanivukovic (London: Bloomsbury, 2017), 263–277.
19. Amy Laura Hall, *Conceiving Parenthood: American Protestantism and the Spirit of Reproduction* (Grand Rapids, MI: Eerdmans, 2008), 10.
20. US Department of Agriculture, Center for Nutrition Policy and Promotion, *Expenditures on Children by Families, 2009* (Alexandria, VA: US Department Agriculture, 2010), 1–32.
21. Cristina Traina, *Feminist Ethics and Natural Law: The End of the Anathemas* (Washington, DC: Georgetown University Press, 1999), 327.
22. Calvin Conzelus Moore and John B. Williamson, "The Universal Fear of Death and the Cultural Response," *Handbook of Death and Dying* 1 (2003): 3–13.
23. Anne O'Byrne, *Natality and Finitude* (Bloomington: Indiana University Press, 2010).
24. Gamal I. Serour, "Islamic Perspectives in Human Reproduction," *Reproductive Biomedicine Online* 17 (2008): 34–38.
25. Marco Luchetti and Giuseppe A. Marraro, "Italy: Where Have We Been?," in *ICU Resource Allocation in the New Millennium: Will We Say "No"?*, ed. David W. Crippen (New York: Springer, 2013), 54.
26. Michael von Wolff, Alexandra Kohl Schwartz, Norman Bitterlich, Petra Stute, and Monika Fäh, "Only Women's Age and the Duration of Infertility Are the Prognostic Factors for the Success Rate of Natural Cycle IVF," *Archives of Gynecology and Obstetrics* 299, no. 3 (2019): 883–889.
27. F. Belva, M. Bonduelle, Mathieu Roelants, Geert Verheyen, and L. Van Landuyt, "Neonatal Health Including Congenital Malformation Risk of 1,072 Children Born after Vitrified Embryo Transfer," *Human Reproduction* 31, no. 7 (2016): 1610–1620.
28. Lucy van de Wiel, "The Speculative Turn in IVF: Egg Freezing and the Financialization of Fertility," *New Genetics and Society* 39, no. 3 (2020): 306–326.
29. Lu-Ting Chen, Fan Qu, Fang-Hong Zhang, Yan-Ting Wu, Lan-Feng Xing, and He-Feng Huang, "Maternal Anxiety Associated with in Vitro Fertilisation (IVF)/ Intracytoplasmic Sperm Injection (ICSI) Outcomes and Risk of Difficult Toddler Temperament: A Three-Year Case-Control Study," *Journal of Obstetrics and Gynaecology* 37, no. 7 (2017): 965–969.
30. Ali Darvishi, Reza Goudarzi, Viktoria Habib Zadeh, and Mohsen Barouni, "Cost-Benefit Analysis of IUI and IVF Based on Willingness to Pay Approach; Case Study: Iran," *PloS One* 15, no. 7 (2020): e0231584.

NOTES 279

31. Ayse Seyhan, Baris Ata, Weon-Young Son, Michael H. Dahan, and Seang Lin Tan, "Comparison of Complication Rates and Pain Scores after Transvaginal Ultrasound–Guided Oocyte Pickup Procedures for in Vitro Maturation and in Vitro Fertilization Cycles," *Fertility and Sterility* 101, no. 3 (2014): 705–709.

32. Nilay Karaca, Aysun Karabulut, Sevgi Ozkan, Hale Aktun, Fatma Orengul, Rabiye Yilmaz, Seda Ates, and Gonca Batmaz, "Effect of IVF Failure on Quality of Life and Emotional Status in Infertile Couples," *European Journal of Obstetrics & Gynecology and Reproductive Biology* 206 (2016): 158–163.

33. Catharina Halkes, "The Rape of Mother Earth: Ecology and Patriarchy," in *Concilium: Religion in the Eighties*, vol. 206: *Motherhood: Experience, Institution, Theology*, ed. Anne Carr and Elizabeth Schussler Fiorenza (Edinburgh: T. and T. Clark, 1989), 99.

34. P. Liang, Y. Xu, X. Zhang, C. Ding, R. Huang, Z. Zhang, J. Lv, X. Xie, Y. Chen, Y. Li, and Y. Sun, "CRISPR/Cas9-Mediated Gene Editing in Human Tripronuclear Zygotes," *Protein & Cell* 6, no. 5 (2015): 363–372.

35. Chen Meng Lam, "Damages for Wrongful Fertilisation: Reliance on Policy Considerations," *Deakin Law Review* 24 (2019): 139–174.

36. Ethics Committee of the American Society for Reproductive Medicine, "Disclosure of Medical Errors Involving Gametes and Embryos: An Ethics Committee Opinion," *Fertility and Sterility* 106, no. 1 (2016): 59–63.

37. Traina, *Feminist Ethics and Natural Law*, 327.

38. National Academies of Sciences, Engineering, and Medicine, "Preterm Births Cost U.S. $26 Billion a Year: Multidisciplinary Research Effort Needed to Prevent Early Births," July 13, 2006, https://www.nationalacademies.org/news/2006/07/preterm-births-cost-us-26-billion-a-year-multidisciplinary-research-effort-needed-to-prev ent-early-births.

39. Maud D. van Zijl, Bouchra Koullali, Martijn A. Oudijk, Anita C. J. Ravelli, Ben W. J. Mol, Eva Pajkrt, and Brenda M. Kazemier, "Trends in Preterm Birth in Singleton and Multiple Gestations in the Netherlands 2008–2015: A Population-Based Study," *European Journal of Obstetrics & Gynecology and Reproductive Biology* 247 (2020): 111–115.

40. M. Roberts, "IVF Multiple Births 'Drain NHS," BBC News, June 19, 2005, http://news.bbc.co.uk/1/hi/health/4120398.stm.

41. Tomáš Sobotka, Martin A. Hansen, Tina Kold Jensen, Anette Tønnes Pedersen, Wolfgang Lutz, and Niels Erik Skakkebæk, "The Contribution of Assisted Reproduction to Completed Fertility: An Analysis of Danish Data," *Population and Development Review* 34, no. 1 (2008): 79–101.

42. Ann Oakley, *The Captured Womb: A History of the Medical Care of Pregnant Women* (New York: Blackwell, 1984).

43. Rahime Nida Ergin, Aslıhan Polat, Bülent Kars, Deniz Öztekin, Kenan Sofuoğlu, and Eray Çalışkan, "Social Stigma and Familial Attitudes Related to Infertility," *Turkish Journal of Obstetrics and Gynecology* 15, no. 1 (2018): 46–49.

44. Kenneth Gannon, Lesley Glover, and Paul Abel, "Masculinity, Infertility, Stigma and Media Reports," *Social Science & Medicine* 59, no. 6 (2004): 1169–1175.

280 NOTES

45. Elisa Camiscioli, "Producing Citizens, Reproducing the 'French Race': Immigration, Demography, and Pronatalism in Early Twentieth-Century France," *Gender & History* 13, no. 3 (2001): 593–621.

46. Erica Åberg and Jarna Huvila, "Hip Children, Good Mothers—Children's Clothing as Capital Investment?," *Young Consumers: Insight and Ideas for Responsible Marketers* 20, no. 3 (2019): 153–166.

47. Nancy Felipe Russo, "The Motherhood Mandate," *Journal of Social Issues* 32, no. 3 (1976): 143–153.

48. Barbara Curbow and Mark Somerfield, "Use of the Rosenberg Self-Esteem Scale with Adult Cancer Patients," *Journal of Psychosocial Oncology* 9, no. 2 (1991): 113–131.

49. Morgan Carpenter, "The 'Normalization' of Intersex Bodies and 'Othering' of Intersex Identities in Australia," *Journal of Bioethical Inquiry* 15 (2018): 487–495.

50. A. B. Corrigan, R. G. Robinson, Tanya R. Terenty, J. B. Dick-Smith, and D. Walters, "Benign Rheumatoid Arthritis of the Aged," *British Medical Journal* 1, no. 5905 (1974): 444–446.

51. Lotte Hvas, "Positive Aspects of Menopause: A Qualitative Study," *Maturitas* 39, no. 1 (2001): 11–17.

52. Piia Jallinoja, Päivi Santalahti, Hanna Toiviainen, and Elina Hemminki, "Acceptance of Screening and Abortion for Down Syndrome among Finnish Midwives and Public Health Nurses," *Prenatal Diagnosis* 19, no. 11 (1999): 1015–1022.

53. N. K. Purewal, *Son Preference: Sex Selection, Gender and Culture in South Asia* (London: Routledge, 2020).

54. Bornstein, Marta, Jessica D. Gipson, Gates Failing, Venson Banda, and Alison Norris. "Individual and Community-Level Impact of Infertility-Related Stigma in Malawi," *Social Science & Medicine* 251 (2020): 112910.

55. Pamela Feldman-Savelsberg, "Plundered Kitchens and Empty Wombs: Fear of Infertility in the Cameroonian Grassfields," *Social Science & Medicine* 39, no. 4 (1994): 463–474.

56. Gudorf, "Western Religion and the Patriarchal Family," 270.

57. G. S. Becker, "Fertility and the Economy," *Journal of Population Economics* 5, no. 3 (1992): 185–201.

58. Mary Condren, "To Bear Children for the Fatherland: Mothers and Militarism," in *The Power of Naming: A Concilium Reader in Feminist Liberation Theology* ed. Elisabeth Schüssler Fiorenza (New York: Orbis Books, 1989), 115–123.

59. Norbert Campagna, *The Contingent Nature of Life* (Dordrecht: Springer, 2008), 109–117.

60. Gemma E. Carey, Melissa Graham, Julia Shelley, and Ann Taket, "Discourse, Power and Exclusion: The Experiences of Childless Women," in *Theorising Social Exclusion*, ed. Ann Taket, Beth R. Crisp, Annemarie Nevill, Greer Lamaro, Melissa Graham, and Sarah Barter-Godfrey (London: Routledge, 2009), 137–143.

61. Traina, *Feminist Ethics and Natural Law*, 327.

62. Eileen Wood, Serge Desmarais, and Sara Gugula, "The Impact of Parenting Experience on Gender Stereotyped Toy Play of Children," *Sex Roles* 47, nos. 1–2 (2002): 39–49.

NOTES 281

63. S. J. Moran, "Unconventual Women: Religion, Politics, and Image in the Court Beguinages, 1585–1713" (PhD diss., Brown University, 2010).

64. Sarah Franklin, "Deconstructing 'Desperateness': The Social Construction of Infertility in Popular Representations of New Reproductive Technologies," in *The New Reproductive Technologies*, ed. Maureen McNeil, Ian Varcoe, and Steven Yearley (London: Palgrave Macmillan, 1990), 200–229.

65. Jane M. Ussher and Janette Perz, "Threat of Biographical Disruption: The Gendered Construction and Experience of Infertility Following Cancer for Women and Men," *BMC Cancer* 18, no. 1 (2018): 1–17.

66. Robert D. Nachtigall, "International Disparities in Access to Infertility Services," *Fertility and Sterility* 85, no. 4 (2006): 871–875.

67. Richard Schmalensee, Thomas M. Stoker, and Ruth A. Judson, "World Carbon Dioxide Emissions: 1950–2050," *Review of Economics and Statistics* 80, no. 1 (1998): 15–27.

68. Anne Dochin, "In Whose Interest? Policy and Politics in Assisted Reproduction," *Bioethics* 25, no. 2 (2011): 100.

69. Dochin, "In Whose Interest?," 100.

70. Anna-Niina Terävä, Mika Gissler, Elina Hemminki, and Riitta Luoto, "Infertility and the Use of Infertility Treatments in Finland: Prevalence and Socio-demographic Determinants 1992–2004," *European Journal of Obstetrics & Gynecology and Reproductive Biology* 136, no. 1 (2008): 61–66.

71. David B. Dunson, Donna D. Baird, and Bernardo Colombo, "Increased Infertility with Age in Men and Women," *Obstetrics & Gynecology* 103, no. 1 (2004): 51–56.

72. Chee-Ruey Hsieh, Lee-Lan Yen, Jin-Tan Liu, and Chyongchiou Jeng Lin, "Smoking, Health Knowledge, and Anti-smoking Campaigns: An Empirical Study in Taiwan," *Journal of Health Economics* 15, no. 1 (1996): 87–104.

73. M. O'Brien, *The Politics of Reproduction* (Boulder, CO: Westview, 1989), 220–221.

74. Marie-Eve Lemoine and Vardit Ravitsky, "Sleepwalking into Infertility: The Need for a Public Health Approach toward Advanced Maternal Age," *American Journal of Bioethics* 15, no. 11 (2015): 37.

75. Dochin, "In Whose Interest?," 100.

76. P. Ghosh, "Older Dads Linked to Rise in Genetic Disorder," BBC News, August 22, 2012.

77. Afsana Islama and Umme Shefa Chowdhuryb, "Engaging Fathers in Care Work: A Study Exploring the Pathway of Preventing Violence against Women and Children in Rural Bangladesh," *Proceedings of 3rd Kantina Postgraduate* 16 (2016): 441–448.

78. Xiana Bueno and Mary C. Brinton, "Gender Egalitarianism, Perceived Economic Insecurity, and Fertility Intentions in Spain: A Qualitative Analysis," *Population Studies* 73, no. 2 (2019): 247–260.

79. Promoting gender equality and empower women is Goal 3 of the UN's Millennium Development Goals. See https://www.un.org/millenniumgoals/.

80. A. M. M. Chandrika, "Feminism and Emancipation: Influence of Feminist Ideas on Women's Socio-Economic and Political Liberation in Sri Lanka," *Sociology Mind* 9, no. 4 (2019): 302–331.

282 NOTES

81. A. Marphatia, Naomi M. Saville, Gabriel S. Amable, Dharma S. Manandhar, Mario Cortina-Borja, Jonathan C. Wells, and Alice M. Reid, "How Much Education Is Needed to Delay Women's Age at Marriage and First Pregnancy?," *Frontiers in Public Health* 7, no. 396 (2020): 1–17.

82. Dochin, "In Whose Interest?," 100.

83. Josef Fuchs, *Moral Demands and Personal Obligations,* trans. Brian McNeil (Washington, DC: Georgetown University Press, 1993), 69.

84. Dorothy Roberts, *Killing the black body: Race, Reproduction, and the Meaning Of Liberty* (New York: Vintage, 2014).

85. Dochin, "In Whose Interest?," 100.

86. Dochin, "In Whose Interest?," 100.

87. Childfreedom, n.d., October 23, 2023. https://childfreedom.blogspot.com/.

88. Amy Blackstone, "Childless . . . or Childfree?," *Contexts* 13, no. 4 (2014): 68–70.

89. Bella DePaulo, "Single, No Children: Who Is Your Family?," in *The Routledge Handbook of Family Communication,* ed. Anita L. Vangelisti (London: Routledge, 2012), 202–216.

90. Stephanie Clare, "Reimagining Biological Relatedness: Epigenetics and Queer Kin," *Signs: Journal of Women in Culture and Society* 45, no. 1 (2019): 51–73.

91. Gary Stewart, Wiliam Cutrer, Timothy Demy, Donal O'Mathuna, Paige Cuningham, John Kilner, and Linda Bevington, *Basic Questions on Sexuality and Reproductive Technology: When Is It Right to Intervene?* (Grand Rapids, MI: Kregel, 1998), 60.

92. Mercy Amba Oduyoye, "The African Family as a Symbol of Ecumenism," *Ecumenical Review* 43, no. 4 (1991): 465–478.

93. Erving Goffman, *Stigma: Notes on the Management of Spoiled Identity* (New York: Penguin, 1990).

94. E. Y. Adashi, Jonathon Cohen, L. Hamberger, H. W. Jones, D. M. De Kretser, B. Lunenfeld, Z. Rosenwaks, and A. J. H. R. Van Steirteghem, "Public Perception on Infertility and Its Treatment: An International Survey," *Human Reproduction* 15, no. 2 (2000): 330–334.

95. Stephanie Rich, Ann Taket, Melissa Graham, and Julia Shelley, "'Unnatural,' 'Unwomanly,' 'Uncreditable' and 'Undervalued': The Significance of Being a Childless Woman in Australian Society," *Gender Issues* 28, no. 4 (2011): 226–247.

96. Maura Ryan, *The Ethics and Economics of ART: The Cost of Longing* (Washington, DC: Georgetown University Press, 2001), 57.

97. United Nations Children's Fund, "United Nations Convention on the Rights of the Child," adopted and opened for signature, ratification, and accession by General Assembly Resolution 44/25 of November 20, 1989; entry into force September 2, 1990, in accordance with Article 49.

98. Hall, *Conceiving Parenthood,* 393.

99. L. S. Cahill, "Adoption: A Roman Catholic Perspective," in *The Morality of Adoption: Social-Psychological, Theological, and Legal Perspectives,* ed. T. P. Jackson (Grand Rapids, MI: Eerdmans, 2005), 148–171.

100. Lucretius, *De Rerum Natura,* quoted in Peter Singer, *Practical Ethics* (New York: Cambridge University Press, 1993), 125.

NOTES 283

101. E. S. Anderson, "Is Women's Labor a Commodity?," *Philosophy and Public Affairs* 19 (1990): 71–92; E. Bartholet, "Beyond Biology: The Politics of Adoption and Reproduction," *Duke Journal of Gender Law & Policy* 2, no. 1 (1995): 5–13; E. Bartholet, *Family Bonds: Adoption, Infertility, and the New World of Child Production* (Boston: Beacon Press, 1999).

102. De Wispelaere and Weinstock, "State Regulation and Assisted Reproduction."

103. The converse can be said of a developing world couple that adopts a national or international child: the carbon impact is much less.

104. Eric Engle, "The History of the General Principle of Proportionality: An Overview," *Dartmouth Law Journal* 10 (2012): 1–11.

105. James A. Nash, "Biotic Rights and Human Ecological Responsibilities," in *The Annual of the Society of Christian Ethics*, ed. H. Beckley (Washington, DC: Georgetown University Press, 1993), 160.

106. Roderick M. Chisholm, "The Ethics of Requirement," *American Philosophical Quarterly* 1, no. 2 (1964): 147–153.

107. Or the "gold standard" of biological children. See Timothy F. Murphy, "Pathways to Genetic Parenthood for Same-Sex Couples," *Journal of Medical Ethics* (2017): doi:10.1136 medethics-2017-104291, published online first.

108. D. Cutas, "Sex Is Over-rated: On the Right to Reproduce," *Human Fertility* 12, no. 1 (2009): 45–52. B. B. Woodhouse, "Waiting for Loving: The Child's Fundamental Right to Adoption," *Capital University Law Review* 34 (2005): 297–329.

109. Rachel H. Farr and Abbie E. Goldberg, "Sexual Orientation, Gender Identity, and Adoption Law," *Family Court Review* 56, no. 3 (2018): 374–383.

110. Kimberly D. McKee, "Monetary Flows and the Movements of Children: The Transnational Adoption Industrial Complex," *Journal of Korean Studies* 21, no. 1 (2016): 137–178.

111. Channary Khun, Sajal Lahiri, and Sokchea Lim, "Why Do US Parents Prefer Private to Foster Care Adoptions? The Role of Adoption Subsidies, Gender, Race, and Special Needs," *Economic Inquiry* 58, no. 4 (2020): 1757–1782.

112. Hall, *Conceiving Parenthood*, 394.

113. Gregory E. Kaebnick, "The Natural Father: Genetic Paternity Testing, Marriage, and Fatherhood," in *Genetics: Science, Ethics, and Public Policy*, ed. Thomas A. Shannon (Lanham, MD: Rowman & Littlefield, 2005), 64.

114. De Wispelaere and Weinstock, "State Regulation and Assisted Reproduction."

115. Cora A. Du Bois, "Socio-Cultural Aspects of Population Growth," in *Human Fertility and Population Problems*, ed. Roy O. Greep (Cambridge, MA: Schenkman, 1963), 259.

116. Nicole Petrowski, Claudia Cappa, and Peter Gross, "Estimating the Number of Children in Formal Alternative Care: Challenges and Results," *Child Abuse & Neglect* 70 (2017): 388–398.

117. Angelique Day, Tamarie Willis, Lori Vanderwill, Stella Resko, Debra Patterson, Kris Henneman, and Sue Cohick, "Key Factors and Characteristics of Successful Resource Parents Who Care for Older Youth: A Systematic Review of Research," *Children and Youth Services Review* 84 (2018): 152–158.

284 NOTES

118. Anca Gheaus, "More Co-parents, Fewer Children: Multiparenting and Sustainable Population," *Essays in Philosophy* 20, no. 1 (2019): 20.

119. Robert Pralat, "Parenthood as Intended: Reproductive Responsibility, Moral Judgements and Having Children 'by Accident,'" *Sociological Review* 68, no. 1 (2020): 161–176.

120. M. P. Auliso, Thomas May, and Geoffrey D. Block, "Procreation for Donation: The Moral and Political Permissibility of 'Having a Child to Save a Child,'" in *Genetics: Science, Ethics, and Public Policy*, ed. T. A. Shannon (Lanham, MD: Rowman & Littlefield, 2005), 88.

121. Ryan, *The Ethics and Economics of ART*, 166.

122. Tapestry Adoption and Foster Care Ministry is just one example of Christians galvanizing to support those seeking to become foster parents and those who are already foster parents. See the Tapestry Adoption and Foster Care Ministry site, 2019, https://tapestryministry.org/.

123. Rebecca S. Trammell, "Orphan Train Myths and Legal Reality," *Modern American* 5 (2009): 3–13.

124. Shulamith Firestone, *The Dialectic of Sex: The Case for Feminist Revolution* (New York: William Morrow, 1970).

125. Gheaus, "More Co-parents, Fewer Children," 5.

126. Jane Ribbens McCarthy, Rosalind Edwards, and Val Gillies, *Making Families: Moral Tales of Parenting and Step-parenting* (New York: Taylor & Francis, 2017).

127. Ryan, *The Ethics and Economics of ART*, 78.

128. TripAdvisor, "Benefits at Trip Advisor—Canada," 2013, http://www.tripadvisor.com/careers/benefits#.UsmlGvaLSKw.

129. Kacie Wielgus, "Family and Medical Leave Act: Happy Sweet 16," *ACLU*, February 5, 2009, http://www.aclu.org/blog/defending-targets-discrimination/family-and-medical-leave-act-happy-sweet-16.

130. Bella DePaulo, "'Having It All'? Four Reasons Why I'm Having None of It," *Psychology Today*, July 9, 2012, http://www.psychologytoday.com/blog/living-single/201207/having-it-all-four-reasons-why-i-m-having-none-it.

131. DePaulo, "'Having It All'?"

132. Mara J. Goldman, Matthew D. Turner, and Meaghan Daly, "A Critical Political Ecology of Human Dimensions of Climate Change: Epistemology, Ontology, and Ethics," *Wiley Interdisciplinary Reviews: Climate Change* 9, no. 4 (2018): e526.

Conclusion

1. Jessica Pierce and Andrew Jameton, "Sustainable Health Care and Emerging Ethical Responsibilities," *Canadian Medical Association Journal* 164, no. 3 (February 6, 2001): 367.

2. John Nolt, "Sustainability and Hope," in *Sustainability Ethics: 5 Questions,* ed. Ryne Raffaelle, Wade L. Robison, and Evan Selinger (Copenhagen: Automatic/VIP,

NOTES 285

2010), 148; Mary Rowell, "Toward a New Paradigm for Bioethics: Ecological and Theological Contributions" (PhD diss., University of Durham, 2005); Jason Lee Fishel, "The Green Staff of Asclepius: Envisioning Sustainable Medicine" (PhD diss., University of Tennessee, 2014).

3. Elizabeth Cripps, "Intergenerational Ethics and Individual Duties: A Cooperative Promotional Approach," in *The Oxford Handbook of Intergenerational Ethics*, ed. Stephen M. Gardiner (Oxford: Oxford University Press, 2021).

4. Willis Jenkins, *The Future of Ethics: Sustainability, Social Justice, and Religious Creativity* (Washington, DC: Georgetown University Press, 2013), 40. See also Malte Meinshausen, Nicolai Meinshausen, William Hare, Sarah C. B. Raper, Katja Frieler, Reto Knutti, David J. Frame, and Myles R. Allen, "Greenhouse-Gas Emission Targets for Limiting Global Warming to 2°C," *Nature* 458 (April 30, 2009): 1158–1162.

5. Thomas C. Schelling, "The Life You Save May Be Your Own," in *Problems in Public Expenditure Analysis*, ed. Samuel B. Chase Jr. (Washington, DC: Brookings Institution, 1968), 127–162.

6. Norman Daniels, "Reasonable Disagreement about Identified vs. Statistical Victims," *Hastings Center Report* 42, no. 1 (2012): 36.

7. Daniels, "Reasonable Disagreement about Identified vs. Statistical victims," 36.

8. Michael S. Northcott and Peter M. Scott, eds., *Systematic Theology and Climate Change: Ecumenical Perspectives* (Florence, KY: Taylor and Francis, 2014), 84n4; Ken Caldeira and David Keith, "The Need for Climate Engineering Research," *Issues in Science and Technology* 27, no. 1 (2010): 57–62.

9. National Health Services Sustainable Development Unit, *Saving Carbon, Improving Health: NHS Carbon Reduction Strategy for England* (London: NHS Sustainable Development Unit, 2009), 21.

10. Marlyne D. Sahakian, and Christophe Dunand, "The Social and Solidarity Economy towards Greater 'Sustainability': Learning across Contexts and Cultures, from Geneva to Manila," *Community Development Journal* 50, no. 3 (2015): 403–417.

11. Pierce and Jameton, "Sustainable Health Care and Emerging Ethical Responsibilities," 367.

12. Immanuel Kant, "Metaphysical First Principles of the Doctrine of Virtue," in *The Metaphysics of Morals*, ed. Lara Denis, trans. Mary Gregor (Cambridge: Cambridge University Press, 1991), 246.

13. Jenkins, *The Future of Ethics*, 116–117.

14. Nancy Kass, "Public Health Ethics: From Foundations and Frameworks to Justice and Global Public Health," *Journal of Law, Medicine and Ethics* 32 (2004): 236.

15. Jane Galvão, "Brazil and Access to HIV/AIDS Drugs: A Question of Human Rights and Public Health," *American Journal of Public Health* 95, no. 7 (2005): 1113.

16. M. J. Iozzio, "Genetic Anomaly or Genetic Diversity: Thinking in the Key of Disability on the Human Genome," *Theological Studies* 66 (2005): 878.

17. Kass, "Public Health Ethics," 234; President's Commission for the Study of Ethical Problems in Medicine and Biomedical Behavioral Research, *Securing Access to Health Care: The Ethical Implications of Difference in the Availability of Health*

286 NOTES

Services, vol. 1 (Washington, DC: GPO, 1983); L. Churchill, *Rationing Health Care in America* (Notre Dame, IN: University of Notre Dame Press, 1987).

18. Jon Sobrino, *The Principle of Mercy: Taking the Crucified People from the Cross* (Maryknoll, NY: Orbis Books, 1994), 150.

19. Robert Nozick, "Distributive Justice," *Philosophy and Public Affairs* 3, no. 1. (1973): 101.

Index

For the benefit of digital users, indexed terms that span two pages (e.g., 52–53) may, on occasion, appear on only one of those pages.

Figures are indicated by *f* following the page number

abortion, 73, 74, 138–41, 175
ACLU. *See* American Civil Liberties Union
Adashi, Eli Y., 75
adoption, 193–95
Affordable Care Act of 2010, 119, 126, 175–76
AI. *See* artificial insemination
American Civil Liberties Union (ACLU), 197–98
American Pregnancy Association, 38
American Society for Reproductive Medicine (ASRM), 42–43, 124–25, 130–32, 133, 136–37
Americans with Disabilities Act of 1990, 155
artificial insemination (AI), 19, 27, 28–29, 31–32, 62–63, 65–66
artificial reproduction, 117, 128, 129, 133
ARTs. *See* assisted reproductive technologies
Asch, Adrienne, 51
ASRM. *See* American Society for Reproductive Medicine
assisted reproductive technologies (ARTs), 9, 38, 45–46, 71
   costs of, 157–59
   as elective choices, 134–35
   fertile people and, 69–71, 135–36
   healthcare insurance and, 125, 126–28, 136
   infertility and, 60–61, 131–36
   prioritization of, 133–36
   regulation in healthcare, 124–27
   reproductive rights and freedom and, 177–78, 179–80
   subsidized, 125–27, 128
   twin delivery costs, 163

assisted reproductive technologies (ARTs), fertilization techniques, 60–64
   adjuncts and add-ons, 61–62
   AI, 62–63
   ICSI, 64
   IVF, 63–64
assisted reproductive technologies (ARTs), gestational options, 65–69
   gestational surrogates, 65–67
   uterus transplants, 67–69

Bayer, Ronald, 120
Beauchamp, Tom, 119
billing codes, 118–19
biohazards, 19–21, 74
biomedical ethics, 14, 15, 44, 94, 119–20
Birenbaum-Carmeli, Daphna, 10–11
Blood, Diana, 41
Botox, 134, 135
Bowers, John, 80–81
breast pumps, 85, 134

Campion, Nicole, 80
cap and trade (C&T), 104–7
Cappa, Claudia, 195
carbon budgets
   individual and family, 111–14, 115–16
   medical, 113
   reproductive, 112–13
carbon capping, 100–4
carbon dioxide (CO_2) emissions
   in climate change, 1, 3–4, 5–6, 7–8
   climate justice and, 199–201
   from C-sections, 83
   C&T, 104–7
   from developed world, 7–8

288 INDEX

carbon dioxide (CO_2) emissions (*cont.*)
　external and internal healthcare, 91, 95
　global rise, 2008-2010, 1
　healthcare in national, 91–93
　from inpatient admissions for
　　childbirth, 80–81
　as metric of sustainability, 92–93
　MR and, 13–14, 96, 102
　MR and, policies for, 98–100, 103–4,
　　106–7, 109–11, 114
　from PGD, 153–55
　pharmaceuticals and, 19–23
　of pornography industry, 162–63
　subsidiarity, MR policies and, 99–100
　in transport of healthcare, 73
carbon dioxide (CO2) reduction
　climate change and, 8–9, 95
　for climate justice, 201
　healthcare and, 91, 92–93, 99–100
　in healthcare delivery, 93–94
　sustainability and, 92–93
carbon footprint
　of children born from MR, 11–12
　of healthcare in industrialized
　　countries, 106–7
　of MR, 11–12, 22, 43, 45, 72–75, 96–97
　of transportation-associated
　　activities, 45
carbon-intensive infrastructure, of MR,
　11–12, 12*f*
carbon legacy, of MR, 11, 96–100
carbon taxes, 108–9
　healthcare and, 109
　individual and family, 114–15
　MR and, 109–11, 114
CCX. *See* Chicago Climate Exchange
Centers for Disease Control, 80
cesarean section (C-section), 12*f*, 78–79,
　80, 81–83
Cheyne, Helen, 80–81
Chicago Climate Exchange (CCX), 105
childbirth, MR and, 78–83
　C-section and, 81–83
　vaginal childbirth, 80–81
Childress, James, 119
Clark, Meghan, 171–72
climate change, 205n.1
　addressing, 6–9
　carbon reduction in addressing, 8–9, 95

　causes of, 3–6
　CO_2 emissions in, 1, 3–4, 5–6, 7–8
　effects of, 1–3
　GHG in, 1
　health impacts of, 1, 2–3
　human population degrowth in
　　addressing, 6–8
　human population levels and, 3–6
　MR and, 9–13, 15, 198, 199
　procreation and, 181
climate justice, 199–201
CO_2. *See* carbon dioxide
condoms, 23–24
contested rights, 172–74
contraception, 133, 139, 140, 142, 166
　access as right, 175–76
contraceptive sterilization, 36, 141–43, 175
co-parenting, 196–97
Corea, Gena, 82
cosmetic afterbirth procedures, 84–85
COVID-19 pandemic, 120–21, 173
Crippen, David, 79
CRISPR, 51–53
CRISPR-Cas9, 48, 51–52, 185
cryopreservation, 27, 34–35, 36–38
cryopreservation units, 27, 38–39, 45–48, 178
C-section. *See* cesarean section
C&T. *See* cap and trade
custom birth packs, 80, 83, 239n.56

Daniels, Norman, 200
designer babies, 59–60, 155, 157
De Wispelaere, Jurgen, 132–33, 157–58,
　177–78
Diderot effect, 8
disabilities
　people with, genetic diagnosis and, 49–53
　selecting for, PGD and, 56–57, 155–56
disability rights movement and activists,
　49–51, 155
Dochin, Anne, 190–92
Doe v. Bolton (1973), 175
Du Bois, Cora A., 194–95
Dworkin, Andrea, 162–63

ECAFS. *See* Ethics Committee of the
　American Fertility Society
Eckelman, Matthew, 20
Edelman, Lee, 168

INDEX 289

Edwards, Robert G., 15
egg assessment, 47–48
egg cryopreservation, 34–35, 36–37
egg retrieval, 25–26
Eisenstadt v. Baird (1972), 175
embryo adoption, 28
embryo cryopreservation, 37
embryos
    PGD, 153–54
    selective reduction of, 73
embryo storage and disposal, 27–30
embryo transfer, 75–77, 163, 164
environmental ethics, 7–8, 10, 14, 94, 95,
    141, 167
Environmental Protection Agency (EPA),
    1, 108–9
environmental racism, 1, 3
EPA. *See* Environmental
    Protection Agency
Ethics Committee of the American
    Fertility Society (ECAFS), 167–68
eugenics, 49–50, 58, 155–56, 174–75
European Journal of Obstetrics &
    Gynecology and Reproductive
    Biology, 77
European Society of Human Reproduction
    and Embryology Capri Workshop
    Group, 77–78
external healthcare carbon dioxide (CO_2)
    emissions, 91, 95

Fairchild, Amy L., 120
Family and Medical Leave Act of 1993
    (FMLA), 197–98
feminism and feminists, 25, 26, 50–51, 64,
    68, 74–75, 146–47, 162–63, 219n.99
fertile people
    ARTs and, 69–71, 135–36
    gamete storage and donation for, 30–32
    MR for, 139–40
fertility pharmaceuticals, 19–20, 21–23, 40
fertility preservation, 36–41
fertility treatments, gametes for people
    who may undergo, 33–36
Firestone, Shulamith, 86, 219n.99
FMLA. *See* Family and Medical Leave Act
    of 1993
fostering children, 195–96
Foucault, Michel, 146–47

French, William C., 110
fresh embryo transfer, 76
frozen embryo transfer, 75–77
Fuchs, Josef, 190

gamete assessment, for genetic features
    unrelated to health, 53–60
    designer babies, 59–60
    HLA compatibility, 54–56
    selecting for disability, 56–57
    sex selection, 57–59
gamete assessment, for genetic
    health, 48–53
    CRISPR, 51–53
    PGD, 48–51
gamete assessment, for viability, 46–48
    eggs, 47–48
    sperm, 47
gamete cryopreservation, 34–35
gamete donation, 28–32
gamete retrieval
    gamete storage and, 32–44
    for long-term access, 32–43
    PMSR, 24, 25, 33–34, 41–43, 149–
        50, 151
    postmortem, 148–52
    process, 23–26
gametes, 19–20, 69
gamete storage
    donation, 28–32
    IVF and, 26–27, 28–30, 31–32
    for long-term access, 32–44
    retrieval and, 32–44
    for short-term access, 26–32, 43–44
genetic counseling, 49
gestational surrogates, 65–67, 69
Gheaus, Anca, 182–83, 195, 196
GHG. *See* greenhouse gases
GINK movement. *See* Green Inclinations,
    No Kids movement
Goffman, Erving, 191–92
greenhouse gases (GHG), 1, 100–1.
    See also carbon dioxide (CO2)
    emissions
Green Inclinations, No Kids (GINK)
    movement, 167
Griswold v. Connecticut (1965), 175
Gross, Peter, 195
Gudorf, Christine E., 181–82

290 INDEX

Hall, Amy Laura, 183–84
Hashiloni-Dolev, Yael, 43
healthcare delivery, carbon reduction
in, 93–94
healthcare insurance, 22–23, 71, 96
ARTs and, 125, 126–28, 136
billing codes, 118–19
biomedical ethics of, 119–20
infertility and, 130–31
medical consumerism and, 119
national healthcare systems and, 118
parameters of coverage, 119–20
PGD and, 152
premiums, 117, 120
right to, 119
subsidized healthcare, 98, 118, 119–20,
127–28, 136, 141, 142, 149–50, 151,
152, 153, 175–76, 178–79
third-party payer systems, 117–18, 119
voluntary sterilization and, 142–44
women's rights and, 140
healthcare insurance companies, 85, 106,
130–31, 142–43
healthcare policies, evaluating, 120–24
healthcare taxes, 117, 120
hemodialysis, 96, 122–23
Herbert, Geoff, 82
HFEA. See Human Fertilisation and
Embryology Authority
HIV. See human immunodeficiency virus
HLA compatibility. See human leukocyte
antigen compatibility
Hofmeyr, Ross, 119
Human Fertilisation and Embryology
(Deceased Fathers) Act of 2003, 41
Human Fertilisation and Embryology
Authority (HFEA), 61–62
Human Fertilization and Embryology
Authority, UK, 126
human immunodeficiency virus (HIV),
81, 123
human leukocyte antigen (HLA)
compatibility, 53, 54–56, 150–51,
154–55
human population
climate change and, 3–6
degrowth in developed world, 7–8
degrowth in developing world, 6–7

growth, MR and, 10–11
human rights, 170–72, 173–74, 178
Hunter, John, 62

Ibn Adham, Ibrahim, 167
ICSI. See intracytoplasmic sperm injection
infertile people
gamete storage and donation for, 28–
30, 32–33
parenting without procreation, 192–97
infertility
artificial reproduction for, 129
ARTs and, 60–61, 131–36
awareness, prevention, and
acceptance, 186–92
biomedical and anthropological views
of, 186
definitions and diagnostics, 46, 129,
130–31, 133, 187, 210n.91
egg assessment and, 47–48
fertility status of single people and, 144–46
male-first approach to, 160–61
PGD and, 48–49, 51, 152–54
posthumous reproduction and, 148–52
same-sex couples and, 146–48
secondary, 136–38
social, 129, 130–31, 143–45, 146, 147,
148–49, 152
sperm assessment and, 47
Innocent III (pope), 167
internal healthcare carbon dioxide (CO2)
emissions, 91, 95
intracytoplasmic sperm injection (ICSI),
28–30, 64, 65–66
intrauterine growth retardation
(IUGR), 77–78
intrauterine insemination (IUI), 31–
32, 62–63
in-vitro fertilization (IVF), 9–10, 63–64
CRISPR and, 52–53
gametes in, 19, 69
gamete storage and, 26–27, 28–30, 31–32
Israeli policies on, 125
procreative ethics and, 167–68
resource use and, 11–12
surrogates in, 65–67
in US, 10–11
uterus transplants and, 68

Israel Attorney General Guidelines, 43
IUGR. *See* intrauterine growth retardation
IUI. *See* intrauterine insemination
IVF. *See* in-vitro fertilization

JAMA. See *Journal of the American Medical Association*
Jameton, Andrew, 19–20, 201
Jenkins, Willis, 21, 200
Joint United Nations Programme on HIV/AIDS, 6
Journal of the American Medical Association (JAMA), 20, 78

Kaebnick, Gregory E., 194
Kant, Immanuel, 54–55, 201–2
Kass, Nancy, 3, 202
Kraft, Rory E., 86–87
Kyoto Protocol, 92–93, 100–1

Lancet, 6, 78
Liao, Matthew, 52
Luchetti, Marco, 184–85
Lucretius, 192–93

male infertility, 160–61
Malthus, Thomas, 167, 168–69
Marraro, Giuseppe A., 184–85
Mayo Clinic, 160
McCoy, Rajiv C., 75
McKibben, Bill, 15
medical carbon budgets, 113
medical consumerism, 13, 82, 119
medical ethics, 97–100
   biomedical ethics, 14, 15, 44, 94, 119–20
medicalized reproduction (MR). *See also* assisted reproductive technologies; in-vitro fertilization; pre-implantation genetic diagnosis
   adoption *versus*, 193–95
   carbon budgets and, 112–15
   carbon capping and, 103–4
   carbon footprint of, 11–12, 22, 43, 45, 72–75, 96–97
   carbon-intensive infrastructure of, 11–12, 12*f*
   carbon legacy of, 11, 96–100
   carbon taxes and, 109–11, 114

children of, mortality and, 184–86
climate change and, 9–13, 15, 198, 199
CO_2 emissions and, 13–14, 96, 102
CO_2 emissions and, policies for, 98–100, 103–4, 106–7, 109–11, 114
cosmetic afterbirth procedures and, 84–85
C&T and, 106–7
as elective treatment, 96, 98
environmental impact of, 9–10
environmental regulation and, 95
ethical assessment of, 13–15
fertility pharmaceuticals in, 22
gamete assessment in, 46–60
gamete retrieval and storage for long-term access, 32–43
gamete retrieval process, 23–26
gamete storage and donation, 28–32
gamete storage for short-term access, 26–32
goals of medicine and, 131–33, 149, 153
infertility awareness, prevention, and acceptance and, 186–92
miscarriage, 75–77
non-infertility-related, 151–52
population growth and, 10–11
pornography and, 161–63
resource use and, 11–13
singleton pregnancies and births, 163–64
subsidized, 135–52, 158–59, 163, 164, 165, 178–80
unsubsidized, 98, 99–100, 103–4, 106–8, 109–11, 113, 115–16, 136, 138, 143, 157–59, 177
medicalized reproduction (MR), pregnancy and, 72, 85–87
childbirth and, 78–83
C-section and, 81–83
miscarriage and, 75–77
premature delivery and, 77–78
selective reduction and, 73–75
medical justice, 202–3
Miller-McLemore, Bonnie, 184
miscarriage, 75–77
MR. *See* medicalized reproduction
multiparenting, 196–97, 198

292 INDEX

Nash, James, 172
national healthcare systems, 106, 117–19, 134
National Health Service (NHS), UK, 20–21, 32–33, 102–4, 117, 121, 126, 144, 147–48, 201
negative rights
positive rights and, 171–72, 173–75
reproductive, 174–76
neo-natal intensive care unit (NICU), 19, 163
NHS. *See* National Health Service
NHS Carbon Reduction Strategy, 121
NICU. *See* neo-natal intensive care unit
Nietzsche, Friedrich, 167
non-human animals and plants, 1–2
Northcott, Michael S., 101–2
Nussbaum, Martha, 177, 178

Oakley, Ann, 74–75, 79
Obstetrics & Gynecology, 78
oncofertility, 36–41, 52
"One Wales: A Progressive Agenda for Wales," 102–3
ovarian tissue, 36–38

Parens, Erik, 51
parental ethics, 44, 50, 137, 141, 157, 169, 181
parenting without procreation, 192–98
Paris Climate Agreement, 9, 92–93
pediatric oncofertility, 38–39
Peterson-Iyer, Karen, 11
Petrarch, 167
Petrowski, Nicole, 195
PGD. *See* pre-implantation genetic diagnosis
pharmaceuticals
carbon emissions and, 19–23
fertility, 19–20, 21–23, 40
Pierce, Jessica, 19–20, 201
Pitts, Victoria, 79
PMSR. *See* postmortem sperm retrieval
polluter pays principle, 3
population reduction, 181
pornography, 23–24, 25, 161–63
positive rights
negative rights and, 171–72, 173–75
reproductive, 176–79

posthumous reproduction, 41, 42–43, 148–52
postmortem sperm retrieval (PMSR), 24, 25, 33–34, 41–43, 149–50, 151
pre-implantation genetic diagnosis (PGD), 48, 52–53, 54, 70
CO_2 emissions from, 153–55
for designer babies, 59–60, 157
in gamete assessment for genetic health, 48–51
genetic disease and, 152–54
HLA compatability and, 54–57, 154–55
infertility and, 48–49, 51, 152–54
IVF and, 64
in selection for disability, 56–57, 155–56
in sex selection, 57–59, 156–57
premature delivery, 77–78
Primary Care Trust, UK, 138
Proceedings of the National Academy of Sciences of the United States of America, 4
procreative ethics, 166–68
arguments against procreation, 167–68
arguments in favor of procreation, 168–70
on rights and procreation, 170, 180

racism
environmental, 1, 3
structural, 3
systemic, 81
rape, pregnancy as a result of, 86
Raymond, Janice, 26
reproduction
social and psychological aspects of, 183–86
sustainability and, 181–86
work policies that do not incentivize, 197–98
reproductive carbon budget, 112–13
reproductive freedom, 132, 159, 173, 177, 182–83
reproductive rights, 173–74, 179–80
negative, 174–76
positive, 176–79
reproductive tourism, 41, 66–67
Roache, Rebecca, 52
Roe v. Wade (1973), 175
Ryan, Maura, 5–6

INDEX

same-sex couples, infertility and, 146–48
Sandberg, Anders, 52
Sanger, Margaret, 167
Saving Carbon, Improving Health: NHS Carbon Reduction Strategy for England, 102–3
savior siblings, 49, 53, 54–56, 70, 150–51, 154
Schicktanz, Silke, 43
SDGs. *See* Sustainable Development Goals
secondary infertility, 136–38
selective reduction, 73–75
sex-reassignment surgery, 36
sex selection, 53, 57–59, 70, 156–57
sexual ethics, 25, 44, 97, 141
Sherman, Jodi, 20
single people, fertility status of, 144–46
singleton births, 163–64
Smith, Janet, 49
social infertility, 129, 130–31, 143–45, 146, 147, 148–49, 152
social justice, 201–2
Society for Maternal-Fetal Medicine, 81–82
sperm assessment, 47
sperm retrieval, 23–25
step-parenting, 196–98
structural racism, 3
Stuebe, Alison, 85
subsidiarity, MR carbon emissions policy and, 99–100
Suleman, Nadya, 70, 137–38
sustainability
    CO_2 emissions as metric of, 92–93
    reproduction and, 181–86

Sustainable Development Goals (SDGs), 6–7
sustainable healthcare, 91, 95, 103, 122, 151, 162–63
systemic racism, 81

Toxic Wastes and Race in the United States, 3
toxic waste sites, 3

United Nations
    Convention on the Rights of the Child, 192
    Population Division, 4
    SDGs, 6–7
    Universal Declaration of Human Rights, 170–71, 174–75
United States of America v. Defabian C. Shannon, 86
uterus transplants, 67–69

vaginal childbirth, 12*f*, 80–81
voluntary sterilization, 141–44
Voluntary Sterilization Act of 1974, 175

Walters, Barry, 114
Weinstock, Daniel, 132–33, 157–58, 177–78
Woodrow Wilson Center for International Scholars, 3–4
World Health Organization, 2–3, 83, 92, 130–32, 133, 136–37, 210n.91

zygotes
    implanting, 63–64, 68, 74
    selective reduction of, 73, 74